DUE

THE JAPANESE MAFIA

To Chiba Shinichi Sensei
自分に厳しい

THE JAPANESE MAFIA

Yakuza, Law, and the State

Peter B. E. Hill

OXFORD
UNIVERSITY PRESS

OXFORD
UNIVERSITY PRESS

Great Clarendon Street, Oxford OX2 6DP

Oxford University Press is a department of the University of Oxford.
It furthers the University's objective of excellence in research, scholarship,
and education by publishing worldwide in

Oxford New York

Auckland Cape Town Dar es Salaam Hong Kong Karachi
Kuala Lumpur Madrid Melbourne Mexico City Nairobi
New Delhi Shanghai Taipei Toronto

With offices in

Argentina Austria Brazil Chile Czech Republic France Greece
Guatemala Hungary Italy Japan South Korea Poland Portugal
Singapore Switzerland Thailand Turkey Ukraine Vietnam

Published in the United States
by Oxford University Press Inc., New York

British Library Cataloguing in Publication Data

Data available

Library of Congress Cataloging in Publication Data

Data available

ISBN 0–19–925752–3

3 5 7 9 10 8 6 4 2

Typeset by Newgen Imaging Systems (P) Ltd., Chennai, India
Printed in Great Britain
on acid-free paper by
Biddles Ltd., King's Lynn, Norfolk

Acknowledgements

Doing research into society's criminal and pathological aspects has the tendency to adversely colour one's view of human nature. The enormous generosity, kindness, encouragement, and guidance from the vast and varied collection of people who assisted me in my research have more than made up for the ugliness and cynicism to which I have been exposed. Without these individuals, not only would the book never have been written, my faith in human nature may well have been irreparably damaged. It would not be possible, short of writing another book, to adequately express my thanks to them; hopefully they know who they are and how grateful I am. For the record, special thanks to the following:

My mentors Kweku Ampiah, Antony Clunies-Ross, Diego Gambetta, Hoshino Kanehiro and Mizoguchi Atsushi.

My teachers, colleagues, and friends at the Scottish Centre for Japanese Studies (sadly no longer with us), the Institute of Social Science at Tokyo University, and, at the University of Oxford, Green College, the Department of Sociology, the Centre for Criminological Research, the Oriental Institute, and the Nissan Institute.

The staff at the National Research Institute of Police Science, in particular Tamura Masayuki, Uchiyama Ayako, and Yonezato Seiji. In Iwate, to Senior Superintendent Numazaki, his wife Setsuko, and the personnel at both the Prefectural Police Headquarters and the Academy.

For their enduring hospitality and support: in Tokyo, the Suzuki family, Takeshi, Sakiko, Kahori, Megumi, and Lucky; in Kōbe, Gotō Sadato, and his wife Akiko; in Iwate, the Chiba family, Shinichi, Keiko, Hideo, Ayako, Sahoko, and Motoki.

For their extremely valuable comments, criticisms, and advice on drafts of various chapters, Tom Gill, Frank Leishman, Iwai Hiroaki, Wolf Herbert, Katalin Ferber, David Kaplan, Jonathan Lewis, Federico Varese, Joy Hendry, Chris Aldous, John Crump, David Johnson and the anonymous referees appointed by Oxford University Press and Social Science Japan Journal.

My many interviewees both named and unnamed. Of the latter category, particular mentions to Miyazawa Setsuo, Nishimura Haruo, Yamada Hiroshi, Yamanouchi Yukio, Miyazawa Kōichi, Katō Naotaka, and the members of the Organised Crime Division of the Association for the Study of Security Science.

My spotters, Patrick Chalmers, Ben Butcher, and Neil McGinty. You are all diamond geezers. My superb editors, Dominic Byatt and Claire Croft. My sponsors, Kyushu Electrical Power Company, the Japan Foundation Endowment Committee, and the British Academy. Thanks are also due to Gotō Takaaki, whose spontaneous generosity made possible my participation at the Twelfth International Congress on Criminology in Seoul.

And, of course, I would like to thank my family (especially my nit-picking, reference-checking, proof-reading, long-suffering father) and many friends (and I will be in trouble here if I do not mention Kate Armor and Haveya Fassil) for their love and support during the darker moments of this project.

In thanking those mentioned above I in no way wish to make them complicit in any errors or deficiencies in the book; such as they are, I take full responsibility. I doubt that many of those consulted during the course of my research will agree with all of that which follows. To them I say this: I have tried to be both fair and honest. My fieldwork, organisational and interpersonal skills have not always been exemplary but, in the immortal words of Samuel L. Jackson, I'm trying real hard.

Contents

List of Figures

List of Tables

Glossary

Amakudari	'Descent from heaven', post-retirement employment for bureaucrats
Ampō	Japan US Security Treaty (the revision of this treaty in 1960 triggered massive demonstrations in Japan)
Bakuto	Gambler/gambling *yakuza* group
Bōryokudan	'Violent group', official term for Japanese OC groups
Bōtaihō	*Bōryokudan* Countermeasures Law
Bōtuisen	Centres for the Eradication of *Bōryokudan*
Chūshi meirei	Stoppage order (*Bōtaihō* injunction)
DKB	Dai-ichi Kangyō Bank
Gokudō	'The extreme way', *yakuza* way of life
Gurentai	Non-traditional Japanese gangster group, racketeers
Habōhō	Subversive Activities Prevention Law
Hamon	Expulsion
Hanzai Hakusho	White Paper on Crime
Heisei (period)	1989–
Hōmu-shō	Ministry of Justice
HSB	Heiwa Sōgō Bank
Ikka	*Yakuza* (fictive) family
Jun-kōsei-in	Uninitiated *bōryokudan* members, apprentices and affiliates
Keisatsu-chō	National Police Agency
Keisastsu Hakusho	White Paper on Police
Keizai Yakuza	Economic *yakuza*—*yakuza* involved in sophisticated financial and business crimes
Kobun	Fictive son, protégé, follower
Kōsei-in	Full gang member
Kumi (-chō/-in)	*Yakuza* group (boss/member)
Kyōbai Bōgai	Auction obstruction
Kyōdai	Brother
LCN	La Cosa Nostra (Italian-American organised crime)
LDP	Liberal Democratic Party, *Jimin-tō*
Meiji (period)	1868–1912
Mizu shōbai	'Water trades', Japan's hospitality/entertainment industry
MOF	Ministry of Finance
MOJ	Ministry of Justice
Nawabari	(Gang) territory

Nichibenren	Japan Federation of Bar Associations
Ninkyō (-dantai)	Chivalry ('chivalrous group' i.e. *yakuza*)
NPA	National Police Agency
NRIPS	National Research Institute for Police Science
OC(G)	Organised Crime (Groups)
Ōkura-shō	Ministry of Finance
Oyabun	Fictive father, patron, boss
RICO	Racketeer Influenced and Corrupt Organizations statute
Saihatsu bōshi meirei	Repetition prevention order (*Bōtaihō* injunction)
Sakazuki	Ritual exchange of sake cups creating fictive familial relations within *yakuza* society
Sarakin	High interest rate loan companies
Shinogi	Any source of *Yakuza* income, fund-raising activity
Shōwa (period)	1926–1989
Sōkaiya	Corporate blackmailer
Songiri	Loss-cutting
Taishō (period)	1912–1926
Tekiya	Peddler/peddler *yakuza* group
Waka-gashira	Sub-boss
Yakuza	Most commonly used term for Japanese gangs and gangsters either collectively or individually (see Chapter Two)
Yama-ichi tōsō	Conflict between the Yamaguchi-gumi and break-away Ichiwa-kai (1984–1989)
Yubitsume	Ritual *yakuza* finger amputation
Zetsuen	Severing of connections, irrevocable expulsion

Conventions

Japanese words are transliterated according to the modified Hepburn system, with macrons used to express long vowel sounds (with the exception of long 'i' sounds as in Ishii). Macrons are not used in commonly known Japanese place names. Thus Tokyo and Osaka do not take macrons: Hokkaidō, Kōbe, and Kotobuki-chō do.

Japanese personal names are given in the normal Japanese order with family names preceding given names. Where it has been impossible to confirm personal names the most likely reading has been given.

Throughout the text the word *yakuza* has been used in preference to *bōryokudan*. Whilst these two words refer to the same social phenomenon, in Japan they carry very different connotations (the former being overwhelmingly more positive than the latter). This choice of terminology is due to the greater recognition amongst a non-Japanese audience of the former term rather than a desire to support these connotations.

Dollar (US) values of Japanese yen (¥) sums are given at the average exchange rate for the year in question. These are given in Table 0.1.

Table 0.1   Yen–Dollar exchange rate 1978–2000

Year	¥/$	Year	¥/$
1978	210	1990	145
1979	219	1991	135
1980	227	1992	127
1981	221	1993	111
1982	249	1994	102
1983	238	1995	94
1984	238	1995	94
1985	239	1996	109
1986	169	1997	121
1987	145	1998	131
1988	128	1999	114
1989	138	2000	115

Introduction

This book is an attempt to make sense of the *yakuza*. My interest in these groups was first aroused by two social encounters with *yakuza* gang members in bars in the northeast of Japan in the late 1980s. To a fresh-faced and impressionable youngster struggling to internalise the accepted norms of Japanese behaviour, these larger-than-life characters, with their ostentatious display of conflicting norms, were compelling. This was a very different side to the community I thought I knew.

My interest was not, however, a purely emotional phenomenon. On sober reflection, the apparent paradox of a number of large, clearly identifiable criminal gangs operating openly within a society widely regarded as one of the industrialised world's most crime-free societies was puzzling. Recourse to the popular English-language literature, such as van Wolferen (1989) and Kaplan and Dubro (1986), suggests that this paradox is resolved by seeing these syndicates themselves as an integral part of the crime-control process in Japan and enjoying a quasi-symbiotic relationship with the legitimate law-enforcement authorities.

This explanation raises two crucial questions: Is this posited social-control function unique to Japan or can we identify similar patterns in the dealings between organised crime groups and their host communities in other jurisdictions? Is it actually an accurate description of the interplay between *yakuza*, law, and the state?

With respect to my first question, examining the available literature on organised criminal groups outside of Japan, it has become clear that the *yakuza* are not *sui generis*; they exhibit behaviour (not least in their ambiguous relationship with the authorities), which is similar to that of groups comprising, *inter alia*, the Sicilian Mafia, the Hong Kong Triads, the Russian *vory-v-zakone*, and traditional Italian-American organised crime. As such, it is appropriate to refer to all such groups as examples of the same phenomenon. Following Varese's excellent study of "the Russian Mafia" (2001), I use the term mafia to refer to these. What is meant by this, and the implications of it, is explained in the theoretical framework of Chapter One. The empirical material in subsequent chapters will hopefully satisfy the reader that the *yakuza* can therefore be considered the Japanese mafia and that the title of this book, adopted in self-conscious mimicry of the work of Gambetta (1993) and Varese (2001), is appropriate.

With respect to my second question, it seems that the relationship is both ambiguous and dynamic. Over the last half-century, both the *yakuza* and the social, legal, and economic environment in which they exist have changed considerably. In light of this it would have been surprising if the *yakuza*-state relationship had remained static. Over the last decade of the twentieth century, the relationship has become yet more strained following the introduction of the 1992 *Bōryokudan (Yakuza)* Countermeasures Law. Although the provisions of this law are mild by the standards of anti-organised-crime laws in other jurisdictions, it has had a non-trivial effect on the behaviour and psychology of both *yakuza* and the authorities. This, and other new laws, combined with the impact of Japan's long-running economic malaise, leave the *yakuza* facing the twenty-first century in a significantly weakened state. Unfortunately, the social consequences of this are not entirely beneficial.

Note on Sources and Methods

Doing research in criminal areas is inevitably problematic and 'much of what has been written on the subject of organised crime is either inaccurate or distorted' (Nelli 1986: 1). Not only do criminal interviewees have an interest in concealing their criminal activities; they also have a countervailing aspiration to enhance their reputation (a *mafiosi*'s most important trading commodity). By the same token, it cannot be said that governmental agencies universally enjoy an entirely unblemished record of openness and honesty in their presentation of information to the outside world and it would be foolish to accept *a priori* that Japan is an exception in this respect.

Given these formidable barriers to ascertaining the truth, how have I gathered evidence by which to make sense of the *yakuza*? My Ph.D. fieldwork research was conducted between January and August 1998. During this time I was based at Tokyo University's Institute for Social Science (Shakai Kagaku Kenkyū-jo) as a visiting researcher. To mitigate the problems outlined above, I cast my net as widely as possible. Not only did I talk to members of *yakuza* groups, academic criminologists, social activists, police researchers, and serving officers at nearly all levels within the police hierarchy, I talked to individuals such as retired *yakuza*, bar-keepers, and lawyers; those familiar with the *yakuza* world, but not of it, and with less apparent desire to impress or conceal.

My principal research sites were Iwate, the Osaka-Kōbe conurbation, and Tokyo. Iwate was chosen because I had an established social network, which facilitated access to the prefectural police. I refrained from approaching *yakuza* in Iwate due to a desire not to upset the social relations of many of my friends there. If I offended people, it would be easy enough for me to go away; they could not. In Osaka I was introduced to three criminal defence lawyers with long and close experience of the *yakuza* world. They in turn were able to introduce me to several of their clients. For obvious reasons these individuals are identified only by pseudonyms. In Tokyo, my interviewees extended from the homeless day-labourers of Sanya, the slum area of Tokyo, to senior policymakers within the National Police Agency.

I have also made use of literary sources disparaged by Japanese academic criminologists such as Japan's downmarket weekly and monthly magazines. I know that they will consequently consider this book less highly than had I stuck to more 'reputable' works such as the annual *keisatsu hakusho* (police white papers) and the *keisatsu-gaku ronshū* (Journal of Police Science). Whilst the relationship that many of these popular magazines' *yakuza*-journalists have with their subject precludes complete objectivity, publications such as *Jitsuwa Jidai* and *Jitsuwa Dokyumento*, specialising in *yakuza*-related issues, are avidly read by both gang members and police alike as a way of keeping up to date with underworld affairs. They also show *yakuza* members to be living, breathing, thinking, feeling actors; something conspicuously absent in the sanitised police sources. Whilst they must not be used uncritically, the works of these *yakuza*-journalists are a valuable resource that we should not ignore. Special mention must be made here of the work of Mizoguchi Atsushi, which, uniquely, was recommended to me by gang members and police researchers alike.

Whilst such sources will offend Japanese criminologists, I am aware that my use of the official sources will diminish the value of this book in the eyes of many non-Japanese scholars. As Baer and Chambliss (1997) show with respect to official crime statistics in the United States, such figures are far from neutral and may be manipulated, either up or down, according to the prevailing political imperatives. Finch (2000) draws our attention to some of the potential pitfalls of uncritical reliance on Japanese police statistics. However, the main points I make in this book that are based on such figures are corroborated by non-police sources.

A more mundane problem with the official literature is that it necessarily concentrates on those aspects of criminal activity which have, in some way or other, attracted the attention of the police. Successful operations, including many of the *yakuza*'s protective activities, pass unnoticed.

Despite these potential problems, Stark, whose superb ethnographic study of *yakuza* in Western Japan remains unsurpassed in this field, found that the official data were superior to those produced by journalistic and academic sources and were corroborated by his own research findings (1981: 10). Given the comparative openness of the *yakuza* world *vis-à-vis* mafias in historically more hostile legal environments, it has been relatively straightforward for the authorities to assemble detailed information on the organisational structures and membership of *yakuza* groups. The police *yakuza*-countermeasures centres I visited in Iwate and Tokyo both showed me files containing such information on their own respective patches.

Inevitably, many of the figures given in this book are estimates and many of them look suspiciously like they have been calculated on the back of a cigarette packet. The truth is that nobody knows the true figures of, for example, total *yakuza* income. Given that most of this income is (a) immediately dissipated in hedonism and ostentatious display and (b) divided amongst a number of groups rather than accruing to some central Crime Inc., it is hard to see how such a figure would actually be meaningful anyway. It might make more sense to try to ascertain the net loss (or gain) the existence of the *yakuza* incurs to Japan as a whole. I am not sure of a satisfactory method by which such a figure might be generated.

It would be dishonest to say that the methodological issues have been resolved to my own satisfaction here. Even after several years' research in this field, I still see through a glass darkly. Owing to the considerable hospitality of many of those who assisted my research, this was often the literal as well as the metaphorical truth. However, despite its inadequacies, I think that this book does make a positive contribution to the existing body of knowledge in two key areas. First, it provides a comprehensive account in English of the development of trends in the *yakuza* and *yakuza*-countermeasures over the last decades of the twentieth century. Second, it sets this account within a theoretical framework derived from rigorous analyses of other manifestations of mafia-like phenomena.

How to Use This Book

In Chapter One, I lay out what I mean by the term 'mafia'. The material presented in this chapter refers almost exclusively to non-Japanese structures. Those who do not wish to be encumbered by theoretical considerations or are uninterested by comparative analyses may go straight to Chapter Two without depriving themselves of any empirical material directly concerning the *yakuza*. Should the reader's objective be simply to know what changes the *yakuza* have undergone over recent decades, they are directed to the central chapters of this book. Chapter Five, which deals with the 1992 *Bōtaihō* (*Yakuza* Countermeasures) Law, will primarily be of interest to those interested in comparative law and may well, in places, be too dry for many readers' tastes. The initial section of this chapter, which outlines the reasons for this law's introduction, is important to understanding the changing relationship between *yakuza* and state. The following chapter explores the twin effects of this law and the bursting of Japan's economic bubble, which have between them dominated the *yakuza* landscape over the 1990s. In the concluding chapter I return to my starting-point and attempt to make sense of the dynamic relationship between *yakuza*, law, and the state.

1

Mafias and the State

During the course of the fieldwork research for this book, it was frequently asserted by interviewees, on both sides of the law, that the *yakuza* were fundamentally different from the (Sicilian) mafia. These claims were generally based on the perception of the mafia as an unambiguously predatory entity locked in bloody combat with the state (exemplified by such crimes as the assassination of the Italian prosecutors Giovanni Falcone and Paolo Borsellino). This was contrasted with the toleration traditionally enjoyed by the *yakuza* exemplified by the open existence of *yakuza* gang offices which, until 1992, explicitly identified themselves as such by proudly displaying the name of their gang, and its crest, and crest at the entrance (many still do).

Whilst on one level this difference is very real—the *yakuza* do not currently blow up judges and other agents of the state—the perception of difference seems to be based on a misconception of what the Sicilian mafia actually is and does. As the first half of its title suggests, this book, *inter alia*, explores the applicability of the term 'mafia' to the *yakuza*. In order to do this we must first make clear exactly what is meant by mafia, which is the purpose of this chapter, and then how that might apply to the *yakuza*, which is one of the purposes of those which follow. Looking at the *yakuza* with reference to the best available scholarship on the Sicilian mafia and similar manifestations of organised crime gives us powerful analytical tools, which show us that many aspects of the *yakuza's* historical and current behaviour are far from peculiar to the Japanese context.

A thorough grounding in these theoretical considerations will also help us to make sense of the relationship between the *yakuza* and the state, and the problems of framing legal countermeasures to this particular type of criminal behaviour. As implied by the second half of the title, these are central concerns of this book.

Definitions

Despite the lack of a commonly accepted definition of 'organised crime', employing this term has been treated by many as unproblematic. Indiscriminate use has undermined the usefulness of the concept of 'organised crime' to the point whereby many scholars have dropped it in preference for 'enterprise crime' (Levi, 2002: 887). The moral panic-mongering tied up with much usage of this former term leads Levi elsewhere to cynically suggest a 'true *social* definition of "organised criminals"': a set of people whom the police and other agencies of the State regard, or wish us to regard, as "really dangerous" to its essential integrity' (1998a: 2). Following the World Trade Center attack of 11 September 2001, the bogeyman mantle has effectively been transferred to international terrorists. However, the problems of using 'organised crime' persist.

This is unfortunate; there is a conceptually distinct pattern of criminal association worthy of a name. Categorising this behaviour with a clearly defined label is not just an academic exercise but is useful in two particular ways. First, providing the definition is constructed in such a way as to throw light on the way in which this pattern of association is distinct (and what good would it be as a definition if it did not), it will provide us with an insight to the processes involved in the phenomenon in question. Second, an understanding of these processes, may well yield insights into any special problems that this type of criminal activity might present to criminal justice systems and thereby have policy implications. Therefore, at the risk of being old-fashioned, let us try to provide a concrete understanding of what is meant here by organised crime.

Schelling observes, and many have reiterated, that organised crime does 'not mean simply "crime that is organised"' (1984: 180). Even a comparatively straightforward felony will require a certain amount of planning whilst a large professional robbery will involve a high degree of division of labour, specialisation, and organisation. This does not make them examples of organised crime; 'project crime' is perhaps a better description of this type of criminal operation. Similarly, highly systematic and sophisticated white-collar crime within legitimate organisations is not considered here to be an example of organised crime. This is not to imply, however, that organised crime will not involve itself in either type of operation; merely that they are not, in themselves, 'organised' in the sense of organised crime.

The 1967 US Task Force On Organized Crime states that 'the core of organised crime activity is the supplying of illegal goods and services—gambling, loan-sharking, narcotics, and other forms of vice—to countless numbers of citizen consumers' (1967: 1). Whilst it is not a definition, this description is useful in highlighting one crucial difference between organised crime and other types of financially motivated criminality. This is the way in which, whilst this latter category of crimes can generally be characterised as unambiguously socially dysfunctional, resulting in a clearly identifiable victim, organised crime exists because it functions as a business satisfying a demand for goods and services among members of the 'legitimate' world. This is an absolutely critical consideration to our understanding of this phenomenon: Whilst we would all be better off if there were no burglars, robbers, and swindlers, some of us would feel the loss if the suppliers of illegal drugs, gambling, and sexual services disappeared.

Schelling, who was himself a member of the 1967 Task Force, developed this idea further asserting that the provision of these illegal goods and services was not, in itself, sufficient to qualify as an organised crime entity. What Schelling considers to be a crucial characteristic is that an organised crime group endeavours to achieve monopolistic control over the illegal markets in which it is active (1984: 181–2).

This view has been criticised by Reuter (1983, p. xi), who suggests that this stress on monopolistic control is not supported by the empirical evidence. Accordingly, he provides a much more general definition of organised crime as 'organisations that have durability, hierarchy, and involvement in a multiplicity of criminal activities' (1983: 175). Though these are all indeed attributes of organised crime, this definition deals neither with this phenomenon's desire to control criminal activity nor with its central involvement in illegal *markets*. It also encompasses, for example, a business corporation that engages in bribery, fraud, and environmental crimes.

Whilst Reuter is undoubtedly right that the reality of organised crime is generally characterised by oligopolistic competition rather than central control, Schelling's analysis of it as fulfilling essentially a governmental role is one that offers powerful insights into the workings of organised crime. This approach has been refined by Gambetta (1993), in his outstanding theoretical examination of the Sicilian mafia. Gambetta argues that the essential characteristic of the mafia is that it is 'a specific economic enterprise, an industry which produces, promotes, and sells private protection' (1993: 1). Gambetta himself maintains that it is a misconception to equate the mafia with organised crime. This is because, he maintains, the mafia is primarily responsible for supplying the 'organising force', whilst the range of criminal entrepreneurs subject to this organisation (which Gambetta apparently identifies as organised crime) are 'usually independent economic agents licensed and protected by the former' (1993: 227).

Varese (2001: 4), following the footsteps of Gambetta, argues that the term 'mafia' may be applied not only to the Sicilian mafia but used as a general term for groups which share the Sicilian mafia's core characteristics. He makes the distinction between the broader set of organised crime groups (OCGs), which 'aspire to obtain a monopoly over the production and distribution of a certain commodity in the underworld' and its subset mafias, which 'are OCGs, but deal in different commodities: they sell and seek to monopolize the supply of *protection*'.

Whilst this is *prima facie*, an attractive distinction, it is not unproblematic. For an OCG to monopolise a criminal market, it must be able to enjoy sufficient military advantage to deter new entrants and protect that monopoly. Should a group have such a military asset there is likely to be a logic for that protective power to be extended to other criminal markets within the same geographical territory. There is a nice empirical example of this revealed in the accounts of a North American drug-dealing gang analysed by Levitt and Venkatesh (2000) in which the group made use of the military power they had built up to protect their core business to tax other criminals engaging in business within their territory.

Schelling himself makes clear that organised crime is not just concerned with the monopolisation of illegal markets but that its central business is extortion/protection of those markets (1984: 185). In this sense organised crime is not just criminal business: it is criminal government. Although Varese's distinction has been informed by Schelling's analysis of organised crime, it seems here that what Schelling has in mind when referring to OC is therefore very close to a mafia and his analysis of organised crime in the United States some three decades ago is still of relevance to our study of mafia-like groups in other jurisdictions today.

Whilst equating the term 'organised crime' with mafias is an extreme minority position, in this book, when referring to organised crime, unless otherwise specified, what is meant is essentially a mafia where a mafia is defined as a set of firms that provide extra-state protection to consumers in primarily, but not exclusively, the illegal market sector.

At a presentation of a prototype draft of this chapter to the organised crime division of the Association for the Study of Security Science (a Japanese think tank comprised of retired and serving senior police officers), the audience criticised this sort of social-science definition on the grounds that it lacked operational and judicial applicability. This is of course true, and the State's organised-crime countermeasures must be founded on an unambiguous legal definition of what it is that is being countered. Definitions of this type are more properly expressed in Chapter Five, which concerns such countermeasures. The purpose of this chapter is to provide a solid theoretical understanding of what mafias are and what they do. For such a purpose, the social science definition provided above is an excellent starting-point yielding numerous insights. Let us now explore these.

Consumers of Protection

If we are to assert that 'mafia' is the collective term for firms that attempt to monopolise the market for private protection, we are immediately making the implicit assertion that, as a market, there are not only suppliers (our mafia), but those who demand their services. Who constitutes the demand side of this equation? Although not all consumers of mafia protection exist in the underworld (as suggested by the earlier use of the term 'criminal government'), it is here that the underlying processes can be seen most starkly. Denizens of the underworld have a major dilemma: because they are operating outside of the law, they are unable to make use of the legal mechanisms afforded to their upper-world equivalents which guarantee their property rights and enforce contracts. These problems might not be insurmountable for thieves whose larceny is necessarily carried out in a clandestine fashion. For those that are operating in criminal markets (and this would include the aforementioned thieves should they try to sell the fruits of their labour), a degree of visibility is essential in order to attract customers. These individuals are therefore highly vulnerable to being exploited by customers, employees, or predatory criminals. The acuity of this dilemma is increased when we bear in mind that participants in these markets have already demonstrated their preparedness to violate one set of rules (the legal, state-enforced one); why should they obey any others? (Gambetta forthcoming: Ch. 9)

This problem can be overcome by several strategies. First, illegal market traders can limit their client-base to known and trusted customers. This strategy of course imposes clear limits on the number of customers and the growth of the trader's market, and may well be an insurmountable barrier to new entrants. Second, traders can trade more openly and rely on being sufficiently tough and smart both to deter predators and to detect and punish those that try to cheat or rob them. Of course, such a course of action is not cost-free. Tracking down cheats and breaking their legs takes time that is more profitably employed running the criminal business. Besides, it is by no means certain that the skills required to run a successful illegal business are the same skills as those required for catching and punishing: even for the genuinely tough, violently punishing others runs the risk of finding oneself on the receiving end of violence; how much more so for those who are not experts (Gambetta forthcoming: Ch. 9).

In an underworld where all traders also operate as their own enforcers, especially one in which nobody has an efficient mechanism for ascertaining just how tough and smart those with whom they transact business actually are, we can see how business may become far more costly, violent, and inefficient than it need be. This might yield social benefits if less illegal business is conducted as a consequence but that is not our concern right now; we are interested in understanding the problems of criminals and how they resolve them. We can therefore see how it may well be not only cost-effective for illegal traders to seek an external supplier of protection, but also yield greater stability.

Although the conditions generating the demand for private protection are most apparent in the underworld, they are by no means exclusive to it. Where the state is unwilling or unable to provide protection
to citizens operating in legitimate markets, there will be a similar
demand. It is not difficult to think of examples where these conditions
obtain: failed states (unable); jurisdictions in which state protection is
only extended to some citizens and not to others (unwilling). Where
this latter case is due to a corrupt jurisdiction in which state-protection
is afforded only to those who pay for it, we have the interesting situation in which mafia and state are directly competing in *precisely* the
same market. The nature of the relationship between mafia and state
will be dealt with at greater length below. Another often-witnessed situation involving partial state-protection is that in which a minority
community distrusts or otherwise imperfectly communicates with the
authorities (and these conditions of trust are of course ones that rival
suppliers of protection will have a vested interest in upholding). In
this case the problem is not one merely of supply but also of the
perceptions of those who have a demand for protection.

Providers of Protection

To consider one way in which the demand for protection may be met,
let us return to our hypothetical Hobbesian underworld in which
illegal market traders individually supply their own. The effectiveness
with which they are able to do this will be essentially a function
of three qualities: how skilled they are in deploying violence, how
smart they are, and how well-informed they are. It should be readily
apparent to anyone with even the most superficial acquaintance with
humanity that some individuals possess these attributes in greater
measure than others. We can expect therefore that some participants in
illegal markets will prove to be more successful in this business than
others. Natural aptitude will of course be enhanced by an environment
which provides training in, or frequent recourse to, the efficient use
of violence. Examples of such an environment are military service or
penal servitude.

If we apply Adam Smith's observation of the benefits derived from
the division of labour and David Ricardo's principle of comparative

advantage, and if we further assume that protection is a genuinely demanded service, we can see how this logic driving the specialisation of the best protectors to that business might yield the greatest overall returns to the criminal economy as a whole. It does not, however, tell us whether all parties gain equally from this more efficient state of affairs. In principle we might expect our specialist protector to set the price of protection at just below the level at which his protectees might find it preferable to supply their own protection (which, if they can do successfully, might encourage them to specialise and sell protection to others) or buy it in from an alternative source. We do of course have the problem that criminal protection is a commodity that is qualitatively different from gambling, sexual services, or drugs in that it relies on the threat, and ultimately the actual use, of violence. We must also remember that we are supposing our protector specialises in this business because he is better at providing violence than his protectees. We can also see that in the cruel world where protection is necessary, those that aspire to this role whilst lacking an advantage in the requisite qualities *vis-à-vis* competing providers will quickly find themselves, at best, looking for alternative sources of employment ultimately leading to a situation in which protection is subject to a territorial monopoly.

Given these two considerations, the options for consumers of protection to protect themselves or shop around for better value protection, are limited. The protector is therefore in a position to charge his protectees for protection not only from other predators but from himself, in which case protection becomes extortion. We will discuss the extent to which protection should be more accurately described as extortion at greater length below.

The Aetiology of Mafias

From the simple starting-point outlined above, we should expect to see mafias arising when the market demand for extra-legal protection is met by supply. If we examine the empirical evidence, we can see that theory does seem to fit the available evidence. If we look at the Sicilian case we can see that the mafia originally arose as a response to the imperfect transition from a feudal economic system during the nineteenth century. This shift generated a large increase in the number of economic transactions but failed, at the same time, to provide efficient mechanisms for resolving disputes arising from those transactions. At the same time there was an ample supply of former soldiers, now unemployed, estate guards, and ex-prisoners who provided a pool of labour with the necessary skills to act as protectors. It is instructive to note that in those areas of Sicily where the structure of land ownership remained essentially unchanged and economic development retarded, the levels of mafia activity were considerably lower than in the more dynamic areas (Gambetta 1993: 86–92).

In the case of the United States, mafia formation was primarily a response to the root and branch transfer of a formerly legitimate industry to the criminal economy with the prohibition of the sale of alcohol between 1920 and 1933. This situation coexisted with a supply of violent and ambitious young men, frequently drawn from immigrant communities disadvantaged in more respectable labour markets, with the necessary skills to protect this market. Although there had been criminal organisations running the illegal prostitution and gambling markets before this period, the Eighteenth Amendment to the Constitution and the Volstead Act resulted in a massive jump in the scale, sophistication, violence, and wealth of the groups protecting illegal markets in the United States (Gambetta 1993: 251–2).

Perhaps the case study where conditions favouring mafia genesis can be seen starkly is the countries comprising the former Soviet Union. The rapid transition from a state command economy to a market economy during the late 1980s and early 1990s entailed widespread transfer of state assets into private hands. Because this transfer was not matched with either the social norms or the state institutions protecting the integrity of market transactions and property rights, potential entrepreneurs were highly vulnerable to predation. This, in turn, presented these individuals with a considerable disincentive to engage in trade. In short, there was a widespread market demand for protection that was not being met by the state (Gambetta 1993: 252–4; Varese 2001: Ch. 1).

This economic reconstruction also entailed a large increase in the level of unemployment within the former Soviet Union as large areas of the state apparatus were dismantled and over-manned industries were subjected to rationalisation. Of particular interest here are the proportion of these individuals with a comparative advantage in the efficient use of violence. During the period of transition many tens of thousands of officers were dismissed from the state's military, police, and security services. The formerly pampered elite of professional athletes, especially those specialising in combat sports, also enjoyed the physical capital qualifying them for participation in the labour market for protection (Varese 2001: 56–8). This pool of labour, combined with freely available military-grade weaponry, has ensured that the market demand for protection has been met.

Varese (2003) has suggested that this pattern might also be applicable to the Japanese context with the *yakuza* qua mafia tracing their origins to the transition of Japan from feudalism to a modern state at around the time of the Meiji restoration in the latter part of the nineteenth century. This transition, the argument goes, resulted in a pool of 'disenfranchised samurai, hoodlums and landless peasants (who) formed the supply of the early *yakuza'*. Implicit to this argument is that this transition also generated a demand for protection by increasing the volume of market transactions outside of official protection. Whether this is indeed the case will be examined in the following chapter dealing with the historical development of the *yakuza*.

At the risk of labouring the point, we should reiterate here that there are two distinct patterns observable in the development of mafias: first, there are mafias which come into existence due to the existence of illegal markets and therefore transactions in these markets lie outside the jurisdiction of the state (as in the Prohibition Era in the United States); second, there are mafias which develop due to the inability of the state to afford protection as a public good within the geographical area over which it claims jurisdiction (Sicily, the former Soviet Union, and, perhaps, Japan).

There are profound policy implications in both mafia geneses. With respect to the former case, criminalisation of goods and services that some politicians or voters deem immoral or harmful but that others consider desirable may be counterproductive; rather than leading to a significant reduction in the volume of these goods and services being consumed they may actually be generating a number of socially undesirable outcomes: first, it encourages a disrespect for the law and brings otherwise law-abiding citizens into contact with the criminal underworld; second, by creating an artificial barrier to entry of legitimate entrepreneurs, it may enable criminals to charge higher prices than would obtain in a genuinely competitive market—prohibition thereby generates even greater revenues to the criminal world than might be expected by simply transferring a market to the criminal economy; because banned commodities lie outside of state regulation, there are no mechanisms to guarantee the purity or safety of these goods, and this may have significant consequences for public health; because mafia protection is typically considerably more violent than its state equivalent, the growth in illegal markets generally leads to a corresponding increase in violence; the social costs of prohibiting a commodity may therefore outweigh any benefits.[1]

In cases in which mafias arise as a response to failure on the part of the state to provide protection, there are clear implications for the international community when dealing with states in transition, war-torn states, and—a topical issue at the time of writing—states subjected to 'regime change' that wish to avoid providing a fertile breeding ground for mafias.

Scale and Structure of Mafias

Within the protection business there are considerable economies of scale. Most obviously this industry depends on military power, which is in part a function of size. Stronger groups more credibly deter both rivals and those wishing to prey on protectees, and as such they are the suppliers that consumers will turn to; success breeds success. We might also expect that the costs of corrupting the authorities of the upper-world can be carried more efficiently if conducted on a more centralised basis; a lone gambler might be able to pay off street-level law-enforcement but lack the resources to have influence at the political or judicial level.

This logic might lead us to suppose that ultimately we will end up with a situation in which the most effective protector is protecting the entire global underworld economy. Unless such a Napoleon of crime has covered his tracks exceptionally well, empirically, this does not seem to happen. Why not? It seems that there must be factors which countervail the tendency to expansion. Most significant of these is the diseconomy of scale presented by the need for good intelligence. In order reliably to supply protection, a mafia group must know its territory sufficiently well to apprehend those who are abusing those protected by the group. Of equal importance, from the mafia group's point of view, they must be able to detect free-riders who pass themselves off as protectees without paying. Both types of transgressors must be visibly punished to demonstrate first, the effectiveness of protection and second, that it cannot be had for free (Gambetta 1993: 35–9, 53, 59).

Protection therefore depends on very precise knowledge of one's market and this depends on remaining close to it. To a certain extent this problem can be circumvented by having a number of employees who provide, *inter alia*, intelligence of their own locality, but this raises problems of its own. Once a gang increases in size to the point where its leader no longer has good knowledge over the gang's territory, he runs the risk of being cheated not so much by his customers but by his employees (and it must be remembered that such employees are hardly the most rule-compliant or honest of men). Once a group gets beyond a certain size, there are also tendencies to schism, especially when factions compete over group leadership succession.

Mafia activity therefore has a strong tendency to parochialism and limited group size. In the Sicilian Mafia, for example, police reports for 1987 gave a figure of 105 groups varying in size from 2 to 120 members per group. Within the American Mafia, groups are less numerous but tend to have a larger membership (75–400) (Varese 2003). Amongst the Hong Kong Triads, the groups that function at street-level generally have between 15 and 20 members, though in some cases this may rise to just under 100 (Chu 2000: 28). Amongst the Japanese *yakuza*, the average size of the gangs comprising wide area syndicates in 1985 was just over 30 (*Hanzai Hakusho* 1989: 346).

What makes these groups seem larger is the tendency they have to develop supra-gang mechanisms for cooperation and the avoidance of conflict. The two main ways in which this can happen is by forming either federations or syndicates. A mafia confederation describes a situation in which autonomous groups agree to respect each others' territorial integrity and establish codes of conduct and procedures whereby inter-group disputes may be avoided and, failing that, resolved. Although confederation members may cooperate on particular criminal ventures, they remain essentially independent groups. In the Sicilian Mafia, these associations are overseen by committees (*commissione*).

These *commissione* exist on a provincial basis and all but two of Sicily's provinces have such groups. According to the mid-1980s testimony of Tomaso Buscetta, in the case of Palermo, the mafia firms had a commission comprising ten members. Although it is not clear to what extent it has played an effective role in coordinating mafia group activity, at some stages there has been a pan-Sicilian *commissione* on which the provincial cartels were represented (though dominated by that of Palermo). A similar system, also called a commission, has existed amongst La Cosa Nostra groups in the United States (Gambetta 1993: 112–13; Stille 1996: 100–10).

A tighter coalescence of mafia firms can be seen in the Chinese and Japanese contexts in which large syndicates operate in a way analogous to a franchise or feudal system. Gangs pay a monthly fee for the right to belong to the syndicate and exploit its collective brand image. Whilst member groups are expected to obey the rules and directives provided by the head organisation, they have autonomy over their own economic activity within their territory. Gangs may be forced to join the syndicate by threat of arms or may apply to join voluntarily but, in most cases within the current Japanese context, groups are formed within the syndicate as members recruit enough followers to set up an internal group of their own. In a sense here subgroups are consumers of the protection provided by syndicate membership. They must, however, also contribute to the collective security of the syndicate by providing military support at the behest of their parent organisation, and operate as local protectors within their own territory, so they simultaneously produce and consume protection.

We can see, in both these mechanisms, attempts by mafia firms to resolve the problem identified by Schelling *vis-à-vis* individual and organised criminality (1984: 172): acts committed by rational, self-interested criminals generate externalities borne by all criminals collectively; if crime is centrally coordinated, criminals as a group have an interest in moderating the behaviour of all. The same might be said of individual groups. For example, killing, especially of police officers or other agents of the state, may generate increased levels of law-enforcement against them. Alternatively, the negative effects of one group's disappearance or another's aggressive expansion, may be moderated. In this way both confederations and syndicates foster greater stability and tranquillity of the business than would exist otherwise.

Extortion or Protection?

Talk of a market in protection and the central role of mafias in it may seem naively benign to many readers. To what extent is mafia 'protection' actually demanded by customers and to what extent is it thrust upon them? Surely, given that an established mafia group has a territorial monopoly on the means to violence, there is nothing to stop it from extorting money from criminals (who by virtue of their law-breaking have denied themselves state-protection) and law-abiding, but poorly protected citizens. Can 'protection', insofar as it exists, be interpreted merely as protection from the protecting group itself?

Whilst there are indeed examples of such purely negative protection, there are good theoretical and empirical grounds for arguing that in many cases protection is an authentic commodity. Because the nature of this commodity is one that tends towards monopoly, it may well be that it is overpriced and service is less than customers might achieve were they able to shop around. But like consumers in other monopolised markets, lacking alternatives, customers grumble and pay up. Authentic protection is, of course, less likely to be visible than its sham variant; it is when the market fails in some way (for example by forcing unwilling customers) that it comes to public attention (Gambetta 1993: 28–33).

As mentioned above, for a market to exist, there must be a demand for the commodity in question. The existence of extortionists, cheats, robbers, and other threats, by generating demand amongst one's client base, is therefore highly functional to protectors. If the world were safe without protection, why pay? It is for this reason that mafia protection is not a public good extended to all; non-customers must be victimised in order to prove protection's value to customers (Gambetta 1993: 24–5). We can see here how a mafia firm might therefore simultaneously operate as a supplier of, and a generator of demand for, protection. In a nice twist pointed out by Gambetta (1993: 31–2) with reference to the Sicilian market and corroborated by Varese (2001: 100) in the Russian one, extortionate demands on a new entrant to a market also act as a way of protecting incumbent businesses that currently pay protection; one of the things from which such businesses require protection is new entrants!

Obviously, if the environment that group operates in is already sufficiently rich in demand, we might expect our group not to waste resources on generating more. Conversely, in conditions where traders might get on very well without purchasing protection, we might expect aspiring protectors to first generate demand. This suggests that we might expect a tendency for mafias to engage in extortion in legitimate markets and protection in criminal ones. As will be shown below, this is not necessarily the case.

Another factor which we might expect to influence the preferences of a mafia firm *vis-à-vis* protection versus extortion (as well as the rate at which their services are charged), is its time horizon (Gambetta 1993: 33). A rational profit-maximising mafia firm, which expects long-term business continuity, might be expected to look after its protectees well: one that expects to go out of business tomorrow has only today in which to maximise revenue. Even if they do not apply such a calculation, rapacious extortionists discourage new business activity, both legal and illegal, within their territory and, in killing the goose that lays the golden eggs, ultimately impoverish themselves.

On the basis of his investigations in Russia, Varese (1996: 133–4) categorised the 'protection' firms he encountered into three types: predatory, extortionary, and protective. The first of these generally imposes ever larger taxes on its subject businesses with fatal results for the tax-payer. The second type of firm typically extracts small taxes in return for bogus protection; 'protection from a danger that the group itself might cause'. The third class, genuinely protecting groups, were actively sought out by firms which would do research in order to identify such a strong and reliable protector. Varese suggests that, over time, it is likely that the former groups will disappear and only the latter will prove successful.

Even in cases when aspiring extortionists attempt to sell bogus protection they may get drawn into providing a genuine commodity. Abadinsky (1983: 150–1) gives as an example of Pete and Figgy who shake down stall-holders with the face-saving assurance that should the stall-holders have any problems, they will take care of it. When problems do in fact arise, Pete and Figgy feel compelled to act in order to maintain their credibility and therefore their capacity to receive payments in the future.

To illustrate the ways in which mafia-type organisations operate as protectors, let us address now the question: who, and from whom, do mafias protect? First, protectors protect themselves. By virtue of an established reputation for efficiently supplying violence, protectors can engage in business (criminal or otherwise) with enhanced confidence that they will not be cheated or robbed. Gambetta argues that in the Sicilian case, mafiosi seldom actually engage in business on their own account and generally do very badly when they try. Members of mafia firms who make use of their affiliation to engage in business activities might therefore be more appropriately considered to be internalised consumers of protection.

Empirically, however, we can see cases of gangsters who extend protection to others, and contribute directly to the military strength of their group whilst making use of that strength to conduct business on their own account: in the example of the street-level drug-dealing gang analysed by Levitt and Venkatesh, for example, the group both operated its own drug-retailing business and taxed, regulated, and protected other criminal activities within its territory; until the mid-1970s,[2] prominent *yakuza* bosses would run their own gambling operations whilst extending protection to a myriad of other operations; senior members of mafia firms in both Sicily and the United States were direct participants in the heroin trade; the made mafia members of whom undercover FBI agent Pistone was supposedly a protectee in his role as a jewel thief, themselves engaged in robberies of various kinds; protectors everywhere engage in money-lending.

The second category of protectees is that of other criminals. Typically, these are participants in illegal markets though this need not be the case; robbers, for example, may find themselves in need of mafia services. Although Schelling (1985: 184) observes that burglary, as a clandestine activity with low barriers to entry, is impossible to monopolise and therefore 'organise', thieves may require protection from themselves being robbed or cheated. They are particularly vulnerable to such predation when they attempt to fence stolen property. A slightly different order of protection a thief might acquire is good intelligence concerning those who may be victimised with impunity; to rob a mafia-protectee may have serious repercussions for the ill-advised robber (see, for example, Gambetta 1993: 173).

Entrepreneurs engaged in illegal markets provide a bigger potential demand for mafia services. The most obvious type of protection is from being robbed, cheated, beaten, or not paid by customers. Prostitutes are particularly vulnerable to this type of victimisation, but it also applies to gamblers, loan sharks, and drug-dealers. Not only are these individuals criminals and therefore denied access to state protection, and not only are they frequently dealing with other criminals (individuals with a proven record of non-rule-compliance), but agreements are rarely written down. This ensures that disputes over agreements are a regular occurrence in the criminal economy. Arbitrating disputes of this nature is apparently a significant aspect of the work of mafia groups (cf. Reuter 1983: 151–73). Where the legal system is, or is perceived to be, partial, costly, or inefficient, mafia dispute settlement services may also be attractive to individuals and firms in legitimate markets, too.

Mafia groups may also protect their clients in illegal markets by neutralising or mitigating the effects of law-enforcement. A third service offered by mafia firms to their protectees in illegal markets is protection from competition. Limiting the number of suppliers of an illegal good within the firm's territory enables protectees to charge monopoly prices secure in the knowledge that they are sheltered from the vagaries of unfettered market forces; because traders know that their peers are similarly paying for protection, they can pass these costs on to their customers (Schelling 1984: 192).

A similar mechanism exists amongst the third category of possible mafia-protectees, legitimate businesses. Bars, nightclubs, and restaurants are the classic example of businesses that are reliant on mafia protection. Such premises are highly vulnerable to the disruption of business because they depend on customers being attracted by a pleasant atmosphere. This is a particularly fragile asset destroyed by drunk and abusive customers, fighting, bad odours round the entrance, a lack of customers (interpreted by potential customers as an indication that there must be something wrong with the premises), and so on. The problem of bad customers creates a genuine need, and places of entertainment will require some means to deal with this problem. This may lead them to actively seek out protection. At the same time, deliberate sabotage of their atmosphere means they can easily be subject to extortion. In an area in which such predators are numerous, bar and restaurant owners may also find it preferable to seek out one protector to defend against others. Here again we can see that the existence of racketeers generates a demand for protectors.

The fact that these establishments also hold a genuine market demand for such protection can be seen by the way in which Britain's night-time economy in recent decades has spawned a large 'bouncer' industry employing thousands of combative young men. Hobbs et al. (2002), in their study of social control in Britain's night-time economy, estimate that nearly 1,000 bouncers work the doors on a typical Friday or Saturday night in central Manchester alone. This might seem a large number unless one is also aware that the clubs, bars, and discotheques of Manchester draw an average crowd of 75,000 predominantly young and alcohol-fuelled people, while official state protection in the same area and time-frame is provided by just 30 police officers.

The existence of Britain's bouncer industry shows that, at least within legitimate industries, the demand for security need not necessarily be met from mafia sources.[3] Indeed, many companies internalise their security demand with guards, rigorous procedures to defend against embezzlement, security cameras, and so on. The solution found by Britain's night-time entertainment industries provides confirmation, were any needed, that the extent of mafia-type organisations in Britain is less than in, for example, Sicily, Japan, Russia, or Hong Kong.

Although there are many reasons for this, amongst these, perhaps the most important are that, first, Britain underwent its transition to a modern state several centuries before and has had the opportunity to develop more or less efficient, and broadly trusted, state mechanisms for protecting legitimate market transactions. Second, the scale of Britain's illegal markets has been reduced by the establishment of a legal gambling industry, and until recently, the official line that drugs should be considered primarily a public health problem rather than a criminal offence. Due to the widespread use of recreational drugs, especially its spread to otherwise respectable middle-class young, combined with relatively poor law enforcement, the drugs industry has developed into a highly competitive one making it very difficult for groups to acquire monopoly or even oligopoly power over it at any level of the distribution chain (see, e.g. Reuter and Hagga 1989: 40, 54; Pearson and Hobbs 2001: 11–12; Naylor 2001: 28). This nicely illustrates Schelling's observation that there is an optimum level of law enforcement to encourage organised crime domination of a criminal market; complete law enforcement means no market at all: not enough means low barriers to entry and too much competition (1984: 174).

The one area of Britain in which the processes we associate with mafia activity can most starkly be seen is Northern Ireland. In this troubled province the paramilitary groups associated with both communities not only protect and control certain criminal markets but a wide range of legitimate ones as well (Maguire 1993). This is enforced by 'beating' those who operate outside the protective fold or who transgress their codes of conduct.[4]

Legitimate businesses may require protection from not only their customers, as in the bar and club industries, but from their employees, the activities of which can seriously impair company performance. Militant trade union activism, for example, may disrupt a firm's production and, if such unionism results in improved pay and minimum levels of safety for workers, imposes increased costs on employers. Businesses have made use of mafia firms to break strikes, obstruct union formation and, in cases where unions have formed, to mitigate their consequences. This service has been well documented in Sicily:

When (as happens with increasing frequency) an agricultural or industrial company passes from the hands of a non-mafia entrepreneur into those of a mafia entrepreneur,[5] trade union struggle in that firm soon slackens off (Arlacchi 1983: 97).

And in the United States:

In response to the many craft unions' power to set unfavourable terms and to engage in extortion, contractors and builders have reached out to actors with power to control unions, ensure labour peace, and provide relief from onerous collective bargaining provisions. For half a century, La Cosa Nostra has had that power (Jacobs, Friel, and Radick 1999: 100).

And, as we shall see in later chapters, in Japan.

Whilst labour control is a protective service provided by mafias to businesses, it should be observed that independent trade unionism directly threatens the interests of mafias. Because unions are essentially bodies aspiring to the collective protection of their members, they are mafia rivals. Moreover, the left-wing ideals associated with trade unionism are directly antagonistic to the mafia: '(I)f work and land are perceived as rights, fairness in labor relations is enforced, and protection is offered for free, the mafia is out of business' (Gambetta 1993: 93).

Because of this, radical trade union and political activists attempting to organise, for example, peasants in Sicily, have frequently met a violent end at the hands of their mafia rivals (Blok 1974: 203–8). Hess (1998: 149) records that four such organisers were murdered in 1920 alone. This has lead some analysts, most notably Pearce (1976), to observe that mafias operate merely as agents of the economically dominant class. As professional protectors we might think that theoretically they would be prepared to sell their services to the highest bidder. Empirically we can see evidence for this in Sicily where local groups of the *Fasci Siciliani*, a peasant movement dating from the last decade of the nineteenth century (and not to be confused with fascism), were dominated by *mafiosi* (Blok 1974: 125). In areas of Sicily that were devoid of socialist political movements 'the *mafiosi* felt no compunction in appointing themselves protectors of the peasantry in the struggle for land; in return they asked for, and received, the lion's share' (Gambetta 1993: 93).

Occasionally, as in this example from New York, protection may be provided simultaneously to employers and employees:

At one time, employers in the garment trades hired Legs Diamond and his sluggers to break strikes, and the communists, then in control of the Cloakmakers Union, hired one Little Augie to protect the pickets and beat up the scabs; only later did both sides learn that Legs Diamond and Little Augie were working for the same man, Rothstein[6] (Bell 1965: 131).

Protection is a particularly valuable commodity in industries which are vulnerable to delay or sabotage and where such problems incur high costs. Construction is a good example of such an industry. When the value of the real estate and materials are all factored into the equation, enormous amounts of capital (typically demanding interest payments) are tied up in a construction project. Contracts imposing penalty clauses for failing to meet agreed deadlines compound the problem for developers. Should a group or individual hold the power to obstruct the smooth progress of a construction project they possess power indeed.

There are many ways in which delay can be caused. The most simple means is to obstruct the entrance to site entrances, find violations of the local planning regulations necessitating reapplication for permission, stealing, or damaging machinery and building materials. These are very low-cost strategies for the perpetrator. A more sophisticated technique, and the classic way in which mafia groups in New York have exerted delaying power, is through their control of the labour supply.

In order to weather the vagaries of business conditions, construction companies have the minimum number of core permanent employees, relying on temporary workers to fulfil contracts. In New York, these labourers are assigned to the employer by the appropriate trade union. This provides the allocating union tremendous power over the employer. As mentioned above, this power in New York has been held by mafia groups.

Whilst, as Jacobs observed, La Cosa Nostra can act to protect employers from trade union militancy, it is clear that this also enables them to make or break these same firms. Depending on one's perspective, the way in which this power has been used can be interpreted either as extortion or protection. This is because, just as Gambetta observed with reference to criminal markets, the mafia here act to protect cartels at the expense of firms outside of the cartel agreement. Outsiders obviously threaten the cartel as they might try to undercut the artificially high prices charged by the colluding firms.

An interesting observation of mafia involvement in the running of business cartels is that the mafia is not just protecting participants from outsiders but from *themselves*. One of the problems with cartels is that there is always an incentive for members to cheat by marginally undercutting the monopoly prices set by the cartel (though higher than would be attained in a free market) thereby gaining more business than the other colluding firms. Once one firm does this, all other firms are going to catch on and follow suit leading to the breakdown of the cartel and all firms worse off than had they all stuck to the agreement. Obviously, because this type of agreement is illegal, it cannot be policed by the authorities. By providing for an effective means of policing the agreement (carrying with it the credible threat that transgressors will be punished) the mafia here provides the conditions of confidence enabling cartel-formation that a lack of trust would otherwise prevent (Reuter 1985; Gambetta 1993; Gambetta and Reuter 1995).

In addition to the construction industry, mafia-policed cartels in New York have included the Fulton fish market, the garbage carting business, and the garment industry. La Cosa Nostra involvement in these industries is brilliantly described in Jacobs, Friel and Radick's outstanding 1999 work 'Gotham Unbound'. Gambetta and Reuter's (1995) examination of mafia involvement in cartel enforcement in markets in New York and Sicily suggests that the main beneficiaries of these arrangements are the colluding firms themselves rather than the enforcers. Presumably the enforcing group judges that, were it to retain the bulk of the monopoly profits itself then there would be little incentive for the participating firms to perpetuate the agreement and the mafia would have to engage in costly coercive measures.

Other legitimate industries that are highly susceptible to disruption are similarly liable to find themselves customers—whether willing or unwilling—of mafias. One example of this is the film industry. Film shoots on location are highly expensive yet can easily be sabotaged by extraneous noises, unwanted people wandering into frame, and vandalism. Moreover, in cases in which stars are frequently involved in a number of films at the same time (as in say India or Hong Kong), rescheduling a disrupted shoot may be impossible. Chu, writing about the Triads in pre-handover Hong Kong, suggests that payments are all but ubiquitous and could run to tens of thousands of Hong Kong dollars per day. In response to widespread harassment, a common strategy would be to pay off the locality's most powerful Triad boss in advance (Chu 2000: 49–52). Such protection cannot therefore be argued to be genuine as it is required only to defend against the extortionate activities of others, or indeed the protecting group in itself.

A significant role played by mafia protectors for their business clients is in the role of dispute resolution. For example, when debts are owed, trying to recover the money through the legal channels might be prohibitively costly both financially and in terms of time. Moreover, there may be a problem proving one's case in court. Frequently the police will be reluctant to involve themselves in this sort of civil dispute.

Owing to superior intelligence concerning the workings of the underworld, mafia groups typically are far more efficient in catching up with absconding debtors:

I reported the matter to the police and months later they had got nowhere. It took the triads only a matter of days to track down the man. I had a phone call at 2 a.m. The man was phoning me from his bed and he was surrounded by triads. One had a knife at his throat. He pleaded with me to call them off. I told them he had 48 hours to pay up or they would be back. I got my money (cited in Chu 2000: 78).

For such services a charge is made. Chu's informants suggest that the commission earned on this type of service was 30 per cent plus an up front starting fee of HK$3,000. Due to the fact that it is recovering a debt rather than preventing a bad-debt problem arising, it is perhaps better to consider this type of collection as post facto protection. A trader with a high risk of incurring such unpaid debts—such as a loan shark—might find it cost-effective to pay for his protection in advance. This of course also carries a powerful deterrent effect, assuming the protectee is somehow able to advertise the fact to his clients.

In a highly uncertain business environment such as that existing in transition stage Russia, protection (tellingly described as a 'roof'—*krysha*) of legitimate business extends to practically every area of commercial activity:

When a business comes 'under the roof' of a ROC (Russian organised crime) group, it is not always seen as a clear case of extortion. Often the krysha offers a range of services. The business can be expected to be defended from other racketeers, including corrupt law-enforcement; effective technical and guard protection of property; debt collection; assistance with customs clearance; legal and business advice froma an adroit 'legal staff'; and banking privileges at criminal controlled banks (Center for Strategic and International Studies, 1997: 29).

Ordinary individual members of the public may also find themselves customers of mafia services. The picture painted of Don Caló's morning walk in the square of a Sicilian village, colourfully describes a mafia prince holding court:

From the shadows of the walls and out of small side streets now emerged the people who . . . had waited in order to speak to him. They were peasants, old women with black shawls on their heads, young mafiosi, men of the middle class. Each one walked a short distance with him, when his time came, and explained his problems to him. He would listen, then call one of his followers, give a few instructions and then call the next supplicant. Many would kiss his hand in gratitude as they left him (Barzini in Hess 1998: 133).

The range of problems that Don Caló and his equivalents might be asked to resolve is broad. Victims might ask that stolen items be returned. This is a service that mafia groups can perform far more efficiently than official protectors; Mori, writing of the Sicilian mafia in the 1930s, estimated that in such cases the police would be successful in only around 10 per cent of cases: the mafia in all but 5 per cent (in Hess 1998: 151–2). More recent examples suggest that not much has changed since then (see, e.g. Gambetta 1993: 171–4).

Assistance might also be sought by supplicants in terms of securing employment, admission to a school or college, approval of official applications. Favours might also be of a more sensitive, non-material nature; in the film *The Godfather*, an undertaker appeals to Don Corleone to avenge the rape of his daughter; in the novel *Gli Inesorabili* an orphan young woman petitions a mafiosi to compel her seducer to marry her. Whilst both these examples are taken from fiction, they are not atypical.

Not all of the services rendered by mafia patrons to their clients are performed as cash transactions. Some are repaid with various types of favours such as employment for relatives, goods and services, odd jobs and so on (Gambetta 1993: 179–182). Other debts may be banked by the patron as social capital providing him with a pool of indebted individuals whose favours may or not be called in at a later stage:

Generosity creates obligations which are recognised by its recipients. Beyond the group of 'parasites' who are completely dependent on his support, there are a large number of corner boys who are at some time or other beholden to the racketeer for money lent to them or spent upon them[7] (Whyte 1993: 143).

In the meantime the demonstration of power implicit in these various social services to his clients contributes enormously to the respect enjoyed by he mafia patron.

The final source of custom for mafia services is provided by politicians. At the most basic level, mafia figures may help client politicians by providing them with positive electoral support. A powerful mafia group or figure will have a wide base of individuals who owe their jobs, livelihoods, or other benefits to the benevolence of their patron. This can provide a significant block of voters. Of course the political influence this provides to a mafia enhances its power to protect: it yields patronage powers over the distribution of state benefits and contracts; it facilitates the neutralisation of the criminal justice system *vis-à-vis* protectees. This in turn makes mafia clients more beholden to their patron thereby swelling their number increasing their potency as a voting block. In this way mafias can be considered to be protecting politicians from their rivals.

Democratic systems attempt to bolster the integrity of the electoral system by handicapping the ability of pressure groups to intimidate or buy voters (or voters to sell their votes) by ballot secrecy.[8] At least in some cases ways have been found to circumvent this. In the past at election time in Navarra in Sicily many voters would mysteriously be struck by temporary blindness and thereby gained dispensations allowing them to be accompanied into the voting booth. Although such devices are no longer apparently practised in Sicily, there are still veiled suggestions that ways exist for mafia patrons to find out how votes have been cast (Hess 1998: 157–8).

Of course, given their reputation for violence, mafias can also protect politicians from their rivals by intimidating and, if this fails, harming opposing politicians or their supporters. Newspapers that print unfavourable stories can be threatened and attacked; scandals silenced.

Needless to say, elected politicians are in a position to protect their mafia protectors so this relationship is a mutually beneficial relationship and mafia support may not be bought with cash but on the understanding that favours will be returned in the future. In Russia, some members of the *vory-v-zakone* have internalised this process by themselves standing for election (Varese 2001: 182–3).

This is a step that the Sicilian mafia, even in their period of greatest strength and influence would not have considered. As the *pentito mafiosi* Calderone observed, 'it is hard for a politician to become a *uomo d'onore*. "Within the Cosa Nostra there is a strong dislike of politicians because they cannot be trusted, because they do not keep their promises, because they constantly play the smart alec. They are false people without principles" ' (Hess 1998: 198).

In order to work as a credible supplier of protection in an uncertain and dangerous world, it is important that ones reputation as a person who will reliably fill one's side of an agreement, no matter what, be unsullied. The aspiring Russian politicians mentioned by Varese, may find that their work as protectors is irreparably compromised by their political ambitions.

Whilst it would be a conceptual mistake to conflate politicians with the state, the discussion on the mafia–politician nexus, naturally draws us to consider the nature of the relationship between mafia and state.

Mafia and the State

As has been made clear from the foregoing discussion, both mafia and state are dealers in the same commodity, protection. As such, they must be considered rivals. At the same time, due to the essentially monopolistic nature of this type of business, protectors can brook no rivalry. As such we should expect to see unremitting hostility between these two parties: 'The mafia does not have to be combated because of its values, which may seem warranted in a disintegrating society, but because of its very essence: there cannot be two systems of government in one society' (Falcone in Hess 1998: 195). As Falcone discovered to his ultimate cost, the relationship can be hostile indeed.

However, this is not the case in all circumstances and empirically the relationship has been more ambiguous. Let us first explore these ambiguities before returning to the breakdown in state–mafia relations in Sicily resulting in Falcone's tragic death.

Pearce (1976), writing from a Marxist perspective, argues that far from being an irreconcilable enemy of the state, 'the underworld' (which, from his analysis, is analogous to what is here understood collectively as the mafia) is in fact its servant. Mafia groups are just one more means of social control and the perpetuation of the existing hegemonic structure. In the light of the catalogue of services provided to various categories of customers given earlier, the suggestion that mafia services might also extend to the state may not be surprising. Let us examine the theoretical and empirical grounds on which Pearce's claim might be supported.

The main argument used by Pearce to support this claim is the way in which mafia groups have been used to suppress radical movements in ways that a democratic state cannot openly itself employ. Examples of this mafia as hammer of the left view have been cited above with reference to Sicily and the United States. Later chapters will show its widespread existence in Japan. In pre-revolutionary China, where the links between the Kuomintang government and the Green gang of triads were so close to make distinction meaningless, the Greens engaged in the White Terror of 1927 in which thousands of people thought to be communists were slaughtered on the streets of Shanghai (Booth 1999: 105–6). It should be reiterated that such behaviour need not necessarily be interpreted as mafia gangs protecting the state; socialist principles and, a fortiori, communist ones with their emphasis on a strong centralised state, represent a serious threat to mafia groups.

There are, however, examples of mafia groups providing less bloody services to different branches of the state. The most striking of such examples are those in which the security/intelligence apparatus of the state has coopted mafia groups. Perhaps most famous of these is the legendary use by US naval intelligence of 'Lucky' Luciano to ensure delay free operation of, and aid counter-intelligence on, the New York waterfront during the Second World War (Pearce 1976: 148). American intelligence agencies have also made use of foreign gangsters to combat communist threats[9] but this is a slightly different kind of relationship as what is of interest to us here is the relationship between a state and its domestic mafia groups.

A splendid case of mafia service to the state can be seen in the system of tax collection in Sicily. Up until 1984, this was carried out as a private concession run by the Salvo brothers (who as early as the 1960s had been identified by the police as mafia members). The Salvos were legally entitled to a commission of 10 per cent of all taxes collected (three times the costs of collecting taxes in other parts of Italy). Unsurprisingly, following the transfer of tax collection to less motivated and intimidating state inspectors, evasion 'increased dramatically' (Gambetta 1993: 163; Stille 1996: 55).

Perhaps the most significant way in which mafia groups can 'serve the state' can be seen in their relationship with law enforcement. Even if we discount corruption of the police (either through bribery or intimidation) by mafia groups, in which case we can consider the police to be protecting mafia protectors, we can see that mafia and police can interact to their mutual benefit. Mafias, as aspiring monopolists, have an interest in eradicating rivals. Providing police with evidence sufficient for such competitors to be successfully prosecuted gives an easy victory to both.[10] The advantages to mafia may be particularly pronounced as alternative (violent) strategies for getting rid of rivals are likely to incur all sorts of costs and risks.

For the same reasons mafias will take other actions to dissuade non-protected criminals from operating within its territory—especially if they are adversely affecting the business climate in which protected businesses operate. It can therefore be conjectured that mafias may paradoxically exercise a *crime-control* function. Whilst this is not done primarily for the benefit of the police, it is of course a situation that a hard-pressed or plain lazy police force might welcome. Empirically, there is evidence to support this surmise. Gambetta, for example, observes that 'the mafia at times polices its territory as if it were responsible for public safety' (1993: 166). The same has been said of the *yakuza* to the extent that it has become a cliché.

Whilst the neo-Marxist view of mafia as servant of the state is not without supporting evidence, it is a simplification of one outcome of a wider potential set. It is more accurate to say that this evidence more properly supports the argument that the state is one possible consumer of mafia services. However, state-patronage of such groups is not a necessary condition for their existence, or even their apparent toleration.

Even if law-enforcement officials and policymakers are opposed to the continued existence of mafias, it is still possible that they may adopt a quasi-cooperative policy. The way in which this might happen is explored by Celantini, Marrelli, and Martina (1995), who use economic modelling to show how the state might regulate organised crime. Celantini, Marrelli, and Martina's model is composed of a repeated fixed-stage game in which the government is facing two criminal groups, both of which are rational discounted-profit-maximisers. The government's objective is the minimisation of the combined profits of the two gangs. The government has at its disposal fixed resources available for action against these two groups, which it can allocate to the two groups in any ratio it thinks fit. The probability that a gang will be put out of business is directly proportional to the level of resources arrayed against it. If a firm is destroyed by government action, then a new one will take its place in the next game cycle.

At the beginning of each game cycle, the three players choose their game plan and, at the end of the game, the result is revealed and they receive their payoff (profits for the gangs and a negative payoff for the state equal to the sum of these profits). As the gangs value future as well as current profits, it will not be in their interests to adopt an aggressive short-term profit-maximising strategy, as this will incur a higher probability of being exterminated by the government in the next game period. A stable equilibrium can be reached in which the government 'rewards' gangs that play by the rules and do not antagonise it.

A pragmatic relationship approximating this model can be seen in the real world. The government must accept that it does not have a total monopoly of power and must therefore come to terms with other power groups. On the other side, organised crime groups will tend to adopt codes of practice (e.g. not killing police-officers) that avoid their coming into direct confrontation with the government. This need not imply any cordiality between the two parties; it can be likened to two powers locked in a military confrontation having a tacit understanding as to the 'limitation of war...and the delineation of spheres of influence' (Schelling 1984: 173).

Schelling (1984: 172) therefore suggests that, from a social point of view, there may be at least one advantage-organised criminality has over an anarchic underworld. This rests on the argument that an organisation may internalise costs that would be externalities to an individual. Whilst an act of violence carried out by an individual criminal in the perpetration of a crime may register as a significant cost to that individual, it also burdens other criminals with additional costs.

Because violence increases public anxiety, it will stimulate law-enforcement efforts to crackdown on crime. If crime is organised in regional monopolies, they will then have an interest in reducing violence. It may well be the case, of course, that in certain circumstances the costs of violence to the criminal organisation will be more than outweighed by the benefits. This does not alter the principle that, *ceteris paribus*, a mafia group will have an interest in maintaining discipline amongst its members not only for the obvious administrative reasons that all organisations have, but to avoid antagonising the authorities.

Tacit toleration of mafias by the authorities may be facilitated by attitudes towards the businesses in which they have traditionally been active. Where these businesses are perceived as victimless transactions between consenting adults, as may be the case with gambling, loan-sharking, and prostitution (whether or not this perception is accurate), there may be a general acceptance of mafias and consequently little pressure to enforce the relevant laws. Even high levels of inter-gang violence may not engender corresponding levels of public anxiety provided it is 'kept inside the ghettos' and resulting deaths are limited to combatants or members of marginal groups. The widespread perception of illegal recreational drugs as a serious threat to society makes a tacit acceptance of mafias involved in those markets much harder. The increasing importance of drug trafficking to the finances of such groups is one major feature, but by no means the only one, in the more overtly antipathetical treatment by governments in recent years.

Even with regard to the drugs trade, law-enforcement resources may well be directed at that aspect, which most directly concerns the public, street-level trading. This is characteristically a level at which there is little direct mafia involvement (under our definition, street-gangs can be seen as, at best, proto-mafia; more frequently they are consumers of protection provided by others). Given that law-enforcement resources are typically seriously constrained, they will be targeted in politically efficient ways; that is, against those crimes that voters are most worried about, such as disorganised violent street and property crimes, and, in so far as the drugs trade is targeted, its relatively 'disorganised' retail end.

The authorities may also invest few resources into combating mafias if they are faced with more pressing priorities. In Italy during much of the second half of the twentieth century, there was a very real threat of terrorism from both extremes of the political spectrum; in Japan and the United States, tackling the perceived threat posed by subversive radicals has traditionally been a far more significant goal than dealing with their respective mafia groups. It is no coincidence that increased efforts in countering the supposed global menace of trans-national organised crime came shortly after the end of the cold war.

As this last sentence and the experience of Sicily, and Falcone, suggest, the relationship between state and mafia is by no means static, and symbiosis and/or cooperation can degenerate into open and violent hostility. Some reasons for this shift will hopefully become apparent in subsequent chapters dealing empirically with the Japanese context. In the final chapter we will return to this problem in more theoretical terms exploring the changing relationships of mafias and states.

Mafias and *Yakuza*

The central argument of this chapter is that the Sicilian phenomenon known as the Mafia exhibits patterns, which can also be discerned amongst other sets of criminal groups such as traditional Italian organised crime in the United States, the Hong Kong Triads, and the Russian *vory-v-zakone*. Because of this, we are justified in categorising these groups as mafias. The central characteristic shared by mafias is their provision of protection to consumers who are either denied access to protection from the state or who desire types of protection that the state is unprepared to provide. This role ensures complex and ambiguous relationships with other sections of society, not least with the state.

Having established above what is meant here by the term 'mafia' and what sort of protection it affords to its protectees, let us now examine the Japanese context: to what extent are the *yakuza* the Japanese mafia?

2

Yakuza Evolution

Historical Antecedents

The groups commonly referred to as *yakuza* lay claim to a long lineage. Whilst much of this is of dubious historical validity, the *yakuza* mythology is important in conditioning the perceptions, held by both the gang members themselves and the wider society, of the place the *yakuza/bōryokudan* hold in Japanese society. Historically the term '*yakuza*' itself is imprecise in that it is commonly used to refer to two distinct groups, the *bakuto* (gamblers) and the *tekiya* (itinerant peddlers). The derivation of the word itself from the '*ya*' (eight), '*ku*' (nine) and '*sa*' (three) making up the worst possible hand in a traditional Japanese card game, shows clearly its original reference to gamblers.

It is probable that as long as there has been commerce there have been traders trying to sell sub-standard merchandise. Pedlars travelling around local fairs and markets using trickery and deceit to sell shoddy goods and cure-all medicines at inflated prices have long existed in Japan and elsewhere. However, due to the fragmentary and largely unwritten history of the underclass, it is hard to say when these traders first banded together into gangs of *tekiya* or, as they were formerly known, *yashi*. It is not even clear what the etymology of the word *yashi* is. Although it can be written with the characters for perfume-goods master (and carries the meanings not only of perfumer but of charlatan, quack, or showman) there are a number of theories suggesting that *yashi* was originally derived from other combinations of characters of which 'medicine master' seems the most plausible, but there is insufficient evidence for any of them (Iwai 1963: 57–8).

It is, however, clear that, for such groups, protection would be an important commodity; employing violence would have been an effective way of limiting competition. By 1740 the Tokugawa had appointed the more prominent gang leaders as supervisors responsible for organising open-air trading within a certain area. This example was followed at the shrines and temples where many markets were held. The supervisor was responsible for allocating sites for each stall as well as collecting rent from each trader.

Iwai (1963: 34) traces the history of the gamblers back to the seventh century; as early as AD 689 an imperial edict had banned gambling, whilst contemporary documents refer to the existence of organised gambling gangs by the Kamakura period (1185–1392). By the early Tokugawa period (1600–1867) recognisable *bakuto* organisations had appeared. The reaction of the authoritarian military dictatorship to these groups was initially highly restrictive with severe penalties for gamblers. Later, however, the central government developed a pragmatic policy of secretly aiding the more powerful of the *bakuto* leaders in order to exercise leverage over them to its own advantage (DeVos 1973: 283). During this period, the police authorities also coopted key *bakuto* and *tekiya* personnel into their intelligence networks. This is an early example of the symbiotic OC-state relationship that was discussed in the previous chapter.

Under this more relaxed political climate, the *bakuto* flourished to the extent that the most powerful bosses of gambling gangs became significant figures in the upper-, as well as the underworld. Some of these prominent gamblers also operated as labour brokers supplying construction workers for the large public-works programmes of this period. One of the responsibilities of the Shōgunate's vassals was to provide labour for these projects, and those lords who did not want to send their own men therefore required the services of these gambler/labour brokers. During this time the houses of gambling bosses operated as rudimentary hostels for itinerants. This had the triple purpose of attracting gambling customers, labourers, and potential gang members.

Labour broking, and raking off a percentage of the labourer's wages (*pinhane*), is therefore another continuous feature of the history of *yakuza* organisations. There is a happy synergy in these two industries;

the lure of gambling attracted potential labour whilst, after work, their wages could be fleeced off them at the gaming dens. Alternatively, it might work the other way round: the boss might lend money to a gambler and, once the money had been lost, the debt could be paid off by labour. The role of money-lending by bosses is clearly reflected in the traditional title of gambling bosses, *kashimoto* (source of loans).

The most famous of these gambler/brokers was Banzuiin Chōbeii. Banzuiin's fame is due to his perceived role as a protector of the common man against arbitrary treatment by gangs of discontented samurai. The unification of Japan under the Tokugawa at the beginning of the seventeenth century brought to an end centuries of warfare and revolt. With peace, came a crisis for the large, and economically useless, warrior class. Whilst many samurai responded by becoming bureaucrats and scholars, others reacted against the change in the political situation by forming gangs, which became known as the *hatamoto yakko* (servants of the Shōgun). These bands set themselves apart by their ostentatious dress and hair, devotion to the martial arts and stress on the *bushidō* code of their forebears. More significantly *hatamoto yakko* committed frequent outrages against ordinary townspeople (Ino 1993: 33).

Banzuiin, and others like him, supposedly set up civil-defence groups composed of his gamblers, labourers, and local firemen (*machi hikeshi*) to counteract the *hatamoto yakko*. These groups, in turn, became known as the *machi yakko*, the servants of the town. Rather than being primarily altruistic anti-*hatamoto-yakko* forces, Ino (1993: 44) maintains that the rationale for the *machi yakko's* existence was as mutual-aid societies. They were largely composed of victims of the Tokugawa regime such as farmers (who had abandoned the land due to land taxes), debtors, and also masterless warriors, some of whom had set up martial-arts schools for townspeople.

The *machi yakko* quickly became folk heroes and the subject of songs, *kabuki* plays, novels and, more recently, films. This Robin Hood mythology is claimed by the modern *yakuza* who assert that they are the descendants of the *machi yakko*. Interestingly, in their profession of reactionary political views, exaggerated attire, elaborate rituals, and defiant self-exclusion, they perhaps share more with the *hatamoto yakko*. Despite the claims made by the *yakuza* to *machi yakko* ancestry, these groups were finally eradicated by the Tokugawa in the late seventeenth century (DeVos 1973: 286).

In Chapter One, it was mentioned that the environment that had favoured the development of the mafia in Sicily had comprised three key components: the end of the feudal system of agricultural production, with a concomitant increase in the number of transactions within that society; the absence of efficient legal mechanisms for protecting the integrity of those transactions; a pool of men able and willing to provide extra-legal protection through their comparative advantage in the use of violence. Varese shows that the same combination of factors generated a Russian mafia following the transition to a market economy in the former Soviet Union.

Can we identify the same sort of mechanism in the rise of the *yakuza*? To ask this question we are making the implicit assumption that historically the *yakuza* have primarily been involved in the provision of protection. This assumption is in fact problematic; early *bakuto* and *tekiya* groups certainly have long used violence to protect their own territorial monopolies, but there is a lack of evidence that these groups exploited this military advantage to specialise in the sale of protection to others.

It would be tempting to draw the analogy with Sicily and assert that the Meiji restoration involved the transition from a feudal system of government to a modern state, and the disenfranchisement of large numbers of samurai (whose martial skills well-qualified them to serve as providers of protection). However, if we look at the available empirical evidence, it seems that, at least as far as the *bakuto* are concerned, the period in which they flourished was actually the end of the Tokugawa period.

The reasons for this golden age are not, however, completely at odds with the mechanism we identify as being responsible for the development of the Sicilian and Russian mafias. By the early nineteenth century, the Tokugawa military government became increasingly weak as the growth of a wealthy merchant class supplanted a hereditary landholding aristocracy as the main source of economic power. In this period of transition, Iwai (1963: 42) notes that, by the Tenpō period (1830–1844), many areas were effectively unpoliced; gambling groups openly defied the law by wearing swords; the regional officials were unable to take steps against them.

Whether the military potential of these *bakuto* groups was exploited by them in mafia-like ways is not clear; the apparent lack of formal controls is suggestive of a potential demand for protection, and

Iwai (1963: 42) mentions that these groups were seen as conspiring with local elites. All this makes the analogy at least plausible but the evidential base is very weak.

During the struggle for supremacy between the decaying regime of the Tokugawa and the pro-imperial faction, the larger *bakuto* groups with their reserves of fighting men became important political forces. They adopted an opportunistic attitude, with different groups supporting whichever side they considered more likely to win. The most well-known of these gamblers-turned-politicians was Shimizu Jirōchō. Jirōchō and his 480 armed followers took over the city of Ise and the surrounding area for the Imperial forces. Following the war there was a problem of warriors loyal to the defeated Shōgunate raiding the highways, and it was decided to make use of gambling groups to counteract them. Jirōchō was made one of the officials responsible for guarding the highways. Not only were his past crimes pardoned in return for his military support, but he was granted the right to wear swords (Iwai 1963: 45; Tamura 1981: 225).

Despite the services that various gambling groups had rendered to the Meiji government in establishing itself, the new administration persecuted gambling and the *bakuto* groups. In 1884 the government implemented an 'Ordinance for the Treatment of Gambling Crimes' under which mass arrests of gamblers took place. This practice by the authorities of making use of gangs when it is advantageous, and restricting them when they are perceived as a threat to public order, is a persistent theme in the history of the relations between Japan's ruling elite and the *yakuza* groups. This particular period of control did not last long and with economic prosperity following Japan's wars with China (1894–5) and Russia (1905), there was a revival in the fortunes of gambling groups.

An important observation to make here is that by this time we can see that these groups were not operating exclusively as gamblers but that they were also exercising a protective function *vis-à-vis* the prostitution, entertainment, and construction industries (Iwai 1963: 45–6). We can therefore assert that, by the end of the Meiji period, the *yakuza* had started to behave in ways that were identified in the previous chapter as those characterising mafias.

It is not clear that the *yakuza* exercised a similar role for other industries at this stage. There was a big growth in the level of economic activity over this period; so there was a corresponding rise in the number of transactions requiring protection. However, we do not have evidence to show that it was the *yakuza* who provided it. This may be due to evidential deficiencies or because the demand for protection was being met by alternatives. One of the differences between Japan and Sicily following the termination of feudalism was that Japan had 'long been familiar with registry systems, complex procedures for adjudication, and sophisticated commercial instruments' and that modern European-inspired legal codes were 'easily integrated into the Japanese cultural and institutional matrix' (Haley 1991: 70–1). It is likely therefore that there were fewer opportunities for *yakuza* to provide protection than were available to the Sicilian Mafia in their respective transitional economies.

With the maturation of an industrial capitalist economy, an increasingly militant labour movement developed in Japan. This received a large boost from the 1917 Bolshevik revolution in Russia. In Japan, riots broke out throughout the country the following year. These disturbances had been triggered by high rice prices, compounded by inflation, but soon spread to the coal mines where the rioting had a more potentially subversive anti-company tone (Lewis 1990: 15–16, 206–13).[1]

In order to counter the threat of an increasingly vociferous labour movement, both the government and industrialists hoped to harness *bakuto* groups as shock-troops to break strikes and enforce labour acquiescence. In 1919, a national alliance of gamblers, the Dai Nippon Kokusui-kai (the Greater Japan National Essence Society), was set up by Interior Minister Tokonami Takejirō at the instigation of the Hara cabinet. This organisation received support from senior military figures and was advised by the famous right-wing extremist Tōyama Mitsuru. Like later attempts to organise such federations, the Dai Nippon Kokusui-kai was wracked by internal conflict and not susceptible to external control. Consequently it had only limited impact (Iwai 1963: 46).

However, links between political and military leaders on one hand and *bakuto* and *tekiya* bosses on the other, increased into the early Shōwa period. *Yakuza* groups played active roles in extreme right-wing groups such as the Kokuryū-kai which were involved in violent strike-breaking, combating left-wing and liberal political movements, and engineering 'incidents' in China and Manchuria[2] (Iwai 1963: 46–7). Whilst some members may have found a political justification for their actions, the *yakuza* also benefited substantially from this relationship.

This was profitable both in terms of increased political influence, and materially from the revenues to be made from protecting the opium dens supplying the Chinese (Vaughn, Huang, and Ramirez 1995: 496).

It might be reasonable to conjecture that *yakuza* gangs had also been responsible for supplying 'comfort women' to the Imperial Japanese Army. However, Iwai, who before becoming one of the foremost authorities on the *yakuza* had served in the Imperial Japanese Navy, disputes this, saying that there was no need for *yakuza* involvement in this business because legitimate merchants were responsible for employing comfort women (interview Tokyo, 1989).

With the mobilisation of the Japanese economy onto a wartime footing, there was no longer any reason to cultivate the *yakuza*. Therefore, gang members who had not been directly incorporated into the war effort were once again the target of official crackdowns. It would not be until the end of the Pacific War that gangs would once again flourish.

Postwar Developments

The 43-year period between the end of the Second World War and the death of the Shōwa emperor (1989) saw enormous changes in Japan and, in response to the opportunities and challenges that these changes offered, organised crime in Japan developed profoundly, too. The 1989 *Hanzai Hakusho* (Ministry of Justice White Paper on Crime) identifies five separate historical periods in this development. These are the Period of Postwar Confusion (1945–50), the Gang War Period (1950–1963), the Summit Strategy Period (1964–1970), the Period of Reorganisation, Expansion, and Oligopolisation (1971–1980), and the Period of Generation Change (1981–1988).

Although the analysis provided by the 1989 White Paper on Crime is by no means exhaustive, this periodisation is a useful starting-point to evaluate the trends in the development of the postwar *yakuza*. These will be presented here in brief outline, and then various points of interest will be discussed in greater depth. A detailed account of the various sources of *yakuza* income will be provided in Chapter Four, and these are therefore mentioned only in passing here.

Period of Postwar Confusion

By the end of the war, Japan was devastated: its major cities lay in ruins; many of its people were facing starvation; unemployment stood at 13.1 million (of which 17.6 per cent were disbanded troops); manufacturing capacity stood at 52.7 per cent of its 1937 level and rice production at 59 per cent (Nakamura 1981: 12–22). To exacerbate matters the police had been disarmed, purged, and discredited and were temporarily unable to enforce public order, whilst the occupying American authorities, faced with budget constraints of their own, did not treat policing the underworld as a priority (Huang and Vaughn 1992: 25).

In the face of these almost impossible circumstances, black-market trading became the only way that people could survive. In one famous incident a young judge, morally unable to condemn the small-time black-market traders whilst remaining their customer, insisted on subsisting only on his allocated official ration; he starved to death (Dower 2000: 99–100).

The speed with which these markets developed is remarkable. On 18 August 1945, just three days after the Emperor's announcement of surrender, the Tokyo-based *tekiya* group the Kantō Ozu-gumi placed the following advertisement in local papers:

Urgent notice to enterprises, factories and those manufacturers in the process of shifting from wartime production to peacetime production. Your product will be bought in large quantities at a suitable price. Those who wish to sell should come with samples and estimates of production costs to the following address:

Shinjuku Market, 1–854 Tsunohazu, Yodobashiku, Shinjuku, Tokyo.

Kantō Ozu-gumi (Whiting 2000: 7)

Elsewhere in Japan similar markets rapidly appeared under the control of local *yakuza* bosses. Only two months after the surrender, it was estimated that there were 17,000 such markets throughout the country (Dower 2000: 140). This extensive black market featured not only the traditional street traders, the *tekiya*, but the *bakuto* and non-traditional gangs of racketeers known as *gurentai*. Whilst some traditional gambling groups attempted to remain aloof from these developments, they tended to be forced out of business or into alliances with the more aggressive *gurentai* (DeVos 1973: 295).

The state was in no position to control these markets and even found itself reliant on the services of *yakuza* gangs. Harry Emerson Wildes, an American journalist who had worked in Japan before the war, writing in 1948, noted that *yakuza* bosses were 'officially designated collectors of Tokyo mercantile taxes' although 'no effective supervision exists to prevent exploitation, nor even to guard against undue delay between collection and final delivery of the tax money' (Wildes 1948: 1157–8). Similarly, the police were forced to accept the reality of *yakuza* control of the markets: this was formalised by a 1946 ordinance giving *tekiya* bosses formal control over the open-air markets in Tokyo (1948: 1157–8).

This is therefore the period by which we can claim that the transition of the *yakuza* to a mafia, as the term has been defined in Chapter One, became complete. This is also the period in which the combination of aetiological factors encouraging mafia emergence are most evident: a market; a lack of official mechanisms for regulating the transactions within that market; and a supply of tough and desperate men, in this case large numbers of returning combat-veterans who were well-schooled in the use of violence and able to provide informal alternatives.

Ironically, government actions in the immediate postwar period inadvertently accelerated the shift of traditional *bakuto* groups into alternative economic activities. In an attempt to increase government revenue by taking over the most popular forms of gambling, the government squeezed the *bakuto*'s main source of revenue thereby forcing them to diversify.

The black market did not just deal in essentials such as food, cooking oil, and utensils such as pots and pans: They also dealt in drugs; in this period, drug use reached epidemic proportions. This was chiefly for three reasons. First, during the war, the government had produced large quantities of amphetamines to boost both workers' productivity and the endurance of troops. With Japan's defeat, the remaining stockpiles, as well as the technical know-how to produce amphetamines, quickly found their way into the hands of criminal gangs. Second, the use of these drugs had been lent legitimacy by their role in the war effort and, since many otherwise law-abiding people were already making purchases from the black market, there was no stigma attached to the use of amphetamines. Third, given the shortage of food, amphetamines were a useful way of suppressing fatigue and hunger (Vaughn, Huang, and Ramirez 1995: 498). It should be noted that the amphetamines-control law was not passed until 1951, so in the immediate postwar period, dealing in this commodity was no more problematic than for other black-market goods.

Amongst the *gurentai* groups were large numbers of Koreans, Taiwanese, and Chinese who had been brought over to Japan as forced labour for Japan's shipyards, mines, and factories. People from these three countries (known as *sangokujin*) had endured years of appalling treatment at the hands of their Japanese masters and many sought revenge in violent reprisals. Therefore the conflicts that inevitably arose over control of the illegal and highly lucrative markets often took on a racial tone with native Japanese gangs portraying themselves as defenders of the common people against foreign hoodlums. Given that many of the participants in these fights were battle-hardened veterans with access to military weaponry, they presented a severe threat to public safety (*Hanzai Hakusho* 1989: 348).

Perhaps the largest of these conflicts occurred in July 1946 when the Matsuda-gumi, who ran the Shinbashi market in Tokyo, came to blows with Taiwanese stall-holders. More than one thousand Matsuda-gumi members and several hundred Taiwanese were involved and, in the final battle, the Taiwanese suffered seven fatalities and thirty-four serious injuries (Dower 2000: 143).

Gang-War Period

During the 1950s Japan's economy started to pick up. This process of recovery received a massive boost when the Korean War created an enormous demand for military equipment. The Jinmu boom of 1955–1956 and the Iwato boom of 1959–1960 generated large construction projects for roads, apartment blocks, and infrastructure of all types. At the same time, this increased economic activity led to a massive increase in shipping cargo. As, by this time, the labour supplies of both the construction and docking industries were largely dominated by *yakuza* groups, they profited handsomely from this development.

Whilst economic growth led to the withering away of the black market for necessities, prosperity spawned a thriving entertainment industry including *pachinko* and public gambling, as well as *mizushōbai* trades such as bars, restaurants, and prostitution.[3] There was therefore

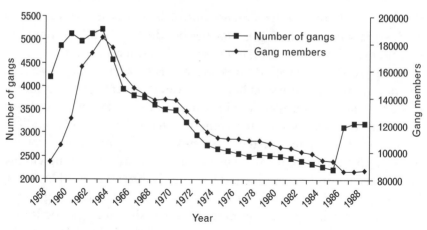

Fig. 2.1 *Yakuza* gangs and gang members 1958–1988
Source: *Hanzai Hakusho* (1989).

considerable scope for protection rackets and extortion. This period consequently saw a considerable growth in the number and member-ship of *yakuza* groups. As can be seen in Figure 2.1, the size of OCGs reached a peak in 1963 with 184,091 members in 5,216 gangs.

The increase in market opportunities also saw increased competi-tion between the various groups over control of these new sources of funds. This is illustrated by Figure 2.2 showing the incidence of vio-lent intergang conflicts from 1960 to 1988. The violence of these con-flicts is demonstrated by the fact that during the peak year of 1963, 48.4 per cent of all *bōryokudan* arrests were for assault, bodily harm, or murder (*Hanzai Hakusho* 1989: 343). This period of warfare resulted in a few organisations achieving national prominence by a process of swallowing up their weaker neighbours in military alliances or by destroying them in open conflict. In particular, seven groups were identified by the police as major syndicates. These were: the Yamaguchi-gumi, the Honda-kai (later the Dai Nippon Heiwa-kai), the Sumiyoshi-kai (Sumiyoshi Rengō), the Kinsei-kai (Inagawa-kai), the Nippon Kokusui-kai, the Kyokutō Aio-kai, and the Matsuba-kai.

In an attempt to control *bōryokudan* crimes, a number of new laws were introduced. In 1958 the criminal law was changed to include the crime of witness intimidation, and provisions were made for the protection of witnesses. At the same time, penalties against lethal

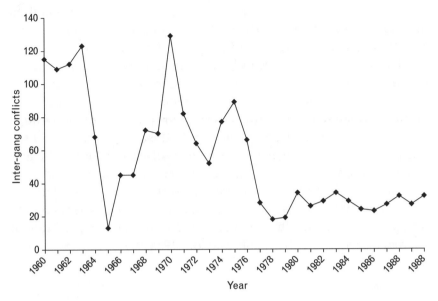

Fig. 2.2 *Yakuza* intergang conflicts 1960–1988
Source: *Hanzai Hakusho* (1989).

weapons such as guns and swords were increased and a law forbidding assembly with weapons was enacted. Given that intergang conflict did not decrease until 1963, these laws seem to have had little impact. Possible reasons for this will be discussed below. In 1964 legal sanctions against crimes of assault with either swords or firearms were further strengthened.

Summit Strategy

In the early 1960s, widespread public discontent, including a 1964 campaign by the *Mainichi Shimbun*, with the high level of gang feuds, put pressure on the police to take more comprehensive anti-OC measures. The forthcoming Tokyo Olympics also spurred the authorities to clean up the capital. The police response was to put into effect its 'summit strategy' of nationally coordinated arrests of gang members, targeting particularly high-ranking personnel of executive (*kanbu*) grade or above. In particular the police made efforts to control illegal sources of income and firearms (Shikita and Tsuchiya 1992: 88). Both the police and crime white papers try to show the success of the summit strategy crackdowns by pointing out that during this period a number of powerful groups including the Sumiyoshi-kai, the Kinsei-kai, and the Honda-kai, as well as a large federation, the Kantō-kai, disbanded. What they do not mention is that, whilst these large syndicates disbanded, in many cases their component subgroups remained in existence. Consequently both the Sumiyoshi-kai and the Kinsei-kai were able to re-establish themselves not long after and today remain, after the Yamaguchi-gumi, the largest *yakuza* syndicates in Japan (Ino 1992*a*: 263). Furthermore, as discussed by Kaplan and Dubro, the Kantō-kai was the result of a politically inspired attempt to set up a nation-wide alliance of *bōryokudan*, which collapsed due to internal dissent rather than police action (1986: 95).

Reorganisation, Expansion, and Oligopolisation

Whilst the summit strategy had a marked effect on the level of inter-gang struggles and caused a number of gangs to disband and total membership to decline, it also had other, unanticipated, consequences. As the police crackdowns targeted primarily traditional *yakuza* crimes such as gambling and extortion, the main brunt of this assault fell disproportionately on the small and medium-sized organisations who depended entirely on these activities for their income. The larger groups, with much more diversified portfolios of legal and illegal businesses, were better able to withstand the effect of police crackdowns.

Furthermore, the top leadership of the big groups quickly developed a system which effectively insulated them from successful prosecution. This system, known as *jōnōkin*, consisted of payments from gang subordinates, and meant that bosses received a substantial income without direct involvement in criminal activity themselves. Therefore the large *yakuza* groups, most notably the Yamaguchi-gumi, were actually in a position to improve their standing during this period. As the overall number of gangs and gang-members dropped, the large syndicates expanded into new territories either by taking over the weakened small gangs or by filling vacuums left by disbanded groups

Table 2.1 Indexed changes in *yakuza* strength 1968–1979

1979 (1968 = 100)	Gangs	Members
Total *yakuza*	69.9	77.2
Seven designated groups	134.9	119.9
Big Three	153.9	140.4

Source: Hanzai Hakusho (1989).

(*Keisatsu Hakusho* 1989: 13). The police summit operations can therefore be considered as, at best, only a qualified success.

The period immediately following the police crackdown era was therefore characterised by a process of expansion as a few large gang syndicates came to dominate the OC landscape of Japan. This tendency was stimulated in the early 1970s by the gradual release of some of the most able bosses and executives who had been arrested during the previous decade. In particular the growth of the big three groups, the Yamaguchi-gumi, the Sumiyoshi-kai, and the Inagawa-kai, stands out. The relative size of these is illustrated in Table 2.1.

As well as geographically expanding their territories, these groups found it necessary to continually seek new business activities, both legal and illegal, due to the pressure of law-enforcement crackdowns on established criminal operations. Diversification was also necessitated by the oil shock of 1973, which had a big impact on *yakuza* income. As a response to economic recession and a more hostile legal environment, the *yakuza* became increasingly involved in new fields, such as organising foreign gambling trips, *sōkaiya* corporate blackmail, finance, and forming spurious social movements and right-wing political organisations as pretexts for raising money.

During this period, *yakuza* also became increasingly heavily dependent on amphetamines as a source of income. Tamura (1992: 102–3) identifies the beginning of the 'second stimulant epidemic', as in 1970, and suggests that this industry provided the cash-generating engine that financed the expansion of the big groups. This agrees with Schelling's observations on the need for a 'core' business providing the resources to build the necessary political and military infrastructure of a large organised crime operation.

Generation Change

Throughout the 1980s the trends of the previous decade continued: the large organisations became increasingly sophisticated and diversified whilst the smaller groups were swallowed up by one or another of the large syndicates, disbanded, or condemned to a marginal existence. However, the seemingly relentless progress of the big three gangs was rocked in July, 1981 when the third-generation *kumi-chō* (boss) of the Yamaguchi-gumi, Taoka Kazuo, died. In February of the following year, his designated successor, Yamamoto Kenichi, also died. The organisation quickly became divided as to who would succeed Taoka. After two years of political manoeuvring, Takenaka Masahisa was finally selected as fourth-generation boss of the Yamaguchi-gumi in 1984 and the organisation was split into two as Yamamoto Hiroshi, another top executive, broke away and formed a rival organisation, the Ichiwa-kai. The resulting gang war lasted five years and was on an unprecedented scale: in nineteen prefectures and two metropolitan areas, over three hundred violent incidents took place causing twenty-five deaths (including the new *kumi-chō*, Takenaka), seventy injuries including four innocent bystanders, and over five hundred arrests for crimes directly related to the conflict (Yamadaira 1993: 287–8).

Although the Ichiwa-kai had initially consisted of 13,000 members, its numbers quickly dwindled due to the fact that the Yamaguchi-gumi successfully lured back many of the defectors. This was aided by many Ichiwa-kai members when they found that, without the established reputation of the Yamaguchi-gumi behind them, it was much harder for them to raise money (Yamadaira 1992: 37). This illustrates the crucial importance of reputation and brand image to mafia groups as discussed in Chapter One. Eventually, in 1989, the defeated rump of the Ichiwa-kai disbanded. Although severely hit by the schism of 1984, the Yamaguchi-gumi quickly restored its pre-eminent position and by the last year of the Shōwa period the organisation consisted of 737 groups and 20,826 members (*Keisatsu Hakusho* 1989: 17) whilst its reputation for invincibility had, if anything, been enhanced.

The problem of generational change affected not only the Yamaguchi-gumi. Other large gangs also had an ageing leadership and, due to the changing age structure of *yakuza* in the last decade of the Shōwa period, it is possible that gangs will find it increasingly difficult to find suitable personnel moving up the ranks to fill their key

Table 2.2 The ageing composition
of *yakuza* groups

	20–29 years old	Over 40 years old
1966	73,259 (49.8%)	21,185 (14.4%)
1976	39,614 (36.7%)	27,523 (25.1%)
1985	22,594 (24.2%)	34, 295 (36.7%)

Source: Hanzai Hakusho (1989).

leadership positions. The trend towards an increasingly aged *yakuza* community is shown in Table 2.2.

The process of *yakuza* gerontification (*kōreika*), is in part a reflection of demographic change in Japan as a whole. When we look at these figures with reference to those for the composition of total working-age Japanese, *yakuza* ageing does not look quite as dramatic. Even so, it is taking place at a faster rate than that of the wider Japanese population;[4] so this cannot be explained purely by recourse to demographic factors. Given that *yakuza* work ultimately depends on the credible threat of violence, a diminishing proportion of young males (statistically the most violent section of society) is a problem for *yakuza* organisations.

'Formerly it had been said that the supply of *bōryokudan* members would never dry up, but now they are facing a severe crisis of new personnel' (*Hanzai Hakusho* 1989: 349). In one extreme case a Hokkaidō-based group found itself so short of personnel that it felt compelled to advertise in an employment magazine for students to work on a part-time basis (Yamadaira 1992: 140). This process of '*bōryokudan banare*' (movement away from the *bōryokudan*) may well be a major long-term problem for these groups. A number of hypotheses are generated by this phenomenon, and the reasons for, and consequences of, the *bōryokudan banare* merit further research.

One possible explanation is that, rather than being seen as glamorous, *yakuza* life is now perceived as *kitsui*, *kitanai*, and *kiken* (arduous, dirty, and dangerous) and, consequently, recruitment is becoming harder amongst an increasingly soft and pampered Japanese youth. Looking at police photographs of Yamaguchi-gumi gang members of the 1950s one is struck by the universally sunken sockets and prominent cheek bones of a malnourished and desperate group of men for whom gang activity was quite simply a means of survival. The faces of young *yakuza* members today lack this lean and hungry look. In the conclusion, changes in other social conditions encouraging *yakuza* recruitment will be discussed.

It does not seem plausible that the decline in the apparent ability of *yakuza* to attract young apprentices was due to a decline in the profitability of the industry in the 1980s. The bubble economy generated enormous wealth, and *yakuza* became heavily involved in real-estate and stock-market speculation. In particular, the *yakuza* developed the lucrative business of *jiage* (land-raising), in which small landholders on adjoining plots would be forced to sell so that a larger, more profitable site for development could be created. The heady economic atmosphere of the late 1980s also engendered financial irresponsibility, in which some *yakuza* were able to acquire enormous loans. At the same time companies, awash with money, were easy prey for corporate blackmail and extortion.

Another development during this period was the increase in crimes targeting ordinary citizens and businesses (*minji kainyū bōryoku*). Traditionally, part of the code of ethics of the *yakuza* had been to avoid inflicting harm on the common people. This is shown by the pride taken in the legends of the *machi yakko* as defenders of the commoners against exploitation by the rich and powerful, expressed in the set phrase *'jaku o tasukete: kyō o kujiki'* (help the weak: crush the strong). Whilst certain sections of society, especially those working in the *mizu-shōbai*/entertainment and construction industries, had long enjoyed a close relationship with these groups, for most of the postwar era the *yakuza* had not directly impinged on the lives of most ordinary people. With the diversification of *yakuza* into new predatory business activities, the perception of a romanticised *yakuza* code became increasingly tarnished in the minds of straight (*katagi*) society.

Throughout the periods of reorganisation and generation change, the modernising, diversifying, and expanding *yakuza* had developed an international dimension to their operations. This process has continued into the Heisei period with gathering momentum. There are a number of reasons for this. First, the modern *yakuza* depend on overseas countries, especially in Asia and the Pacific Rim, as a source of drugs, firearms, and prostitutes. These are all commodities that play an important part in Japan's criminal economy. Second, international investment, especially real-estate, provides an avenue for both money-laundering and the securing of assets outside the reach of Japan's tax and law-enforcement authorities. Third, the boom in overseas travel from Japan, spurred by the strong yen, created opportunities for the *yakuza* and, in conjunction with local criminal groups, they became involved in organising sex-tourism and gambling trips in various Asian countries for Japanese businessmen.

From about 1970 onwards, the *yakuza* have become increasingly well-armed, and there has been a marked shift from swords and daggers to modern firearms. This tendency has become especially pronounced since the mid-1980s, though seizure rates from that period may be attributed to the abnormal circumstances of the Yamaguchi-gumi's internal conflict. It is possible that the *yakuza* are trying to compensate for their manpower crisis by increasing their firepower through investing in efficient modern weaponry (*Hanzai Hakusho* 1989: 353).

Behind the Scenes

The historical development outlined above is largely derived from official sources and in particular from the *Keisatsu* and *Hanzai Hakusho*. One question that arises from the official picture is how, given the apparently concerted attempts by the police to eradicate the *yakuza* (especially since the mid-1960s), did OC manage to remain such a large and vibrant aspect of Japan in the late Shōwa period? Indeed the largest groups actually grew in both relative and absolute terms during this period. To answer this question it is necessary to go behind the surface (*tatemae*) of official arrest-rate statistics.

The links between the postwar *yakuza* and, usually right-wing, politicians are well known. This is not so much due to fearless investigative journalism or mass-arrests of corrupt politicians as to the extraordinary degree to which these links were openly displayed for much of this period. In some cases during the period of immediate postwar chaos, the links were in fact so close as to make it impossible to differentiate between the authorities and gangsters. During the immediate postwar period in Nagahama city in Shiga prefecture, the boss of the Hakuryū-sha *yakuza* group not only sat on the city council, but also served as head of the city's police commission (Iwai 1963: 692). The Hakuryū-sha therefore ultimately controlled both formal and informal markets for protection. This was largely made possible due to attempts by the occupying authorities to impose a decentralised system of policing on Japan. With the reversal of this policy and the passage of the police law in 1954, such flagrant and extreme cases of *yakuza* monopolisation became highly unlikely.

One of the most prominent gangsters of this period was the leader of the Kantō Ozu-gumi, Ozu Boss, who controlled the Shinjuku black market. Having refused an invitation to join the Socialist Party, Ozu was persuaded to run for the Diet by the leadership of the Liberal Party with which he had very cordial relations; the foreword to his autobiography was penned by the then Finance Minister, Ishibashi Tanzan, whilst another senior Liberal Party figure, Ōno Banboku, was his sworn blood-brother (Iwai 1963: 693). As conditions returned to normal and the police reasserted their control over the more overt abuses, exceptional cases such as the above disappeared. However, politicians still found it useful to maintain links with the *bōryokudan*.

Initially, the occupying American forces under General MacArthur had intended to purge Japan's government and business elites of extreme right-wing figures. With the onset of the Cold War and the fear of Japan's indigenous communists and trade union activists, this policy underwent a *gyaku kōsu* or 'reverse course'. Just as had been the case in 1919, certain members of the government saw the *yakuza* as a means to counteract trade union militancy and the threat of socialism. Various anti-communist organisations such as the *Jiyū Kurabu* (liberal club) and the Meikyō-kai brought together conservative politicians, *yakuza*, and right-wing extremists in an alliance reminiscent of the *ingaidan* (political lobbying groups) which characterised Japan's pre-war politics (Iwai 1963: 693).

The role played by these links is graphically illustrated by an incident during 1952 in which socialist Diet members and left-wing students were trying to oppose the passage of the Subversive Activities Bill (*Hakai Katsudō Bōshi Hō* or, for short, *Habōhō*). Fearing that the Diet was to be invaded, Justice Minister Kimura and Chief Cabinet Hori contacted Unabara Seitaira, a prominent Liberal Party politician, who also happened to be the chairman of one of these associations, the Dōkō-kai. Unabara quickly arranged for a composite force of the strongest fighting men from the main *tekiya* groups in Tokyo to surround the Diet and the Bill was passed (Iwai 1963: 693; DeVos 1973: 299).

In 1951, Justice Minister Kimura was also responsible for attempting to organise a 200,000-strong force of assorted rightists, gamblers, *tekiya* and *gurentai*. This organisation, known as the *Battō-tai* (literally, 'drawn-sword squad'), was to act as an anti-communist shock-troop opposing the revolution that Kimura believed to be imminent. As a sweetener to this arrangement, Kimura revised the criminal law so that gambling offences were only indictable on the basis of red-handed arrests. Only when Kimura presented a request for the *Battō-tai*'s proposed annual budget of ¥370 m to Prime Minister Yoshida, was this plan scrapped (Hori 1983: 137–8; Ino 1993: 254–7).

A more well-known example of governmental purchase of *yakuza* protection took place in 1960. Amidst widespread discontent and rioting opposing the Japan–America Security Treaty, the government had fears for the safety of President Eisenhower during his projected visit. Preparations were therefore made for a protective force comprising *yakuza*. The visit was eventually cancelled but the *yakuza* had already agreed to help and had made their plans. Between ¥500 and ¥600 m had been provided by the government to finance Eisenhower's protection but, following the cancellation, the money disappeared (Kaplan and Dubro 1986: 85; Ino 1992a: 269). The link-man between the Kishi government and the *yakuza* in this operation was an extreme right-winger, Kodama Yoshio.[5]

In addition to providing muscle to oppose truculent radical elements and silence opposition, the *yakuza*-politician link has proved to be very useful to politicians in terms of fund-raising, organising voters, and discrediting opponents. It is for this reason that throughout the 1950s and 1960s large floral wreaths, with the donating politician's name prominently displayed in the centre, were a common feature at *yakuza* succession ceremonies, weddings, and funerals. Important politicians would often be the guests of honour at such parties. This relationship did, however, go far beyond the ritual exchange of social pleasantries; in 1958 a petition calling for the release of a gang member arrested for his participation in a territorial gangwar was signed by the prefectural governor, the mayor, and the head of the prefectural assembly as well as several Diet members (Iwai 1963: 692–5).

Even as late as 1971, bail for a Yamaguchi-gumi boss arrested for murder was guaranteed by former Prime Minister Kishi and former Education Minister Nakamura (Kaplan and Dubro 1986: 116). However, the exposure of the Lockheed scandal in the mid-1970s and the generally worsening public perception of the *yakuza* generated a climate in which the open flaunting of *yakuza*-politician links was becoming electorally disadvantageous. This is not to say that such connections no longer existed; merely that they became more discreet. By the time that Stark was carrying out his fieldwork in the late 1970s they were firmly part of the *ura* (behind-the-scenes) of Japanese society.

Stark's description of 'the clique' composed of the locality's prominent businessmen, politicians, representatives of the bureaucracy, and with Noda Boss of the Araki-gumi as its nexus, shows how these different worlds interact and make use of their clique connections to further their own particular interests (1981: 196–209). The business members provide money to the other clique members. In return the other members of the group aid the business interests in the competition for contracts. Businessmen may also be useful to politicians in mobilising employees and dependents as a voting block. The political figures are responsible for the awarding of public-works contracts and consequently wield considerable power within the clique. The bureaucrats play the relatively minor role of flexible application of regulations concerning contract bidding. The bureaucrats' rewards are correspondingly minor, consisting of money and perks such as free entertainment in gang-owned or associated bars and clubs.

The role of the *yakuza* within the clique is to fulfil the 'quasi-governmental functions' of adjudicating and enforcing clique decisions (Stark 1981: 198). As discussed in the Chapter One, when business transactions are of dubious legality, the participants are unable to seek legal enforcement of contracts. The gang boss, with expertise in clandestine extra-legal control and access to the machinery with which to carry it out, is therefore uniquely placed to provide the structure within which the clique operates.

The *Yakuza* and the Police

Another factor widely held to be responsible for the continued existence of *yakuza* organisations is the relationship between the police and the gangs. The English-language literature generally stresses the 'symbiotic' nature of this relationship (Ames 1981; Kaplan and Dubro 1986; van Wolferen 1989; Huang and Vaughn 1992). Consequently it is claimed that 'no serious attempt to break the gangs has ever been made' (van Wolferen 1989: 103). This bold assertion seems to be in direct contradiction to the police white papers with their constant references to repeated and intensified crackdowns and widespread arrests. To assess the validity of these rival views of the nature of OC-law enforcement interaction in Japan, it is necessary to look at the evidence.

The periodisation of the *yakuza*'s postwar development given earlier in this chapter demonstrates the dynamic nature of these groups. Similarly the police have undergone massive changes over the same half-century. From this we might expect that the relationship between the *yakuza* and the police will not be an unchanging one. The historical record shows this to be the case.

During the period of postwar chaos and the flourishing black market, one of the preconditions for *yakuza* control over this market was the absence of efficient alternative providers of protection. This was in part due to a reluctance of the various sections of the occupation authority to intervene in areas over which they did not have a jurisdictional monopoly (Wildes 1954: 171). A more significant factor was the weakness of the Japanese police during this period, and here too we can see the hand of MacArthur's staff.

One of the ways in which SCAP proposed to promote the democratisation of Japan was through root-and-branch reform of the police, which had enjoyed an enormous and all-pervasive influence over preoccupation Japan. One of the central pillars of this reform was the decentralisation of the police, with independent police forces for every town of over 5,000 inhabitants and a separate force for policing rural areas. It was this decentralised system that allowed the head of the Hakuryū-sha to become head of the local public-safety commission responsible for overseeing the police. At the same time, Wildes reports, 'it was common knowledge that many local Public Safety Commissions were packed with gangsters' (1954: 188).

One of the problems with this decentralised system was that of funding. Even those, like Oppler, who supported the ethos on which police decentralisation rested, questioned whether it would be realistic. Given the extreme economic scarcity of this period, 'the financial resources of local entities (were) too inadequate to allow every small town to have its own police administration' (Oppler 1976: 171).

One way in which local forces overcame this problem was by accepting donations from 'Police Supporters Associations' and 'Crime

Prevention Societies'. Inevitably contributions included those from *yakuza* groups seeking to insulate themselves from police interference in their activities. In March 1949, the *Jiji Shinpō* identified a 'conspiracy between local bosses and police officials since the police must depend on local citizens for funds' (Aldous and Leishman 1997: 138). In one case *yakuza* from Sakamoto donated an expensive official residence for the head of the local police force (Wildes 1954: 188).

Corruption was not the only debilitating factor that police decentralisation generated; the small autonomous forces were inevitably unable to adequately coordinate their operations or share information. This deficiency, compounded by a lack of trained personnel[6] and equipment, left the police largely powerless to deal with criminal *yakuza* activities. For example, a man discovered his stolen overcoat on sale for ¥3,500 in the local black market. When he reported this to the police they suggested he discuss the problem with the market's controlling boss. He did so and was 'graciously' allowed to recover his coat for only ¥500 (70 per cent of his monthly salary) (Dower 2000: 144).

In another case, stall-holders who had refused to pay protection money to Ozu, protested to the authorities after he had destroyed their stalls. Although the US Provost Marshal had instructed the police to safeguard the interests of these stall-holders, they sided with Ozu. Protection of Ozu extended to the Japanese criminal justice system; when he was finally convicted after lengthy pressure from SCAP officials, prosecutors and judges declared him too ill to serve his sentence. Similarly, poor health also prevented convicted gang boss Sekine from serving his sentence. In fact very few *yakuza* arrestees during the occupation period suffered greatly; about half would be released immediately due to lack of evidence whilst, even if they were convicted, sentences (typically light) were suspended in two-thirds of cases (Wildes 1954: 175–80).

As was mentioned earlier, the immediate postwar period witnessed considerable violence committed by *sangokujin*, the Chinese, Koreans, and Taiwanese that had been brought into Japan as forced labour for wartime industries. Following Japan's surrender, these individuals were outside the jurisdiction of the Japanese police due to privileged status granted them by the Occupation authorities (Whiting 1999: 319). According to the autobiography of third-generation Yamaguchi-gumi boss Taoka Kazuo, much of this *sangokujin* violence was directed at the police. The Kōbe police, unable to defend themselves from attacks by these *sangokujin*, requested the help of Taoka in controlling them. Taoka recalls: 'Feeling regret and anger at the powerlessness of this defeated country's police, I accepted this proposal. For the safety of the people and the maintenance of the public peace, everybody had to unite to eradicate *sangokujin* violence' (Shinoda 2001: 4).

Whether or not the police actually asked for Taoka's protection, it is immediately apparent that a *yakuza* group will necessarily be intolerant of alternative sources of violence within their territory. Police requests for their eradication merely legitimised a group's pre-existing objectives. Given that they established territorial monopolies of power, successful *yakuza* groups did maintain some sort of public peace. Shinoda asserts that the role of the *yakuza* in stabilising the underworld by driving out competitors during the period of postwar chaos generated the argument that the *yakuza* were a necessary evil (*hitsuyō aku*) (2001: 4). Whilst this is a somewhat flawed argument, in that the successful groups went on to engage in territorial conflicts with each other, it still had a wide currency at the time.

The relationship between the police in this period was therefore one in which a weak, fragmented, and disorganised police force was frequently financially beholden to, or under the governance of, *yakuza* groups. Insofar as this relationship was symbiotic, it was also based on a large asymmetry of power in favour of the *yakuza*. If Taoka is to be believed, then the imbalance was extreme indeed.

By 1950 it was recognised that the police reforms had not been successful, and, in June 1951, following the departure of MacArthur, towns and villages were allowed to hand over their policing responsibilities to the National Rural Police. Eventually less than 200 of the 1,600 local police forces were retained (Wildes 1954: 191). This policy U-turn, part of the wider 'reverse course' following the outbreak of war in Korea, was completed with the passage of the Police Law in 1954, which set up a system of prefectural forces under the central control of the National Police Agency (NPA). This recentralisation effectively removed *yakuza* elements from control of the local police forces, as in the case of the Hakuryū-sha in Nagahama, as well as putting the police on a more secure financial footing.

The police were considerably strengthened by these developments, and as we move into the gang-war period, the police–*yakuza* relationship does shift to a perceptibly more hostile one; this is evinced by the introduction, and use, of new laws as well as efforts to drive *yakuza* out of racecourses and pachinko parlours. However, the relationship was by no means unambiguously hostile. Given that in 1959 Kōbe harbour police felt the need to flatter Taoka Kazuo by making him station commander for a day (Shinoda 2001: 6), the extent of this shift is problematic.

With the first 'summit strategy' of 1964 the police started to have a real impact on the size and number of gangs. Does this then mark a real change in the nature of the *yakuza*–police relationship? After the summit strategy their relations have been too complex to admit simple categorisation as hostile or otherwise; there have been aspects of both.

It has been widely argued in recent decades that *yakuza*–police connection is founded on more than an uneasy coexistence. Ino (1993), Kaplan and Dubro (1986), van Wolferen (1989), Huang and Vaughn (1992), amongst others, suggest that, tacitly, the police have actively welcomed the existence of the *yakuza*. In addition to their supposed role as a hammer of the left, they are also seen to have played a part in controlling disorganised crime within their *nawabari*, thereby contributing to Japan's reputation as a 'crime-free society'.

As we saw in Chapter One, this perception is by no means unique to Japan, and frequently such behaviour is in the interests of the gang itself. Whilst this mechanism can be clearly seen in the immediate post-war era, has it survived the renaissance of police power? The closest indirect evidence for the retention of this type of relationship post-summit strategy is the frequent visits made by police officers, primarily detectives from the *bōryokudan* countermeasures squads, to gang offices. There they would sit down and discuss what was happening on the streets whilst sharing coffee and cigarettes with their *yakuza* hosts. Whilst the main function for the police of these visits was the gathering of information, it is clear that these diplomatic links might enable the ground-rules concerning the limits of tolerable behaviour to be defined. Such links no doubt also facilitate the eradication of rivals.

One potential pitfall in discussing the nature of the *yakuza*–police relationship is to treat these two protagonists as monolithic bodies. *Yakuza* is a collective term for many independent groups, the subgroups of which retain a degree of autonomy over their activities. The general consensus amongst interviewees on both sides of the law was that, traditionally, the Tokyo groups have been much more prepared to moderate their behaviour and avoid antagonising the police than the gangs in Western Japan, and in particular the Yamaguchi-gumi.

Just as the term '*yakuza*' should not be interpreted as a single united entity, the modern police force also comprises different groups with different objectives. In particular, the main bifurcation within the Japanese police force that is of relevance here is that between the elite career bureaucrats, who staff the NPA and the senior positions within the prefectural forces, and the officers responsible for the actual business of street-level policing. It is not hard to imagine a scenario in which a policy of increased crackdowns on the *yakuza*, formulated by the elite career officers, is less than wholeheartedly endorsed by police officers on the front line who might find peace within their own patch to be better served by a nod and a wink over coffee and cigarettes at the local gang office. However, there is no hard evidence to suggest that this imagined scenario reflects the reality of the policing of the *yakuza* at the close of the Shōwa period.

Ames, during his fieldwork with the police in Western Japan in the late 1970s was struck by the 'remarkable cordiality' between *yakuza* members and police officers (1981: 105). Even during interrogations of arrested gang members, both sides would maintain a jocular banter. Ames, however, does point out that this is not necessarily indicative of close friendship, interpreting excessive joking as suggestive of a potentially hostile relationship. Ames (1981: 107) notes that it is recognised by both parties that it is not in their interests for this underlying hostility to manifest itself:

The relationship is mutually beneficial: Police and gangsters each find it advantageous to maintain rapport and to enhance it with a façade of cordiality. This nucleus of goodwill and understanding seems to remain when the police must severely crack down on a gang after a major incident. A complete rupture in the relationship would be counter-productive for both sides.

It is also important to note that this cordiality does not necessarily imply corruption. Given that these organisations exist and that they, or their replacements, will continue to exist, the police may conclude that it is preferable to adopt a pragmatic strategy in their dealings with them. This is exactly the conclusion reached by Celantini, Marrelli, and Martina in their model discussed in Chapter One; both organised crime and law-enforcement players adopt a non-aggressive stance *vis-à-vis* each other.

In contrast to Ames, Stark (1981: 16–17) describes the relationship between the Araki-gumi and the local police in less glowing terms. Whilst there is contact between gangs and the authorities, the 'limited amount of co-operation with law-enforcement personnel is all behind-the-scenes, marked by mutual contempt, and necessitated only by their respective self-interests'.

This antagonism was reflected in the poor relations that Stark had with the police authorities within his fieldwork area. Despite Stark's backing by the National Research Institute of Police Science, the local police saw his research as 'promoting the gang's public image and lending it legitimacy' (1981: 16–17). Consequently, they attempted to frustrate his research by intimidating his informants.

At a micro-level of analysis, *yakuza*–police relations over the four decades following the 'summit strategy' can be anything but cosy; one veteran mid-level Yamaguchi-gumi interviewee's recollections of the beatings he received from officers whilst in police custody in no way resonate with the 'cordiality' observed by Ames.

So far as it exists, police tolerance of the *yakuza* in the postwar era has been aided by a number of factors. First, the well-known links existing between conservative politicians and prominent gang leaders have not encouraged the police to actively pursue *yakuza* infringements of the law. As mentioned above, these connections have become more discreet in response to increasingly negative public perceptions of the *yakuza*. Part, but by no means all, of this attraction between right-wing politicians and gangsters was the supposed utility of the latter in the battle against left-wing activism. With mass affluence and, *a fortiori*, following the end of the Cold War, the threat posed by the left has lost any vestiges of credibility.

Second, as noted in Chapter Two, organized crime acceptance is facilitated when such groups activities can be characterised as 'consensual' and 'victimless'. Despite the evidence to the contrary, the *yakuza* of the postwar era have profited from romantic associations with the outlaw heroes of the past and a perception that throughout, this period, they have remained essentially concerned with gambling and peddling. As they have moved into other areas of business, tolerance has become progressively scarcer.

Another factor encouraging police acceptance of *yakuza* groups is the degree of sympathy found amongst the police for the idealised value system of traditional *yakuza* chivalry expressed by such terms as *jingi, ninkyō,* and *kyōkaku.* This is evinced by the widespread following enjoyed by *yakuza* films (also known as chivalry films—*ninkyō eiga*) amongst both police and *yakuza* circles. These films typically depict extreme devotion to a code of honour and such traditional Japanese virtues as endurance (*gaman*), duty (*giri*), humanity (*ninjō*), and self-sacrifice and, as such, appeal to the tough, masculine, and traditional cultures of both policemen and gangsters.

Ames suggests that a degree of identification between the *bōryoku-dan* and police might also be fostered by the fact that both groups have, in the past, recruited members from comparable social and educational backgrounds. Given that almost two-thirds of the recruit intake for the prefectural police were university graduates in 1995, this can no longer be considered a relevant factor.

In contrast to the state of the Japanese police during the chaotic years immediately following 1945, they have, more recently, enjoyed a reputation for competence and honesty. This reputation has been enhanced both by Japan's low crime statistics, and by a number of highly laudatory books written by Americans (Bayley 1976; Clifford 1976; Parker 1984). In recent decades, however, a number of corruption scandals have broken, which suggest that the cordial relationship described by Ames is occasionally based on more than a desire to avoid rocking the boat.[7] Kaplan and Dubro give evidence of one case in Osaka in which police officers routinely took bribes to provide advance warning of raids on gaming-machine operations. Eventually 124 officers in the Osaka police force were either dismissed or disciplined, whilst the former police chief, who had also been implicated, committed suicide (1986: 157–9).

Bornoff, writing about the sex industry in Japan, also notes that premises are usually aware beforehand of impending raids due to 'a lot of money changing hands under the table' (1994: 495). Similarly, the Osaka-based Sakaume-gumi gambling group always knew when the police were due to appear at their illegal book-keeping operations. In frustration senior officers from the NPA resorted to going themselves without telling police headquarters in Osaka (interview veteran former NPA employee, 1998). One ex-*yakuza* interviewee recounted to the author how he used to 'by chance' bump into various police officers on their day off and slip some money into their pockets 'for *pachinko*' (interview Osaka, 1998). Ames suggests that the high-profile raids since the days of the summit strategy 'assume almost a ritual air' and most arrestees are quickly released due to a lack of concrete evidence or the insignificant nature of any crimes proved. Sometimes the *yakuza* have been informed prior to a raid, thereby enabling them to hide incriminating evidence, weapons, and drugs. However, often they will enable the police to confiscate a few weapons in order to save face (1981: 127).

Corruption in Japan is notoriously hard to pin down. This is largely due to the deep-rooted culture of gift-giving, reciprocity, and obligation in which all major social occasions are marked by presentations of envelopes filled with cash. On a more subtle level, just as retiring bureaucrats find rewarding employment in the industries they formerly regulated (a process known as *amakudari* or 'descent from heaven'), it is not unknown for retired police officers to be employed in industries concerned with the sale or distribution of gambling machines.

Whilst individual cases of corruption may still persist, it still seems that the cosy picture of symbiosis portrayed by van Wolferen (1989) can no longer be sustained. As will be shown in the later chapters, since the mid-1960s, police activities have been the driving force behind the evolution of *yakuza* business. This fact powerfully undermines a simple symbiosis thesis. As we shall see rather than being consumers of *yakuza* services in the form of street-policing, in recent years the police have become competitors in the ways in which they regulate businesses traditionally within the world of the *yakuza*.

Insofar as we can generalise about the state of the relationship between the police and the *yakuza* since the summit strategy period of the mid-1960s, there was a progressive increase in the level of hostility and a corresponding decrease in the factors encouraging symbiosis. Despite his observations of 'cordiality', Ames accepted that the police had been adopting an increasingly hard line against the *yakuza* over this period (1981: 124–9). This manifested itself not only in high-profile arrests and harassment of gang members but in the development of public awareness campaigns, education programmes, and the initiation of, and support for, the citizens' anti-*bōryokudan* movement. As the gangs had become perceived as increasingly violent and involved in non-consensual crimes in which ordinary citizens have become victims, the police have come under growing pressure to take serious steps against them. In the two decades since Ames did his fieldwork, this trend has continued.

3

The Modern *Yakuza*: Structure and Organisation

In December 1988, there were 3,197 *bōryokudan* groups with a total membership of 86,552 men, recognised by the police. Of these 1,397 gangs (34,492 men) were affiliated to one of the three national syndicates; the Yamaguchi-gumi, the Inagawa-kai, and the Sumiyoshi-kai, whilst 737 (20,826 men) of these groups were connected with the Yamaguchi-gumi (*Keisatsu Hakusho* 1989: 17). As mentioned in Chapter Two, whilst in the previous two decades there was a decline in overall *bōryokudan* statistics, the three large gangs have grown in both relative and absolute terms.

These syndicates are composed of *ikka*, or (fictive) families. *Ikka* (sometimes also referred to as *kumi*) are the fundamental organisational units of the *yakuza* (Iwai 1986: 214). Stark (1981: 62–88) identifies three distinct overlapping internal structures within the *ikka*: (1) a formal administrative hierarchy; (2) a hierarchy based on the traditional Japanese model of the household (*ie*); and (3) the hierarchy within internal groups. These structures give 'cohesion and tightness to the group and counter the factionalism inherent in the three hierarchies' (1981: 62).

The administrative, or 'rank and duty' hierarchy is the most visible feature of Stark's structures. It comprises the formal structure of the organisation with clearly defined strata; each entailing specified tasks, duties, status, and privileges. These are: *Kumi-chō* (family head/boss);

Kumi-chō

⇩   *Kōmon*

Waka-gashira

⇩

Saikō-kanbu

⇩

Kanbu

⇩

Kumi-in

⇩

Jun-kōsei-in

Fig. 3.1 *Yakuza* rank hierarchy

saikō-kanbu (senior executives); *kanbu* (executives); soldiers (*kumi-in*); and *jun-kōsei-in* (trainees) (Stark 1981: 65). The category of *jun-kōsei-in* also includes peripheral figures (*shūhensha*), such as *kigyō shatei* (business brothers), who are not officially connected with the *ikka*, but who profit from maintaining informal links (see Figure 3.1). With respect to this formal hierarchy the gang is similar to a legitimate corporation or military organisation. It is also practically identical to the formal rank structures of the American La Cosa Nostra and Chinese Triads.

Ultimate responsibility for the *ikka*'s business activities rests with the *kumi-chō*. He is advised on gang business by his advisors (kōmon)[1] and by the senior executives, one of whom may act as under-boss (usually known as *waka-gashira*). Both *dai-kanbu* and *kanbu* are entitled to form their own internal groups, though not all may have sufficient funds to maintain the branch office and personnel that this entails. The *kumi-in* are responsible for guard duties, driving, manning the telephone, cleaning, serving guests, and supervising the apprentices. The *kumi-in* may also be employed in businesses owned by the *kumi-chō* or *kanbu* or otherwise connected with the *ikka*. The apprentices are usually given the most menial tasks. As well as working for their boss, *kanbu* and *kumi-in* often operate on their own account, though, where such business activities are illegal and make use of the *ikka*'s reputation, some of these earnings will usually be passed on to the boss. Until the 1970s these payments were generally a percentage of earnings, but the system was subsequently changed to a fixed amount as too many gang members were under-reporting their incomes (Hoshino interview Yokohama, 1998).

In the Araki-gumi, the organisation studied by Stark, of the roughly 125 men below the Araki *kumi-chō*, 12 per cent held *kanbu* rank, 68 per cent *kumi-in*, and 20 per cent *jun-kōsei-in*. These figures deviate from the national average for the same period in which 3.2 per cent are *kumi-chō*, 26.9 per cent are *kanbu*, 54.2 per cent are *kumi-in*, and 15.7 per cent are *jun-kōsei-in*. Recent rank structure data are not currently available and this needs to be rectified, as the situation is likely to have changed in the last two decades. *Ceteris paribus*, the ageing structure of the *yakuza* mentioned above, combined with the increasing sophistication of *yakuza* crimes, might be expected to have encouraged a positive skew towards the upper echelons of *yakuza* rank structure. However, other changes to be discussed in later chapters can be expected to have impacted on this structure in non-trivial ways.

The type of formal hierarchy and division of labour outlined above has been used by researchers, such as Cressey and Salerno, to assert that OC groups are effectively bureaucratic organisations. What Cressey failed to realise is that there are parallel hierarchy structures within both Japanese and traditional Italian OC groups, based on traditional kinship ties, that coexist with this corporate/bureaucratic structure. Within the *ikka* these social bonds are based on the family relationships of father–son (*oyabun–kobun*) and brother–brother (*kyōdaibun*). It is important to note that these bonds connect individuals to each other rather than to a group. These fictive kinship links are seen as crucial in maintaining group cohesion both vertically (*oyabun–kobun*) and horizontally (*kyōdaibun*) (Stark 1981: 64–70).

These relationships are established by the ritual exchange of *sake* in the *sakazuki* ceremony. The nature of the relationship is determined by the ratio of *sake* in the recipients' cups; for example, an equal *kyōdai* relationship would involve equal quantities of *sake* whilst an unequal *aniki–shatei* relationship would be reflected in a six-to-four or a seven-to-three distribution of *sake*. OC groups are considerably more meritocratic than traditional large Japanese enterprises characterised by seniority promotion. Consequently, the social kinship hierarchy within the *ikka* is fluid and this is reflected in the way that an equal *kyōdai* relationship can become a six to four relationship as one member progresses faster than his less able brother. Equally, a *kumi-in*, on promotion to *kanbu* status, may become the *shatei* (younger brother) to other executives who may have formerly been his uncles or even his *oyabun*.

This system of artificial kinship relationships is by no means unique to the *yakuza* in Japan. Liza Dalby, in her participant observation study of *geisha*, noted that a similar system of mother–daughter and sister–sister links, established by the ceremonial drinking of nine sake cups, exists. This is not, however, an exact correlate to *yakuza* kinship structure in that sibling bonds are of greater importance than the parent–child ones amongst *geisha* society; for the *yakuza* it is the other way round (Dalby 2000: 40–2). Perhaps more interestingly, a similar, though less formalised, system of *oyabun–kobun* relationships exists within the rationalised, bureaucratic, organisational structure of the police force. This researcher's own fieldwork with the police in Iwate prefecture was greatly facilitated by the fact that his access had been arranged by a senior officer who had many *kobun*, largely adopted whilst he was head of the prefectural riot squad.

The third hierarchy within the *ikka* is the internal group, which forms when an executive takes on his own *kobun*. Within the *ikka*, individual members occupy two different positions; that within the *ikka* as a whole and that within the internal group. Most internal groups tend to be small groups composed of less than ten members. Due to their small size and the fact that most day-to-day business and interaction is carried out at this level, internal groups tend to be the most cohesive and intimate units within the *yakuza* world.

Stark stresses that it is vital that these three structures are flexible enough to accommodate the constantly changing vicissitudes of gang fortunes (1981: 76). Arrest, imprisonment, intergang conflict, temporary cessation of certain business activities due to law-enforcement harassment and new market opportunities make OC a highly precarious and dynamic process unsuited to a rigid bureaucratic structure.

A large area syndicate may form when a strong group subsumes weaker ones into its organisation either voluntarily or through military pressure. The *kumi-chō* of the weaker group will become a *kobun* of the boss, or the younger brother of an executive, of the dominant one. Alternatively, internal groups may expand out, forming semi-autonomous *ikka* in new territory. In a national syndicate such as the Yamaguchi-gumi, this results in a multi-tiered pyramidal arrangement in which executives within the central group are themselves

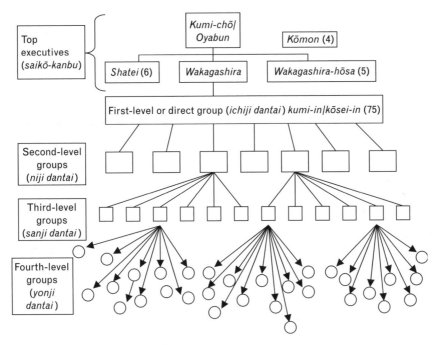

Fig. 3.2 Structure of the Yamaguchi-gumi 1989

oyabun heading *kumi*, the executives of which also have their own groups, and so on. This is shown in Figure 3.2.

Alternatively, a syndicate can arise when groups voluntarily form an alliance of equals. The obvious benefits of such an arrangement are the economies of scale, security from outside predation, and reduction in competition arguments put forward in Chapter Two. The group studied by Stark was a member of a nine-member alliance in the West of Japan, which had formed to block the spread of the Yamaguchi-gumi. Alliances of this type are cemented by *sakazuki* rituals in which the leaders of the participating groups become brothers.

Another example of a federation of gangs is the Sumiyoshi-kai[2] in which the leaders of the large component groups retain control over their own organisations although a president is selected from among their number (refer to Fig. 3.3). The president is responsible for maintaining the overall smooth running of the organisation and adjudicates in cases of intra-federation disputes (Iwai 1986: 225–6).

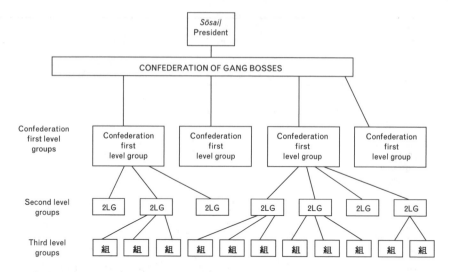

Fig. 3.3 Structure of the Sumiyoshi-kai
Source: Iwai (1986).

Within large-scale syndicates of either type, control exerted over sub-gangs by the parent body is usually confined to major decisions that will have ramifications beyond the sub-gang's established territory (*Keisatsu Hakusho* 1989: 32–3). For example, approval from above will be required when dealing with problems such as succession of leadership, expansion of the gang's *nawabari*, the dissolution of the gang, and the use of punishment torture. Most gangs do not require permission to sell drugs or move into new areas of criminal activity. In part this may be because large syndicates officially maintain a policy of non-involvement in the drugs business.

Although the Japanese syndicates have not managed to forge a nation-wide governmental organ along the lines of the commission of the Italian-American crime families or the *cupola* of the Sicilian Mafia, within the Kantō area the major *bakuto* gangs have a loose association, which fills a similar function. The Kantō Hatsuka-kai traces its lineage to the Kantō-kai set up by Kodama in 1963. Although the Kantō-kai was disbanded the following year due to the increased police pressure on the *yakuza* brought about by the summit strategy, in 1972 the original members formed the new organisation. The membership consisted of the two largest Tokyo-based groups, the Inagawa-kai and the Sumiyoshi-kai, plus the Matsuba-kai, the Kokusui-kai, the Gijintō, the Tōā-kai, the Kōwa-kai (all of which had been in the former Kantō-kai), the Nibiki-kai, and the Soai-kai.[3]

The Kantō-kai had originally been politically motivated but the Kantō Hatsuka-kai was set up purely as a mechanism for promoting peaceful coexistence between the various *bakuto* groups within the Kantō-plain area and for ensuring that, when conflict does break out between subgroups, this trouble does not escalate and is quickly resolved. This is officially carried out through a rotational system of chairmanship (*tsuki tōban*) by which the member groups take it in turns to be responsible for resolving problems within the association. In reality, however, if there is a serious problem, then the stronger two groups end up playing a role in its resolution even if they are not on *tōban* duty. The original charter of the Kantō Hatsuka-kai provides for strict penalties for those who jeopardise intra-association harmony.

The Kantō Hatsuka-kai derives its name from its habitual meeting on the twentieth day of every month (unless this clashes with an important event in which case it is shifted to the preceding or following day). The meeting is composed of two parts. The first of these is the business meeting attended by the headquarters chiefs of all the component groups at which any areas of inter-group friction or other problems are discussed. The second phase of the monthly meeting is a purely social affair in which senior executives of the member groups share a meal in the private room of a restaurant and then take turns in singing *karaoke*. As this second meeting is conducted in a non-secure environment, announcements concerning gang-related business are not made.

To further minimise the risk of trouble within the Tokyo area the Kantō Hatsuka-kai also maintains fraternal relations with the Kantō Shinnō Dōshi-kai, which is the federation comprising the Tokyo-based *tekiya* groups. This group has observer status within the Kantō Hatsuka-kai and each February a formal dinner is held in order to further the amicable relations between these two groups (*Jitsuwa Jidai*, July 1999: 94–6).

The group studied by Stark in Okayama prefecture was also the member of a loose association of independent groups. However, in this case the prime motivating force had been a desire to withstand the relentless advance of the Yamaguchi-gumi, rather than an attempt to restrict conflict between the component groups (although doubtless this was an important side product) (Stark 1981: 49–56).

It should be stressed that associations such as the Kantō Hatsuka-kai are not themselves monolithic gang organisations under the guidance of some 'Mr Big'. Decisions concerning the internal discipline, economic activities, or military endeavours of member groups remain entirely at the discretion of these individual member groups' bosses unless they directly impinge on other federation members. It should also be pointed out that the Kantō Hatsuka-kai has been very successful in reducing trouble within the Tokyo area. This is indicative of the way in which the Kantō-based *yakuza* groups have traditionally been much more sensitive to the need to prevent provocative displays of violence than Kansai *yakuza* groups in Western Japan (interviews: Iwai Tokyo, June 1998; Yoshimura Tokyo, June 1998).

In cases where there are not inter-group links, conflict resolution becomes harder. In order to maximise the chances that a cessation of hostilities between two parties will hold, a ceremony will be held at which a trusted and respected third party will act as guarantor for the reconciliation. Should one of the disputants then break the terms of the reconciliation, the dignity of this third party is gravely affronted and this insult will have to be avenged. A ceremony further reinforces this agreement because it increases the number of witnesses to this agreement and therefore raises the potential loss of face to the guarantor should the dispute re-erupt. The disputants, by handicapping themselves in this way, enable an agreement to be reached in conditions of mutual suspicion and enmity. These ceremonies are known as *teuchi* (literally, 'hand-striking').

Internal Control

As self-governing entities, operating in a hostile environment with no recourse to legal protection, *yakuza* organisations must create and enforce their own rules. Essentially there are five cardinal rules which have remained unchanged for centuries: (1) do not disobey, or cause a nuisance to your superiors; (2) do not betray your gang or your fellow gang members; (3) do not fight with fellow members or disrupt the harmony of the gang; (4) do not embezzle gang funds; and (5) do not touch the woman of a fellow gang member. These norms bear a remarkably close similarity to those of Sicilian, Russian, and Chinese mafia groups (Morgan 1960: 157; Gambetta 1993: 147; Varese 2001: 151). This suggests that such groups are continually subject to the same sorts of pressures and that these structural conditions transcend cultural differences.

Whilst the propaganda of mafia groups themselves, as well as that of those seeking to portray them as evil empires, accentuate the idea of an iron code of discipline, the empirical evidence, both from Japan and elsewhere, suggests that this ideal is far from realised. The fact that these rules exist at all, suggests that the temptations to maximise self-interest at the expense of the group, or more usually the boss, are strong. For example, the universal rule against skimming profits from gang-related activities is one over which bosses must always maintain extreme vigilance.

Consequently, the most important virtue within the *yakuza* code is unquestioning obedience, even in defiance of logic. This is reflected in the well-known traditional *yakuza* saying, which states that if the *oyabun* says that the passing crow is white, then the *kobun* must agree. A police survey of members of large syndicates carried out in 1985 found that 64 per cent of their interviewees said that they would unquestioningly carry out the orders of their *oyabun*. A further 21 per cent said that they would carry them out if they agreed (*Keisatsu Hakusho* 1989: 30). The opinion of the remaining 15 per cent is not recorded but it can be seen that this virtue is largely, but not universally, recognised.

A graphic illustration of *kobun* obedience is the phenomenon of *migawari*, in which low-ranking *kumi-in* hand themselves in to the police and admit to crimes committed by their superiors. Such obedience is rewarded by promotion, financial remuneration, and an elaborate ceremony on the release from jail (*demukae*) of the individual concerned. During his incarceration, maintenance will be paid to his dependants. For a *kumi-in* of low ability, *migawari* may actually be the best career move he could make. Hoshino suggests that incidence of *migawari* is in decline as sentencing patterns become more severe. In addition to this, one case related to the researcher in Iwate prefecture concerns the local boss forcing a subordinate to go to prison in his place and then failing to provide adequate support or remuneration on the subordinate's release. Both these points show that the relationships governed by traditional *yakuza* codes are under strain.

Whilst Hoshino's observation suggests that this strain has increased in recent years, the fact that codes of loyalty are stressed and reinforced by elaborate rituals and fictive familial bonds can be taken as indicative that the obedience of subordinates has always been a potential problem. Although intra-gang bonds and socialisation imbued during the period of apprenticeship go someway to fostering this spirit of blind, self-sacrificing obedience and *kumi*-harmony, the authoritarian nature of *yakuza* groups can put the *oyabun–kobun* relationship under great tension. Referring to this, Iwai (1986: 222) writes: 'Frequently this gives rise to a strong, usually unspoken, antipathy between the leader and his followers which may threaten the *oyabun's* authority and the cohesion of the group at large. In spite of the obsequious displays of loyalty and fealty, it is not rare for a *kobun* to reject his *oyabun*.'

It is therefore necessary for control within *yakuza* organisations to be reinforced by a system of rewards and punishments. As mentioned above, cases of *migawari* are rewarded by money and promotion. Similarly money and promotion[4] are the two major reward mechanisms for other outstanding examples of obedience, ability, and results. At the other end of the scale there are a number of punishments available to the *kumi-chō* in order to enforce discipline. For relatively light offenses these include shaving off hair[5] (narcissism is an accepted facet of the *yakuza* subculture), confinement, fines, and temporary expulsion from home (Yamadaira 1992: 48). More serious breaches will be punished with beatings (known confusingly as lynching, which is Japanised to *rinchi*), *yubitsume* (finger amputation), *hamon* (expulsion from the *ikka*), and *zetsuen* (the irreversible severing of links); the ultimate sanction is death.

Yubitsume (also known within *yakuza* circles as *enkozume*) is perhaps the most famous aspect of traditional *yakuza* culture and one that arouses considerable fascination outside Japan. It is significant that both of the most widely known American films concerning Japanese organised crime, *Black Rain* (1989) and *The Yakuza* (1975), include scenes depicting this custom. Frequently *yubitsume* is not demanded as a punishment but will be the pre-emptive decision of the transgressor to show atonement for his misdeeds in the hope of escaping a heavier punishment.

It is commonly said that the custom of *yubitsume* is becoming less prevalent amongst younger gang members who prefer to pay fines. Whether this is due to an increased desire to avoid identification as a gang member as the *yakuza* become less open, or whether it reflects a weakening of traditional *yakuza* ethos amongst the gangs is not clear. In 1971, 42 per cent of members of *bakuto* groups, 45 per cent of *gurentai*, and 30 per cent of *tekiya* had at least one amputated finger (Mugishima, Hoshino, and Kiyonaga 1971: 133). By 1994, police data suggested that the national average of finger amputees amongst *bōryokudan* had declined to 33 per cent (Yonezato et al. 1994: 43).

The alleged preference for fines amongst younger *yakuza* is certainly not universal and, in the areas of high *yakuza* density, such as Nishinari-ku in Osaka, young finger-amputees are to be seen wandering the streets. One nineteen-year-old Yamaguchi-gumi subgroup member I met in 1998 had lost his left pinkie the previous year. Given that this young man had the Yamaguchi-gumi's diamond crest tattooed on his forehead, a desire to obscure *yakuza* identity was certainly not a relevant consideration for him.

Yubitsume exists not only as a punishment/sign of atonement but may also be undertaken for positive reasons. Whilst a finger cut off to erase some misdeed is referred to as a 'dead finger' (*shinu yubi*), a 'living finger' (*iki yubi*) is one which is sacrificed to show one's commitment to 'resolve an issue or conflict that one is not directly responsible for' (Stark 1981: 113). Both of the gang bosses in Stark's fieldwork had lost more than one *iki yubi*, usually in order to bring peace between conflicting gangs. This second type of finger-cutting, as a means of signalling one's sincerity in a way that would be prohibitively costly to fake, is reminiscent of prostitutes in medieval Japan who would cut off a finger to demonstrate their devotion to a particular client (Iwai 1963: 225). For both *yakuza* and prostitutes there is clearly an upper limit to the number of times such sincerity can credibly, and physically, be expressed.

Originally the main cost of *yubitsume* to *yakuza* was that it weakened one's grip on a sword, therefore limiting self-defence ability (Hoshino 1971: 8). Stark maintains that in pre-modern Japan, *yubitsume* would have effectively ended one's *yakuza* career (1981: 116); when the famous gambler Shimizu no Jirōchō cut off the fingers of three followers of a slain enemy leaving them with thumbs and forefingers only, the implied meaning was that they were permitted only to eat. According to a golf-professional acquaintance, the more recent implication of *yubitsume* is the adverse affect it has on amputees' golf swings.

A more significant punishment than *yubitsume* is expulsion (*hamon*). *Hamon* differs from *zetsuen* in that there remains a possibility of return for expellees depending on the nature of the offence and their behaviour whilst outside the gang. On expulsion, special postcards known as *hamon-jō* are sent to all *yakuza* groups throughout the country with which that group enjoys friendly relations, informing them that the person concerned no longer has any connection with the gang and respectfully asking them not to employ or help him. *Hamon-jō* are printed in either black or red ink with red indicating a more severe punishment and a correspondingly smaller possibility of rehabilitation (*fukuen*). Obviously for an *ikka* to employ, or otherwise help, an expelled gangster from another group without that group's consent, is both a severe breach of the traditional code of the *yakuza* and a grave affront to the dignity of the group, that will demand redress (Yamadaira 1992: 48). More recently it appears that *hamon* messages have come to be sent by fax (Hoshino interview Yokohama, 1998; Shūkan Jitsuwa *passim*).

A typical *hamon-jō* taken from police sources reads, in translation, as follows[6]:

GANG CREST

HAMON-JŌ

Gentlemen,

We take great pleasure in the growing prosperity of all members of your esteemed family.

Expellee's gang name and position.

Expellee's name, age, place of residence.

It has been decided after consultation with our whole family that the above-mentioned person, having lost his conscience and due to many acts of impropriety violating the ways of chivalry, has been expelled as of . . . date.

We therefore respectfully inform you that, as of this date, he has absolutely no connection with the XX-ikka of the OO-kai.

Accordingly, we firmly and absolutely prohibit any alliance, hospitality, friendship, or pick-up, regardless of any extenuating circumstances, between your wise and esteemed selves and this individual.

Respectfully yours,

                                                                              Date

OO-kai President (name)

XX-ikka boss (name)

XX-ikka General Headquarters

    Address

    Telephone

                                        (*Source*: *Keisatsu Hakusho* 1993: 20)

An expellee is forbidden to take part in illegal activity, to make use of his former affiliation with the gang, or even to adopt the loud dress and arrogant behaviour patterns of a gang member. Those that disobey may be challenged, beaten, or, if they persist, killed (Stark 1981: 109). Expulsion is severe for gang members because it is not easy for them to make a living outside their group's protective fold. Engaging in criminal activity as a 'lone-wolf' (*ippiki ōkami*) not only puts the expellee at risk of maltreatment from his former gang-mates and makes him an easy target for other groups; he now lacks the reputational asset that membership entails. Whilst he has been deprived of illegal employment, few employers will want to take him on in the legitimate sector. It is particularly difficult for those that have been permanently stigmatised as *bōryokudan*, through either *yubitsume* or a body tattoo (*irezumi*[7]), to conceal their former status.

If, after an appropriate length of time, expellees have conducted themselves properly outside of the gang and show a reformed attitude, they may be reinstated. This will be accompanied by the sending of reinstatement cards (*fukuen-jō*) to the recipients of the *hamon-jō*.

Girikake

Control within *yakuza* groups is also encouraged in less direct ways. One of these is through the use of ceremonies, known collectively as *girikake*, to mark important events within the group. Examples of this include not only the obvious examples such as those establishing father–son and brotherhood bonds and leadership succession, but jail-release (*demukae*) ceremonies, new-year ceremonies (*koto-hajime*), funeral ceremonies, and so on. These ceremonies can be interpreted as fulfilling many different functions. The first of these is to reinforce the individual's sense of belonging to a group with traditions, history, social-bonds, and a specific identity. One effect of this sense of historical continuity contributes to the consciousness held by *yakuza* members that they are not just organised criminals (although it is not argued here that ceremonies are held purely because of this).

Similarly *girikake* re-establishes the individual's place within the organisation. One way in which this is done is through the seating arrangements at ceremonies and, as Stark noted in his observation of a jail-release ceremony, the relative positions occupied by the various subgroups and, within them, members as they stood outside the prison to greet the releasee. Such considerations are not *yakuza*-specific; generally speaking, seating arrangements, reflecting the relative status of those attending, are given greater priority in Japan than in contemporary Britain.

Whilst individual parent–child and brother–brother bonds are most obviously manifested at the *sakazuke* ceremonies at which the bonds are formally created, the *girikake* event most clearly stressing group cohesion is *koto hajime*. *Koto hajime* (literally 'the beginning of things') is said to be 'the most solemn ceremony within *yakuza* society' (Yamada 1994*a*: 172). It traditionally occurs on 13 December in Western Japan, though in Tokyo and elsewhere it is sometimes combined with a year-end or new-year party and is not so firmly attached to any particular date. At this ceremony, gang members collectively go to the home or office of their boss, give him their compliments of the season and swear their loyalty to him. At the same ceremony, the boss will formally present them with the gang's policy for the coming year (*Bōryokudan Taisakka* materials).[8] In the case of the Yamaguchi-gumi, these are expressed in pithy four-character formulations like the exhortation for 1989 '*wa chū kyō sai*' (peaceful mind: accomplish together) (Yamada 1994*a*: 328).

Yakuza ceremonies also operate as a way of advertising the size and power of the group both to society generally and to other gangs (*Keisatsu Hakusho* 1989: 35). Apart from the obvious indicators of these three factors, one way in which the host-group's influence might be demonstrated would be by the large floral or paper rosettes outside the hall where the event in question is to take place. Such rosettes, known as *hanawa*, are commonly used at non-*yakuza* events in Japan at funerals, weddings, and shop-openings. The prestige of the donors of these rosettes lends itself to the host of the function. A *yakuza* event to which rosettes have been donated by prominent politicians, business figures, or powerful underworld bosses is therefore demonstrating that the hosting group is well connected. The same obviously applies if such individuals attend the function.[9]

Perhaps the most insidious role played by *girikake* is as a mechanism for transferring money within the *yakuza* world. When attending *girikake* the participants typically pay money for the honour. In the case of a funeral, the money will be divided up between the deceased's family and his gang. In Iwate prefecture, where, according to both *yakuza* and police informants, the *yakuza* are amongst the least affluent in Japan, the funeral of the boss of the largest gang in the prefecture (just under 50 full members) raised ¥1.5 m (Iwate police interviews 1998). The amount raised at the funeral of a Yamaguchi-gumi direct boss (a member of the first-level or head family) would typically be ¥20 m (Yamada 1994*a*: 223).[10]

One former *tekiya* interviewee estimated that he typically attended three *girikake* ceremonies a month and that between them these, combined with the various costs (comparatively low) of serving duty roster at the gang's headquarters office (transport etc.), cost him just under ¥120,000 per month. Given that this was the expenditure for a reasonably low-ranking member from an area not well-known for the wealth of its *yakuza*, it seems that the police are correct to observe that *girikake* has become a mechanism by which groups can extract large amounts of money from subordinates and affiliated groups (*Keisatsu Hakusho* 1989: 36). Given this situation, one must ask the question, why do people join these groups?

Recruitment

In order to make up for the wastage in numbers due to imprisonment, retirement, illness, and members leaving for other reasons (too many parties?), *yakuza* are constantly under pressure to maintain their existing strength. As mentioned in the 1989 *Hanzai Hakusho*, in the late

1980s the process of recruiting new, young members, seems to have become particularly problematic. Recruitment is important not only at the gang level; advancement within the organisation is aided by an individual's ability to bring in suitable new blood. This is especially important for an executive wishing to create his own internal group. Gang members are therefore always on the lookout for likely material. *Yakuza* life is obviously not suited to everybody and recruitment tends to be concentrated within certain clearly defined groups.

The underlying rationale behind the theory of ethnic progression put forward by Bell (1965) and Ianni (1974), is that, when certain ethnic groups are denied access to legitimate means to self-advancement, criminality may remain the only route by which these disadvantaged groups can attain their material goals. This argument is often applied to Japan, where it is held that discrimination against *burakumin* and *sangokujin* (particularly ethnic Koreans) is a prime motivation forcing members of these groups into criminal associations. Although supposedly liberated in 1871, discrimination against *burakumin* has persisted. Many *yakuza* leaders play on this idea of discrimination to justify their existence: society is to blame, not them, moreover (they say), the *yakuza* play a vital social role in providing a niche for society's outcasts.

Owing to the sensitivity publishers, editors, and even official publications have in dealing with *burakumin* issues (van Wolferen 1989: 342), there is no recent hard data on the levels of *burakumin* and Korean participation in the *yakuza*, and it is not in anybody's interest to provide any. Even for the police to conduct surveys would be considered discrimination, whilst the legitimate *buraku* liberation movements are not keen for their public perception to be tainted with *bōryokudan* associations.

It is, however, widely believed that the proportion of minority groups within the *yakuza* is disproportionately high: whilst roughly 0.5 per cent of the population is considered ethnically Korean and 2.5 per cent to be of *burakumin* origin, unofficial police estimates cited by Ames (1981: 112) suggest that within the Yamaguchi-gumi 10 per cent of total gang strength is Korean and 70 per cent is *burakumin*. These figures are, however, problematic, and illustrate the dangers of inappropriate extrapolation of data. Whilst in areas of Japan with high concentrations of such minorities, such as Okayama prefecture where Ames conducted most of his research, these figures are credible; it is highly dubious that they apply to the country as a whole.

Attempts to establish the extent of minority representation within the ranks of the *yakuza* during the course of my fieldwork were not successful. Criminal defence lawyers Shimamura and Yamanouchi agreed that it was 'still high' but were reluctant to give even a rough figure. One group of third-level Yamaguchi-gumi executives estimated that about two-thirds of Yamaguchi-gumi members were of Korean extraction but this does not seem credible and, at best, probably only reflects the composition of their own immediate group. Their own gang office was situated in the Nishinari area of Osaka, which has a high percentage of residents of Korean ancestry.

The sensitivity of issues relating to *burakumin* is indicated by the fact that, when Ames' book was translated into Japanese, it was only after changing publishers and standing up to considerable informal pressure from various quarters to excise the relevant sections that Ames managed to publish the fully translated book. The full events surrounding this translation provide a fascinating insight into many aspects of Japan and it is to be hoped that, now that the protagonists are retired, Ames reveals them to a wider audience. Typically, authors have not been so adamant. This self-censorship is not an uncommon defence mechanism adopted by publishers to forestall denunciation by *buraku* organisations and, as we shall see in the Chapter Four, by *yakuza* groups masquerading as such.

This problem makes ascertaining the exact extent of discrimination against *burakumin* at the end of the Shōwa period problematic. By the mid-1980s, affirmative action and investment in public facilities in neighbourhoods designated as *dōwa*[11] areas had significantly raised the material conditions in which most *burakumin* lived. In some cases these measures actually created envy amongst non-*burakumin* (Kitaguchi 1999: 98–9). Despite these improvements, by most objective criteria, the life-chances of *burakumin* were still considerably worse than those of their compatriots: in a 1984 survey it was found that there were 800 *buraku* areas that were not officially designated and had therefore failed to receive special-measures investment; the same survey showed that average household income for *burakumin* was 60 per cent of the national average; young *burakumin* were twice as likely to drop out of school as other Japanese and were half as likely to enter university. Cases of illicit trading of registers of *burakumin* names and addresses for purposes of vetting potential employees and marriage partners persisted (1999: 41–8). As late as the mid-1970s, when Ames was doing his fieldwork, the police were included amongst the large organisations that did not employ *burakumin*.

Discrimination also exists against those who fail to meet the demands of Japan's *gakureki shakai* (school-record society). Police statistics show that 80 per cent of recently joined gang members had either left school after completing compulsory schooling or dropped out during high school. In their last year at school 66 per cent had played truant for one month or more (*Keisatsu Hakusho* 1989: 37–8). This contrasts with national educational advancement rates of 95 per cent for high school, and 30 per cent for university (*Tōkei Kyoku* 1990: 666). Of course, educational and ethnic discrimination need not necessarily be mutually exclusive. Given that informal barriers to employment remain in many high-prestige occupations, why bother with overcoming the formal ones?

Another significant aspect of *yakuza* recruits is their domestic background. Whilst it is not surprising that they tend to come from poorer families, what is surprising is the high levels who come from single-parent families (43 per cent) or feel they have been neglected as children (50 per cent) compared to those who had been 'doted upon' or 'looked after too much' (10 per cent). One third had run away from home (Ames 1981: 112–3; *Keisatsu Hakusho* 1989: 37). More recently, it seems that the significance of single-parent families has been declining, but parental neglect within conventional two-parent families has increased as a factor contributing to *yakuza* recruitment (Hoshino 1994: 139). It seems reasonable to assume that the tight, closed, social structure of the *yakuza*, and the kinship bonds of the *sakazuki*, take on an added significance in the light of the dysfunctional family background of many gang entrants.

Of course, not all members of these disadvantaged groups become members of *yakuza*. *Yakuza* 'talent scouts' do not try to induct individuals *because* they are Korean, or *burakumin*, or have no educational qualifications, but because they are suitable. In *yakuza* terms, suitable recruiting material is to be most readily found amongst those who have already embarked upon a career of deviancy.[12] In the 1989 police survey of recent *yakuza* recruits, 11.3 per cent were shoplifters, 33 per cent solvent abusers, 75 per cent had been arrested prior to joining a *yakuza* group, and 50 per cent had been arrested more than once. Of the survey's interviewees, the majority (60 per cent) had been involved in delinquent groups, especially *bōsozoku* hot-rod groups and local street-gangs (*Keisatsu Hakusho* 1989: 38–9).

Yakuza 'talent scouts' will patrol game-centres, street-corners, and other delinquent hangouts making contact with likely individuals (Yamadaira 1992: 141). Potential recruits may be given pocket money, meals, or drugs. They may then be employed on errands and slowly drawn into the talent scout's circle. Herbert reports that karate clubs at some of the less-prestigious universities have also been targeted as potential recruiting grounds; whilst this has not been corroborated by other sources it is not unfeasible.[13] Martial-arts schools have long been run by Chinese Triad groups purely as recruiting and training vehicles (Booth 1999: 173, 212), whilst I am aware of at least one foreigner who used his credentials as a *karate-ka* to gain part-time employment as a driver and 'acrobat' for a Tokyo-based gang.

Recruitment need not be a one-way process. All the interviewees who commented on their motives for joining had joined of their own volition. Tanomura, a *tekiya* in Iwate prefecture, had been attracted to the bright lights and excitement of festivals. In contrast to this, Fujimura joined in his mid-1920s because his bars were consistently pestered by *yakuza* seeking to squeeze money out of him in some way or other; membership insulated him from this harassment.[14] Most of the interviewees had joined at an early age having spent a childhood apprenticeship. In one police survey of 291 *yakuza*, 27 per cent had asked to join rather than waiting to be invited, 49 per cent had joined immediately after being invited, whilst only 3 per cent had joined against their will (*Keisatsu Hakusho* 1989: 40). This attraction to the *yakuza* life is reflected in the reasons given by interviewed *yakuza* arrestees for joining their organisations (see Table 3.1).

It is significant that gang members themselves see the flashy image and *giri-ninjō* value system, beloved by Japanese film makers, as more important than the perception that the *ikka* will recognise even people like them (whilst society doesn't). This does not necessarily contradict the discrimination thesis. Narcissism is a common factor within organised crime subcultures (Hobbs 1994: 448–9) and, when manifested by extremely 'flash' attire, suggests a defiant rejection of societal judgement.[15] At the same time such clothing signals the wealth, which within the *yakuza* world as elsewhere, itself acts as an indicator of success. Demonstrating one's wealth, whether through clothing,

Table 3.1 Motivational factors for joining *yakuza*

Factor	Agreement rating (%)
Attracted by the *yakuza* image (*kakko-ii*)	36.5
Attracted by the world of *giri-ninjō*	29.1
They will recognise even someone like myself	17.1
You can achieve an enjoyable lifestyle	16.7
To support immediate lifestyle	12.2
Feel attraction for controlling through violence	9.5
Convenient for work	7.2
It is easy economically	7.1
It is easy work	3.9
Forced to join against will so no motivation for joining	3.5
No reason in particular	4.1

Source: *Keisatsu Hakusho* (1993: 31).

jewellery, or cars, is therefore a way of advertising that you are a successful gangster and, by implication, a worthy protector.

Notice that the police survey skirts around the issue of discrimination as a possible factor encouraging individuals to join *yakuza* groups.
The statement 'they will recognise someone like myself', which registered an agreement rating of 17 per cent, may be seen as a rough proxy
indicating the extent to which the respondents felt discriminated
against, for whatever reason, prior to joining. Given that the possible
causes of this include discrimination against Koreans/*burakumin*, low
educational attainment, and a criminal record, it is surprising that this
figure is so low.

Whilst most members join in their youth, this is not necessarily the
case. Released convicts, dismissed policemen, and failed salarymen
(possibly fired for fraud or similar irregularities), may all find themselves deprived of legitimate employment. The latter two categories
may bring particular skills to the organisation. Due to the increasing
proportion of white-collar activities amongst *yakuza* sources of
income, computer and financial expertise are especially welcome.

Although it is not given above as a major motivating factor in joining,
interviews of *kumi-chō* frequently reveal that economic considerations
are also important. Whilst money itself is not necessarily given as a

reason for joining, the status and power that money gives is undoubtedly important (Yasuda 1993: 207). This is reflected in the ostentatious display of wealth, which is such an important part of the *yakuza* image. An often-overlooked factor in this is that people join *yakuza* groups for the simple reason that, for the successful, crime pays extremely well.

Education

Vocational apprenticeships in Japan are traditionally based on the concept of *minarai*, or 'learning by looking'. Within the *yakuza* world this process is reinforced by hitting trainees when they commit some error. Thus, by a process of observation, imitation, and filtering out behaviour patterns that incur blows, *yakuza* initiates typically learn their craft (Yamaguchi-gumi subgroup interviewees, Osaka 1998). Just as *geisha* initiates are adopted by an elder sister who is primarily responsible for the apprentice's behaviour and education (Dalby 2000: 41), *yakuza* trainees typically have an elder brother to act as their sponsor and mentor.

According to Yamadaira, the modern *yakuza* apprenticeship lasts for a period of between six months and three years (1988: 141). In the gang studied by Stark the period was six months, though during the 1960s it had lasted for one year (1981: 96). During the period of training, new recruits typically live in the gang office, in the boss's house, or the house of another gang executive. This *sumi-komi* (living-in) training involves such menial domestic chores as cleaning, cooking, walking the dog, running errands, and driving. In addition to these tasks, trainees must pay close attention to matters of etiquette: when a boss, executive, or guest picks up a cigarette, a trainee quickly proffers a flame; similarly, on exiting the lavatory, he will be presented with a hot towel; when the boss enters or exits the office, the trainees bow outside the door; trainees run to open and close the car door for the boss; and shoes left at the entrance must be arranged perfectly. It is an appealing way to be treated.

Although *yakuza* education typically seems to be informal on-the-job training, we have evidence of one area of technical expertise in which, during the 1970s, trained *yakuza* members were sent to serve apprenticeships with non-*yakuza* whilst serving as their protectors.

This is the field of corporate extortion operated by *sōkaiya*, which will be discussed in greater detail in Chapter Four.

In prewar *yakuza* society, an important aspect of training was the learning of *jingi*. Literally, *jingi* translates as humanity and justice, though it later came to be used by *yakuza* to refer to correct *yakuza* conduct and in particular to the formal greetings peculiar to this world. *Jingi* takes three distinct forms: *aitsuki-mentsu*, *mawari-mentsu*, and *goro-mentsu*, which are used as a form of *yakuza* self-introduction in one-to-one, group, and threatening situations respectively. Trainees who failed to correctly recite *jingi* greetings in public could be beaten with impunity by *yakuza* from other groups. By 1971, Hoshino notes that *jingi* had fallen out of use and that only senior members knew how to perform these greetings correctly (Hoshino 1971: 41–2; Hoshino, Mugishima, and Kiyonaga 1971: 144–5). More recently, during the course of my fieldwork, one boss's knowledge of traditional *jingi* was given as supporting evidence for the claim that he was something special within the *yakuza* world.

The fact that extensive training was required to master it suggests that *jingi* was used as a way of establishing one's authenticity as a *yakuza*, and therefore the existence of potentially violent backup, in a way that others would find difficult to mimic. Given that the modern alternatives, typically name-cards and badges, are less costly to acquire (and therefore to fake), it is interesting to speculate why the use of *jingi* has fallen out of favour. The most probable reason is the mass influx of new entrants following 1945. However, one device that traditionally signals *yakuza* identity and is costly to acquire remained in wide currency at the end of the 1980s: the tattoo.

Tattoos

Tattoos (known in Japanese as *irezumi*, *horimono*, or *kurikara monmon*) are, along with *yubitsume*, the most widely known aspect of the *yakuza* amongst non-Japanese. For much the same reasons, they serve as powerful means by which one's identity as a *yakuza* can be established. They are expensive to acquire, highly visible, widely recognised as *yakuza* brands, and, consequently, stigmatised by mainstream Japanese society. The signalling function of finger-amputation is of secondary importance to its role as a punishment and it is doubtful if many *yakuza* actually *want* to cut off their fingers. Tattooing is another matter.

According to Japan's earliest historical records (the *Kojiki* and *Nihonshiki*, both dating from the eighth century), tattoos were traditionally used as a way of punishing criminals. Similarly, following a law of 1720, small thefts, vagrancy, elopement, and other light crimes were punished with bands tattooed onto the criminals' arms or the head (Herbert 1995: 8). These tattoos therefore served as a record sheet. One police document claims that many such individuals attempted to disguise these marks by more extensive tattoos (*Bōryokudan Taisakka*, undated/unpaged). This seems surprising. Whilst big tattoos are today frequently used to obscure smaller 'mistakes' (such as self-inscribed prison tattoos or the names of former girlfriends), surely the wilful, and highly visible, destruction of state records must have met with penal sanctions from the state.

During the Edo period, tattoos were popular amongst those engaged in tough masculine jobs such as firefighters and steeplejacks. Interestingly, during the same period, several state officials were ordered into retirement on discovery of their tattoos (*Bōryokudan Taisakka*). Similar cases exist more recently of company employees being fired on the discovery of their tattoos (Herbert 1995: 9). During the Meiji period, the authorities, identifying tattooing as a barbaric practice unbecoming a modern state, formally prohibited it, though with little success (Herbert 1995: 8).

During the early 1970s, NRIPS research showed that just over 70 per cent of *yakuza* had tattoos. There was no great variation amongst the various grades. The vast majority of these had been done in the traditional Japanese way of hand-pricking the skin with a tight cluster of needles dipped in ink. Only 10 per cent of tattoos had been made with modern tattooing machines. When asked for their motivations, by far the most popular reasons given were ostentation and intimidation (53 per cent and 17 per cent, respectively). The next most significant motivating factor was curiosity (7 per cent) (Mugishima et al. 1971: 137–9). Although there is no similar study conducted for the late 1980s, later figures suggest that the 70 per cent figure is essentially unchanged (*Zen-Bōtsusen* 1994: 33). Herbert's research with the tattoo master Horitsune (1995), suggests that modern tattooing machines are becoming more prevalent. It seems unlikely that ostentation has ceased to be the main motivational factor.

Tattoos are ostentatious. Any ostentatious act by definition suggests that the actor wishes to give some message and can therefore be studied as a signalling device. This is certainly true for *yakuza*-style tattoos,[16] which carry all sorts of messages. The most obvious one is that it identifies the wearer as a *yakuza*. Not all tattooed men are in fact *yakuza*, though the majority are or were, and those that are not are running the risk not only of societal disapprobation (namely the case of the dismissed salaryman), but also of penalties for brand-infringement. Outside of the *yakuza*, the most common possessors of tattoos up to the end of the 1980s were those employed in the *mizu-shōbai* world of clubs and hostess bars.

For a sign to be a strong indicator of some attribute, it should only be manifested by those who genuinely possess that attribute and difficult for impostors to acquire (as in the case of correct mastery of *jingi*). Tattoos would seem to be easier to acquire but there are, in fact, significant costs in acquiring a tattoo, over and above their social stigmatisation, that act as deterrents to all but the most committed aspiring signaller. First, they are very expensive in terms of both time and money. It can take three years to complete a full tattoo using traditional techniques. This might cost a few million yen. Using a machine, this would be reduced to a year on the basis of one session a week and would also be cheaper (though still not cheap).

Tattoos also place significant physical costs on the wearer: they hurt. Not only does the traditional needle hurt on entry, but also the pigment injected into the wounds causes fevers and, frequently, liver problems in later life; liver-related illnesses are a significant cause of death amongst *yakuza* (though this is in no small part exacerbated by their high rates of alcohol consumption). A tattoo is therefore demonstrating the wearer's ability to endure pain and, perhaps less consciously, a disregard for the future. Unfortunately, the strength of this signal too has been undermined by modern, less painful, machine tattooing.

The final cost to the bearer of a tattoo is its permanent nature. Once acquired, it is very hard to remove. This fact, combined with society's general intolerance of tattoos, makes their acquisition a strong statement of commitment to the *yakuza* life and, by implication, to the tattoo-bearer's group. By wearing a tattoo, a gang member is telling mainstream society not only that he is not part of it, but that he never wants to be so.

Given that the 70-per-cent tattoo rate is roughly similar for senior executives, executives, and ordinary *kumi-in*, the un-tattooed 30 per cent cannot be explained as being due to new-entrants' not yet having had time to become tattooed. It seems plausible to conjecture that un-tattooed *yakuza* are those whose commitment is weakest. The evidence suggests this is only a partial explanation.[17] Given that such a committed, wealthy, and tough *yakuza* as fourth-generation Yamaguchi-gumi boss Takenaka did not bear tattoos, the costs mentioned above do not adequately explain why a minority of *yakuza* fail to make use of this available trade mark.

Financial Flows

In 1989, the police estimated that the total income of *bōryokudan* groups in Japan was over ¥1.3 trillion ($9.4 bn) (*Keisatsu Hakusho* 1989: 46). This translates into an average annual per capita income of ¥15 m ($109,000). Police data on *bōryokudan* income from 1979 (the first year such measurements were made) put total *bōryokudan* income at ¥1 trillion and average annual income per head at ¥10 m (Mizoguchi 1986: 183). Such figures suggest that *yakuza* income had grown by 30 per cent. However, due to the smaller less competitive *ikka* being forced out of business, *yakuza* per capita earnings would have increased by 50 per cent. However, as will be discussed in Chapter Four, there are large question marks appended to these figures.

Of course, *yakuza* groups are not egalitarian organisations and the distribution of their income reflects this. Uchiyama (1989: 89) in a survey of 925 *yakuza* arrestees found that the average annual income for bosses (¥26.7 m) was nearly eight times that of the average *kumi-in* (¥2.46 m); executives averaged ¥7.7 m. During the same year, the average annual salary of a regular company employee was ¥3.6 m (*Tōkei Kyoku* 1992: 98). It should be noted that these figures are averages; for senior bosses this differential will be considerably higher. Retired third-level Ichiwa-kai boss Fujimura states that most ordinary young *kumi-in* are permanently broke, living a parasitical hand-to-mouth existence off the income of girlfriends, parents, or their *oyabun* (Fujimura interview Osaka, August 1998). Most of the proceeds from organised crime end up in the higher echelons of the various groups.

Large syndicates operate on a system of tribute known by the police as *jōnōkin* (literally 'upward payment money') whilst the *yakuza* themselves prefer the term *'kaihi'* (association fees). Under this system, gang members typically pay a monthly amount of *jōnōkin* to their gang. Similarly subordinate gangs give *jōnōkin* to their parent organisation. This system evolved as a direct consequence of the first and second police summit strategies of the mid-to-late 1960s. Because of these concentrated arrests of senior executives and bosses, it became necessary to insulate the top leadership from direct criminal involvement whilst retaining a secure and stable source of income. As a result of the *jōnōkin* system the number of arrests of senior *yakuza* figures declined dramatically and this remains a serious problem for police *bōryokudan* countermeasures (Ino 1992*a*: 264).

It should be noted that, within second- and third-level gangs, there is no hard rule concerning *jōnōkin* and it remains at the discretion of the boss of the gang in question. Fujimura states that within his old *gumi* (a second-level group within the Yamaguchi-gumi and then the breakaway Ichiwa-kai) there was no *jōnōkin* but he voluntarily paid the telephone bill for the gang headquarters (Fujimura interview Osaka, August 1998).

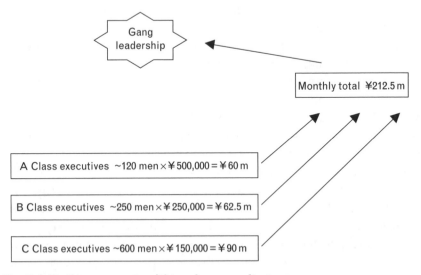

Fig. 3.4 *Jōnōkin* payments within a large syndicate

Source: Keisatsu Hakusho (1989). Where does this money come from? From *yakuza shinogi*.

The *jōnōkin* structure of a typical large syndicate is shown in Figure 3.4. The example in the diagram shows that the syndicate leadership receives a monthly income of ¥212.5m ($1.5m) without recourse to direct criminal involvement. Between its introduction and the end of the 1980s, there was a trend for *jōnōkin* to rise. Within the Yamaguchi-gumi this process started with a reorganisation of the syndicate's finances under the then waka *gashira*, Yamamoto Kenichi, in 1971. At that time, members of the first-level Yamaguchi-gumi would each pay ¥50,000 per month. By 1982 this had doubled to ¥100,000. Over the next decade *jōnōkin* increased over thirteen-fold to a hefty ¥1,340,000 yielding the headquarters an annual income of ¥21.26 bn ($167 m)[18] (Mizoguchi 1997: 54, 58). Consequently, meeting the burdens of *jōnōkin* payments has become problematic for many *ikka*, especially for the second- and third-level gangs on whom the financial responsibility ultimately rests. In some cases this has resulted in the dissolution of the gang (Ames 1981: 118). Since Ames was writing this problem has become yet more acute.

Where does this money come from? From *yakuza shinogi*.

4

Shinogi—Sources of Income

Within the *yakuza* world, all types of economic activity from which gangs or gang members derive money are known collectively as *shinogi. Shinogi* is defined in Kenkyusha's New Japanese-English Dictionary as 'to be in a helpless condition; be driven to the wall; be quite at a loss how to tide over difficulties'. This captures quite well the desperate and transient nature of the hand-to-mouth existence of many low-ranking *yakuza*. However, the apparent wealth of successful senior *yakuza* during the highly affluent years at the end of the 1980s, is at odds with the etymology of '*shinogi*'.

Whilst the police estimates of gang income given in Chapter Three may seem large, many sources consider the figures to be highly conservative. One source of doubt is that the previous official police estimates of *yakuza* income, conducted in 1979, yielded two figures of ¥1 trillion (itself suspiciously round) and ¥1.37 trillion (Mizoguchi 1986: 183). In the succeeding ten years, *yakuza* sources of income substantially diversified and became more sophisticated. In the light of this, even allowing for the decline in *yakuza* numbers, it is unlikely that *yakuza* income remained stagnant or increased merely by 30 per cent over this period whilst, to provide a rough comparison, real GDP growth of the Japanese economy between 1980 and 1990 was just a whisker below 50 per cent (Kawai 1999: 80). However, criticising one estimate on the basis of another is only a useful exercise if we hold some degree of confidence about the accuracy of our comparator.

The 1979 figures were estimated by two distinct methods. In the first case, the *yakuza* were categorised into five different classes; the average income and size of each of these categories was estimated; the two figures from each group were then multiplied and totalled. The second figure was produced by estimating the income generated from the various business activities engaged in by *yakuza*. Mizoguchi, writing in the mid-1980s, suggests that this under-reports the contribution played by various forms of extortion and exaggerates the role of drugs revenue. Instead he presents a figure of ¥7 trillion as being nearer the mark, though he describes this as *yakuza* turnover rather than profit (which he estimates at 70–80 per cent of this total arguing that most *yakuza* businesses have very low costs) (1986: 182). From his direct observations of the standard of living of senior *yakuza* bosses, Mizoguchi does not find such a figure surprising. Hoshino also admitted to the researcher that, having visited the homes of high-ranking *yakuza* and seen their lifestyles, he felt the official estimates were likely to be on the low side (interview Yokohama, 1998).

The 1989 figures were generated from the same basic sectoral analysis as the second 1979 estimate. As such, they are liable to similar criticisms. One of the research officers at the National Research Institute for Police Science (NRIPS), who had been responsible for creating the methodology by which the 1989 estimate was obtained, pointed out in interview that some sources of funding were seriously under-represented in the final figures. In particular the amounts of money that *yakuza* groups extract from legitimate businesses were significantly underestimated and the interviewee asserted that this had been a politically motivated decision made by superiors within the NPA; it would have been embarrassing to show the extent to which many large mainstream companies were bank-rolling these groups (interview NRIPS, Tokyo, March 1998).

Another senior researcher at NRIPS confessed with unnerving cheerfulness that, despite a never-ending stream of journalists and researchers beating a path to his door with requests for the figures his institute churns out to the nearest tenth of a percentage, he was unsure to what extent the data his institute produced bore any relation to the real world (interview NRIPS, Tokyo, February 1998).

Bearing these caveats in mind, let us look at the 1989 estimate, as broken down by sector, given in Figure 4.1.

According, therefore, to the official police estimates, the overwhelming majority of *yakuza* income as of 1989 was derived from illegal sources.

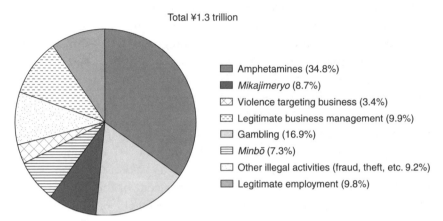

Fig. 4.1 Sources of *Bōryokudan* income—police estimates 1989
Source: Keisatsu Hakusho (1989).

What is more surprising, given the changing nature of *yakuza* activity, is that conventional, established sources of income, namely, gambling and bookmaking, amphetamines, protection, and other traditional forms of *shinogi*, were still considered to account for over 60 per cent of this total.

Whilst it is beyond the scope of this chapter to try to suggest exactly what are actual relative contributions to total *yakuza* income of the various types of *shinogi*, it seems highly likely that, at the end of the 1980s, the proportion of *yakuza* income derived from protection and activities collectively categorised by the police as the 'violent intervention in civil affairs' (*minji kainyū bōryoku*, or *minbō* for short, in Japanese) were far more significant than the police figures suggest.

Although no attempt is made here to improve on the police estimate, this chapter tries to show the various types of *yakuza shinogi* and their place in the *yakuza* economy at the end of the Shōwa period.

Protection

As we have defined mafia-style organisations in Chapter One, it is the provision of protection which gives such groups their special characteristics. It is the ability of OC syndicates to provide protection to their members and other consumers, as well as to deny it to others, which enables them to obtain all other forms of *shinogi*. Protection therefore overarches the diverse set of business activities, both legal and illegal, in which *yakuza* members are active.

Whilst protection is therefore implicit in their other business activities, in this section I deal with the narrow conception of protection; that afforded to businesses to reduce the threat of disruption to their operating environment by bad customers, suppliers, employees or predators. More specific forms of protection will be dealt with later. Traditionally the main focus of *yakuza* protection has been the entertainment industries comprising restaurants, bars, night-clubs, and sex industry known collectively as *mizushōbai* (water trades). In these businesses *yakuza* protection is referred to as *mikajimeryō*.[1] There are many ways in which *yakuza* can gain money from shops and bars. The most straightforward form of *mikajimeryō* is to receive *yojimbōdai* (bodyguard fee). A more subtle approach is to get the protectee to buy goods and services from gang-run businesses at inflated prices. *Oshibori* (hot hand-towels) and *tsumami* (snacks) are often provided to bars and restaurants in this way. Alternatively, pictures, potted plants, and other decorations may be leased at above market rates.

A 1988 questionnaire of 1,500 traders carried out by the police in Ishikawa prefecture yielded the data shown in Table 4.1.

Although these percentages are not high, within the sample population this represents total monthly payments amounting to roughly ¥2.2 m. When it is considered that *yakuza* protection activity has traditionally been concentrated in Japan's vast[2] *mizushōbai* (entertainment)

Table 4.1 Payment of *mikajimeryō* (%)

Currently paying *mikajimeryō*	6.6
of which ¥1,000/month	0.1
¥5,000/month	6.5
Have paid *mikajimeryō* in the past	5.4
Being forced to buy goods	19.6
of which ¥5–10,000/month	0.5
¥3–5,000/month	19.1
Have made use of *bōryokudan* in the past	1.4
of which, used to sort out trouble	1.0
recover money owed	0.4

Source: Keisatsu Hakusho (1989).

industry, then they become more significant. A 1980 survey carried out by police in the Yokohama area, showed that more than 70 per cent of enterprises in the *mizushōbai* sector paid *mikajimeryō* to *yakuza*. This yielded an annual figure of approximately ¥1.5 bn ($6.61 m) (Kaplan and Dubro 1986: 169). A rough estimate by a *yakuza* associate working in the entertainment area of Shinjuku suggests that two thirds of the 3,000 bars and clubs in Kabuki-chō were paying an average of ¥30,000 per month. This gives an annual pay-out of ¥720 m (Hinago 1992*b*: 75). The figures cited by Mizoguchi for typical *mikajimeryō* payments in the Kōbe area are ¥100,000 per month for a club and ¥300–500,000 for a *pachinko* (pinball) parlour. In the fashionable Ginza district of Tokyo, some clubs reportedly pay as much as ¥1 m per month (1997: 82).

Although it is a significant and arguably necessary expense to the operators of entertainment facilities, such proprietors are not able to deduct protection payments for tax purposes. In *Miura* v. *Meguro* Tax Office 1989, the owner of two 'special public bathing facilities' claimed tax-deductible expenses of protection money varying between ¥5–7 m per month. The court decided against Miura on the grounds that were the deduction to be allowed, 'the country would effectively be using firms to subsidise the mob' (Ramseyer and Nakazato 1999: 231, 286).

Protection covers not only the entertainment industry. Sagawa Kyūbin, the parcel delivery company, reputedly paid ¥2 bn per year to Ishii Susumu, Inagawa-kai boss (1986–1990), to ensure trouble-free business (1999: 231, 286). In total the Tokyo Metropolitan Police estimate that roughly ¥100 bn flowed to Ishii from Sagawa Kyūbin (Nakagawa 1992: 235). Such delivery companies have characteristics that make them particularly dependent on protection; it is a highly competitive business, employing largely unskilled labour, in which consignments can get delayed, damaged in transit, and lost.

The construction industry is also one in which *yakuza* protection is significant. Like the trucking industry it is vulnerable to the pilfering of materials and delays. It is also dependent on a large, unskilled workforce. As argued in Chapter One, such industries are more likely consumers of protection than capital-intensive industries with a small, highly skilled workforce. As will be shown below, *yakuza* involvement in construction is facilitated by partial control over the supply of labour to this industry (see labour-broking). Owing to the high value of land in Japan, astronomically so at the time of the bubble economy, construction costs are a lower proportion of the total project than in most other countries. Delays may also therefore be more expensive than elsewhere. For these reasons, the Japanese construction industry is especially susceptible to *yakuza* protection.[3]

The standard fee to ensure trouble-free construction is 3 per cent of the total construction cost[4] (interview Fujimura, Osaka 1998). In 1985 total investment in construction reached ¥50 trillion, or 16 per cent of GNP for the same year. Of this ¥30 trillion was private sector investment and the remaining ¥20 trillion, public (Hasegawa 1988: 2–3). Assuming that protection is extended to just one-third of this total, in 1985 *yakuza* earned ¥500 bn from this industry alone. Such a figure is just under 40 per cent of the total police estimate of *yakuza* income for 1988 and this suggests more powerfully than anything else that the police figure is unrealistic. Although it is not clear to what extent the construction industry pays protection, one-third is probably an underestimate; former Ichiwa-kai boss Fujimura suggested that payment was the norm rather than the exception, whilst the two-thirds payment rate in the *mizushōbai* sector, which is seen as having a similar relationship to the *yakuza* as that enjoyed by the construction industry, suggests a higher proportion would not be surprising.

Of course, *bōryokudan* involvement in construction operates at more than one level. The other ways in which criminal groups extract funds from this industry are more properly dealt with in the sections concerning legitimate business and activities targeting legitimate business.

The term '*mikajimeryō*' carries wider connotations than the provision of protection in that it also applies to payments made to a group in return for permission to conduct business within that gang's territory. Therefore, traders at the economic and legal margins such as outdoor stall-holders, drug-dealers, and street prostitutes pay a street-tax to the relevant gang. For women on the streets of Shin-Ōkubo this amounted to ¥3,000 per woman per day (police interviewee, Tokyo 1998).

This tax need not be an entirely exploitative relationship. One Israeli stall-holder[5] explained why he had little trouble with the police in the following way: 'The bosses (those running the Israeli jewellery hawkers) have a relationship with the *yakuza* and they (the *yakuza*) have a relationship with the police. It is a good system and it works well' (stall-holder, Kōbe 1998).

For bar-keepers, protection ensures that problems involving unruly customers, or those that refuse to pay their bill, can be resolved quickly. In one incident I witnessed in a bar in central Japan, the local boss arrived within 5 minutes of a situation developing. Whilst it is not to be argued that payers of protection get value for money, the protection relationship is not a purely exploitative one and many entrepreneurs actively seek out protection rather than finding it thrust upon them.

The need for this service is not confined to traders in the entertainment business; as has been discussed above, both politicians and businesses have long found it useful to maintain a relationship with *yakuza* elements. Although, by the late 1980s, overt *yakuza* connections were no longer a political advantage, many politicians retained such links behind the scenes as the Sagawa Kyūbin scandal, to be discussed in Chapter Six, illustrates. The business–*yakuza* nexus is discussed below in the section dealing with *minji kainyū bōryoku*.

Drugs

As is the case with Great Britain, Japan's history with recreational drugs is far from unambiguous. During the 1930s and early 1940s Japan had a twin-track narcotics policy. Within Japan the use of drugs was strictly prohibited, whilst in the occupied territories, opium trafficking was seen as both a source of revenue and a means of keeping the populace docile. On taking control of Manchuria, Japan quickly established an opium monopoly. By 1939 this industry was yielding $90 m in tax revenues to the Japanese government. As this industry was legal, legitimate traders could operate, though *yakuza* groups provided protection at the numerous opium dens (Vaughn, Huang, and Ramirez 1995: 495–6).

At the same time, amphetamine-based stimulants were freely and legally available in Japan. The first such product came on the market in 1931 under the brand name Hiropon and was sold either as ampoules of injectable liquid or as lozenges. At the time amphetamines were widely regarded as an almost miraculous panacea and used to treat a number of conditions ranging from low blood pressure to obesity (Abadinsky 1994: 382–3). They were also recognised as having considerable military application not only for raising the stamina of combat troops, but also for ensuring continued industrial production despite an increasingly malnourished workforce.

At the end of the war, huge stocks of military amphetamines came onto the civilian market where they became a popular means of combating the fatigue and hunger resulting from chronic food shortages. The consequences of this were that amphetamine abuse exploded in what became known as the 'first epidemic period' (1945–1955). At its peak in 1954, it involved an estimated 2 million (2.2 per cent of the total population). By 1948, amphetamine had become officially recognised as a 'dangerous drug' (though still legal) and the potency of the ampoules was reduced. In 1951, the Stimulant Drug Control Law (*Kakuseizai Torishimari Hō*) was passed. This was followed in 1953 by a widespread public awareness campaign (Brill and Hirose 1969: 179–80).

As a response to the harsher penalties imposed by the revision of the Stimulant Drug Control Law in 1954, there was a rapid decline in amphetamine consumption and by 1957 the problem was effectively over.[6] However, as pointed out by Brill and Hirose, 'as amphetamine abuse declined, there was a sharp rise in heroin addiction' (1969: 179–80). This is interesting because it is frequently claimed that the current absence of heroin in Japan is due to its not suiting the 'Japanese temperament'.

The second period of epidemic amphetamine abuse started in 1970. It peaked in 1984 and by 1988 was slowly starting to decline. In contrast to the first epidemic, the *yakuza* played a crucial role in its development. As the senior *yakuza* figures who had been arrested due to the police summit strategies of the mid-1960s were released from prison, they needed an easily developable cash-generating activity on which they could re-establish their syndicates. The epidemic started in the Osaka area and spread from there to the rest of Japan. It is reported that this was facilitated by construction workers, who had gathered in Osaka to build the Osaka Expo World Fair, later returning to their homes taking their newly-acquired habit with them (Tamura 1992: 102–3).

Although illegal drug abuse in Japan overwhelmingly involves the injection of methamphetamine (known colloquially as *shabu* or *pon*), other types of substance abuse are not unknown. Narcotics abuse is a relatively minor problem; in 1988 only 105 arrests were made for narcotics violations and 1,464 for cannabis whilst 20,399 were made for stimulant violations. Police interviewees reveal that the *yakuza* are not seriously involved in cannabis trafficking, which is seen by the police as being largely carried out on a disorganised basis by individuals involved with what the police identify as 'alternative' lifestyles such as surfing, the arts, and rock music. Cocaine-related arrests in 1988 numbered a comparatively negligible 35 (*Keisatsu Hakusho* 1997: 140). More significant, however, is the number of cases of solvent abuse amongst juveniles.[7]

The trade in amphetamines is monopolised by the *yakuza* as only they have the organisational networks, connections and ability to deploy sufficient protection to operate, or allow those paying the appropriate 'street-tax' to operate, within this illegal market. Furthermore, many gang members are themselves users of stimulants (Tamura 1992: 101–3). However, by no means do all *yakuza* participate in this type of *shinogi*. Nor does any one particular group hold monopoly power over this market. The three large syndicates maintain a formal policy of non-involvement in the amphetamine trade. The Yamaguchi-gumi has taken this a step further by forming the *Zenkoku Kokudō Jōka Dōmei* (National Purification League), which is supposedly dedicated to the eradication of amphetamine abuse.

The police dismiss this as, at best, a poor public-relations exercise or a cynical attempt to run the competition out of town. However, amongst most *yakuza* and related interviewees there was undisguised contempt for drug-dealing *yakuza* whom they dismissed as those lacking either the strength or the brains to succeed at any other type of *shinogi*. There are also very good reasons why these organisations would wish to distance themselves from this particular business. As it is perceived in Japan as a more pernicious crime than gambling, protection, or prostitution, involvement in amphetamine dealing is likely to incur more rigorous law enforcement and severe penalties. It is also likely to exacerbate a negative public perception of organisations involved in this business.

Despite this, it seems clear that the pressure to pay the expenses which a *yakuza* lifestyle entails, forces many subgroups into the amphetamine business. However, Yamaguchi-gumi members arrested for drugs-related offences are formally expelled. In the case of Pao, a young *kumi-in* expelled from a Yamaguchi-gumi Yamaken-gumi subgroup visited during fieldwork, rehabilitation was achieved after a year. It seems reasonable to suggest that as long as *jōnōkin* payments are forthcoming, a blind eye is turned to discreet trading. In Britain, professional criminals reputedly had a similar disdain for the drugs industry and similarly many have lost this disdain once its lucrative nature became fully apparent (Morton 1992: 399).

Gauging just how lucrative Japan's market for methamphetamine is exactly, is of course problematic. Tamura (1988) illustrates these problems in a 1988 review of the various attempts by the NPA to estimate the scale of amphetamine use in Japan. Early police estimates rested on a number of questionable assumptions that render their results highly dubious. For example, a 1978 estimate rested on the heroic assumptions that the volume of amphetamine seizures represented 5 per cent of the total amount of the drug in circulation. Similarly, drug-related arrest was reckoned equivalent to 10 per cent of all consumers. This led the NPA to conclude that roughly 2 tons of amphetamine were imported in 1978 and consumed by 200,000 individuals. Making the further, but more reasonable, assumption that the average consumer injects one shot of 0.03 g per day gives a total annual consumption of 2.19 tons ($0.03\,g \times 365 \times 200,000$), which is not so far off their estimate for circulation.

To evaluate the level of profit generated by this trade, the NPA multiplied this figure by the street price minus initial wholesale price (at the time, ¥250,000/g and ¥10,000/g, respectively). This yielded a total profit of ¥4.6 trillion ($21.9 bn). It was further assumed that all this profit accrued to *yakuza* traders and those actively participating in dealing were numbered at 40,000 (working on the assumption that 20 per cent of all dealers are arrested per year). The NPA therefore calculated the average annual profit per *yakuza* dealer in 1978 at ¥11.6 m ($55,200).

Even disregarding the NPA assumptions concerning the ratio of seizures and arrests to the 'dark figures', the estimates as to profit levels are too simple. For example, they disregard the facts that street-level dealing is often carried out by non-*yakuza* members and that many dealers are also users who withdraw a certain amount, at whatever level of the distribution chain they occupy, for their own consumption. The 1978 methodology also falls down when applied to 1987 arrest and seizure statistics. This was because the volume of drugs seized had increased by over six times whilst the number of arrests had remained roughly constant.

By the late 1980s a more sophisticated picture had emerged due to the collation of intelligence gathered by the various prefectural police headquarters. The results of the 1987 NPA survey of the amphetamine situation were considered by Tamura to be much more dependable than anything hitherto conducted (1988: 54). It was estimated that 2,125 *yakuza* groups were involved in the sale and distribution of amphetamines (this represented 85 per cent of all gangs in Japan). Of these groups, 300 were considered to be operating at the wholesale level (dealing in kilograms rather than grams). About 50,000 *yakuza* members were dealing and this was augmented by 50,000 non-*yakuza*, which gives us a total employment of 100,000. Of this, 90 per cent (including all non-*yakuza*) were dealing in units of 1 g or less.

From interviews of arrestees it appeared that each dealer had an average of five customers. In addition it was apparent that most dealers were themselves consumers. The total number of consumers was therefore estimated to be 550,000 ((90,000 × 5) + 100,000). This is roughly 27 times the number of drug-related arrests made each year. Total consumption was estimated by assuming that the amphetamine-consuming population could be broken down into five equal groups according to usage frequency as shown in Table 4.2. Whether this frequency is based on police-interview data or not is unclear; however, the all too tidy breakdown of the figures urges caution. Despite this, the total consumption figure of just over 7 tons seems reasonable given that 620 kg (or 8 per cent of the total supposedly imported) was seized by the police in 1987.

There are a number of ways of attempting to estimate the revenue this 7 tons generates. The most elementary is to simply subtract the

Table 4.2 Usage frequency of amphetamine-consuming population

Usage frequency	g/p/a[a]	# users	Total (kg)
3 × /day	30	110,000	3,300
2 × /day	20	110,000	2,200
1 × /day	10	110,000	1,100
2 × /week	3	110,000	330
2 × /month	1	110,000	110
TOTAL			7,040

Source: *Tamura* (1988)
Note (*a*) g/p/a grams/person/year

amount that the 100,000 dealers themselves consume and then multiply the remainder by current street prices as follows:

Street price	¥100,000/g	= ¥100 m/kg
Total consumed		
by non-dealers	7,040 × 0.82	= 5,760 kg
Total revenue	5,760 × 100 m	= ¥576 bn ($4 bn)

This, however, assumes that dealers share the consumption patterns of their customers. It seems plausible that dealers, with ready access to supplies, will be heavier consumers than non-dealing users. Given that we are interested in *yakuza* income rather than dealers' income we should perhaps not exclude non-*yakuza* dealers from our calculation. To complicate matters, these individuals, as dealers themselves, are not purchasing at street price.

Taking into account the differing prices at the various stages along the distribution chain, the NPA have constructed a diagram representing the structure of the amphetamine trade in Japan as of 1987. This yields total sales of ¥450 bn and profit of ¥209 bn (roughly $3.1 and $1.4 bn, respectively). Tamura, with characteristic scepticism, stresses that these estimates should be treated with caution and that there is a need for further research to clarify the nature of this industry (1988: 60). However, as of the end of the Shōwa period, they were the best figures available.

Most of the groups involved at the importation level of the business are relatively small. Typical of these is the 'M-gumi' a subgroup of the Fukuoka-based Dōjin-kai consisting of about twenty members. This group imported several hundreds of kilograms per year, meeting with Taiwanese exporters on the open sea, where amphetamines would be exchanged for ¥1,000/g. This would be distributed via parcel-delivery companies to Dōjin-kai subgroups in Hokkaidō and Kyōsei-kai subgroups in Hiroshima. At a wholesale price of ¥4,500/g, M-gumi had annual sales of ¥600 m (Mizoguchi 1997: 85–6).

The monthly finances of 'S-gumi', a lower-level drug dealing organisation, are given in Table 4.3.

This clearly shows that, at the level of a small-scale drug-dealing gang, this trade is economically attractive. After allowing for the necessary

Table 4.3 Breakdown of drug dealing group's finances

Sales	¥9,400,000
Purchase cost	¥600,000
Gross margin	¥8,800,000
Expenses	
Jōnōkin	¥250,000
Food for duty *kumi-in*	¥90,000
Gang office building rent	¥250,000
Land rent	¥300,000
Heating/lighting	¥300,000
Insurance	¥70,000
TOTAL	¥1,260,000
Distribution to subgroups etc.	
A Gumi	¥300,000
B Gumi	¥200,000
Kumi-in A	¥120,000
Kumi-in B	¥120,000
Living-in *wakashu*	¥360,000
Boss's children's education	¥100,000
TOTAL	¥1,200,000
Savings etc.	
Boss's accounts	¥1,200,000
Boss's family accounts	¥300,000
Imprisoned *kumi-in* accounts	¥120,000
Loan repayments	¥1,000,000
Boss's safe	¥3,720,000
TOTAL	¥6,340,000

Source: Mizoguchi (1997: 87).

expenses of maintaining gang infrastructure, the group is able to clear ¥75.4 m a year, most of which accrues to the boss. As illegal income, this is obviously not subject to tax. It should, however, be noted that the boss will also be expected to attend various *yakuza* ceremonies each month. At each of these he is obliged to present a gift of money. This can be a considerable drain on resources.

As of 1988 purity levels remained high, as the drug is uncut with other materials. This is because consumers are experienced users who would seek out alternative sources of supply if sold a substandard product (interviews Drug Countermeasures Rooms—Iwate Police Headquarters, April 1998 and Fukugawa Police Station, Tokyo,

May 1998). Price levels are unresponsive to major drug seizures suggesting sufficiently large stockpiles of amphetamines exist to maintain steady supply (Tamura 1988: 60).

Stimulants are almost entirely imported from other countries in Asia as domestically produced drugs are hard to manufacture secretly; the raw materials are controlled; and the high exchange rate makes them uncompetitive *vis-à-vis* foreign imports. Originally Korea was the main source of supply; in 1980 police analysis of confiscated drugs indicated that 79 per cent came from Korea and 21 per cent from Taiwan. However, due to Korean attempts to 'purify' the country in the run up to the 1988 Seoul Olympics, there were widespread crackdowns on Korean OC groups. Consequently, there has been a shift in purchasing patterns and, according to police estimates, by 1987, 78 per cent of amphetamines were imported from Taiwan and just 11 per cent from Korea (Tamura 1992: 104).

In both of these countries, *yakuza* groups have good, established links with local criminal organisations. In particular, the Four Seas and United Bamboo Triad organisations in Taiwan (and the 14 K in Hong Kong) have mutually beneficial associations with *yakuza* groups. Japanese drug-manufacturing technology has been provided to Chinese OC groups (Booth 1990: 142). This close cooperation extends beyond merely supplying amphetamines to the Japanese market; Japanese and Chinese criminal groups are now apparently involved in joint heroin ventures. Owing to its significance as a leading trading nation, Japan has become a major transit point for heroin shipments to Europe and America (Vaughn, Huang, and Ramirez 1995: 506–7). Chinese heroin dealers have also allegedly proposed setting up partnerships with *yakuza* selling heroin in Japan but they have been turned down (Booth 1999: 199). It is likely that this lack of interest was due to the perception that heroin is a much more socially pernicious substance than amphetamines and thereby attracts greater attention from the criminal-justice system.

Gambling

Gambling has long been illegal under Japanese law. The current criminal law of 1907 provides no break with this tradition and provides two categories of gambling: 'simple criminal gambling' (*tanjun tobaku zai*) and 'habitual criminal gambling' (*jōshu tobaku zai*). However, special laws provide exemption for gambling on certain types of officially sanctioned racing and lotteries (Sibbitt 1997: 571). *Yakuza* participation in gambling in Japan takes three quite distinct forms: organising various types of card, dice and, latterly, roulette games (*bakuchi*); illegal bookmaking (*nomikōi*); involvement in Japan's *pachinko* (a kind of electronic bagatelle).

Prior to postwar legal changes, it was difficult to prosecute individuals for habitual criminal gambling because arrests could only be made when gamblers were caught red-handed. In addition, as a victimless crime, gambling was generally accorded a low priority by the law-enforcement officials. However, with the police summit strategy of 1964, this change in the law allowed the authorities to prosecute *yakuza* for gambling-related crimes purely on the testimony of two witnesses regardless of when the offence took place. Over half of the arrests of gang bosses and top executives made during the first summit strategy period were arrests of this type (Yamadaira 1992: 88). As mentioned before, in this way the first summit strategy was largely instrumental in causing a reduced dependence on gambling as a source of income and the diversification of the *yakuza* into alternative economic activities.

Despite this, some organisations were still actively engaged in this type of business throughout the 1980s. For example, Takenaka Masahisa, the Yamaguchi-gumi's fourth-generation boss, was a pure gambler. It was reputed that his organisation, the Takenaka-gumi, made ¥1 bn in the 3 years 1979–1982 (Yamadaira 1992: 88).

The diversity in scale of *yakuza* gambling operations offers a good illustration of the different levels at which *yakuza* economic activity exists. At the bottom end of the market, one-man dicing operations at a minimum stake of ¥100 exist on the streets of the day-labourers' quarters. The stall of this type in Kotobuki-chō visited by me during the course of my fieldwork existed openly. However, not long after my appearance, protection arrived with a bulge under the waistband of his trousers to ensure that the researcher posed no threat.

At the other end of the spectrum are luxury gambling trips for the seriously wealthy (thereby excluding academic researchers). These take place at private country villas, hot-spring resorts, mountain retreats, or, since the late 1960s, abroad. The foreign gambling trip was pioneered by the highly able and innovative Inagawa-kai executive (and later boss) Ishii Susumu in an attempt to create gambling income, which was secure from police interference. (Ishii had himself been arrested for gambling during the first summit strategy.) The standard procedure was to provide flights, luxury accommodation, and sumptuous entertainment (including female company) free of charge. Suitably pampered, clients would then be allowed to win small amounts before being systematically fleeced. Usually customers would pay up as they had been entertained so well. In 1976, however, Ishii was arrested when a client on a Korean trip complained of cheating. Apparently the dealer had attached a small mirror to the shoe enabling him to read the cards (Nakagawa 1992: 227–8). The fact that flights, accommodation, and entertainment were provided free suggests that there were serious sums on the table.

At a more typical level an apartment will be rented and the windows heavily blacked out. Clients will be directed to park their cars some distance from the gambling place and then will be escorted there by a low-ranking member. A number of lookouts (*tachiban*) surround the premises to maintain security. These precautions illustrate that, although it is a low priority target for law-enforcement, gambling still exists in a hostile legal environment.

Illegal bookmaking exists in direct competition with government-run bookmaking, and police intervention becomes effectively a defence of the government's monopoly, a fact not lost on the manager and lookout of one-bookmaking premises in Kamagasaki visited during my fieldwork. At such places bets are placed on the horse, cycle, and motorboat races of the officially sanctioned industry. However, because they are illegal operations, they do not pay the 10 per cent tax that the legal bookmakers at racecourses or 'television tracks' are obliged to. The odds offered by illegal operations are, however, the same as legal bookmakers and therefore illegal operations generally offer much better value to the customer. However, unlike their legal equivalents, illegal bookmakers impose a ceiling on the payout on a single bet (¥10,000 on an initial stake of ¥100 and a total maximum of ¥1 m) (Yamanouchi 1992*b*: 129).

Although most illegal bookmaking has been successfully driven out of racecourses, apparently the Osaka-based Sakaume-gumi successfully avoided this fate due to a highly efficient advanced-warning system, which enabled them to disappear before the police arrived. Apparently this warning system functioned satisfactorily even when top-ranking NPA officers decided to make a snap inspection without informing the Osaka police (retired NPA-related interviewee 1998).

Security at an off-course illegal bookmaker's premises, such as the one visited in Kamagasaki, is maintained by a watch-man manning a heavy steel door. This was augmented by a system of lookouts at cross-roads further up the street. Twice in the course of conversations with watch-men they disappeared mid-sentence to slam their doors shut and await the all-clear signal. Because such businesses are heavily concentrated within a small number of streets within the Kamagasaki area, the costs and benefits of maintaining this lookout system are shared. *Yakuza* involvement insures that there are no freeriders.

Within the bookmaker's premises itself, security is further enhanced by limiting communication between the trading floor and the office by a small trap-door in the ceiling through which the paperwork, and presumably also takings, on each race are passed via a small basket on a string. Security at similar premises in Kotobuki-chō seemed much lower. Possibly this reflects the reputation for laxity of Kanagawa prefectural police.

The standard penalty for bookmaking is a fine as well as the confiscation of television monitors and other paraphernalia. Given that the site visited was equipped with eleven large-screen monitors as well as two closed-circuit television cameras, seizure would present a very real financial penalty. Partly for this reason, but more significantly for reasons of security, most bookmaking is carried out by telephone. Usually an apartment will be rented and a number of telephone lines installed. These lines will be manned and all calls recorded. As a security precaution powerful magnets are kept on hand to wipe cassettes should the police try and break through the doubly locked doors.

Telephone bookmaking offers a convenient service to the customers as they can conduct betting from the comfort of their own homes. Typically the customer's account will be cleared on a weekly basis by a gang member. Alternatively, the customer may pay money into a special bank account. In addition to boat, horse, and cycle racing, telephone bookmakers also accept bets on baseball, *sumō*, and other popular sports. In order to reduce their exposure to risk, bookmakers adopt a system of point spread or handicaps. Setting the handicap of any given event is a highly skilled job requiring close attention to the sporting press and the likely preferences of customers.

Reputedly a very profitable business with margins of about 25 per cent of total sales, telephone bookmaking offers a good income on minimal overheads. One typical third-level boss cited by Yamanouchi received a monthly income of ¥8–10 m/month from four phone lines manned by three *kobun* (1992b: 129), whilst another Yamaguchi-gumi executive generates a profit of ¥6 m/racing day (Mizoguchi 1997: 79). However, success in this business is not automatic and requires a sharp assessment of customers' likely betting patterns and the reduction in exposure through lay-off betting with other bookmakers.

Pachinko is a staggeringly large industry in Japan. The most reliable estimates as to the turnover of this business vary from around ¥26 to ¥31 trillion ($243–$290 bn). The profits generated are even less clear (the tax authorities consider this industry second only to bars and clubs for the inaccuracy of their tax returns) (Tanioka 1998: 18, 113). The *pachinko* industry in Japan occupies an 'amorphous legal space' in that, whilst this business is not unambiguously excluded from the gambling provisions of the criminal law, the Public Morals Law categorises *pachinko* as a 'type seven business'. As such these businesses are subject to police restrictions as to the value and type of prizes they issue (Sibbitt 1997: 571–2).

To get round this, successful *pachinko* players take their prizes to a small booth situated close to the *pachinko* parlour and exchange their prizes for cash. Under the provisions of the Public Morals Law it is considered illegal if this exchange booth (*kōkansho*) then resells prizes directly to the *pachinko* parlour. It is also held to be illegal if both exchange booth and *pachinko* parlour are owned by the same person. It is, however, permissible for the exchange booth to sell prizes on to a third company (*keihin monya*) (Mizoguchi 1997: 83). The legal grey area of this stage of the *pachinko* industry makes it one which easily falls victim to *yakuza* predation. It should, however, be noted that, due to close police supervision of the *pachinko* parlours, under the auspices of the Public Morals Law, *yakuza* members are unable to directly run *pachinko* businesses (an estimated 70 per cent of *pachinko* owners are ethnic Koreans resident in Japan (Tanioka 1998: 112)).

Originally *yakuza* developed the prize-exchange industry. When, in the face of fierce competition, parlours started issuing cigarettes as prizes, gang members would stand outside the parlour and purchase them at 70 per cent of their retail value. They would add a percentage then resell them directly to the parlours. Since about the mid-1960s and the first summit strategy, the police in most parts of Japan started to put pressure on the *pachinko* industry to sever links with organised crime. Because the police, through their control of the Public Morals Law, exercise considerable regulatory power over the industry, this was largely effective; in most areas of Japan the *yakuza* were effectively excluded from this source of funds. In particular, Hyōgo prefecture and Osaka have developed a system by which the exchange business became the preserve of public-welfare businesses (the top executive positions of which are held by retired police officers) and there is consequently no *yakuza* involvement in this area of the business.

Up until the end of the Shōwa period the two noticeable exceptions to this, otherwise successful, eradication of *yakuza* from the exchange business are Tokyo and Hokuriku (the northern part of Japan). The available literature fails to offer any explanation as to why this should be. As far as Hokuriku is concerned, it seems likely that this was not deemed necessary as the local *yakuza* were not perceived to be a major social problem during the period currently under consideration. The police in Iwate prefecture (which is part of Hokuriku) responsible for *yakuza* countermeasures certainly admitted as much during my fieldwork.

In Tokyo it seems plausible that the *pachinko* industry was left untouched by the police as a stick hanging over the *yakuza* to ensure good behaviour *vis-à-vis* less socially acceptable forms of organised crime activity. Discussions with police interviewees repeatedly emphasised the more sophisticated and politically savvy behaviour of the Kantō *yakuza* compared to their much less socially responsible colleagues in the west, and suggested that this is reflected in the different styles of policing in the two regions.

Whatever the reasons, continued access to the prize-exchange business yielded enormous funds for the Tokyo syndicates. The Tokyo metropolitan police estimated that the exchange business generated by the roughly 1,500 *pachinko* parlours in the capital yielded Tokyo *yakuza* groups ¥60 bn/year (Hinago 1992a: 201). Even in areas in which *yakuza* had been driven out of the exchange business, they had by no means severed all links with the industry as a whole, and *pachinko* remains a highly attractive target for extortion and protection type activities.

Tekiya

Most modern treatments of the contemporary *yakuza* completely ignore this traditional source of income (e.g. it does not even feature in the police estimates of gang income). The notable exception is Raz, who conducted fieldwork with *tekiya*. The group he studied travelled from town to town setting up their stalls at over 200 festivals per year (1996: 198). The goods sold by *tekiya* are extremely cheap and cheerful in appearance but sold at a considerable mark-up. However, not all of the profit accrues to the stall-holder himself. First, he must pay a fee for the use of his stall site to the boss of the *tekiya* organisation in whose territory[8] the festival is. According to the two former *tekiya* I interviewed in Iwate prefecture, this varied from ¥2,000 to ¥10,000. Included in this would be electricity and cleaning fees. Because the potential profits of a stall are dependent on where the stall is situated, the allocation of sites is highly important (interviews Iwate, August 1998). Originally this was decided by threats and pressure from the bosses of the various groups attending the festival. More recently this came to be decided by precedent (Raz 1996: 202).

Second, the *tekiya* typically buy their 'special' festival goods from their boss. These are, of course, more expensive than those that could be purchased from other commercial outlets. However, because all stall-holders stock similarly sourced wares, this additional cost can be transferred to the festival-going public who, in turn, generally keep less tight control over their purse-strings at such times.

Third, like all other *yakuza* members, they are obliged to pay *jōnōkin* and give gifts at the various *yakuza* events and ceremonies. One of the former *tekiya* interviewed in Iwate had been paying ¥2 m a year to his group in *jōnōkin* and *girikake* gifts. Unless the *tekiya* member has other sources of income or occupies a senior position within the organisation, this is not one of the more lucrative *yakuza* career paths. However, as the same interviewee pointed out, his motivation to join the *tekiya* had not been financial, nor had it been due to any attachment to the world of *giri-ninjō* or a fascination with violence; he just loved the noise and colour and buzz surrounding traditional Japanese festivals and wanted to be part of it.

Labour-Broking

As mentioned in Chapter Two, the early history of the *bakuto* was closely linked with the history of the brokers responsible for assembling labour for the large public construction projects of Edo Japan. This has remained a role traditionally filled by *yakuza*. The construction industry in Japan depends on a pyramidal structure in which a few very large companies subcontract work to medium-sized companies, which in turn subcontract work to smaller companies. This enables these firms to maintain a small core of skilled labour, based on the lifetime-employment system, which can be almost instantly, and cheaply, augmented by unskilled and semi-skilled labour. At the base of this labour market are the day labourers (*hiyatoi rōdōsha*[9]) who assemble at dawn each day in the labour markets (*yoseba*), most notably San'ya in Tokyo, Kotobuki-chō in Yokohama, and Kamagasaki in Osaka. Before containerisation transformed the docking industry, *yakuza* brokers performed a similar function in the great ports of Kōbe, Yokohama, and Tokyo.

The labour-brokers (*tehaishi*) responsible for supplying these workers to the construction industry are overwhelmingly either themselves *yakuza* or in some way connected to the *yakuza*. The workers' wages are paid to the broker rather than to the labourers themselves. From this sum the broker takes his cut (known as *pinhane*) before paying the labourers. Although wages vary according to the level of demand, the going rate for an unskilled labourer would typically be ¥13,500, whilst that for a skilled steeplejack (*tobi*) would be ¥18–20,000 per day. From this, the *tehaishi* skims between ¥2,500 and ¥3,000. Occasionally brokers find some pretext to refuse payment to labourers, though if this happened too often, labourers would presumably find a more reliable broker. Inagaki San, a remarkable guardian and protector to the day-labourers of Kamagasaki, states that in cases of non-payment the official channels for complaint do not work effectively though he is usually able to resolve the problem with a telephone call to the broker in question (interview Kamagasaki, June 1998).

Although there exists a formal labour exchange for the employment of day labourers in the form of the *shokuan* (*kōkyō shokugyō antei sho* or public employment security office) and the local labour centre, these only account for the minority of employment in the *yoseba*; Fowler (1996: 33) suggests a figure of less than one-quarter whilst a political activist interviewed in Kotobuki-chō (1998) gives a figure of between 20 and 30 per cent. This is because, even when their commission has been removed, *tehaishi* offer higher rates of pay than the official labour market as they exercise greater quality control over those they employ (Fowler 1996: 34). It is also observed that construction companies prefer using *yakuza*-related *tehaishi* as their involvement is seen as facilitating trouble-free labour-relations (interviews Inagaki, Yamanouchi et al., Osaka, 1998).

During the late 1980s there were over one hundred labour-brokers operating in the San'ya labour market (interview San'ya, July 1998). The much larger market in Kamagasaki would have had at least three times that number during the same period. At the beginning of the 1970s there was a police movement to drive out the *yakuza* from the *tehaishi* business in the Kamagasaki labour market. This was partially successful and the Yamaguchi-gumi and the Matsuda-gumi temporarily disappeared. Not long after, however, they returned. Since then, observers on the ground report that, although there are occasional raids on gambling and drug-dealing, no police efforts have been made to eliminate gang members from the labour-broking business. It is hard to escape the conclusion that the police in these areas see the *yakuza* as a useful bulwark against the unpredictable and potentially dangerous day-labourers of the *yoseba*. Certainly this is the analysis provided by the communist activists in such areas: 'When we are fighting the fascists (*yakuza*) the police have their shields facing towards us!' (San'ya 1998).

Prostitution

Until the passing of the Prostitution Prevention Law (*baishun bōshi hō*) in 1956, prostitution was not illegal in Japan. Indeed for much of Japan's history, rulers have encouraged a system of licensed prostitution, which was seen not only as an essential component of maintaining public order but as a useful means by which the police, through their brothel-keeping informants, could keep a close eye on the population. Even such noted advocates of European Liberalism, monogamy and women's rights, as Fukuzawa Yukichi could claim in 1885 that licensed prostitution was 'the only way to preserve social peace' (Garon 1997: 101). Although the system of military prostitution, known euphemistically as 'comfort stations', adopted by the Imperial Japanese Army may be seen as a logical development from the licensed prostitution system, this type of arrangement was by no means unique to the Japanese: the brothels run by the legions of imperial Rome bear a 'remarkable similarity to (those of) the Japanese military' whilst parallels also exist with the British Army in India and the Wehrmacht in occupied Europe to name but two (Hicks 1994: 29–30).

As prostitution was legal until 1956, it was not an industry directly managed by *yakuza*. This is not to say that it was not a consumer of protection. However, close links between brothel-keepers and the police, reinforced with free entertainment for some police officers, may have entailed that this was not as necessary as is the case under different legal regimes.

After 1956 the situation became more complex. The Prostitution Prevention Law has been described to me as a *kagohō*[10] (a 'bamboo-cage law', i.e. full of holes) (interview Hoshino, Yokohama June 1998). Under Article 2 of the 1956 law prostitution is defined as 'sexual intercourse with an unspecified other party for compensation or for a promise of compensation'. This means that any sexual services that exclude vaginal penetration fall outside the provisions of this law.

As a consequence, Japan has spawned a large and legitimate sex industry ranging from 'soapland', in which naked, soap-covered women massage customers with their bodies, to 'fashion-health' massage parlours offering masturbation and fellatio services. As these industries come under the jurisdiction of the Public Morals Law, and consequently require police certification, it is difficult for *yakuza* to directly manage such businesses. Even the overt traditional brothels of the Tobita area of Osaka are officially licensed as eating and drinking establishments and, as a consequence, are not managed by *yakuza*. Yamanouchi claims that a further barrier to *yakuza* entry into this end of the market is provided by the high degree of capital outlay required for the installation of suitable premises[11] (interview Yamanouchi, Osaka August 1998; Yamanouchi 1992*a*: 51).

There are, however, two areas of the sex industry that are mono-polised by the *yakuza*. These are 'dateclubs' and the management of street and foreign prostitutes. The advantage of these types of businesses is that they require very little fixed-capital investment, which runs the risk of police seizure. Dateclubs require little more than a number of telephone lines, a driver, a receptionist, and a collection of sex-workers. Clients telephone the number advertised on fliers fixed to the interior of public telephone boxes and are directed to a love hotel where they will be met by a prostitute.

If run successfully, dateclubs are an attractive source of revenue. Fujimura, a retired third-level boss from the Kansai area, earned profits of roughly ¥20 m per month on sales of ¥60 m during the early 1980s from his workforce of 80 women (interview Fujimura, Osaka, August 1998). Unlike the Sicilian mafia, Japanese gangsters have no compunction about living off the earnings of prostitutes, and about one-third of the women working in date clubs have *yakuza* boyfriends (Yamanouchi 1992a: 59). According to both police data and interviewees, a high proportion (28 per cent) of *yakuza*, usually low-level members, are financially dependent on their girlfriends, wives, or mistresses (Mizoguchi 1997: 64; interviews Osaka, 1998).

To minimise potential problems with the police it is in the dateclub manager's interest to look after his employees well. According to one of Yamanouchi's interviewees, it is also important for pimps to screen employees for drug-users, as well as underage and runaway girls. The former tend to have violent mood-swings, which cause problems with both colleagues and customers. The latter group is subject to greater police vigilance, and the employment of minors carries heavier legal penalties. Dateclub employees can enter and exit this sector of the labour market freely, though many reportedly find the financial rewards and flexible working hours such that it becomes difficult to readjust to other sources of income (Yamanouchi 1992a: 59–60).

The treatment of foreign prostitutes is an altogether different matter. As these women have usually either entered the country illegally or are overstaying their visas, they are unable to seek legal protection. Most of these women are recruited in Asian countries such as Thailand, the Philippines, Malaysia, and Indonesia (though more recently Chinese and South Americans have increased) by brokers promising them jobs as waitresses, factory workers, hostesses, and nannies (although one-fifth of the women in a survey conducted by Salā[12] intended to work as prostitutes). On arrival in Japan, the broker typically sells them on to a second broker for between ¥1.5 and ¥2 m (which covers the cost of ticket, passport, visa, and overheads).

The secondary broker then sells or auctions these women on to clubs for between ¥3.5 and ¥4 m. Generally the initial broker will be a native of the country concerned and the second broker will belong to a *yakuza* group.

These women therefore start their careers as indentured labourers with a substantial debt, which must be paid off before they can earn any money for themselves. In addition they are expected to pay for their own food and clothing, though accommodation is often provided. Frequently a woman about to repay her debt, or found to be pregnant, will be resold to another club and therefore incur a new debt. In addition to these debts, foreign prostitutes are subject to fines for such offences as putting on weight or failing to have a customer in three days (Sālā 1996: 1–7).

The clubs at which foreign indentured prostitutes typically work are 'closely tied to the *yakuza*' either directly or through the payment of protection money (Human Rights Watch 2000: 14). In this context, protection includes protecting the club from bad (non-paying) customers and disciplining disobedient or fleeing prostitutes. In addition, it has been suggested that *yakuza* involvement in this industry is 'a key reason behind the lack of adequate police responses to abuses' (Human Rights Watch 2000: 14).

Much of the information concerning this business comes from women who have successfully fled their employers. It is hard to know whether their tales of brutality and confinement are representative of the business as a whole. The facts that some women return to Japan for another stint whilst others end up being driven to murder their managers suggest that the range of experiences is broad.

Foreign prostitutes typically work on the streets in areas such as Shin-Ōkubo near Kabuki-chō in Shinjuku, or in foreign clubs where they formally work as hostesses. In the early 1990s, there were reportedly between two and three hundred such clubs in Kabuki-chō alone (Hinago 1992*b*: 70).

Loan-Sharking

The modern Japanese banking system has primarily concerned itself with serving the needs of its business clients, and consumer-banking services remain extremely poor. Many Japanese use post-office accounts or credit unions (*shinyō kinko*), rather than bank accounts, to deposit their savings. As a consequence of this, commercial banks are not active in the market for loans to small businesses and individual citizens. This niche has generally been filled by companies known as *sarakin*. These organisations offer loans at very high rates of interest to small businesses and individuals experiencing short-term liquidity problems.

Money-lending in Japan is governed by several laws. The Interest Rate Limitation Law (*Risoku Seigen Hō*) limits the interest rates charged by deposit-taking financial institutions (such as banks) to 15 per cent per year for loans of more than ¥1 m, 18 per cent for those between ¥1 m and ¥100,000, and 20 per cent for loans of less than ¥100,000. The second law, the Investment Law (*Shusshi Hō*) limits the interest rates on loans to 109.5 per cent/year. In 1983, the *Sarakin* Regulation Law (*Sarakin Kisei Hō*) was added. Under the provisions of this law, *sarakin* loans were limited to annual rate of interest of 73 per cent. Since then this rate has been reduced to 40.004 per cent. The 109.5 per cent limit of the Investment Law only applies in particular circumstances; so for most purposes the two other laws cover the majority of cases.

Provided that they stay within the limits of the *Sarakin* Regulation Law, *sarakin* businesses are legal. Contrary to public perception, these *sarakin* operations are not, except for very small outfits, run by *yakuza* groups. Under the provisions of article six of the 1983 law, those who have been punished for violating the Finance Law, the Violent Acts Law, the Price Control Ordinance or any criminal-law provisions within the past three years are unable to register as *sarakin* businesses. This limitation had the express purpose of removing *yakuza* from this business. *Sarakin* do, however, retain links with *yakuza* (as well as the police) as an insurance policy (*Keisatsu-chō* 1997: 623, 281; Mizoguchi 1986: 191 and private correspondence 1999; interview Fujimura, 1998).

For those who are denied access to *sarakin* finance, either because their credit rating is too poor or they are operating in wholly illegal markets, there exists a parallel system of financing. *Yakuza* loan-sharking generally operates on a system known as *tō-ichi* (ten-one). This means that every 10 days, a charge of one-tenth of the principal is paid to the lender until the principal is repaid in full. The annual rate of interest, assuming the loan was kept outstanding for one year but that the 10% charge was paid on time, would therefore be 365 per cent $((365/10) \times 10)$. Because many borrowers are themselves *yakuza* requiring short-term finance, there is always the risk of a strong gang member defaulting on a debt to a weaker one (interviews Fujimura, Osaka, 1998; Ujihara, Nagoya, 1998).

Minji Kainyū Bōryoku

Perhaps the most significant development in the *yakuza* in the postwar period is their adoption of new techniques of money-earning known collectively as *minji kainyū bōryoku* (usually abbreviated to *minbō*). As was the case with their increased involvement in the drugs trade, this type of business was a response to increased police pressure on traditional sources of income like gambling. The *jōnōkin* system, also a response to the police summit strategies, further encouraged this development.

Minji kainyū bōryoku, literally the violent intervention in civil affairs, can be defined as acts in which individuals 'attempt to acquire an illegal or unfair profit by intervening in the everyday affairs and economic transactions of members of the general public by adopting the form of those holding some legitimate connection or right under civil law' (Fujimoto 1997: 11). The police have a number of sub-classifications of *bōryokudan* activities falling under this definition. These are:

1. Debt-collection (*saiken toritate*).
2. Activities targeting company annual shareholders meetings (*sōkaiya* and *kaisha goro*).
3. Incidents related to finance.
4. Incidents related to promissory notes.
5. Bankruptcy management (*tōsan seiri*).
6. Real-estate and rent-related problems (esp. *jiage*).
7. Out-of-court settlements of traffic-accident disputes.
8. Disputes over prices of goods and other everyday matters.
9. Other civil disputes.

As will be seen from a brief analysis of these different activities, *minji kainyū bōryoku* effectively consists of different types of protection. The justification for dealing with it as a separate topic is that it is characterized as a new (post-summit strategy) development in Japanese organised crime. In particular, it is significant in that it involves the increasing penetration of legitimate society and business by the *yakuza*.

Yakuza intervention in civil affairs represents a particular problem for the authorities for three main reasons. The first of these is that, in many of these activities, the perpetrators are not committing a crime as defined by law. Although a threat is being made, it is usually implicit and falls short of the legal definition of intimidation. Consequently, many *minbō* activities occupy, at best, a legal grey zone. Secondly, there is a market demand for certain categories of *minbō*. Many of these activities take place due to inadequacies of the legal system. In particular, the cost in both time and money that civil cases take to reach a conclusion means that potential litigants may find it advantageous to employ *yakuza*, rather than official, channels for the resolution of their civil disputes. In their analysis of the *yakuza* as suppliers of extra-legal dispute resolution services, Milhaupt and West (2000) coin the memorable term "the dark side of private ordering" to refer to this role.

Thirdly, whilst there are clearly beneficiaries to this type of private ordering, there are also victims: protectees can settle disputes to their advantage; the unprotected lose out. Therefore, unlike more traditional *yakuza* activities, it directly impinges on the lives of ordinary members of the public, as opposed to marginal elements such as day labourers, prostitutes and bar-keepers. There will consequently be a greater political pressure on the authorities to be seen to be doing something about the *bōryokudan*.

Pretext Racketeering

At the most basic level of *minbō*-type operations, *yakuza* exploit some injury, real or invented, to gain financial advantage. The most well known example is *yakuza* intervention in traffic disputes. The legal machinery involved in insurance claims is complex and time-consuming. These problems can be circumvented if the injured party subcontracts his or her claim to a *yakuza* group. In the face of pressure from such groups, insurance companies have generally paid much more quickly than they would otherwise. For this service, *yakuza* groups typically charge a commission of between 30 and 50 per cent (Hiraoka 1987: 71).

Operations of this type once more show that the relationship between criminal organisations and members of the business community/civil society may not be a universally predatory one. In an imperfectly functioning world, such groups may have a competitive advantage in the provision of protection services *vis-à-vis* legitimate alternatives. However, this system of intervention in discussions has also degenerated into one whereby *yakuza* deliberately engineer incidents for their own advantage.

Another type of pretext for racketeering commonly used by *yakuza* is to find some fault with a good or service. For example, the boss's expensive suit sent to the dry-cleaners may have been 'ruined' and compensation demanded. Alternatively, a product purchased may be sub-standard or overpriced and, therefore, recompense appropriate. The examples of this type of activity given in the Juzo Itami film '*Minbō no Onna*', though fictitious, show the breadth of *minbō* extortion: A cooked cockroach is 'found' in a plate of lasagne; a bag containing money is mislaid; guests at a hotel are unable to use the swimming pool and sport their expensive new swimming trunks because they have extensive body tattoos.

A further twist is given to many of these racketeering practices by being performed under the guise of social or political movements. These are dealt with in greater detail below.

Whilst activities of this kind may cause the most inconvenience to ordinary members of the public, they are largely at the bottom end of the scale of *yakuza* economic activity. Many of the more sophisticated fund-raising techniques falling under the broad definition of *minji kainyū bōryoku* are far more lucrative.

Debt-Collection

Under Japanese law, only lawyers are authorised to collect debts. However, the length of time and expense involved in employing the appropriate channels means that many creditors prefer to cut legal corners. The standard rate charged by *yakuza* debt-collectors is 50 per cent. In addition, they may charge expenses (known as *ashidai* or leg-fee) (Yajima 1992*b*: 22–3). As a consequence of this, the majority of the money involved usually accrues to the debt-collector rather than the creditor. As both parties are officially criminal conspirators, the creditor is unable to seek legal redress should he be charged exorbitant expenses. However, 30 per cent of a debt collected is preferable to 100 per cent of one that is not.

Former gang boss Yajima evaluated this form of activity as one that earns a lot of money if conducted successfully, and it is relatively easy to carry out. For this reason, it is one form of *shinogi* with which even the least able *yakuza* member can be involved in. However, as it frequently involves intimidation, it is a business in which the risk of imprisonment is high and, as a consequence, could not be said to be a terribly good source of income (Yajima 1992*a*: 11). Despite Yajima's assessment, the criminal law's provisions concerning intimidation only governed explicit threats. For the implicit threat involved with *yakuza* turning up at a debtor's house, in a highly conspicuous fashion, and at a time when the neighbours would be in, the criminal law could do very little. It is only when such an implied threat is insufficient that collectors escalate to legally actionable intimidation or the actual use of violence.

Jiage

Another recent development in *yakuza* activities in which ordinary citizens are victimised is the business of land-sharking (*jiage*). *Jiage* refers to the practice of forcing small landholders on adjacent plots to sell up and lease holders to give up their lease. This renders a larger, more lucratively developable site. Common tactics involve the playing of loud music and banging of metal sheets at night, threats, crashing of cars into targeted property, and even arson. On one occasion, a *jiageya* from Osaka went to the extent of installing one hundred live chickens next to a property he had targeted in the hope that the smell would drive out the occupants (*Business Week* 29 January 1996: 15). *Jiage* reached its heyday during the bubble economy of the late 1980s when land prices reached absurd levels. During the period of the bubble economy *jiage* became the biggest single source of income for *yakuza* in both the Kansai and Kantō regions (Mizoguchi 1997: 66).

The key reason for the existence of this type of activity is that Japanese property law makes it enormously difficult to evict tenants, even when they violate the terms of their lease (Ramseyer and Nakazato 1999: 38). There is, therefore, a clear demand for what Milhaupt and West (2000) refer to as "private ordering" mechanisms to circumvent this legal obstacle to real estate development.

The complicity of real-estate companies in the *jiage* process once more indicates the ambivalent relationship existing between organised crime and the 'straight' world. Initially the *yakuza* were employed by real-estate agents to clear a given site. For this service they would typically receive a commission of 3 per cent of the market value of that site (2 or 1.5 per cent if it was a particularly valuable property). On discovering the scale of profits to be made in this industry, the more astute *yakuza* executives became directly involved in the property-development business. In order to maximise profits they developed the tax-evasion technique of using the land as collateral on a loan so as to obscure ownership of the property in question. Alternatively, the site would be sold on to a number of bogus intermediaries before its final disposal (Mizoguchi 1997: 66).

Most prominent of the *yakuza* involved in *jiage* operations was the quintessential white-collar gangster (*keizai yakuza*), Ishii Susumu of the Inagawa-kai. On his release from prison in 1985, Ishii used his prison-release-celebration donations to start up Hokushō Sangyō, Kasen Sangyō, Daishin, and other companies, which he then used to move in on Tokyo's real-estate business. The extent of his success in *jiage* operations, largely in the Shinjuku area of Tokyo, is illustrated by the rapid increase in the turnover of Hokushō Sangyō from ¥250 m ($1.48 m) in 1986 to ¥12.2 bn ($84.1 m) the following year (Nakagawa 1992: 233–4). Much of the immense profits which the more able *yakuza* members, such as Ishii, made from *jiage* were ploughed into stock-market speculation.

Bankruptcy Management

Bankruptcy management (*tōsan seiri*) is one of the most sophisticated and skilled techniques by which *yakuza* members make money. When a company goes bankrupt in Japan, the legal machinery for the settlement of the various creditors' claims usually takes several years (occasionally up to ten) and the amount of debt eventually repaid is a small percentage of that actually owed. Creditors may therefore find it advantageous to sell their debt to a specialist bankruptcy manager (*tōsan seiriya*) even for as little as 5 per cent of face value (Mizoguchi 1986: 189). Emotionally fragile managers of bankrupt firms may also prefer to bring *yakuza* on board to protect them from the wrath of angry creditors (interview Fujimura, Osaka 1998).

The two most important things for bankruptcy management specialists are speed of action and the accumulation of more debt than other creditors. What *seiriya* will often do is identify a company on the point of collapse and then move in with short-term financial support. From this position of strength, the *seiriya* will force the manager to write and seal a document granting power of attorney and gain possession of the firm's books, seals, and deeds. The *seiriya* may then forge promissory notes and other documents in his favour. Once the company has finally gone bankrupt, it is important to occupy the company's premises and collect any money outstanding from credit sales before any other creditors, or *yakuza*, can get their hands on the company's assets.

Speed is important because, once a company has been declared bankrupt, the courts appoint a lawyer as the legal trustee (*kanzainin*) of the company to ensure that it is disposed of lawfully. The trustee is, however, weak *vis-à-vis* the major creditor. From his position as major creditor in possession of the company's assets, the *seiriya* can have himself nominated chairman of the creditors' meeting and can consequently control its proceedings and cow opposition into submission. Through this mechanism, the skilled *seiriya* can therefore ensure that the lion's share of the bankrupt firm's realisable assets ends up in his hands. If there are items, which can be quietly appropriated before the trustee appears, so much the better. However, excessive concealment may undermine the *seiriya*'s credibility (Yajima 1992*a*: 16–21).

Although any attempt to estimate the revenue generated by *yakuza* bankruptcy management would be foolhardy, the potential sums are not trivial. In 1977 there were 18,000 bankruptcies in Japan (the comparable figure for the United States, supposedly an exemplar of risk-taking entrepreneurialism, was 800) and the total liability of Japan's bankrupt businesses in this year was valued at ¥4.3 trillion (Saxonhouse 1979: 290). Throughout the first half of the 1980s, the rate of bankruptcy remained at around 18,000 per year, though, after a 1984 peak (of over 20,000 with total debts of ¥3.6 trillion), the rate declined; by 1988 only 10,123 companies went bankrupt with total liabilities of ¥2 trillion (*Tōkei Kyoku* 1985: 384, 1990: 386). The high rate of bankruptcy in Japan is largely due to the precarious position of small companies who are forced to act as shock-absorbers for the big firms for which they carry out subcontracting work. Given the high rate of bankruptcy in Japan and the cumbersome machinery for the legal unravelling of such incidents, it is reasonable to assume that this is a significant source of income for those capable *yakuza* who choose to specialise in it.

Sōkaiya

Sōkaiya translates literally as 'general meeting specialist' and this well illustrates their *modus operandi*. *Sōkaiya* are essentially corporate blackmailers. Having bought one share (until changes to the commercial code in 1982) in a company's stock, *sōkaiya* are entitled to attend that company's annual general meeting. They then use this right to extort money from companies by threatening to disclose sensitive information about either its financial status or irregular management practices (including scandals concerning the private lives of managers), or simply to disrupt the shareholders' meeting. This is facilitated by the fact that the commercial code of Japan does not oblige companies to issue annual financial reports or allow transparency into their business operations at all. Information concerning a company's performance has traditionally been privileged information only available to favoured major stockholders.

Sōkaiya first started to appear in the rumbustious and murky beginnings of modern Japanese capitalism at the end of the nineteenth century. However, with the notable exception of the gambling boss Takebe Kosaku, these individuals were unconnected to the traditional *yakuza* groups of that time. It was not until the late 1960s that *yakuza* involvement in this business became a significant phenomenon. As had been the case with the development of other non-traditional sources of *yakuza* income, the stimulus for this phenomenon was essentially the first summit strategy of the mid-1960s in which traditional *yakuza* activities were targeted by the police.

One of the first of these *yakuza-sōkaiya* was Ogawa Kaoru, of the Hiroshima-based Kyōsei-kai, who formed the 'Hiroshima Group'. In 1971, this group became involved in a violent conflict with a traditional *sōkaiya*, Shimazaki Eiji, at a shareholders' annual general meeting in Tokyo. This confrontation was resolved by a traditional *yakuza*-style reconciliation (*teuchi*) in which Shimazaki relied upon a retired Matsuba-kai boss for support. This incident (reportedly the first of its kind) was significant as it illustrated the way in which the traditional *sōkaiya* were to become dependent on the protective umbrella of the *yakuza* (Szymkowiak 1996: 91–4).

As has been mentioned above, the inability of groups or individuals to benefit from legitimate sources of protection creates a market niche for providers of alternative protection. As companies found themselves unable effectively to combat or pay off all *sōkaiya* targeting them, many companies found it expedient to employ *sōkaiya-yakuza* to protect them from other groups. This gave rise to the sub-classification of *sōkaiya* into '*yotō-sōkaiya*' (insider or protector *sōkaiya*) and '*yatō-sōkaiya*' (outsider or aggressor *sōkaiya*).

Protection was helpful not only in dealing with predatory extortionists but also with demonstrators protesting at the company's business practices. Most notable of these were the protests directed at the Chisso Corporation, by victims of that company's dumping of mercury compounds into the sea off Minamata, and at Mitsubishi Heavy Industries, by peace campaigners criticising MHI's profiting from the Vietnam war. In both these incidents the companies concerned relied heavily on *yakuza* and extreme right-wing groups to violently confront protestors attempting to disrupt their shareholders' annual general meetings. Szymkowiak identifies these protests as a 'watershed in Japan's postwar corporate history' as they revealed the full extent to which companies' reputations were vulnerable to criticism through disruption of shareholders' meetings. As a consequence of this, companies became increasingly reliant on the services of protective *sōkaiya* (1996: 98–104).

Following this watershed, the numbers of *sōkaiya* rose rapidly throughout the 1970s. In 1973, the police estimated a *sōkaiya* population of 1,763; by 1982 this number had risen to 6,783—an increase of 285 per cent in a decade. The increase in *yakuza* involvement in this industry was even more dramatic, jumping by 515 per cent over the same period (Szymkowiak 1996: 70).

Yakuza involvement in *sōkaiya* activities was not only due to their provision of protection to existing groups and *yakuza* intimidation of *sōkaiya* at the behest of business contacts. Szymkowiak reports that throughout the 1970s, promising *yakuza* executives served apprenticeships with *sōkaiya* groups after which they set up their own organisations. As a consequence of this process, by 1982 the police estimated that, of the total *sōkaiya* population, 2,012 (30 per cent) were *yakuza* members (1996: 70).

In response to the rapid increase in the number of *sōkaiya*, the Commercial Code was revised in 1982 to make it harder for them to operate. There were two legal changes affecting the operation of these groups. The first of these was the introduction of a threshold of ¥50,000 worth of stock below which an investor was denied full shareholder's voting rights and, more importantly, the right to attend shareholders' meetings. Second, it became illegal for companies to pay money to *sōkaiya* (Szymkowiak 1996: 145–7; Okumura 1997: 13).

The immediate effect of the minimum stock rule was a drastic 75 per cent reduction in the numbers of *sōkaiya* identified by the police from 6,783 in 1982 to 1,682 the following year. The drop amongst *yakuza-sōkaiya* was even more pronounced, falling from 2,012 to just 167 over the same period. Rather than reflecting a real change in the situation, however, this drop was largely due to different accounting practices. In order to act as a *sōkaiya* under the post-reform regime, an individual required ¥50,000 worth of stock in a given company. Those that fell short of this threshold were, by definition, no longer *sōkaiya* regardless of the way in which they made money.

The police were therefore forced to create a new category to accommodate those extortionists who fell short of the post-reform requirements. Such individuals became known as *shinbun goro*, *zasshi goro*, and *kaisha goro* (newspaper, magazine, and company ruffians, respectively). Instead of disrupting shareholders' meetings, these groups would extort money from companies by such techniques as threatening to disclose company scandals in their publications. Other groups developed fronts behind which they could continue extortionate activity. Most noticeable of these were fake *burakumin*-liberation movements (*ese dōwa*) and fake right-wing political organisations (*ese uyoku*). *Ese dōwa* groups are dealt with in greater detail below.

The second anti-*sōkaiya* measure of the 1982 Commercial Code reform also failed to have a decisive impact on this problem. Although it became illegal for companies to make pay-offs from company funds to *sōkaiya*, there were a number of ways in which these payments could be disguised. Most commonly, *sōkaiya* groups would set up research organisations, business consultancies, or bulletins supposedly containing economic analysis. Alternatively, they might set up front companies leasing art works or potted plants to companies (Alletzhauser 1990: 284). Entry fees to golf tournaments, or parties are another means of camouflaging payments. Szymkowiak relates how at least one company even resorted to paying excessive bonuses to the employees working in the general-affairs section, which were then returned to the department in order that the money could be paid out to *sōkaiya* (1996: 147).

The 1982 reform of the Commercial Code cannot be described, therefore, as a success. This is illustrated by a succession of *sōkaiya* scandals during the 1980s. These included some of the most prestigious companies in Japan. For example, in 1985 Japan Air Lines called upon the research department of Rondon Dōyūkai, a well-known *sōkaiya* organisation, to ensure a smooth shareholders' meeting following a particularly unprofitable year. Another case involving the payment of *sōkaiya* with the then rapidly appreciating MHIs convertible bonds was dropped by the police when it became apparent that numerous senior politicians had also received allocations of these bonds (Alletzhauser 1990: 286–90).

One puzzle about the *sōkaiya* is why such individuals flourish in Japan yet do not exist in many other places[13] in anything like the same numbers. Certainly blackmail is not unknown elsewhere, but this particular type of corporate blackmail is rare outside Japan. A cultural explanation might be that Japanese directors do not like to lose face and are therefore prepared to pay up whereas their equivalents elsewhere are prepared to brazen it out. Differences in business culture undoubtedly go some way to explaining the existence of *sōkaiya* in Japan and their absence in Britain and America; to Anglo-American observers the behaviour of *sōkaiya* seems to resemble the healthy exercise of shareholders' rights. However, West (1999) argues persuasively that institutional factors are of far greater significance than cultural ones in explaining this puzzle. This happens in a number of ways.

First, Japanese accounting practices demand much lower levels of information disclosure by companies concerning their financial performance than is the case in other industrialised capitalist economies. In addition, such legal requirements as exist in Japan are enforced much less rigorously than those in the United States. This lack of transparency creates a bigger range of sensitive information that a blackmailer can threaten to reveal. This is compounded by the fact that, due to the greater level of regulation of business in Japan than in West's comparator, America, there are more ways in which Japanese organisations can make legal shortcuts, which can then in turn become grounds for blackmail.

A second consideration that West draws to our attention is that, in America, those in possession of sensitive information can legally and profitably make use of that information in ways which are not viable options in Japan. One course open to American shareholders is to launch a class-action lawsuit against the firm's directors: In Japan there is no financial incentive to litigate in this way. Similarly, in the United States, those in possession of damaging information can profit by short-trading in the relevant company's stock and disclosing the information: In Japan short-trading is not legal and, although other financial instruments, such as options, exist which would theoretically enable strategic disclosure of such information to yield a legal profit in the stock market, high regulation, commissions and tax make them unattractive. A third way in which negative information about a company might be used profitably is by selling it to financial institutions. Here too, Japan does not encourage this strategy; as West observes, 'the securities houses themselves are so often deeply mired in *sōkaiya* activity that pointing out the mistakes of others could simply be a suicide request' (1999: 795).

Perhaps the most telling explanation for why *sōkaiya* persist in Japan but not America is that in Japan companies which have their annual general meetings seriously disrupted by *sōkaiya* (measured by the length of time that the meeting exceeds the ideal of 30 minutes) typically suffer a drop in their share price over the following days as the disturbance is taken as indicative that the company is in trouble. American investors do not attach the same significance to meeting length as they generally have access to more reliable data pertaining to corporate health. Due to the impact of meeting length on stock-price, it may well be a cost-effective strategy for Japanese companies to pay *sōkaiya* to ensure a short shareholders' meeting (West 1999: 805–9).

Fake Social Movements

A more recent development in *yakuza* activities is the hijacking of social movements, which can then be exploited for financial gain. In particular, the development of *yakuza*-related organisations pretending to be dedicated to the liberation of *burakumin*, usually known collectively as *ese dōwa* (*dōwa* now being the politically correct term for *burakumin*), became noticeable in the mid-1980s. In 1986 the NPA identified the new category of 'Fake Social Movement Thugs' (*shakai undō hyōbō goro*) as a target for police countermeasures (Hiraoka 1987: 67).

There have been legitimate organisations dedicated to fighting *burakumin* discrimination since the early 1920s. In more recent years, however, this movement has been characterised by division as rival political parties formed their own *dōwa* associations,[14] which have been characterised by ineffective leadership and intragroup struggles (Herzog 1993: 74).

After ignoring the problem of *burakumin* discrimination, in 1969 the government introduced the *Dōwa* Countermeasures Special Measures Law (*Dōwa Taisaku Jigyō Tokubetsu Sochi Hō*) to ameliorate the condition of the *buraku* communities. In particular, this law provided financial help for developing housing, roads, social amenities, educational programs, and the like. As a consequence of this, obtaining government money 'became the main business of the *buraku* organisations'[15] (Herzog 1993: 74).

Due to increased police pressure on traditional *yakuza* activity and the change in the Commercial Code in 1982 targeting *sōkaiya* activities, a pattern of *yakuza* groups changing their organisations into spurious *dōwa*-liberation groups began to appear. By 1986, over two thousand groups purporting to be dedicated to *buraku* liberation were in existence (Mizoguchi 1986: 194–6).

In 1986 the Ministry of Justice Human Rights Protection Office published the preliminary findings of a nation-wide survey of 5,030 companies in seventeen different industries concerning the extent of *ese dōwa* activity. Of the survey's respondents, a total of 26 per cent had been victimised by groups of this kind. In the Osaka area (a major concentration of people of *buraku* extraction), this figure rose to 36.5 per cent. The construction industry was the most heavily targeted, but banks, credit unions, and insurance companies also reported victimisation rates of over 50 per cent (Hiraoka 1987: 66–7). Fake-*dōwa*-group victimisation of the business community first caught the attention of the Osaka police in July 1985 when a group started sending bulletins to companies which were asked to purchase them for the edification of their employees. Those that refused would be angrily confronted and asked what measures they were taking to deal with the *burakumin* problem. The persistence and vehemence of these confrontations often resulted in firms' agreeing to purchase the bulletins. The finances of this classic technique are seen from another case brought to the attention of the police. Every month a group would receive 500 copies of a bulletin from its parent group. It would sell five copies each to 100 companies, from each of which it would receive ¥10,000/month. This therefore yielded annual sales of ¥12 m. Of the respondents to the MOJ survey, 19.8 per cent had been subject to such demands (Hiraoka 1987: 68–9).

Another area in which fake-social-movement racketeers have been active is in the standard *yakuza* activity of intervening in traffic disputes. *Ese dōwa* have similarly been employed by *sarakin* for the collection of debts, by businessmen seeking an official permit and by ordinary citizens wanting authorities to pay attention to a complaint (Mizoguchi 1986: 194; Hiraoka 1987: 71).

Insurance companies are also subject to fraudulent claims by *ese dōwa* groups. Fraud is employed by these groups in other ways as well. In one case a group instructed people in techniques for evading inheritance tax by forging spurious debts for the deceased. This group naturally took a commission on the money saved. When tax officials became suspicious and started to investigate, they were subject to threatening phone calls at their homes (Mizoguchi 1986: 196).

In addition to these techniques, *ese dōwa* groups are constantly on the lookout for pretexts for extortion. For example, construction companies that are breaking building regulations or causing a nuisance in the neighbourhood are blackmailed with threats of court injunctions. One group, in little over one year, targeted one hundred such firms; was successful in half these cases; and extorted ¥16 m. Owing to cases like this, construction firms frequently find it advantageous to have links with *yakuza* groups to deter predation by others. Another suitable pretext for extortion is denouncing those publishing material detrimental to the cause of *buraku* emancipation. Consequently, publishers are extremely sensitive to publishing any material concerning this issue.[16] Alternatively, *ese dōwa* groups make demands for subcontracting work, the purchase of goods and services at extortionate prices, or loans on favourable terms. Those that refuse are aggressively denounced for discriminatory practices.

The MOJ survey, however, gives an incomplete picture of fake *dōwa* activity in that it ignores the extensive abuse of government measures to help *burakumin* under the provisions of the 1969 Special Measures Law. These measures were actually responsible for the bulk of *ese dōwa* revenue. There were a number of ways in which *ese dōwa* groups could exploit the special measures law: the 1969 law provided tax breaks for *dōwa*-promotion activities and *ese dōwa* racketeers could extract rebates and commissions from these; they could gain licenses for developing land, ostensibly for the benefit of *buraku* communities, which could then be sold on to real-estate developers at a substantial profit; they could extract government money for spurious *buraku*-related projects; the list goes on. These activities were backed up by a highly aggressive and confrontational attitude towards public officials who opposed them; Mizoguchi (1986: 196) reports that after they became pseudo-*dōwa* groups, former *yakuza* actually employed more violence than before and that government officials are particularly afraid of this type of violence.

In his 1988 book examining the *dōwa* problem and *dōwa* groups, Takagi Masayuki drew a number of conclusions concerning the aetiology and persistence of the *ese dōwa* phenomenon. The first of these was that executives within the legitimate *dōwa* movement had become corrupted by the money-making opportunities their position afforded. The splintering of the movement and internal conflict within the main groups exacerbated this problem and resulted in a number of independent groups and lone operatives. At the same time, increased police pressure on established *yakuza* economic activity and the *sōkaiya* encouraged the adoption of this less dangerous business (Takagi 1988: 152–3).

The development of these groups was facilitated by three key factors. The first of these was the low level of understanding of the nature of the *burakumin* problem by most people. This misunderstanding engendered a high degree of fear. Second, Takagi identifies an attitude amongst both businesses and government officials to accept peace at any price. It is also likely that victims of *ese dōwa* activity have been confused by the protection that the Special Measures Law affords to legitimate *dōwa* activity; they think that they are powerless to confront pseudo-*dōwa* activists. Third, the measures taken by the police have been inadequate to deal with this problem (1988). This is evinced by the remark made by a victim, cited by Hiraoka, explaining why he had not notified the police because he had been in doubt as to 'whether or not the police were really serious about getting to grips with it' (1987: 74).

Fake Right-Wing Movements (*Ese Uyoku*)

Although there have long been links between the right-wing and *yakuza*, fake right-wing movements as a front for *yakuza* fund-raising became a significant problem at around the same time as the *ese dōwa* phenomenon and for the same broad reasons. The activities in which they participate are also remarkably similar. In addition to these standard practices, which fall largely under the category of *minji kainyū bōryoku*, fake *uyoku* activity also includes the use of armoured cars (*sendensha*) fitted with enormously powerful speakers and Japanese flags. The most common practice is to position one of these vehicles outside a targeted company, which is then bombarded with high volume martial music and political speeches, usually demanding the return of the Russian-occupied islands in the Chishima (Kuril) chain, until the group's demands for political contributions have been accepted.

Within all prefectures there are administrative ordinances governing excessive noise pollution (*bōsōon jōrei*), which theoretically should provide a legal antidote to the problem of right-wing propaganda trucks. The ordinance in Iwate prefecture, for example, limits publicity trucks to 85 decibels. Unfortunately, these ordinances are limited to empowering the police to tell the noise-polluter to stop. Only if the offending activity continues can action be taken against them. Dealing with fake right-wingers is also problematic because they skilfully exploit the constitutional guarantees to freedom of speech and freedom of association.

Legitimate Business

Throughout the late Shōwa period, there was an increasing trend for *yakuza* to involve themselves in legitimate business. Individuals involved in organised crime generally find it advantageous to establish legitimate sources of income to reduce the risk of seizure and mitigate the other uncertainties inherent in illegal activities. As police pressure on *yakuza* criminal activities increased, these considerations became more important.

Police pressure on traditional *yakuza* crimes also encouraged the process of these groups' moving into other crimes, known collectively as *minji kainyū bōryoku*, targeting both civil society and the business world. This growing proximity to corporate Japan, in which business was frequently a willing accomplice, further encouraged this process; as mentioned above, having been employed by real-estate companies to perform land-sharking services, it was no great jump for *yakuza* to directly participate in real-estate speculation on their own account.

An increasingly aggressive attitude taken by the police towards *yakuza* crime has also made it more important to have a legitimate front through which illegal income can be channelled and criminal activity organised. Frequently, the owner of this business will attempt to further insulate it from law-enforcement intervention by registering the business in the name of a wife, relative, or girlfriend.

The wealth generated by the system of *jōnōkin* payments also led high-ranking *oyabun* to seek new legitimate sectors in which to invest their money. Although businesses traditionally associated with Japanese organised crime, such as construction, outdoor stalls, trucking, and the entertainment industry (typically a bar or club run by the wife or mistress of the gang member), are still heavily represented, the *yakuza* have been moving into real-estate, finance, English-language schools, private hospitals, and hotels. In short, anything that will provide a legitimate front whilst earning a good return on their capital.

Whilst it might be argued that criminals going straight represents a net social benefit, increased *yakuza* involvement in the legitimate business is not necessarily to be welcomed. This is because, all too often, gang members retain their former operating procedures when shifting from the illegal to the legitimate market sector of the economy. For example, *yakuza* businessmen might use the threat that their gang-affiliation implies to demand loans on favourable terms and reduced prices from suppliers of goods and services, whilst their own customers might be expected to pay a premium. Alternatively, competitors might be given disincentives to underbid *yakuza*-owned firms.

A variation on this theme became apparent with the development of *kigyō shatei* (business brothers). *Kigyō shatei* refers to businessmen who, whilst not formally members of *yakuza* organisations themselves, make use of their affiliation with such a grouping to achieve an unfair competitive edge in the marketplace. Such people may be former gang members who retain their underworld links, or alternatively businessmen who have formed a quasi-brotherhood relationship with a senior gang member to further their business interests. Needless to say, this development presents particular problems for law-enforcement authorities in that identifying these seemingly legitimate businessmen is much harder than dealing with well-known criminals. This problem is exacerbated by the fact that these businessmen do not advertise their relationship through ostentatious displays of *yakuza*-style attire or tattoos. Furthermore, the nature of the influence that *yakuza*-affiliation gives is often such that the criminal and commercial legal codes existing as of the end of the Shōwa period were incapable of effectively combating the activities of the business brothers.

One industry in which *yakuza* find they have a competitive advantage is industrial-waste disposal. The waste-disposal business in Japan is said to be worth ¥4 trillion. Since the rampant pollution of Japan's high growth period, typified by the tragedy of mercury poisoning at Minamata and elsewhere, environmental controls and regulations governing the disposal of rubbish have become progressively stricter. As *yakuza* are less scrupulous in their adherence to these regulations than legitimate waste-disposal companies,[17] they are able to operate much more cheaply and can pass on some of these savings to their customers in the shape of lower haulage costs. Moreover, the low start-up costs of this type of business, consisting merely of the cost of a four-tonne lorry or large dump-truck, make this an attractive business for even low-level *yakuza* to enter (Mizoguchi 1992*a*: 142). This type of business may also be attractive to a criminal organisation as it facilitates the disposal of incriminating evidence.

In order to participate in this business it is first necessary to receive a licence from the prefectural governor. This is not granted to those who have spent time in prison within the previous three years; so in many cases, *yakuza* members conduct this business under another name. Licences are much harder to gain for the management of rubbish dumps themselves, especially those dealing with hazardous material. However, many gang members simply ignore these obstacles.

An example of this is the case of S, an executive in a second-level Yamaguchi-gumi gang in Hyōgo prefecture. This man, who ran his own contracting company, collected rubbish from construction companies in several cities in Hyōgo prefecture. S charged only ¥1,000/tonne for this service, which was less than half the going rate amongst his legitimate competitors. The rubbish would then be taken at night to nearby publicly owned mountains where it would be burned and buried. Despite complaints from local residents, this enterprise was given no more than repeated official warnings, which were ignored. Although S was eventually arrested for violations of the Industrial Waste Disposal Law, this was not before he had illegally dumped several tens of thousands of tonnes of waste. Mizoguchi suggests that one interpretation for this lack of effective measures is that such is the amount of rubbish, that the local Public Health Centre must rely on illegal dumping to get rid of it all (1997: 144).

In another case, an executive of a Yamaguchi-gumi front company rented land in the mountains, which he then opened up as an illegal industrial waste dump. Because none of the expensive legal requirements concerning the treatment of such waste were observed, he was able to undercut legitimate dumps charging only half the industry standard. Every night, about ninety trucks would come to deposit rubbish at an average charge of ¥13,000. This therefore yielded a daily gross income of ¥1.17 m and, in total, the executive and partner netted several tens of millions of yen (Mizoguchi 1997: 144).

As well as involving themselves directly in business management, during the 1980s many ambitious *yakuza* became aggressive speculators in the Japanese stock market. Frequently, this was financed by borrowing money. As in their investment in legitimate businesses, *yakuza* investment strategy has not been hindered by an excessive concern for the finer points of the law. In one incident in 1985, the Shinjuku branch manager of Nomura Securities passed on to some of his underworld clients information concerning a miracle drug at Yamanouchi Pharmaceutical. Unfortunately for him rumours concerning unpleasant side-effects of this drug caused a drop in the share price and, after months of stalling, one of these irate customers beat him up severely, leading to a coma followed shortly by the broker's death (Alletzhauser 1990: 205–6). More typically, when faced with a stock that fails to perform up to their expectations, *yakuza* investors approach their broker and demand that they be reimbursed for their losses.

The most famous of these *yakuza* speculators was Ishii Susumu of the Inagawa-kai. Ishii's involvement in the Heiwa Sōgō Bank takeover and his subsequent investment in the Tōkyū Corporation made him a household name in Japan. This scandal is discussed in Chapter Six.

Although such high-profile cases as Ishii's hit the headlines, it was not only the elite of the *yakuza* world who were active in stock-market speculation during this period. At a time of extremely low interest rates and when banks were actively pressuring their clients to borrow more money, riding the wave of rapidly rising land and stock prices was seen as too good an opportunity to miss. It would not be until things had gone horribly wrong with the collapse of this bubble and even more so with the disaster of the *jūsen* problem that the extent and implications of this became appreciated.

Conclusion

The *yakuza* economy at the end of the 1980s encompassed an extremely diverse set of activities ranging from highly profitable financial and real-estate speculation (aided by the bubble economy) to the man with his two dice and a cup taking ¥100 bets on the dirty streets of Kotobuki-chō. This economy was also massively fluid, with evolution being driven by market opportunity and, perhaps more importantly, the legal environment (itself a function of both the law and the level of enforcement) in which these groups existed.

The historical fact that legal changes and varying police enforcement of the law have had such a massive impact on the types of activities which the *yakuza* engage in shows that the *yakuza*–police relationship cannot simply be described as symbiotic. Unfortunately, the effect of new legal measures or increased police enforcement has frequently led to the development of *yakuza* activities, which have attracted greater social disapprobation than those they replace.

Despite this, as should be clear from the description of *yakuza shinogi* given above, the environment in which the *yakuza* operated at the end of the Shōwa period presented them with greater economic opportunities than those enjoyed by equivalent groups in other industrialised capitalist economies. However, by this time, there were also a number of forces at work which militated against the continuation of this environment. The interplay of these various forces resulted in the first Japanese law to specifically identify the *bōryokudan*: The *Bōryokudan Taisaku Hō* or, more simply, the *Bōtaihō*.

5

Bōtaihō: Organised Crime Countermeasures— Japanese Style

From the historical overview of the *yakuza's* development in the Shōwa period it is apparent that there was a large gap between the declared aim of the law-enforcement community, as given in such publicly available material as the *Keisatsu Hakusho* and the *Keisatsu-gaku Ronshū*, of 'the annihilation of the *bōryokudan* and the eradication of illegal violent activity' (*Keisatsu Hakusho* 1989: 70) and the reality of the widespread existence of highly visible *yakuza* groups which, through continual evolution of new business practices, seemed relatively impervious to police action. Existing *yakuza* countermeasures, as they were enforced, were clearly inadequate to satisfy these proclaimed aspirations.

In May 1991, a 'Law Regarding the Prevention of Unjust Acts by *Bōryokudan* Members' (*Bōryokudanin ni yoru Futō na Kōi no Bōshi nado ni Kan-suru Hōritsu*) was passed into law and implemented the following March. This title was usually dropped in favour of the more manageable ' "*Bōryokudan Taisaku Hō*" or *bōryokudan* countermeasures law, which itself truncated to "*Bōtaihō*" '. Gang members themselves, as always rejecting the label '*bōryokudan*', preferred to refer to this law as '*yakuza shinpō*', or the new *yakuza* law.

In order to make sense of this law we must not only understand its main provisions; we must examine it in context. The description of the

Bōtaihō's framework provided in this chapter is therefore prefaced with a number of sections enabling us to assess the significance of this law and draw conclusions as to whether or not this law marks a break with the past and unites police rhetoric with their real intentions.

Background to the *Bōtaihō*

What were the factors causing this law to be introduced in 1991? Does the introduction of the *Bōtaihō* indicate that the *yakuza* were becoming less socially acceptable, or does this legal change suggest a more profound underlying change in the political and legal administration in Japan? An alternative explanation might be found in external factors with the nature of both the gangs and authorities remaining constant. A final hypothesis is that all of these factors were working in interplay to create the conditions in which it became necessary for Japan's legislators to pass this law.

As has been shown in previous chapters there was an evolution of traditional, locally based *bakuto* and *tekiya* groups involved in gambling, labour-broking, and open-air vending to *gurentai* organisations conducting black-marketeering and extortion. The most successful of these became the large-scale *yakuza* syndicates that came to exert oligopolistic control of the underworld economy. With increased pressure on their traditional sources of income and the relentless demands for *jōnōkin* payments, members of these organisations were continually seeking new ways of raising money. Oligopolisation was therefore accompanied by diversification and increased sophistication.

One of the most important of these diversifications was that of *minji kainyū bōryoku* (violent intervention in civil affairs or *minbō*). *Minbō*, though initially a dispute-resolution service capitalising on the inadequacies of the civil courts, quickly became a form of extortion, targeting sections of society that had not traditionally been prey to *yakuza* groups. The theoretical discussion in Chapter One shows that organised crime tolerance may be facilitated by the characterisation of such crimes as consensual, victimless activities. The increase in *minbō* as a source of revenue for these groups can be expected therefore to have had the effect of increasing public perception of *yakuza* as sociopathic organisations.

Under the then existing criminal law, *minbō* occupied what the Japanese literature almost universally refers to as a *gurē zōn* (grey zone). The *yakuza* members obtaining money through this type of activity would typically ensure that their requests for money were couched in such a way as to avoid infringing the law's provisions regarding intimidation or extortion. The member would handover his name card, with his organisational affiliation prominently displayed in the top right-hand corner, or ensure that his tattoo and amputated fingers were visible. The organisation's reputation for violence was therefore clearly displayed and the recipient of the request left in no doubt as to the consequences of non-compliance. However, no explicit threat had been made. Technically, much of this activity was not illegal, and that which was illegal was very difficult to prosecute.

From the last decade of the Shōwa period onwards, the increasing *yakuza* involvement in the affairs of ordinary members of the public was matched by an increased involvement in quasi-legitimate business activity. Although *yakuza* had long been involved in various industries such as running bars and construction firms, the economic conditions of the bubble encouraged much greater *yakuza* participation in the legitimate economy.

The first of the factors encouraging this development was that cash-flush banks during this period were so desperate to lend that some of them even resorted to threatening their clients that, if they would not borrow whilst conditions were good, then credit would be denied them in the future. In such a climate, little effort was made to assess the creditworthiness of borrowers, and *yakuza* members were easily able to raise money based on the collateral of unrealistically valued land.

The funds raised in this way could then be employed in real-estate and stock-market speculation. Although, in this respect, the *yakuza* were behaving no differently from anybody else, what was different was that at each stage there was the possibility that the *yakuza* would use their organisational leverage to achieve loans and purchases either on favourable terms or on credit. When a share price behaved less well than expected, *yakuza* speculators might demand compensation from the firms that had sold them the shares.

Another factor contributing to diminishing public tolerance of the *yakuza* was the continuing outbreak of intergang conflicts in the years preceding and following the imperial succession. It is clear that from the time of the Yama-ichi *tōsō*, the major gang conflict of the 1980s, members of the NPA responsible for *yakuza* countermeasures had felt the need for new legal powers to control these groups. Similarly, it is reported that in 1986 during this conflict, Ishii Susumu, the then head of the Inagawa-kai, had tried to persuade the Yamaguchi-gumi leadership to bring the war to an end. He argued that it was adversely affecting public opinion, bringing increased police attention on the *yakuza* world as a whole, and that the police were currently considering a new *yakuza* law (Mizoguchi 1992*b*: 247–8).

However, there is a time-lag between the peak of the Yama-ichi *tōsō* in 1985 and the final decision to introduce new anti-*yakuza* laws. This suggests that the Yama-ichi *tōsō* was not by itself the prime causal factor. It is clear that by 1988 senior members of the NPA were considering that a change in the law was overdue; in reaction to a 1988 incident in Hamamatsu-chō involving the Ichiriki-ikka,[1] the then head of the NPA's Criminal Investigation Bureau was quoted (Miyagi 1992: 97) as saying: 'The most effective *bōryokudan* countermeasure is to seal off their sources of income. In America there is a law that cuts off the Mafia from their financial base. The time has come when in Japan also we should investigate a similar kind of law.' After the conclusion of the Yama-ichi *tōsō* there were two significant intergang violent struggles both of which had a significant impact on public opinion and police attitudes.

The first of these conflicts preceding the introduction of the *Bōtaihō* was the Hachiōji war in the western outskirts of Tokyo. In February 1990, two executives the Takumi-gumi subgroup of the Yamaguchi-gumi were battered and stabbed to death in Hachiōji by members of the Nibiki-kai, a locally based group. Although officially the Yamaguchi-gumi had an understanding with the Inagawa-kai that they would not raise the Yamaguchi-gumi diamond crest in Tokyo, at the time it is reported that there were over thirty Yamaguchi-gumi-related offices and nearly 300 men in the capital. On not one of these offices did the gang's diamond emblem appear (Yamada 1994*a*: 265–8).

In order that honour be satisfied, the Yamaguchi-gumi mobilised a 150-man revenge force composed largely of Takumi-gumi members. In a ten-day succession of revenge attacks, two people were killed and a number of revenge shots fired on buildings before the Yamaguchi-gumi called a halt and a settlement was reached with the Kantō Hatsuka-kai, the Tokyo groups allied to the Nibiki-kai. The reason for the truce was not so much fear of the Tokyo gangs as the response of the authorities to this conflict. The Tokyo Metropolitan Police mobilised 1,200 officers specifically to deal with this incident, and increased pressure was put on the organisation's other activities. At the same time a hostile press reaction further damaged the syndicate's public image.

Despite the comparative unimportance of this conflict, the Tokyo Metropolitan Police viewed it with alarm as they feared that it might have a more profound significance; 'although it was sparked off by a drunken quarrel, this (incident) has deep roots in that, with the establishment of the fifth-generation leadership, the expansion into Tokyo brings (the Yamaguchi-gumi) into opposition with other groups' (Yamada 1994a: 266). The Tokyo Police have long held the view that there is a profound difference in the organisational culture of the Kantō-based and Kansai-based *yakuza* groups. The former are seen as much more concerned to avoid antagonising the police. Yamaguchi-gumi expansion into the capital would also inevitably lead to widespread conflict with the incumbent groups including a collapse of the stabilising relationship with the Inagawa-kai. The police were obviously highly concerned that this should not happen.

The second, and perhaps the more significant, conflict was the Okinawa war, which lasted from September 1990 to February 1992. Although this war was fought between the third-generation Kokuryū-kai and the breakaway Okinawa Kokuryū-kai, at the time it was called a proxy war between the Yamaguchi-gumi and the Inagawa-kai. The cause of this conflict was the expulsion of a group of executives from the third-generation Kokuryū-kai because they refused to support a move to increase links with the Yamaguchi-gumi (against which they had fought in the 1970s; several of their fellow members were still serving prison sentences for attacks made during that struggle). These expelled executives then formed the Okinawa Kokuryū-kai.

Although the Yamaguchi-gumi top executives urged resolute treatment of the renegade group, this was problematic for two reasons. First, the new Okinawa Kokuryū-kai had six hundred members whilst the third-generation group remained with only four hundred. Second, the expelled executives had gained the support of the Inagawa-kai, with which the Yamaguchi-gumi officially enjoyed friendly relations. In the ensuing conflict, seven people were killed and nine injured. Included amongst this total was a high-school student who had been mistaken for a gang member whilst he was painting a fence at a gang office in order to earn pocket money. Two police officers were also injured in the course of this fight (Mizoguchi 1997: 42–4). Uchiyama Ayako, of the National Research Institute of Police Science, identifies this conflict, and in particular the death of the high-school boy, as the single most important factor in changing public opinion concerning the nature of the *yakuza* and consequently as a major stimulus in the creation of the *Bōtaihō*.

The increasing reliance on *minbō*, the increased intrusion of the *yakuza* into the legitimate economy, and the victimisation of innocent bystanders and the police in intergang conflicts are the standard reasons given in the Japanese literature for the introduction of the *Bōtaihō*. There are also, however, underlying political and international factors, which have not been given due consideration in these accounts.

As mentioned in an earlier chapter, the authorities made use of criminal syndicates as agents of social control in the postwar period. The two key factors for this were the weakness of the police and the fear of large left-wing organisations. Throughout this period, however, changes in both these factors meant that the basis for this relationship was gradually eroded throughout the latter part of the Shōwa period. The increase in police power, and especially the growth of the security police since the early 1960s (Katzenstein 1996: 61), has meant that the police are now confident of their ability to deal with violent opposition without recourse to outside groups.

Over the same period, the perceived threat posed by extreme left-wing groups has largely been diffused, as Japan's economic success has undermined the support for the large labour and student organisations advocating radical change during the 1950s and 1960s. Such groups as remain are small marginal organisations and, though the security police seem to take their existence very seriously, they present no mortal threat to the continued existence of the Japanese state. This contrasts with the postwar situation as perceived by Justice Minister Kimura at the time that he attempted to establish his anti-communist *yakuza* shock-troops, the *Battōtai* (Hori 1983: 137–8). The end of the Cold War, with the collapse of the Soviet empire, underlined this development.

On a more immediate political level, events involving the ruling Liberal Democratic Party must also be considered as possible factors for the introduction of new *yakuza* control measures. In September 1988, it became apparent that a number of senior figures within the

LDP had received cut-price shares in Recruit Cosmos, the real-estate branch of the Recruit business group, prior to the company's official listing on the Tokyo Stock Exchange. By the following month, police investigations had revealed that a large proportion of the former (Nakasone) cabinet had purchased unlisted shares whilst many members of the current cabinet, including Prime Minister Takeshita himself, had received money from the company. A number of senior bureaucrats were also implicated (*The Economist* 12 November 1988; Mitchell 1996: 124–5).

Eventually Takeshita resigned as Prime Minister (though he continued to exert considerable influence within the party) to be replaced by the ineffectual Foreign Minister Uno; largely because he had not been considered worth bribing, Uno was one of the few senior LDP politicians untainted by the scandal. Uno's leadership lasted for two months, during which time he was undermined by a sex scandal (unusual in Japanese politics) in which a former mistress complained of his meanness and coarseness. The mainstream Japanese press had ignored this story until the *Washington Post* ran it, whereupon they felt obliged to follow suit. Popular contempt for Uno, and for the LDP, was compounded by the highly unpopular consumption tax to create widespread public dissatisfaction with the governing party. It seemed to many voters that those in the government were forcing austerity on the general public whilst lining their own pockets (Mitchell 1996: 125).

These factors combined to reduce the LDP's electoral support to a mere 27 per cent in the Upper House elections of July 1989. The opposition, which had campaigned on a platform of anti-corruption and opposition to the 3 per cent consumption tax, for the first time gained mastery of the Upper House (*The Economist* 27 July 1989; *T ōkei-Kyoku* 1990: 708). Taking responsibility for this defeat, Uno resigned, and in August was replaced as Prime Minister by Kaifu Toshiki.

Kaifu struggled to repair the tarnished image of the LDP with such measures as reform of the consumption tax, the introduction of two women to the cabinet, and promises to reform the political system, specifically the ways in which it was funded, in order to reduce corruption. It was also under Kaifu's leadership that the political go-ahead was given for the NPA to draw up its proposals for new *yakuza*-control measures that would become the *Bōtaihō*. It is not therefore a large jump to postulate that the *Bōtaihō* was part of a wider effort to present a cleaner image to the electorate.

The domestic audience was not, however, the only political pressure on Kaifu's government. Since the early 1980s there was an increasing awareness amongst American law-enforcement officers, particularly the FBI, that Japanese crime syndicates were operating in the United States (Kaplan and Dubro 1986: 241–2). This was largely confined to those areas with large Japanese communities and tourist destinations, such as Hawaii and California. With the rise of the *keizai* (economic) *yakuza*, overseas *yakuza* activity started to include real-estate development as well as more overtly criminal activity. At a time when Japan's enormous trade surplus with America was a serious stumbling block in the two countries' relations, the fact that Japan was now exporting its crime as well was a gift to the media, providing it with excellent ammunition for 'Japan-bashing'.

Yamada Hitoshi of the *Nichibenren*'s (*Nihon Bengoshi Rengō-kai* or Japanese Federation of Bar Associations) *bōryokudan*-countermeasures group, suggests that this was indeed a significant factor:

The consciousness of the police has changed. The most sensitive ones are the police executives who attend international meetings . . . at these meetings they are frequently asked how Japan's *bōryokudan* counter-measures are going. It would be no good if they weren't doing anything so they made it, this law (the *Bōtaihō*) (interview Tokyo, 1998).

Whilst Yamada asserts that on a police-executive level foreign pressure (*gaiatsu*) was a factor, something police interviewees indignantly reject, there was also pressure at the diplomatic level. With the end of the Cold War, there was considerable political rhetoric concerning the establishment of a 'New World Order'. Under this new system the rich industrialised countries, having defeated communism, were to switch their attention to the fight against the new bogeymen of organised crime and the international menace of drugs.

The major motivating force behind this was the American War on Drugs, which George Bush, Sr had enthusiastically inherited from Reagan. Whilst, as far as American political interests were concerned, the War on Drugs and the fight against organised crime were synonymous, the reality of Japan's position was very different. The *bōryokudan*, according to police statistics, made one-third of their income from drug dealing, though, given that the official figures underplay the amount of money received from business, this figure is probably too high. Also the drugs with which the United States were concerned, cocaine and heroin, have not recently been a significant problem in Japan, which has an overwhelming preference for amphetamines.

However, despite these differences, in September 1989, Kaifu publicly united with Bush in 'declaring a global partnership in the war against drugs' (Friman 1996: 64). Friman goes on to identify the reason for this partnership:

(T)he extent of co-operation has been largely determined by domestic factors. Japan's participation in the global partnership reflects the link between drug issues and bilateral economic relations with the United States. Faced with increasing threats of economic retaliation, Japanese policy makers have viewed co-operation on drug issues as a means to defuse broader bilateral tensions.

At the 1986 G7 Tokyo Economic Summit, the participating countries issued a joint declaration supporting improved international cooperation in anti-drugs measures. The following year the United Nations held a special drugs conference and this led directly to the 1988 United Nations Convention against Illicit Traffic in Narcotic Drugs and Psychotropic Substances. Under this convention, signatory countries were required to cooperate with other countries in the punishment of money-laundering, and the identification and seizure of illegal profits from drug-dealing (*Hōmu-shō Keijikyoku Keijihōeika* 1997: 1).

At the time, Japan did not sign. This was considered to be due to the fact that Japan's laws did not contain the provisions necessary for compliance, although newspaper reports at the time indicated that both the NPA and the MOJ were considering the required legal changes. Failure to show concrete achievements towards this end meant that, at the Paris Summit of July 1989, US Secretary of State Baker criticised Japan and urged it to adopt a more proactive attitude. It was in this international context that the newly installed Kaifu entered into his 'global partnership' (Friman 1996: 77–8).

The roles of summit embarrassment and direct *gaiatsu* as causal factors in Japanese legal change is clear. The evidence is, however, strongest for the new Drugs Law of 1991, anti-money-laundering measures, and the three organised crime countermeasures laws (*soshiki hanzai taisaku hō*) passed in August 1999. The comments of Miyazawa Kōichi, a member of the specialist research group assembled by the NPA to consider *bōryokudan* countermeasures (the findings of which became the initial draft of the *Bōtaihō*), confirm that international considerations also played a part in the creation of the *Bōtaihō*:

The *bōryokudan* problem is not just an internal problem. We cannot ignore the fact that the Japanese *yakuza* are causing a nuisance in various other countries, especially several nearby Asian countries...As a country governed by law, it is a very grave problem to leave *bōryokudan* crimes as they are. Considering the strength that Japanese business has in the world economy and this sort of strange existence forever prevalent on the surface of Japanese society and continuing to exert an influence on the economy, these illegal groups stir up international opinion and provide good material for Japan-bashing when they proceed into European and American society. In this situation, we must do something (*Jurisuto* 1 January 1991: 14).

There were therefore a number of political, diplomatic, and attitudinal changes, as well as changes in *yakuza* behaviour, which encouraged the introduction of new anti-*yakuza* legislation. There is no conclusive evidence to support any simple monocausal explanation as to why the *Bōtaihō* should have been introduced. It seems likely, however, that all the factors discussed above were influential in creating an environment in which legal change became expedient.

Problems of Organised Crime Countermeasures

There is an inherent strain within every constitutional liberal-democratic state regarding its efforts to maintain law and order. In classical liberal political theory, in order to protect the rights and freedoms of citizens, paradoxically, laws partially restricting some of these rights and freedoms, and officers of the state empowered to enforce these restrictions, are deemed necessary. In order that these officers, or the state itself, do not exceed or abuse their powers, restrictions are in turn placed on these powers. Law enforcement must itself be carried out within the law; evidence gained and arrests made through extra-legal means are, according to this legal principle, inadmissible in a court of law. Law-enforcement officers within liberal-democratic states therefore are at a disadvantage *vis-à-vis* their colleagues in authoritarian or totalitarian states in that they have considerable constraints of due process placed on their ability to identify and apprehend criminals. Disregard for the moment whether the reality of this situation is quite as tidy as this simple exposition, or whether classical liberal theory is relevant when discussing Japan. The point is that those countries with a written constitution that can satisfactorily be described as liberal-democratic, of which Japan is one, have these clearly defined formal constraints on police and judicial powers. Similarly, in such systems, individual citizens have clearly stated rights.

Whilst the problem of due process is general to all crime-control efforts, there are a number of peculiarities of organised as opposed to other categories of crime that make organised-crime-specific counter-measures problematic. The most basic of these is that, given our observation that organised crime provides goods and services to consumers of both the upper and under worlds, and that some of these consumers occupy elite positions in the political sphere, the whole concept of organised crime countermeasures is itself open to question. If the existence of organised crime is beneficial to key constituencies, possibly including judicial, political, and law-enforcement personnel either at street or at administrative level, are all of these actors seriously committed to the enactment, implementation, and enforcement of such measures? Given these possibilities, it is no great jump to postulate that the introduction of new 'countermeasures' may have a purely symbolic role.

The most obvious way in which OCGs may provide benefits to the constituencies identified above is via a straightforward exchange of money or goods in exchange for immunity. The ability of a large criminal syndicate to corrupt those in positions of authority will typically be greater than that of an individual criminal operator.

Even if we are to accept that organised crime control measures are genuine in their intent and actively enforced, there are severe obstacles to their success. As many such crimes are consensual transactions providing goods and services to consumers, they will not be reported to the authorities. Even predatory organised crime may tend to have low reporting rates as those victimised are themselves frequently operating within the criminal economy. A purely reactive police strategy is therefore inappropriate for organised-crime-control.

As the main asset of organised crime is the reputation for, rather than the actual exercise or explicit threat of, violence, it is very difficult to prosecute the significant category of activities in which economic advantage is gained through the exploitation of that reputation. To construct laws concerning intimidation and extortion which include this type of unstated, but universally recognised, threat is problematic.

The criminal organisation's reputation for violence and penalties against cooperating with the authorities are further obstacles to effectively controlling organised crime. Even when gang members are brought to trial, if witnesses refuse to testify against them, then even the best-planned of control measures may come to naught. Credible witness-protection schemes are therefore an integral part of any viable organised-crime-control strategy. In extreme cases such as Sicily, Colombia, and the former Soviet Union, it may be necessary to routinely extend this protection to judges and prosecutors as well.

As has been seen from the account of *yakuza* development in previous chapters, organised crime is a highly amorphous phenomenon, which is constantly adapting to changes both in economic opportunity and in the legal and administrative environment. Given that it is typically involved in a number of different economic activities, increased enforcement *vis-à-vis* one of these sources of income may be successful in inflating arrest statistics and driving out gang members from that sector, only for those displaced to seek alternative employment in other areas of the criminal economy. 'It is hardly a net gain to society if bookies become drug dealers or hold up men' (Maltz 1990: 14).

With specific reference to the Japanese experience in the 1960s and 1970s, increased police targeting of traditional *yakuza shinogi* had not only exactly the effect described above, but drove the smaller, locally based *gumi* into extinction to be replaced by the more highly diversified wide-area syndicates. Such considerations show the importance of clearly defining one's strategic goal (even if it can not be explicitly stated in public) and designing a set of control measures that offer the best hope of achieving that goal.

Although most criminal-law codes contain provisions concerning conspiracy, it is usually much harder to prove collective responsibility for a crime, in which only one or two actors may have been directly involved, than for the individual criminal liability of those one or two gang members. Giuliani (1987: 104), writing from an American perspective, clearly identifies this problem:

We have a system of justice in which laws defining crimes for the most part focus upon individual behaviour and proscribe conduct in the context of isolated criminal episodes... Even the crime of 'conspiracy', generically defined as a criminal partnership, requires each member of the conspiracy to join in the same criminal scheme.

Typically, those at the higher end of the hierarchy will attempt to dissociate themselves from direct participation in criminal activity, especially crimes which carry a high risk of arrest. As these higher-echelon figures often receive much of their income from taxes, tribute, or dues paid by their subordinates, they are effectively insulated from indictment. Therefore, arrests of gang members may be made but, without access to special legal provisions and surveillance techniques, these arrests are typically of lower-level members on an individual basis for an individual crime. Consequently, the organisational infra-structure remains intact and business carries on much as before. Katō (1991: 50–8) likens this to *mogura tataki* (mole-bashing), the fairground entertainment in which the object is to hit mechanical moles with a mallet as they randomly stick their heads out from a number of different holes.

Even control measures specifically targeting and successfully indict-ing the leadership of a criminal group, may have only a limited effect if the gang's infrastructure is untouched despite the favourable publicity such high-profile arrests may generate. The Japanese 'summit strategy' of the 1960s and American arrests of La Cosa Nostra (LCN) family leaders in the 1970s both show clearly that, in isolation, this type of strategy is ultimately ineffective.

There is therefore a need for special legal devices, specifically designed to combat organised crime, which take into consideration these problems. In particular, consideration should be given to the problem of dealing with organisationally conducted crimes by using laws intended for individual criminal activity. Before the creation of the *Bōtaihō* there were two main approaches to which those responsible for drafting the new law could refer: the European and the American, and the debate within Japan on framing anti-*yakuza* laws was essentially conducted within the parameters of these two approaches.

OC Laws 1—European Model: The Crime of Criminal Association

The origins of the European approach to organised crime control laws can be traced back to the French 1810 criminal law under the Napoleonic code (Morishita 1997: 290). The countries which are most usually cited as examples of laws targeting criminal association, France, Italy, and Germany, have all been heavily influenced by this code. This approach is without doubt the most direct and straightforward legal strategy for dealing with organised crime. Quite simply, the law in these three countries criminalises membership of a criminal organization.[2] Whilst this is straightforward it is not completely unproblematic. The most obvious difficulty is that of framing an operationally enforceable definition of criminal association without infringing the rights of individuals to join legitimate associations.

Although German criminal law has various provisions referring to criminal gangs, 'in Germany, there is no legal definition of organised crime' (Kühne, private correspondence 1998). However, in January 1991, a working definition was drawn up by the Interior Ministers of the various Länder as a guide for German federal police (*Bundeskriminalamt*) and prosecutors. This definition states that:

Organised crime is the planned violation of the law for profit or to acquire power, for which offences are each, or together, of a major significance, and are carried out by more than two participants who co-operate within a division of labour for a long or undetermined time span using

(a) commercial or commercial like structures, or
(b) violence or other means of intimidation, or
(c) influence on politics, media, public administration, justice and the legitimate economy.

Although this definition is widely adopted by European law-enforcement bodies, Kühne asserts that 'everybody—including the ministers of justice—agrees that this definition is pretty vague and can only give some hints to describe this phenomenon'. For example it remains open to interpretation exactly what is meant by 'major significance' (Levi 1998*b*: 2).

Under Article 416 of Italian criminal law, a 'mafia-type association' is defined as one in which, in order to commit crimes, or to gain an unfair profit for themselves or others, the members of that association directly or indirectly control economic activity, sales, or the allocation of public contracts and licenses, by making use of a rule of silence, based on the power of the organisation's threat (Katō 1991: 56). Under the provisions of the same article, members of such a grouping composed of three or more persons are liable to between three and six years' imprisonment.

Katō, a hawkish critic of Japanese organised-crime countermeasures, evaluates this approach highly, crediting it for the absence of organised-crime groups in Germany (1991: 57). This line of argument was also reflected in the comments of several retired police bureaucrats in their reaction to a paper I presented in Tokyo, 1998. This argument is surprising given that the existence of the Mafia, the Camorra, and the 'Ndrangheta in Italy suggests that this law, by itself, was by no means sufficient to eliminate, or even control, organised crime. It is also unreasonable to assert that there are no organised-crime groups in, for example, Germany. Whilst, for reasons given in Chapter One, Germany does not have a tradition of syndicated crime such as can be found in Italy or Japan, representatives of many different criminal syndicates are operating in Germany, especially since the fall of the Berlin wall and reunification (Freemantle 1995: 23–4, 272–3; Sterling 1995: *passim*).

Morishita (1997: 291) suggests that, in fact, very few guilty court verdicts are reached under this type of law. For obvious reasons, if membership of a criminal association, however that is defined, is made illegal, then such affiliation is concealed. It is arguable that this in itself is a desirable strategic goal; if OCGs are going to exist, then let them at least be consigned to the darkest reaches of the underworld. However, in terms of organised-crime eradication, or even control, this type of law promises little chance of success.

OC Laws 2—The American Model: The Rico Statutes

The Racketeer Influenced and Corrupt Organisations Act (RICO) is the 'most important substantive and procedural law tool in the history of organized crime control' (Jacobs 1994: 10). Passed on 15 October 1970, with the express purpose of seeking 'the eradication of organized crime in the United States' (OCCA, 84 Stat. at 923 in Randolph 1995: 1191), RICO shares with the crime-of-criminal-association approach the aim of targeting the criminal organisation itself rather than the individual crimes of its members. Whilst it also makes membership of an organisation falling under the jurisdiction of the RICO statutes a crime, the main significance of this law is that it makes possible the 'single prosecution of an entire multidefendant organized crime group for all of its many and diverse criminal activities' (Giuliani 1987: 105). The RICO law also makes possible the sequestration of the organisation's assets gained through RICO violations. In short, it is 'a law that leaves the

"crime" to other laws and addresses the idea of being "organised" '
(Rebovich 1995: 141).

Although there are other crimes under the provisions of the RICO
law, the most often used and overwhelmingly the most significant is
Section 1962(c):

It shall be unlawful for any person employed by or associated with any
enterprise engaged in, or the activities of which affect, interstate or foreign
commerce, to conduct or participate, directly or indirectly, in the conduct of such
enterprise's affairs through a pattern of racketeering activity or collection of
unlawful debt.

The three crucial considerations here are the definitions of
'enterprise', 'pattern', and 'racketeering'. Under Section 1961(4)
' "enterprise" includes any individual, partnership, corporation, association, or other legal entity, and any union or group of individuals
associated in fact although not a legal entity'.

With respect to our second term, 1961(5) states: 'A pattern of racketeering requires at least two acts of racketeering activity, one of which
occurred after the effective date of this chapter (15 October 1970) and the
last of which occurred within ten years (excluding any period of imprisonment) after the commission of a prior act of racketeering activity'.
Racketeering is defined in Section 1961(1) to include 'any act or threat
involving murder, kidnapping, gambling, arson, robbery, bribery, extortion, or dealing in narcotic or other dangerous drugs, which is charge-
able under State law and punishable by imprisonment for more than
one year'. This is supplemented with 'a "laundry list" of federal
offenses' (Abadinsky 1994: 453) including loan sharking, obstruction of
justice, fraud, Hobbs Act violations (labour or commercial racketeering), counterfeiting, contraband cigarettes, and white slavery.

Those found guilty of RICO violations are liable to a fine of up to
$25,000 or imprisonment of up to 20 years, or a combination of the
two. In addition to these considerable penalties, there are even more
substantial costs to RICO violators. Under the provisions of 1963(a),
those found guilty of RICO offences are liable to the sequestration of
any assets or interests acquired, either directly or indirectly, in violation of these statutes or acquired with the proceeds thereof. This forfeiture includes gross profits, thereby precluding a defendant from
claiming reductions for overheads or taxes paid on illegally gained
proceeds. RICO also allows for citizens who have suffered materially
due to these violations to sue with respect to this loss and to claim for

threefold damages and legal costs. Whilst RICO is a federal statute confined to federal crimes or violations carried out in an inter-state or international context, as of 1995, twenty-nine states had enacted their own anti-OC legislation closely modelled on this law (Rebovich 1995: 141–2).

As can be seen from the brief outline above, RICO clearly circumvents one of the most significant problems of legal organised-crime countermeasures, that of Katō's mole-bashing; rather than prosecuting individual members for individual crimes leaving the organisation itself intact, RICO enables blanket prosecution of the organisation's membership. Moreover, the 'second major purpose of RICO is to attack the economic infrastructure of organized crime, depriving it of its life blood, by providing for criminal forfeiture and civil injunctive relief' (Giuliani 1987: 107).

Despite the attractiveness of this approach and its evident potency as an organised-crime-control measure, RICO has met with a number of criticisms. First, the courts have applied the provisions of this law to groups, such as anti-abortion activists, and individuals, such as the 'junk-bond king' Michael Milken, whose activities fall outside the initial objectives of this law (Randolph 1995: 1189; Rosoff, Pontel, and Tillman 1998: 158).

The severity of the law's provisions are such that their application provides a potent threat for prosecutors and has been crucial factor in breaking down the code of *omerta* amongst Italian-American gangsters. The danger of this is that defendants may be intimidated into settling a case they would otherwise have disputed. At the same time RICO's civil provisions for threefold damages present such an enticing prospect to litigants that cases are brought under RICO when they would otherwise not be considered worth the trouble. This runs the risk of unnecessarily clogging up federal courts. To avoid this courts have fined lawyers who have filed spurious RICO claims (Abadinsky 1994: 456).

Another important question mark concerning RICO is the way in which forfeiture has actually been applied. Forfeiture is considered to be a major tool in organised crime and drug countermeasures where the size of the financial rewards often far outweighs the costs of incarceration. The potency of this approach is evinced by the comments of a *pentito mafioso* (Sterling 1995: 287): 'What bothers us most is when you take our money away. We'd rather stay in jail and keep the money than be free without the money; that's the main thing'. Forfeiture is a very appealing measure to the authorities for the added reason that it provides them with government revenue without taxation.

Despite these attractions, there must be clear restrictions on the ability of the state to seize the assets of citizens without satisfactory proof that the assets in question were derived, either directly or indirectly, from crime. As this is often extremely difficult to do, in America the onus has been shifted so that citizens must prove that property confiscated under civil forfeiture provisions (for which no criminal conviction is necessary) has been acquired through legitimate means. With the escalation of America's War on Drugs, in the 1980s and early 1990s, the burden of proof for civil forfeiture became progressively lighter (Baum 1996: 112, 172, 196).[3]

In addition, since 1985, the proceeds from asset seizure are paid in to the National Assets and Forfeiture Fund. The Fund then distributes this money to the various law-enforcement agencies, which are obliged to use it in some way on the War on Drugs. The consequence of these two factors is that the system has been abused, with over-zealous law-enforcement officers seizing property out of all proportion to the scale of the crimes committed and occasionally when no crime had been committed at all (Baum 1996: 243, 317). It is important that seizure provisions are framed in such a way as to prevent the law-enforcement community behaving effectively as bounty-hunters. It seems that recently these abuses have been recognised by the authorities, and the Supreme Court has recently made decisions demanding proportionality in the level of seizures (Levi 1998a: 20–1).

The radical and complicated nature of the RICO statutes meant that initially courts and law-enforcement agencies were unsure as to how this law should be applied. Consequently, it took some time before the full impact of this law could be ascertained. It is now clear, however, that RICO has been an extremely effective tool in combating organised crime in the United States.

The effectiveness of RICO depends, however, on the availability of sufficient evidence for a successful prosecution. Owing to criminal organisations' stress on organisational security, problems connected with the reliability of informers, and the reluctance of victims or witnesses to provide useful intelligence to the authorities, gathering this kind of evidence is difficult when using conventional police techniques. Attempts have been made to plug this gap through the use of such measures as electronic surveillance. In order to prevent abuses of this tool, investigative agencies in the United States, and most other liberal-democratic states, wishing to tap a suspect's phone or bug his/her property, are required to obtain a court warrant authorising this. This authorisation is typically limited in both duration and scope.

Owing to these restrictions, the heavy costs in manpower such an investigation requires, and the obvious countermeasures taken by professional criminals to limit their susceptibility to electronic eavesdropping, surveillance of this type is actually limited in its effectiveness. According to Abadinsky the cost of an average 30-day operation in the United States is 'in excess of $40,000 . . . and less than 20 percent produce incriminating evidence' (1994: 484). In contrast to Abadinsky's down-beat assessment of electronic surveillance, Jacobs (1994: 8) identifies it as one of the three 'most important legal weapons deployed in the (US) government's attack on organized crime' (along with RICO and the Witness Security Program).

Controlled delivery,[4] undercover investigators, and sting operations are also considered major tools whereby the authorities can gather evidence in organised-crime and drugs cases. Whilst these are not without their problems they can yield spectacular results, as in the six-year undercover operation involving FBI Special Agent Pistone, which contributed to the successful conviction of more than one hundred members of various LCN families.

Japanese organised-crime countermeasures must therefore be considered not just with reference to the substantive laws of other countries but to the investigative techniques available to, and used by, the officers entrusted to enforce these laws. The legal framework within which the Japanese police have operated in the postwar period has precluded extensive use of the investigative techniques outlined above.

The *Bōtaihō*—Draft One

In November 1990, the NPA set up a research group composed of external academics and legal experts with the express task of

preparing an anti-*bōryokudan* law. At the time, with the exception
of the chairman, Professor Narita of Yokohama University, and the
two representatives from the *Nichibenren*, the identities of the members of the fifteen-man committee were kept secret. Originally the
group had been told that they had two to three years to prepare this
law but this was soon cut down radically and their initial proposals
were published after only four meetings, the last of which was held on
6 February 1991. The extraordinary speed with which this draft was
produced has led some observers to suggest that the NPA had already
done provisional work towards the drafting of this bill (Miyagi 1992:
97–8). Shimamura (1992: 9) claims that the way in which this law was
prepared was unusual in that it did not proceed through a legislative
deliberative committee and then a legislative office under the oversight of the MOJ. Instead it was drafted under conditions of secrecy by
the NPA.

On 27 February 1991, the NPA produced its 'Basic Considerations on
the Bill Concerning *Bōryokudan* Countermeasures' (*Bōryokudan Taisaku ni
Kan-suru Hōan no Kihonteki na Kangaekata*). Whilst in many respects the
'Basic Considerations' was what became the *Bōtaihō*, there were a couple of important provisions included in this document that were
dropped from the draft bill. These were the seizure of illegally gained
profits and the exclusion of *bōryokudan* members from certain industries.

The seizure of illegally gained profits was seen by the research group
and the NPA as an important part of their general anti-*bōryokudan* strategy and was clearly influenced by the American RICO seizure provisions. These provisions were dropped from the bill not only due to the
operational problem of identifying what were illegally gained assets
and what legitimate, but also because there were more profound legal
implications in seizure. If assets were seized under the criminal law
(*keiji bosshū*), then it was considered that there would be the risk of
double punishment (Shinozaki, Takebana, Narita et al. 1991: 24).

It should be noted, however, that the 'Basic Considerations' had
been drafted in such a way as to avoid this problem; technically,
illegally gained assets were not to be subject to seizure (*bosshū*) but
subject to a surcharge-payment order (*kachōkin nōfu meirei*) in which
'violation money is levied administratively' (interview NPA bureaucrat, Tokyo March 1998). As the *Bōtaihō* was drafted by the NPA, rather
than the MOJ, this type of administrative approach, which operates
without recourse to the courts, was employed. As will be seen from

the finally enacted version of the law, the *Bōtaihō* relies entirely on administrative law (*gyōseihō*) rather than criminal law (*keihō*).

The other reason that this type of seizure/surcharge payment was not included in the finally enacted law was that at the same time the MOJ was drafting a law, which would enable Japan to conform to the requirements of the UN Convention Against Illicit Drugs and Psychotropic Substances. Included amongst the proposed provisions for the law were the seizure (under the criminal law) of the proceeds from drug trafficking and it was therefore felt a good idea to wait and see how the new drugs law ended up. Some members of the committee also felt that, given the various legal problems and the pressure to create this law quickly, it would be better to omit it for the time being and consider it at greater length at a later date (Takebana in Shinozaki, Takebana, Narita et al. 1991: 24).

The other item dropped from the bill was the proposal to exclude *bōryokudan* members from certain industries such as construction, real estate and finance. However, it was concluded that attempts to include provisions to exclude *bōrykudan* members from the relevant industries would possibly conflict with Article 22 of the 1947 Constitution. This guarantees the freedom of individuals to choose their own occupation, though this guarantee is qualified in that this freedom shall exist 'to the extent that it does not interfere with the public welfare'. It seems, therefore, that a good legal case could have been made for the retention of this provision.

On a more practical level, it seems that to have included this measure would have resulted in interminable discussions with the various ministries controlling the industries from which *bōryokudan* members were to be excluded. It seems more likely therefore that, rather than for constitutional reasons, this proposal was dropped in the interests of speedy enactment and implementation of the whole (Takebana 1991: 25).

The *Bōtaihō*

Only one month passed from the date of cabinet approval for the submission of this legislation to the date of its being passed by the Diet in May 1991. This was exceptionally fast. Moreover, it was passed unanimously with no parties or individual members offering criticism. Miyagi (1992: 100) suggests that, due to the media build-up to this law, 'an atmosphere had been created in which it was hard for the communist and socialist (opposition) parties to oppose (this law) even if they thought it strange'.

The central aspects of the *Bōtaihō* were the designation of *bōryokudan* groups by the Public Safety Commission, administrative control over certain prescribed activities by members of these groups, increased limitations on the use of gang offices during inter-group conflicts, and the establishment of regional centres to assist the victims of *bōryokudan* activities and forward the cause of *bōryokudan* eradication.

Under the provisions of the new law, a *bōryokudan* is defined as 'a group of which there is the risk that its members (including members of its component groups) will collectively or routinely promote illegal violent behaviour' (Article 2 paragraph 2). 'Illegal violent behaviour' (*bōryokuteki fuhō kōi*) is in turn defined as those 'illegal acts which meet the criteria at the discretion of the National Public Safety Commission' (Article 2 paragraph 1). Having provided these definitions, the law empowers the regional Public Safety Commissions (hereafter Public Safety Commissions) to designate *bōryokudan* groups. A designated *bōryokudan* is defined as a '*bōryokudan* of which there is a *high* risk that its members will collectively or routinely promote illegal violent behaviour' (Article 3 emphasis added).

Despite the definitions of designated and undesignated *bōryokudan* differing only with respect to one word—a 'high risk' rather than just a 'risk'—there are three concrete criteria, all of which the Public Safety Commission must judge a *bōryokudan* to meet, in order for it to be designated. The first of these is that it has been shown that, 'regardless of the ostensible purpose, a member of a *bōryokudan* makes use of that *bōryokudan*'s influence' to gain some kind of financial advantage (Article 3 paragraph 1).

The second factor required for designation is that a certain proportion of the group's members have a criminal record. This proportion declines as the size of the group increases: Whilst 66.6 per cent or more of the members of a three to four-man group are required to have a record to merit designation, this proportion drops to 4.2 per cent for a group, or syndicate, of 1,000 men or more. For the purposes of this law the criminal record of an individual is no longer taken into consideration if a certain period of time, varying according to the severity of the offence, has elapsed.

The third and final criterion for designation is that the individuals controlling the management of the *bōryokudan* in question, have beneath them an organisation constructed on hierarchical lines.

When a Public Safety Commission attempts to designate a *bōryokudan* group it is obliged to hold public hearings in which representatives of the group in question are able to put forward arguments and evidence in their defence. The organisation must be informed in advance of the time, place, and reason for these hearings, and this notification must also be publicly displayed. The obligation on the Public Safety Commission to hold a public hearing is waived if it is not possible to locate members of the group in question and if they fail to attend the hearing when due public notification has been given.

Once the Public Safety Commission has satisfied itself that a group meets the criteria for designation, it must present the appropriate evidence and a record of the official hearing to the National Public Safety Commission for official confirmation. For the National Public Safety Commission to confirm this designation it must base its judgement on the opinion of a specialist examining board. Once the National Public Safety Commission has reached a decision, it is obliged to quickly inform the relevant Public Safety Commission.

If designation is confirmed then the Public Safety Commission must inform a representative of that *bōryokudan*. Designation is also publicly notified in the official gazette (*Kanpō*), from which time the *bōryokudan*'s designated status is effective. If designation is not confirmed then the group in question cannot be designated as a *bōryokudan*. Designation remains in force for a period of three years.

Once a *bōryokudan* group has been designated, then its members are forbidden to carry out a number of activities by means of which they could attempt to gain some kind of financial advantage through making 'violent demands' (*bōryokuteki yōkyū*). For the purposes of this law, a 'violent demand' describes a demand or request which is made by a member of a *bōryokudan* whilst in some way using the influence of the organisation to which that member belongs. Therefore, referring to one's group or passing over a name card on which gang affiliation is shown, combined with a request coming under the provisions of Article 9, is a 'violent demand'.

The categories of demands prohibited under the provisions of Article 9 are as follows:

1. Demanding money, goods, or other benefits in return for not revealing secrets about the victim of these demands.
2. Demanding donations and contributions for whatever reason.
3. Demanding contract work or the supply of goods.
4. Demanding that individuals pay a fee in order to conduct business within the designated *bōryokudan*'s territory.
5. Demanding that businesses operating within the *bōryokudan*'s territory purchase goods, or certificates, or that they pay for bodyguard or other services.
6. Demanding payment of interest rates in excess of the maximum rate allowed under the 1954 Interest Limitation Law. Demanding compensation for non-payment of debts in contravention of the same law. Making a nuisance, on behalf of creditors, in connection with debt repayment.
7. Demanding postponement or non-repayment of debt either in part or in full.
8. Demanding loans on favourable terms, demanding loans in spite of refusal, demanding loans of individuals not involved in the money-lending business.
9. Demanding that site or building occupiers leave and give up title to that site or building.
10. Entering into discussions concerning a traffic dispute or other incident and demanding compensation for damages incurred.
11. Demanding compensation for damage or injury due to a traffic accident or other incident. Demanding compensation for losses due to changes in stock or goods prices.

If a member of a designated *bōryokudan* group makes a demand falling under the provisions of Article 9 then the victim of the demand can notify the authorities and the Public Safety Commission is empowered to issue an injunction (*chūshi meirei*) preventing the member from making these demands. In cases where the Public Safety Commission judges that a designated *bōryokudan* member is likely to make similar demands in the future it can issue an injunction prohibiting a recurrence of that type of demand (*saihatsu meirei*). This type of injunction remains in force for no more than a year. The Public

Safety Commission is also empowered to issue an injunction prohibit-ing designated *bōryokudan* members from making violent demands in order to force juveniles (under Japanese law those under 20 years of age) to join their gang.

Before a *saihatsu meirei* injunction is issued, the Public Safety Commission in question must hold a public hearing concerning that injunction. The time and place of this hearing must be publicly displayed beforehand and the *bōryokudan* member responsible for the alleged demands informed of the time, place, and reason for the hear-ing. These hearings may, however, be held in private if it is thought necessary for reasons of confidentiality. If it is not possible to contact the *bōryokudan* member in question or if he does not show up within 30 days of the public notification, then the injunction can be issued with-out recourse to a public hearing. A provisional injunction (*kari no meirei*) can also be issued in cases of great urgency when there is not time to arrange a public hearing. Provisional orders are effective for a period of no more than 15 days, within which time a hearing must be held.

As well as dealing with 'violent demands' by members of desig-nated *bōryokudan*, the Public Safety Commissions are able to issue injunctions concerning the use of gang offices. During times of inter-gang conflicts and if the Public Safety Commission judges that there is a risk that this office will be used for assembling groups of gang members, or command and control, or the storage or construction of weaponry concerned with this conflict, then it can issue an order lasting for up to three months preventing the use of this office. An injunction can also be issued if it is judged that office use during periods of intergang conflict endangers the public. This injunction can be extended for a further three months.

Even during periods of peace, there are certain restrictions imposed by this new law on the use of gang offices. Publicly displaying signs in the vicinity of gang offices (or inside in such a way that they can be seen by passers-by) that the Public Safety Commission judges likely to intimidate members of the general public are liable to a Public Safety Commission order for their removal. Acts in the vicinity of gang offices, which are judged to similarly upset the general public, are also potentially subject to an injunction prohibiting their repetition.

The penalties for violating an injunction issued by a Public Safety Commission under the provisions of this law are, at their most severe, up to 1-year imprisonment, a fine of up to ¥1,000,000 or a combination of the two. Less serious violations carry the penalty of six months' imprisonment, a fine of up to ¥500,000 or a combination of the two. For the least significant infractions a fine of up to ¥250,000 is payable.

In addition to the provisions concerned with controlling *bōryokudan* violent demands and limiting the use of their offices, the *Bōtaihō* also takes measures designed to encourage the eradication of these groups and assist their victims. Central to this end is the designation of Centres for the Elimination of *Bōryokudan* (*Bōryoku Tsuihō Undō Suishin Sentā*) in each administrative region (*Todōfuken*). Designation of a centre is at the discretion of the National Public Safety Commission but each region is to have no more than one centre and, to qualify, an applicant must meet certain minimum requirements. First, it must be a legal entity (*hōjin*) under the terms of the civil law. It must also have personnel with the necessary expertise and be otherwise capable of accomplishing the various tasks required of it.

There are ten separate responsibilities that the centres are given under the provisions of the *Bōtaihō* and they are as follows:

1. Running publicity campaigns to increase public awareness of the threat posed by *bōryokudan*.
2. Providing help to non-governmental anti-*bōryokudan* movements.
3. Holding discussions with, and offering advice to, victims of *bōryokudan* demands.
4. Taking measures to remove the harmful influence of *bōryokudan* on juveniles.
5. Taking measures to help *bōryokudan* members who wish to leave.
6. Operating training courses for employees of businesses particularly susceptible to violent *bōryokudan* demands.
7. Providing assistance to the appropriate bodies dealing with information on *bōryokudan* violent demands.
8. Providing help for victims of *bōryokudan* violent demands with civil suits, making contact with *bōryokudan* groups to facilitate the return of goods and money, and providing sympathy money (*mimaikin*).
9. Conducting training for youth instruction officers.
10. Conducting the administration necessary for the above-mentioned tasks.

Under the provisions of the law the National Public Safety Commission also designates a body as the National Centre for the

Elimination of *Bōryokudan* (*Zenkoku Bōryoku Tsuihō Undō Suishin Sentā*). This centre is responsible for overseeing the operations of the regional centres, providing the necessary training for their specialist staff and conducting research on the social impact of *bōryokudan*.

Revisions of the *Bōtaihō*

Since the law was introduced it has been revised twice, once in May 1993, and then again in May 1997. The purpose in both cases was, mainly, to expand the scope of the law to take into account ways that designated *bōryokudan* had adapted their operations to avoid the main provisions of the *Bōtaihō*.

The 1993 revision had four main themes. The first of these was concerned with encouraging the process of secession and rehabilitation of members of these organisations. Whilst the original law had attempted to restrict the manpower of the designated *bōryokudan* by prohibiting forcible recruitment of juveniles, it had not taken adequate steps to encourage secession and rehabilitation of gang members. To rectify this, the 1993 revision contained provisions prohibiting the obstruction of members wishing to leave their organisation. In particular, demanding either finger amputation or money as a mark of contrition before leaving, could be subject to an injunction. As both amputated fingers and body tattoos were identified as major obstacles to successful rehabilitation, demands that a juvenile member have a tattoo also came under the provisions of the revised law. In order that these provisions could be deployed against the gang bosses and executives as well as ordinary *kumi-in*, it was also prohibited to request or order another gang member to make these demands.

The second measure of the 1993 revision was concerned with tightening up the provisions concerned with forcible recruitment of juveniles. It had become apparent that, rather than putting direct pressure on the juvenile in question, designated *bōryokudan* members were putting pressure on close relatives or people with a close relationship (*missetsu kankeisha*) with that juvenile. Such activity was therefore included under the provisions of the revised law. Similarly ordering, entreating, or relying on other people to make demands that a juvenile join a designated *bōryokudan* group became liable to an injunction.

From the limited success at attempts to rehabilitate gang-seceders, it became apparent that the vaguely worded duty of the Centres for the Elimination of *Bōryokudan* to 'assist those people who wish to leave *bōryokudan*' must be expanded. In particular the regional centres were required to provide the necessary advice to those gang members wishing to leave (*ridatsu kibōsha*) and facilitate their transition to a normal social environment. The most important aspect of successful rehabilitation is employment; so the centres were also obliged to conduct public-awareness campaigns to reduce discrimination against former *bōryokudan* members. It was also recognised that the centres would have to increase cooperation with related groups such as probation officers (*hogoshi*), correctional institutions (*kyōsei shisetsu*), and the Employment Security Administration (*Shokugyō Antei Gyōsei Kikan*).

The final part of the 1993 revisions was the increase in the categories of violent demands covered by the provisions of Article 9. There were three new categories and they were a direct response to developments in *bōryokudan* activity since the introduction of the *Bōtaihō*. The first of these prohibited designated *bōryokudan* members from demanding that stockbrokers should let them conduct share-trading on credit or that they should waive the usual conditions for credit-trading (Article 9 paragraph 9). Second, demanding that companies sell shares, or demanding that shares be sold on favourable terms, also became liable to an injunction (Article 9 paragraph 10). Finally, in response to the increased involvement of *bōryokudan* in auction obstruction following the collapse of the bubble (see Chapter 7), prohibitions were made against making demands for compensation with respect to leaving premises or removing gang paraphernalia (Article 9 paragraph 12).

In addition, several of the pre-existing categories of violent demands contained in Article 9 were expanded. Paragraph 5, concerning demands for bodyguard fees etc, now includes a prohibition against selling entrance tickets to *bōryokudan*-connected shows or parties. Demands for discounts on the sale of promissory notes was included in paragraph 8, and the provisions of paragraph 14 were enlarged to cover making demands for compensation on a spurious or inflated pretext.

Although the pre-revision law had forbidden non-gang members from asking, or hiring, designated *bōryokudan* members to make violent demands, there were no provisions covering non-member participation in these activities. This was rectified in the 1993 revision, which made the act of assisting a designated *bōryokudan* member to make violent demands liable to a *Bōtaihō* administrative order.

The 1997 revision of the *Bōtaihō* contained five changes, which further expanded the scope of this law. The first of these was to create another category of demand coming under the umbrella of Article 9. This was the 'collection of debts under unjust circumstances' (*futō na taiyō ni yoru saiken toritate*). Under Article 9 paragraph 6 of the pre-revision law there had been provisions concerning the collection of debts that violated the Interest Limitation Law but not of normal fully legitimate debts. Under Article 9 paragraph 6.2 of the revised law, the use of 'phone calls, visits, and rough language or other actions causing a nuisance', by members of designated *bōryokudan* demanding repayment of these debts, became actionable.

The second change brought about by the 1997 revision was the widening of the scope of the possible subjects of Public Safety Commission injunctions. Under the original law, an injunction would be issued with respect only to the perpetrator of a violent demand. This meant that typically lower-level *kumi-in* would become subject to such injunctions whilst the higher authority responsible for directing violent demands would remain untouched. To remedy this it became possible under Article 12 paragraph 2 of the revised law to issue injunctions to those designated *bōryokudan* members in positions of authority over those violating the provisions of Article 9 (*jōisha sekinin seido*).

Since the introduction of the *Bōtaihō*, it had become clear to the authorities that a large number of designated *bōryokudan* members were successfully circumventing the provisions of the law. This was achieved by what the NPA came to describe as 'semi-violent demands' (*jun-bōryokuteki na yōkyū*). Semi-violent demands are those acts, which would come under the provisions of Article 9 were they carried out by designated *bōryokudan* members, but are instead carried out by people who, though not members themselves, employ the threat of a designated group to reinforce these demands. The 1997 revision therefore took account of this development by expanding the scope of Article 9 to include demands made by peripheral figures (*shūhensha*), such as *jun-kōsei-in* and *kigyō shatei* (Article 12 paragraphs 3–6).

Owing to the inclusion of semi-violent demands within the remit of Article 9, a further revision was made to expand the provisions concerning assistance for victims of *bōryokudan* demands so as to include people who had been subject to this class of demands (Article 13).

Another trend in the post-*bōtaihō bōryokudan* was the further oligo-polisation of the large wide-area syndicates. This process, combined with reduced opportunities to make money following the collapse of the bubble economy, meant that different groups within the same syndicate increasingly came into conflict with one another. This increased the risk of intra-syndicate warfare. Whilst, under Article 15 of the pre-revision law, it was possible to restrict the use of gang offices in times of intergang conflicts, intra-group struggles had not been included. This was rectified in Article 15 paragraph 2. As will be shown in Chapter Six, the timing of this was most fortunate for the police.

Analysis of the *Bōtaihō*

As can be seen from the description of this law above, the *Bōtaihō* is a very different type of organised-crime countermeasure from either the European model of outright criminalisation, or the American RICO statutes with their use of whole-organisation prosecution and substantial seizure provisions. The fundamental difference is that both RICO and the European model are parts of the criminal legal code (although RICO also contains extensive civil components), whilst the *Bōtaihō* falls under the category of administrative law (*gyōsei hō*). The significance of this difference is that acts that violate the criminal law can be subject to prosecution and punishment whilst behaviour coming under the provisions of administrative law is subject to an injunction directing the perpetrator to stop. It is only when that injunction is violated that punishment can be administered.

Comparatively, therefore, the *Bōtaihō* seems at first glance to be a weak weapon in the fight against organised crime. It should, however, be noted that this law also differs from RICO in that it is essentially concerned with only one type of organised crime activity, namely the exploitation of a group's reputation in order to secure financial or other advantage. As has been noted above, these *minbō*-type activities fall short of extortion or intimidation as defined under the criminal law. It would be practically impossible to frame provisions under the criminal code, which could effectively tackle this type of activity without the law also applying to legitimate social exchanges. Owing to this fact, it is arguable the use of administrative law is more appropriate to deal with *bōryokudan* intervention in civil disputes and other 'grey-zone' operations.

Whilst it is very different from the two foreign models, the *Bōtaihō* combines features of both. In creating a separate class of individuals who are to receive different treatment under the law because of their connection with a criminal organisation, the *Bōtaihō* has similarities to the European model. At the same time, in creating a new category of actionable behaviour ('violent demands' or 'pattern of racketeering') supposedly specific to OCGs, there are similarities between RICO and the *Bōtaihō*. Although the *Bōtaihō* is, in this respect, a hybrid organised-crime countermeasure, it lacks the most potent features of either RICO or European-style criminalisation.

From the comparative weakness of the penalties and the restriction of the *Bōtaihō* to one area of *yakuza* activity, it is apparent that, *ceteris paribus*, the introduction of this law cannot achieve the goal, declared by the police, of eradicating these groups. At best, and assuming that it actually works as described, it will only drive out gang participation in *minbō*, protection, and those other categories of 'violent demand' covered by Article 9, without reducing the many other, more overtly criminal, enterprises in which the *yakuza* are engaged.

In fact, there are very good reasons for believing that the *Bōtaihō* will fail to achieve even that. First, and at a most basic level, it must be noted that the *bōryokudan* have not refrained from acts just because they are out-with the bounds of legality. If we accept that economic rationality is applicable to OCGs,[5] then if the projected costs are only marginally raised by a change in the law (or level of enforcement) and benefits remain constant and above expected costs (the costs of punishment multiplied by the probability of being caught), then little or no change is to be expected. It can be seen from the description of the *Bōtaihō* above that the penalties are light compared to those for either RICO violation or membership of a mafia-style association in Italy. Moreover, because *bōryokudan*[6] 'violent demands' are first to be met with an injunction rather than a concrete penalty, there are no immediate material costs to making these demands until an injunction has been issued. It is, of course, possible that less tangible costs such as the loss of face incurred in backing down when confronted by an injunction may be taken into account.

The theoretical analysis expounded earlier suggests the relationship between organised crime and other socio-economic entities is complex and not entirely predatory. Although they may be overpriced, there are services provided by organised-crime groups especially to those for whom the law fails to provide adequate protection. In particular, those involved in *mizu shōbai*, such as bars and sexual-entertainment establishments, may rely on these groups for protection not just from organised-crime predation, but from problematic customers. To what extent the *Bōtaihō* can be expected to limit protection racketeering (*mikajimeryō*) cannot therefore be determined *a priori* but it is unlikely to eliminate it totally.

Despite these potential weaknesses, the *Bōtaihō* was seen as 'epoch making' by many commentators, both opposing and supporting this law (Ino 1992*b*: 50; Boku 1997: 27; Uchiyama et al. in interview). This was not just because the new law was targeting activities that were hitherto immune from legal intervention, or because of the novel way in which it tackled them. The *Bōtaihō* was seen as a clear break in that, for the first time, there was a legal definition of *bōryokudan* and a law existed that specifically and explicitly identified these groups as a social evil to be subject to special controls. In addition, therefore, to the substantive provisions of the new law, the symbolic significance of the *Bōtaihō* must be considered in evaluating the impact of this legal change. The full significance of this will be seen when we examine post-*bōtaihō yakuza* behaviour.

Although the *Bōtaihō* was passed unanimously by both Houses of the Diet, this should not be interpreted as an indication of universal approval. In fact, it met with criticism both from those considering it excessive and from those who felt the new law to be risibly feeble and quite inadequate for the task of eradicating the *yakuza*. Boku (1997: 28) categorises these groups as the anti-control lobby and the pro-control lobby, respectively. The anti-control group had effectively five main criticisms of the law: its conflict with the constitution; its potential extension to groups other than *yakuza*; the increase in police powers it introduces; the possibility of the police hi-jacking the autonomous anti-*yakuza* movement; the lack of attention to underlying causal factors; and the role played in Japanese society by *yakuza/bōryokudan* groups.

The major criticism of the new law put forward by those opposing the increase in state powers was that it conflicted with the constitution. Fukuda (1992: 24) sees the attitude one has towards this law as a 'litmus test' as to whether or not one understands the values on which the postwar constitution was based.

Article 98 of the 1947 Constitution states:

This Constitution shall be the supreme law of the nation and no law, ordinance, imperial rescript or other act of government, or part thereof, contrary to the prescriptions hereof, shall have legal force or validity.

The charge that the *Bōtaihō* conflicts with the Constitution is therefore a most serious one. Under Article 21 of the Constitution, the freedom of assembly and association is guaranteed. This is usually cited as the reason why the Japanese could not adopt a European-style law criminalising membership of a *bōryokudan* group. It was argued by these critics of the *Bōtaihō* that this law interfered with this freedom and was therefore unconstitutional. As the *Bōtaihō* does not actually penalise membership *per se*, but acts which these members commit, this criticism can be questioned. What is much harder to refute is the argument that the new law conflicts with Article 14, which affirms the equality of all citizens under the law and that there shall be no discrimination 'because of race, creed, sex, social status or family origin'. The second criterion for *bōryokudan* designation under the *Bōtaihō* is the proportion of members with a criminal record. This, it was argued, is a clear case of discrimination. Whilst this is the case, it should be noted that discrimination against those with a criminal record is not specifically covered by Article 14 of the Constitution.

However, the equality-under-law argument seems more telling. Under the *Bōtaihō*, an action committed by the member, or following the 1997 revision, an associate, of a designated *bōryokudan* is subject to legal prohibition, whilst this is not the case when the same action is carried out by a person with no *bōryokudan* connection. That this conflicts with the letter and the spirit of Article 14 appears to be unambiguous. However, as can be seen from the existence of the Self Defence Forces despite Article nine's assertion that 'land, sea and air forces, as well as other war potential, will never be maintained', it has long been possible to interpret the constitution in more than one way.

The second main argument deployed by the opponents of increased legal controls was that these new powers would be deployed against not only *bōryokudan* members, but also left-wing groups and trade unions. This fear is based on historical precedents. For example, the 1926 Law Concerning the Punishment of Violent Activities (*Bōryoku*

Kōi nado Shobatsu ni Kan-suru Hōritsu) was used to repress the labour movement during the early Shōwa period. This was despite the fact that at the time of its introduction the cabinet issued assurances that it was 'a law to control *yakuza* ... it won't be applied to the left-wing movement' (Endō 1992: 28).

Similarly, in 1958, the criminal law was amended to include the crime of assembling with lethal weapons. Contemporary Diet records show that the government made similar assurances that it was a law designed to control gang conflicts and would not be used to combat the left. However, two years later, this law was frequently used in an attempt to control students and unions during, and after, the *Ampō* disturbances (1992: 28). The way in which these laws have been employed out of their original ostensible remit has left those on the political left with a deep-rooted suspicion of the police.

To support this argument, a number of critics, such as Fukuda (1992: 26) and Ino (1992*b*: 51), have pointed out that the foundations on which this law is built are vague: the two key definitions, 'illegal violent activity' and '*bōryokudan*', ultimately rest on the subjective interpretation of the National Public Safety Commission. 'Illegal violent activities' are those illegal acts which are so defined at the discretion of the NPSC. Endō (1992: 29–33) argues that many of the legal provisions included amongst those categorising illegal violent activities are measures which have traditionally been deployed against left-wing groups. Some of these 'illegal activities' are not typical of *bōryokudan* such as the use of fire-bombs. Moreover, employing the implicit threat of an organisation's power in order to gain some economic advantage, which is the central concern of Article 9, is hardly unique to the *bōryokudan*; it is, for example, the *raison d'être* for trade unionism.

Police interviewees have pointed out that these arguments are groundless in that there is the additional, and more objective, necessary criterion for designation: the presence of a given proportion of members with criminal records. Indeed, they argue that the reason for including this criterion was precisely to exclude the possibility that the law would be applied to suppress legitimate political expression. The third main criticism deployed against the *Bōtaihō* by the anti-control lobby follows on from the second. Given the widespread fear and mistrust of the police amongst left-wing and many liberal commentators, an extension of police powers will inevitably be a cause for alarm. From a reading of the law, it seems at first that at each stage of its operation there are checks on the police provided by the provisions requiring hearings and ratification by the various Public Safety Commissions. If these bodies actually operated as envisaged in the 1954 Police Law, then they would provide oversight of the *Bōtaihō*'s implementation. However, as will be discussed later, the work of the Public Safety Commissions is effectively carried out by the police. The checks provided for by the *Bōtaihō* are therefore an irrelevance. As so much of the detail required for the actual operation of the law is 'left at the discretion of the Public Safety Commission', and because the law provides for no appeals procedure further than the National Public Safety Commission, the introduction of the *Bōtaihō* does indeed represent a significant, unchecked increase in police powers.

The introduction of the Centres for the Elimination of *Bōryokudan* also came in for criticism from the anti-control lobby. It was argued that the official imposition of anti-*bōryokudan* centres would stifle the pre-existing citizens' movements opposing gang activity. These movements had sprung up spontaneously as an expression of local communities' reactions to their own experiences of the *yakuza*. Imposing bureaucratic or police control over these groups would radically change their character so that they no longer reflected the needs or aspirations of the communities from which they had sprung.

Whilst there is nothing in the law that explicitly states that these centres will be police-controlled, the fact that designation of regional centres is in the power of the NPSC suggests that this would be a strong possibility. As will be shown in Chapter Six, this has in fact happened and, despite formal independence, the regional centres are located within the prefectural police headquarters, and the permanent staff are retired police officers. Whilst there may be ample justification for this on the grounds for expertise and experience, it does leave the police open to the charges of empire-building and generating *amakudari*[6] positions for former employees.

The final charge of the anti-control tendency was that the law is fundamentally flawed as an anti-*bōryokudan* measure in that it fails to recognise the close links which exist between these groups and members of Japan's political, financial, and law-enforcement communities. As has been mentioned above, attempts to eradicate organised crime without adequately dealing with the various aetiological factors cannot be expected to meet with complete success. If the *Bōtaihō* were really to be judged as the central pillar in a *yakuza* eradication programme, then this criticism would be pertinent. However, if we accept that it has the more limited aim of removing *yakuza* from civil disputes and legitimate industry, this argument loses its relevance.

It can also be argued that the work for which the Centres for the Elimination of *Bōryokudan* are responsible includes tackling some of the broader social considerations concerning the *yakuza*'s place in Japanese society. It is debatable, however, just how effective public-awareness campaigns and training of employees responsible for dealing with *yakuza* can be when their employing companies are benefiting from links with these same groups. As the Centre's propaganda implicitly accepts when it exhorts the public 'don't make use of *bōryokudan*', these groups have been used. A comprehensive *yakuza*-eradication programme must take this into account.

The *yakuza* themselves took on board these arguments as well as putting forward several of their own. There were essentially three supplementary arguments employed by *yakuza* groups against the new law. The first of these is that they provide a valuable control function within the Japanese underworld. They operate as employers of last resort to violent, ill-educated, and otherwise unemployable young males, subjecting them to a hard code of discipline and control. Without this, these individuals would be wandering the streets causing random trouble. It is true that newly inducted trainees are subject to a harsh regime of training in which correct manners are beaten into them. However, this argument lacks the validity it would have had in the days when the primary sources of *yakuza* income were gambling and festival stall-holding. In an age of *minbō* and corporate blackmail, the question must be asked whether centrally controlled, organised violence is preferable to its disorganised, random equivalent.

The second *yakuza* critique of the *Bōtaihō* is that the protection role they have traditionally played within the entertainment industry has had the valuable social side-effect of policing the streets of their respective territories. Gang members argued that, without this service, the level of disorganised street-crime would rise as there would no longer be an effective deterrent to juvenile delinquents. Similarly, it is argued that, with the disappearance of *yakuza* from the *mizu shōbai* industry, their place would be filled with less-scrupulous Chinese and other foreign criminal groups (Ino 1994: 10–15).

Even if we accept that there is a policing function, this argument is open to question; if the *yakuza* actually provide a service within the

mizu-shōbai industry, then the *Bōtaihō* is not likely to have any noticeable effect on *yakuza* participation in this sector. With respect to displacement by Chinese criminal gangs, it can be argued that these
groups can equally be subject to designation as *yakuza* under the provisions of the *Bōtaihō* as well as those of the criminal law (though
admittedly police intelligence concerning these groups is harder to
accumulate than that for the native Japanese groups).

A more significant criticism of this law coming from the gangs themselves is that the effect of the law will be to exacerbate the problem that
they pose both to the police and the wider Japanese society. Driven out
of business activities at the margins of legality and unable to make open
use of their gangs' reputations, gang members will become increasingly
reliant on income from amphetamines and theft in order to survive. As
they become more overtly criminal in nature, the *bōryokudan* will necessarily sink further underground and become increasingly like America's
LCN (which, the *yakuza* insist, they have never resembled). The *Bōtaihō*
will therefore prove to be counter-productive.

As has been seen from the description of police, anti-*yakuza* efforts
in the 1960s and 1970s as presented in Chapter Two, and the general
discussion of the problems of organised-crime countermeasures
provided in this chapter as well, increased enforcement in one sector
of gang activity can result in displacement to new areas of criminality.
This may well result in a net loss to society. Therefore, this prediction
seems highly plausible, and cannot be refuted *a priori*. For this reason,
special attention must be paid to this point when we examine the
effects of the *Bōtaihō*.

On the other side of the ideological barricades, the pro-control lobby
criticised both the liberal and left-wing proponents of the arguments
above as anachronistic *yakuza*-apologists, and the law itself for its lack
of teeth. Although the arguments outlined below are largely derived
from Katō (1991), they are representative of views held by senior
police-related interviewees unable to speak on-record. The first major
drawback, according to this perspective, is that the most potent items
contained in the research group's report, 'Basic Considerations', were
dropped from the final legislation. With the watering-down of the law,
the 'movement to eradicate the *bōryokudan* ends up as a mere declaration' (Katō 1991: 52).

In particular, the failure to include provisions for seizure of *yakuza*
assets was a major object of criticism. On this point, the pro-control

critics divided into those who demanded the introduction of a tough RICO-style law and those who suggested that this was unnecessary as the existing criminal law already contained provisions for seizure (Article 19). It was argued by the second group that these little-used provisions should be more pro-actively deployed against *yakuza*. The problem with this line of argument, the RICO advocates point out, is that the existing law would fail to deal with the considerable assets held by top-level bosses and executives derived from *jōnōkin* (1991: 53); under the provisions of Article 19 of the criminal law, only assets that can be directly linked to crimes can be seized (*Bōryokudan Taisaku Roppō* 1997: 480).

Katō also attacks the failure to include outright criminalisation of *bōryokudan* membership in the new law. Having gone to the trouble of providing a legal definition of *bōryokudan* clearly identifying them as criminal organisations, why stop at administratively curtailing their 'violent demands'? Given that the constitutionality of the *Bōtaihō* is already questionable, and that the constitution is interpreted loosely in other areas, the argument that criminalisation would violate the constitution's guarantee of freedom of association lacks force. It seems reasonable to assume that there are therefore more practical reasons for excluding this measure from *yakuza* countermeasures.

One such reason is that, despite the apparent simplicity of criminalisation, there are clear operational problems in applying it within the Japanese context. Police figures for 1989 give total *bōryokudan* membership of 86,552 identified men (*Keisatsu Hakusho* 1989: 15). The Japanese prison population in the same year was only 45,736 (*Hanzai Hakusho* 1997: 252). Would criminalisation result in almost trebling the overall prison population? Regardless of the cost of such a measure, would it be desirable? In the vacuum left by mass *yakuza* incarceration, what sort of groups would appear to meet consumer demand and take control of legally prohibited markets? Even mass fines could overload Japan's creaky judicial system to the point of collapse.

Katō argues that, even if a criminalisation law is not introduced, it is possible to employ the Subversive Activities Prevention Law (*Hakai Katsudō Bōshi Hō* or, more simply, *Habōhō*) to order the disbanding of organised-crime groups. This law has fallen into disuse (largely because of its discredited history as a tool for attacking left-wing students and other radical groups) and its use remains politically sensitive. It would indeed be ironic for it to be used as an anti-*yakuza* measure, because politicians had mobilised a shock-force of *tekiya* street-fighters to counteract the demonstrators trying to prevent this law's enactment.

It is similarly argued that other laws, already existing in the criminal code, could be more robustly employed to drive *yakuza* groups out of existence. Katō identifies the 1926 Law Concerning the Punishment of Violent Activities (*Bōryoku Kōi nado Shobatsu ni Kansuru Hōritsu*) as being particularly useful since it includes provisions dealing with collective violence and the showing of a group's threat (Article 1), customary and collective blackmail, and intimidation in interviews and discussions (Article 2), and entrusting others to commit acts of violence (Article 3) (*Bōryokudan Taisaku Roppō* 1997: 516). As mentioned above, although this law was used largely to suppress left-wing dissent, at the time of its introduction it was claimed to be a law specifically to combat the *yakuza*. Although Katō claims that Article 2 of this law could be used to deal with *minbō* and *sōkaiya* scams, the way in which many of these activities are at the margins of legality would make practical application very difficult. It is precisely this grey zone, which the *Bōtaihō* is designed to tackle.

It would be satisfying to show that the existing criminal law contained all the necessary provisions to adequately combat the *yakuza*. If this were the case, then it would be reasonable to conclude that the *Bōtaihō* had been introduced for the purely symbolic reason of showing, to both the domestic and international audience, that the authorities were 'getting tough' with the *yakuza*. Several academic, as well as senior and retired law-enforcement-related, interviewees asserted that the legal structure prior to the *Bōtaihō* was indeed sufficient to control these groups. However, it is by no means certain that courts would accept stretching the law to encompass scams which the *yakuza* had painstakingly developed to avoid infringing those same laws. In this respect, the *Bōtaihō* does seem to have a role that is not adequately filled by other laws.

The criticism that the existing laws should be employed more robustly does not seem to be a coherent criticism of the *Bōtaihō*. The introduction of this new law does not logically preclude a more aggressive use of these other laws. The mistake of many critics of the *Bōtaihō* was to fall under the spell of its hype and to see it as an all-encompassing *bōryokudan*-countermeasures law. If we view it more realistically as one weapon in a wider armoury, then this criticism loses relevance. Whether the introduction of the *Bōtaihō* was matched with stricter enforcement of other laws, will be investigated in Chapter Six.

Conclusion

The *Bōtaihō*, despite its description as epoch-making, is a comparatively mild organised-crime-countermeasures law. Compared to either the European model of criminalisation, or the United States' RICO statutes (both of which were highly influential in the debate within Japan on framing the *Bōtaihō*), its scope and penalties are small. Given that this is the case, the question must be asked whether the authorities are serious in their professed aim of *yakuza* eradication. For a comprehensive anti-*yakuza* drive, the introduction of the *Bōtaihō* would need to be accompanied by significantly increased use of the existing criminal law.

The influence of foreign pressure and the reaction to repeated political scandals as catalysts in the creation of this law suggest that a certain degree of symbolism may be involved. However, it seems fair to accept that the new law does have a role to play in reducing the adverse effects of *yakuza* intervention in the private and business affairs of law-abiding members of society. To what extent this has been successful will be examined in the following chapter.

6

Heisei *Yakuza*—Burst Bubble and *Bōtaihō*

Scandals

Around the same time as the *Bōtaihō* was being prepared and passed through the Diet, a succession of scandals came to light, which provided the world with a glimpse of the nature of the relationship that the *yakuza* enjoyed with both business and political elites. These incidents also illustrated clearly that the police estimates for *yakuza* income discussed in Chapter Four significantly underplayed the amounts of money that these groups were generating from financial and business sectors through both the provision of various protection services and more straightforward extortion. Most significant of these incidents were the Sagawa Kyūbin scandal (with its related scandals of the Kōmintō and Heiwa Sōgō Ginkō incidents) and the Itoman scandal.

Although throughout the early postwar period of the 1950s and 1960s, the links between politicians and underworld figures had been, more or less, openly displayed, since the 1970s it had been generally felt that such open connections were no longer an electoral asset. By 1979, when Stark was conducting his fieldwork, the operation of the *yakuza*-centred 'clique' occurred behind closed doors. Whilst cases of *yakuza*-related politicians appeared from time to time, they tended to involve individuals who had fallen into serious debt and lacked more acceptable financial backing. However, the complex web of the

Sagawa Kyūbin scandal revealed that the two most powerful and well-funded politicians in Japan at the end of 1980s were making direct use of the *yakuza*.

In 1992, prosecutors started investigating the activities of Sagawa Kyūbin, a parcel-delivery company. During the course of these investigations it became apparent that, in 1989 Watanabe Hiroyasu, the then president of Tokyo Sagawa Kyūbin, had provided Kanemaru Shin, the then LDP vice-president and king-maker, with ¥500 m ($3.6 m) in cash. Approximately 100 other politicians also received money, totalling more than ¥2 bn, from Watanabe, including those in positions of influence in the Ministries of Transport and Labour. Because of the highly regulated nature of this particular industry, Sagawa Kyūbin had found it prudent to maintain good relations with important political figures.[1] Watanabe also used his connections with Kanemaru to keep Tokyo Sagawa Kyūbin's bankers from causing trouble over the company's outstanding debts, which at the time stood at around ¥500 bn ($3.6 bn) (*Japan Access* 31 August 1992). As the investigation continued, however, it revealed more than a simple case of business–political corruption.

In May 1987, a party was held at the Tokyo Prince Hotel in Minato ward as part of Takeshita Noboru's campaign to gain the LDP nomination for Prime Minister in the forthcoming general election. During the course of this event, seven armoured trucks, equipped with public-announcement equipment (*sendensha*), circled the hotel with their speakers blaring out exhortations to 'support Takeshita for prime-minister for the straight reform of politics'. Over the following months, these trucks cruised round Nagatachō, Japan's political centre, encouraging people to 'make Takeshita prime-minister—in all Japan he's the best at making money'. Far from furthering Takeshita's political ambitions, the purpose of this campaign was to destroy Takeshita's career by 'killing with praise' (*homegoroshi*).

This black propaganda campaign was launched by an obscure extreme right-wing organisation, of about forty members, from Kagawa prefecture, called the Nihon Kōmintō (which translates roughly as the Emperor's Subjects' Party of Japan). This group had been founded by the former Shirakami-gumi gang *wakagashira* (underboss), Inamoto Torao, who had left his gang to follow a political career, when it was taken over by the Yamaguchi-gumi in the early 1970s. Inamoto retained his links with his former gang through gang boss Shirakami Hideo, who became the Nihon Komintō's advisor.

He also held a brother relationship with Takumi Masaru, the then Yamaguchi-gumi *wakagashira hōsa* (assistant under-boss).

In response to the Kōmintō's *homegoroshi*, a number of parliamentarians from Takeshita's faction approached Inamoto to try and persuade him to cease this attack. Most notable of these politicians was Hamada Kōichi, who had formerly been a full member of the Inagawa-kai and still, some felt, retained a nodding acquaintance with the underworld. Despite this persuasion, Inamoto refused to call his trucks back to Kagawa prefecture.

Therefore, late in the summer of 1987, Kanemaru approached Watanabe, the Tokyo Sagawa Kyūbin president, and discussed the problem with him expressing the fear that, if the Kōmintō continued to undermine Takeshita, then prime minister Nakasone might withdraw his nomination of Takeshita as his successor. In response to this, Watanabe suggested that Ishii Susumu would be the person best qualified to deal with the Kōmintō. Kanemaru therefore entrusted Watanabe to seek Ishii's help.

In turn, Ishii approached Mikami Tadashi, the boss of an Aizu-kotetsu subgroup, with whom Ishii enjoyed a close relationship. Mikami also knew Inamoto and was therefore capable of introducing the two men. Inamoto refused to accept money but agreed to stop his propaganda campaign if Takeshita were to go and apologise to his former patron, Tanaka Kakuei, for betraying him. Mikami fixed the day for this visit for 5 October. However, when Takeshita went to make his apology, he called it off at the last minute due to the large number of press reporters waiting at the gates for him. Eventually, the following day, Takeshita appeared at the gates of Tanaka's compound in Mejirodai to pay his respects only to find that, once more, the assembled ranks of the press were waiting for him. Both Inamoto and Mikami had tipped them off.

In February the following year, Kanemaru approached Ishii directly to resolve another problem. Hamada Kōichi, the former Inagawa-kai member and parliamentarian, had publicly called a colleague a murderer. Kanemaru wanted Hamada to resign from his position as chairman of the Lower House Budget Committee as penance for this and secured Ishii's help in persuading him to do this. Ishii was also responsible for silencing right-wing criticism of Kanemaru following his trip to North Korea in 1990. In December 1988, Kanemaru personally thanked Ishii by inviting him to a high-class traditional

Japanese restaurant. The public testimony given later by one of those present reveals that both Kanemaru and Ishii offered the other the place of honour at the head of the table. Furthermore, Kanemaru praised Ishii's 'thing' as 'real chivalry' (*Kyōdō* 1993: 118–28; Mizoguchi 1997: 114–25; Schlesinger 1997: 246; *Japan Access* 10 August 1992; *Reuters* 5 November 1992).

These extraordinary revelations generate two questions: first, why did Inamoto launch his negative publicity campaign against Takeshita? Second, why did Takeshita and Kanemaru treat such a small and insignificant political group as the Kōmintō so seriously? The usual answer provided at the time by the press to the first question is that Inamoto was outraged by the way in which Takeshita had betrayed his mentor and patron, Tanaka Kakuei. Takeshita had secretly created a faction within the Tanaka faction and, alongside Kanemaru and their lieutenant Ozawa Ichirō, used this to usurp Tanaka's position as power broker and financial fountainhead. The fact that Inamoto refused offers of ¥3 bn at the time (though he later received a small 'political contribution' of ¥50 m from Ishii) would seem at first glance to support that.[2]

Kyōdō (1993), however, suggests an alternative explanation that Inamoto had had a financial relationship with Takeshita's office in his home constituency in Shimane prefecture. This had later been terminated and Inamoto intended to wreak his revenge on Takeshita for this. *Kyōdō* cites an executive of the Nippon Seinensha, a right-wing organisation with links to the Sumiyoshi-kai, to illustrate the prevalence of this type of link in Japanese politics:

In elections, a number of LDP candidates are running in the same constituency. If a local right wing group backs one candidate, then other right wing groups quickly appear on the scene. Nearly all LDP Diet members have these links.[3] However, in front of the microphone, they make out that *bōryokudan* and right wing extremists are disgraceful (*Kyōdō* 1993: 130).

If this hypothesis were correct, it seems probable that other commentators would have picked up on the Kōmintō's links to Takeshita. Admitting this link to the public prosecutors during the subsequent investigation of this scandal would have been perhaps the best revenge that the Kōmintō could bring on Takeshita.

Another, more murky, explanation is put forward by Mizoguchi Atsushi in *Gendai Yakuza no Ura-chishiki* (1997), in which he connects the Kōmintō incident to an earlier scandal surrounding the takeover of the Heiwa Sōgō Bank (hereafter HSB) by the Sumitomo Bank in 1986. By 1985 HSB was extensively debt-ridden and threatened by takeover. It did, however, have an extensive network of branches in the Tokyo area and this made it attractive to Sumitomo Bank, which lacked a strong presence in the capital. After a power struggle within the company, Komiyama Eiichi, whose family had founded the firm, retired and sold his 33 per cent holding of HSB to one of the bank's major creditors, Satō Shigeru, for ¥8 bn ($33.5 m) in 1985. Satō, president of Kawasaki Teitoku, was a businessman with extensive connections within both legitimate and underworld economies.

Within the HSB a group of senior executives was desperate to reject the attentions of Sumitomo. To this effect they contracted Ishii Susumu to prevent a takeover. This was facilitated by the fact that Ishii felt a debt of gratitude towards the bank after it had helped finance his mistress's mansion block whilst Ishii himself had been in prison.

In order to secure their position, HSB also made efforts to purchase Satō's 33 per cent block of shares. Satō, however, refused to sell. HSB was then approached by Manabe Toshinari, director of Yaesu Gallery in Tokyo. Manabe was a friend of Satō's and claimed that, if HSB purchased a gold lacquer-work folding-screen, he would persuade Satō to sell the shares. The price Manabe demanded for his folding screen was ¥4 bn ($23.7 m) whilst it had an estimated market value of only ¥120 m. At the negotiations for this sale was Takeshita's private secretary, Aoki Ihei. At the time, Takeshita was Minister for Finance and had the power to block or approve the proposed takeover. Part of the money from this sale was shared out by Satō and various Takeshita-related politicians and it is widely believed that Takeshita also received a cut.

Despite this, the shares were not sold to HSB. Moreover, Ishii had been persuaded to drop HSB. This was accomplished by giving him the chance to fulfil his lifelong ambition, that of owning a golf course. HSB owned a subsidiary company, the Taiheiyō Club, which owned a number of courses throughout Japan. Once it had taken over the HSB in August 1986, Sumitomo Bank disposed of the Taiheiyō Club's assets and agreed to sell the Iwama Country Club Development Company to Watanabe of Tokyo Sagawa Kyūbin for ¥4.8 bn ($28.5 m). The company was placed under the management of Satō and a trusted associate of Ishii's. Not long after the development permission for this had been granted in 1988, 60 per cent of this company was obtained by one of Ishii's front companies (*Kyōdō* 1993: 94–115; Mizoguchi 1997: 119–25; *Tokyo Business Today* December 1994).

Mizoguchi argues that, having been swindled over the sale of the folding screen, the HSB executives resisting Sumitomo's takeover made use of their right-wing connections to strike back at Takeshita for permitting the takeover. This is made credible by the fact that HSB had earlier made use of the right-wing fixer, Toyoda Kazuo, to lobby the Diet over a scheme involving one of HSB's bad investments. Toyoda had been responsible for introducing Inamoto's former gang boss and Kōmintō political advisor, Shirakami Hideo, into politics (Mizoguchi 1997: 21).

A further twist to this scandal was provided by Ishii in 1989 when the Iwama Country Club issued receipts for fake membership licences through which Ishii raised ¥38.4 bn ($280 m). The companies from which Ishii received this money included two of Japan's largest securities companies, Nomura and Nikko, as well as Tokyo Sagawa Kyūbin and two large construction companies. These 'memberships' were essentially worthless as the Iwama Country Club was public and did not operate a system of preferential membership. For all of these firms, however, Ishii had provided bodyguard or trouble-resolution services (Nakagawa 1992: 234).

With this money, Ishii started to purchase shares of Tōkyū Dentetsu, a railway and property-holding company. By the end of 1989, Ishii's holdings in this company had reached 29 million shares (26 per cent of the company). Nomura Securities then ramped up the value of these shares by advising other clients to purchase Tōkyū Dentetsu. By November 1989, the share value peaked at ¥3,060, making Ishii's block worth on paper ¥88.74 bn ($643 m). Unfortunately for Ishii, however, in January 1990, the Tokyo Stock Exchange collapsed before he had realised this capital gain.

It seems that Ishii then sold the shares to a company belonging to his business partner, Satō, with the intention of pressuring Tōkyū Dentetsu to buy them back at a higher price (a technique known as green-mailing). When this did not happen, Satō later claimed that Inagawa-kai personnel came back to him and requested that he let them handle the situation. These Inagawa-kai executives implied that they would kill some Tōkyū bosses, if necessary, to encourage the others. Satō apparently persuaded the *yakuza* not to follow this strategy through (*Kyōdō* 1993: 241–2; *Tokyo Business Today* December 1994).

The other case with which we are concerned is the Itoman scandal. This incident was the largest single financial scandal in postwar Japanese history and resulted in an unprecedented flow of capital from the legitimate economy to the *yakuza* and their associates. Although the full details of this incident remain unclear (due to Sumitomo Bank's taking over the Itoman Corporation before too many embarrassing revelations became public), enough is known to show another important facet of modern *yakuza* fund-raising activity.

Itō Suemitsu was a typical product of the bubble economy of the 1980s. After aggressively expanding his father's wedding-hall business in Hokkaidō, Itō quickly diversified into real-estate speculation in the Tokyo area and elsewhere. In 1985, he made his biggest investment by purchasing 1,300 square meters of the Ginza area of Tokyo for ¥83.8 bn ($351 m), on which he built a large development, the Ginichi Building. This building was then used by Itō as a never-ending source of funds.

In 1988, Itō raised a loan of ¥27 bn ($211 m) using the Ginichi Building as collateral. He then lent this money to Ikeda Hōji, a former member of the Yamaguchi-gumi and, at the time, a business brother (*kigyō shatei*) of the same organisation. Not long after this, Itō also became a business brother of Takumi Masaru, the Yamaguchi-gumi's under-boss (*wakagashira*). It was at this point that the financial scandal began.

When Ikeda disappeared that year, Itō was left with Ikeda's collateral, shares in a sightseeing company, but no capital. However, in 1989, Nagoya Itoman Real-estate Corporation gave Itō ¥46.5 bn ($337 m) in exchange for equal rights on the Ginichi Building, which it wanted to use as its new Tokyo headquarters. In June the following year, Itō was made a director of Itoman. Thereafter, Itoman was systematically raped by Itō and his associates. Artwork was purchased at several times its market worth; money lent without adequate security; and equal rights on other properties held by Itō transferred for large sums. By the time of Itō's arrest in July 1991, it was estimated that between ¥500–600 bn ($3.7–4.4 bn) had been diverted from Itoman to the criminal economy. Of that, ¥200 bn ($1.5 m) had reached the Yamaguchi-gumi (Mizoguchi 1998: 193–6; *Tokyo Business Today* December 1994).

Taken together, these three incidents show the extent to which the modern *yakuza* were playing an integral role in the operations of both business and political life. They also show that, whilst in the case of the Itoman scandal, the relationship between *yakuza* groups and legitimate commercial interests may be wholly predatory, this may not always be the case, and both political and business elite groups have been unforced consumers of the protective services that these groups provide. Moreover, as can be seen by the behaviour of Nomura Securities, these firms may be willing accomplices in the questionable business practices of *yakuza* groups.

Most significantly (and disturbingly) for the purposes of this research is, however, the glimpse allowed by the Kōmintō incident into the relationship between the elite power brokers of the Liberal Democratic Party and Ishii, the then head of one of Japan's largest criminal syndicates. In a world where such individuals are disputing over who should occupy the seat of honour at banquets in high-class restaurants, the sincerity of the political establishment in its avowed commitment to eradicate the *yakuza* must be viewed with suspicion. This must be borne in mind whilst we look at the introduction and implementation of the *Bōtaihō*.

There are further grounds for scepticism as to the likely effectiveness of the *Bōtaihō*, in the light of what these scandals show us about the nature of *yakuza* in the Heisei period. In particular the use of front companies and business associates, such as *kigyō shatei*, meant that such activities are not only harder to identify, but, until the second revision of the *Bōtaihō* in 1997, fell outside the provisions of the new law altogether.

Bursting of the Bubble

The analysis provided in Chapter Four of the various ways in which *yakuza* made money shows clearly that, by the end of the 1980s, they were actively involved in many areas of the legitimate economy. Therefore, as mentioned above, an appraisal of the *Bōtaihō*'s impact on the *yakuza* is made problematic by the effect of economic changes occurring around the time that the law was implemented. The most significant of these was the collapse of Japan's speculative bubble. From its peak in February 1989, the Nikkei Index fell by 63 per cent in just 18 months whilst, between 1990 and 1994, the total market value of Japan's land dropped from ¥2,389 to ¥1,823 trillion. It has since been estimated that, in sum, this crash resulted in a total theoretical loss in value of ¥800 trillion (Hartcher 1998: 98–100).

Real-estate and Stock-market Speculation

In Chapter Four it was claimed that, by the late 1980s, the largest single source of revenue for the *yakuza* was generated through land-sharking (*Jiage*). With the collapse of land prices, this activity dried up, as property developers no longer saw a profit in large projects. Chapter Four also related how the more ambitious and capable *yakuza* members were themselves involved heavily in real-estate and stock-market speculation. Frequently, their investment portfolios had been high risk ones and were entirely dependent on ever-booming stock and real-estate markets: money would be borrowed to invest in real-estate; this would then be used as collateral for further loans to reinvest in shares or more land.

When the markets crashed, *yakuza* were left holding property that was worth a fraction of their total outstanding debt. It should be emphasised that this investment strategy had not been unique to the *yakuza*, and many businesses and individual investors were left with debts that they were quite incapable of repaying. As we shall see, however, *yakuza* debtors represented particular problems to their creditors.

The most spectacular manifestation of the *yakuza*-related bad-debt problem came to light with the collapse of the housing and loans companies known as *jūsen*. *Jūsen* first appeared in the early 1970s to fill a gap in the market for housing loans.[4] As non-bank financial institutions, *jūsen* were unable to take deposits and were therefore dependent on other institutions, such as the banks—under which most of these companies had been set up—for loans, which could then be re-lent to customers.

During the 1980s, however, the business environment in which the *jūsen* existed underwent a profound change. Businesses no longer relied on banks for finance, but started to raise capital by share issues in the buoyant stock market. As a consequence, the banks were forced to seek other customers for bank loans and they came into direct competition with the *jūsen* companies. This seriously undermined the *jūsen*'s market; because the *jūsen* had been dependent on bank loans to finance their lending, the banks were able to offer more competitive rates of interest to the final customer. Furthermore, many *jūsen* had been dependent on their parent banks to introduce customers to them.

The *jūsen* were therefore obliged to lend to those businesses that failed to raise all their capital requirements from banks. Such businesses tended to be those where the risk of failure was higher. However, such was the desperation of *jūsen* companies for business, the level of scrutiny of prospective customers was low. In financing real-estate investment, however, *jūsen* reasoned that, with land as collateral, even if the debtor could not repay the loan, they would be able to recover their costs. This was, of course, dependent on continued high land prices.

By 1990, the Ministry of Finance (MOF) became worried about the level of land prices and, in March that year, it issued administrative guidance to the finance industry to restrict the funds made available to real-estate speculators. Unfortunately, MOF left a loophole in this arrangement by not placing any restrictions on *jūsen* to borrow from agricultural cooperatives (*nōkyō*) and pump this money into the real-estate market. The volume of money flowing through this route quickly swelled as the agricultural co-operatives had confidence that the *jūsen*, which were subsidiaries of the top banks in the country and headed by former elite MOF officials, knew what they were doing (Mabuchi 1997: 10–15).

Unfortunately, this was not the case:

All seven top *jūsen* commonly made loans against collateral with a value lower than that of the loan itself. They made loans to borrowers whom they knew to be using false names. They loaned for speculative stock buying, for *pachinko* parlours... and for sex hotels. Many loans were made to companies associated with politicians. Most of the *jūsen* loans made after the 1990 restriction were paid to the companies of criminal syndicates (Hartcher 1998: 128).

By January 1996 the total scale of the bad debt held by the seven *jūsen* companies was estimated at ¥6.4 trillion ($5.9 bn). In addition, these companies had a further ¥2.1-trillion non-performing but salvageable loans (*Australian Financial Review* 23 January 1996). The proportion of this loan, which was *yakuza*-related, was not clear. One sample of ninety-three loans made by the Sōjō Jūkin Company contained forty, which had been made to *yakuza* (*National Business Review* 15 March 1996). Whilst it would be unsound to extrapolate from this small statistical base to conclude that 43 per cent of all *jūsen* bad debt is held by *yakuza* members, this sort of proportion is in the mid-range of journalistic estimates (generally between one-third and a half) as to the total scale of the problem. MOF sources cited by the *South China Morning Post* (31 May 1998) admitted that '*yakuza* gangs and their front companies borrowed at least five trillion yen' from the *jūsen*.

When the names of the main *jūsen* debtors were eventually made public, the largest single borrower was an Osaka-based property development company called Suenō Kōsan. Suenō Kōsan had taken ¥186bn ($1.7bn) from five *jūsen* companies as well as ¥54bn from other sources. Such was the strength of suspicion that Suenō Kōsan's president was himself a *yakuza* affiliate that a press conference was arranged by him to deny these charges (*Los Angeles Times* 24 February 1996). Whatever the accuracy of these protestations, it was clear that several of the company's buildings were occupied by Yamaguchi-gumi subgroup members whilst the nominal ownership of many of the most valuable assets had been transferred, therefore rendering the loans irrecoverable (Hartcher 1998: 128).

Whilst the *jūsen* debacle was the most spectacular manifestation of Japan's bad-debt problem, it was just one aspect of it. Although Japanese accounting practices allow banks and companies to conceal much of their debt,[5] by July 1998 the official figure for bad debts held by Japan's banks and non-bank financial institutions, was put by the new Financial Supervisory Agency at ¥35 trillion ($267bn) (*Financial Times* 18 July 1998). Although journalistic estimates vary widely from between 80 per cent (*Los Angeles Times* 14 February 1996) and 5 per cent (*Daily Yomiuri* 5 August 1998), the most frequently quoted estimate of the degree of *yakuza* involvement with this total was 40 per cent. This commonly accepted figure seems to be based on a survey of forty-nine loans carried out by an American private security and investigation company, Kroll Associates, for a prospective investor client. This survey was cited in an article by David Kaplan in *US News and World Report* in April 1998. This article was then picked up by a number of newspapers and magazines, both in Japan and outside, and, as a consequence, the 40 per cent figure has acquired a quasi-official status.

The small statistical base on which this figure is built does not engender confidence. However, support for this 40 per cent figure comes from Miyawaki Raisuke, formerly of the NPA and currently a consultant on *yakuza*-related problems, who suggests that 10 per cent of bad debt is directly tied to *yakuza* groups whilst 30 per cent has some probable, indirect, connection (*Financial Times* 12 December 1995).

In December 1995, *Newsweek* magazine published an article, which effectively blamed Japan's bad-debt problem and attendant economic woes on the *yakuza*. This is clearly not the case; the *yakuza* were simply part of a wider phenomenon of reckless speculation. If blame is to be apportioned, it should be directed largely at the banks, non-bank financial institutions, and MOF bureaucrats for their lamentably poor scrutiny and regulation. *Yakuza* involvement does, however, make this problem much harder to resolve.

In August 1993, Koyama Toyosaburō, Vice President of Hanwa Bank, was shot dead on his way to work. Koyama's duties had included recovering debts and, although his assailant was not apprehended, at the time it was widely accepted that his death was caused by *yakuza*. Several months before his death, Koyama had been responsible for approving a ¥590-m loan to a real-estate company run by the wife of a Yamaguchi-gumi sub-boss, Nishihata Haruo. This approval had been granted because Nishihata's group had been instrumental in silencing a monthly political magazine, which had been running a serial campaign exposing various scandals associated with the bank. It is possible that his death was related to this incident. Mizoguchi (1998: 192), however, reveals that there were various other *yakuza*-related problems concerning Hanwa Bank. Most alarming is the disclosure that bitterly competing factions within the bank made use of political organisations and *yakuza* to thwart their rivals. When, in 1996, MOF announced that Hanwa must stop trading, a list of 'special investments' containing categories for *yakuza* and political-group debts was discovered.

Also in 1993 a number of fire-bomb attacks on Sumitomo Bank executives' homes were recorded. Several branches were disrupted after their locks were filled with glue. In September of the following year, Hatanaka Kazufumi, the manager of the Nagoya branch of the Sumitomo Bank, was shot dead as he opened his front door to talk to what he thought was someone apologising for damaging his gate with his car. Police investigating this murder, convinced that the bank was not entirely forthcoming with relevant information, took the unusual step of impounding Hatanaka's desk and filing cabinets. An NPA official, writing under the pseudonym of Sakurada Keiji, attributes the bank's reticence to the links Sumitomo had forged with *yakuza* figures during their highly aggressive business activities in the years of the bubble economy. Sakurada further floats the hypothesis that the murder relates to Sumitomo's involvement in the Heiwa Sōgō Bank Scandal (*Tokyo Business Today* December 1994).

However, Yamada Hitoshi, head of the Japan Bar Association's anti-*bōryokudan* committee, more plausibly identifies the cause of the Hatanaka killing in this way:

Sumitomo had a policy of collecting collateral no matter what and they started using crime syndicates to collect on loans connected to other crime syndicates. Sumitomo's loan collection efforts drove the head of the Aizu-kotetsu gang into suicide in Kyoto and then another gang leader killed himself in Tokyo. At this point, gangsters started to realise they could be next so they murdered the Nagoya branch manager who had been most aggressive at trying to collect on such loans (*South China Morning Post* 31 May 1998).

As a consequence of this attack, MOF granted Sumitomo Bank permission to write off ¥500 bn worth of *yakuza*-related debts as losses for tax purposes. The other major banks were also all allowed to similarly write off their most problematic loans (Mizoguchi 1998: 192). In total, by 1997, 21 major financial institutions had been allowed to write off ¥20.5 trillion ($169 bn) (Konishi 1997: 101).

When I made attempts to confirm this analysis of the Hatanaka murder at the NPA, one interviewee chuckled that Sumitomo was by no means exceptional in its links with *yakuza*.

This type of problem has not been confined to Japanese financial executives. In 1998, there was a spate of newspaper articles concerning increased interest amongst foreign investors in salvaging problem Japanese loans. This was, in part, stimulated by an attack on two employees of Kroll Associates who were investigating the ownership of various properties in which their clients were interested. In another case, in 1997, a fire at the home of an executive of Cargill, a large American company, which had invested in Japanese bad debt, was widely interpreted as *yakuza*-related arson though no arrests were made. By May 1998, Ishizawa Takashi, of the Long Term Credit Bank's economic research division, was reported as claiming that American financial institutions investing in Japanese bad debt were subject to five attacks per month (*South China Morning Post* 31 May 1998). *Shūkan Jitsuwa* (25 June 1998) claimed that two representatives of the American CIA had been sent to Japan earlier that year to gather information and liaise with MOF about *yakuza* involvement in Japan's bad-debt problem.

The circumstances surrounding the murders of Koyama and Hatanaka illustrate two important points. First, that, in the words of lawyer Miyazaki Kenrō:

Generally speaking, if a company has trouble with *yakuza*, it is fair to assume that it had a friendlier relationship with them in the past... This cynical marriage of convenience is at the root of the troubles besetting the Sumitomo group and others.... The rule is: if you hire *yakuza* for any reason, you leave yourself open to attack by them later on (*Tokyo Business Today* December 1994).

Second, the collapse of the speculative bubble and the consequent economic recession generated new business opportunities for the *yakuza*, in this case, an increased market for debt collection, just as established economic activities, such as *jiage*, lost viability. The rapid adaptation of the *yakuza* to the changing economic climate illustrates once more the highly flexible and amorphous nature of organised crime. These developments will be considered below.

Bankruptcy Management

The level of bankruptcies in Japan, historically high by international standards, became considerably more severe in the 1990s. In 1990, the total number of bankruptcies stood at 6,468: By 2000, the annual figure had almost trebled to 19,071. In terms of total liabilities, Japan's bankruptcy growth is even more pronounced; the total liabilities for firms going bankrupt in 1990 was ¥1,996bn: The corresponding figure for 2000 was ¥23,987bn (Japan Economic Institute of America, Teikoku Data Bank). This might seem to present a golden opportunity for specialists in bankruptcy management.

However, despite the larger pot of money available, in various ways bankruptcy management has become harder than in the 1980s (Yamada 1994*b*: 300). Mizoguchi (1998: 190–1) identifies a number of reasons for this. The first is that companies increasingly rely on lawyers to oversee their liquidation. Alternatively, companies may undergo the procedure set up under the provisions of the Company Resuscitation Law. In addition, the police *bōryokudan* countermeasures sections (*bōtaishitsu*), set up in the early 1990s, are now prone to intervene

quickly when they suspect *yakuza* involvement in bankruptcy management. Finally, and perhaps most significantly, Mizoguchi claims that
people are now less afraid of *yakuza*.

As a consequence of these problems, it is easier instead to attach
oneself to a company before it goes bankrupt and exploit it from the
inside. A classic case of this was the Itoman scandal discussed earlier.

Auction Obstruction—*Kyōbai Bōgai*

In the light of these problems facing *yakuza* if they involve themselves
with bankruptcy management, other techniques for exploiting bankrupt companies have come to prominence. The most significant of
these has been *yakuza* obstruction of property auctions (*kyōbai bōgai*).
This type of activity can take many forms, but effectively *kyōbai bōgai*
involves artificially depressing the value of a property to be sold. The
ability to do this can be profitable to *yakuza* in three different ways.
First, they may continue to use the property as before following the
auction's collapse. Second, they may hope to acquire the property
cheaply and then sell it on at its market price. Third, they may be paid
money to vacate the premises by those wishing to sell it.

Originally, auction obstruction had been rampant in the real-estate
industry, leading to the creation of the term '*kyōbaiya*' to describe individuals involved in this business. These specialists would turn up at
auctions and intimidate other potential purchasers. If a property had
not been sold on the first day of auction, its reserve price would drop
by 20 per cent. *Kyōbaiya* would make use of this fact to purchase property cheaply. In 1979, in an attempt to clean up this business, a system
of sealed bids (*kikan nyūsatsu*) was adopted under which, it was
hoped, such intimidation would no longer be possible. However, as
we have seen before, a change in the law does not necessarily eradicate a problem; more frequently it causes the form that the crime in
question takes to change. In this case, the auction specialists evolved
into occupation specialists (*senyūya*).

There are five main ways in which *yakuza* come to occupy property
under threat of auction (Konishi 1997: 102–7). The most direct route is
for the *yakuza* group or individual members themselves to have purchased the property concerned with borrowed money that cannot be

repaid. The property is then lawfully occupied by the group concerned, or let to another group.

Alternatively, *yakuza* might enter premises via the high-interest-rate-lending route. As a company's financial position deteriorates, it will often turn in desperation to high-rate moneylenders with *yakuza* connections or *yakuza* themselves. As collateral the lenders will acquire the short-term leaseholder's rights to the property. This is the typical mechanism by which *yakuza* become involved in auction obstruction.

The third way in which criminal syndicates can occupy threatened property is through their involvement in conventional bankruptcy management. Having hijacked a financially distressed company, the *yakuza* 'consultant' uses the company's seals to dispose off its assets and therefore take control of the property.

Surprisingly enough, property owners themselves frequently approach *yakuza* groups, enter into conspiracy with them, and grant short-term rights to them. In these cases, the objective is to deter the owner's creditors from closing in and recovering their debts. In many cases of problem real-estate-related loans, the properties in question have multiple mortgages on them. Should the property be sold, the first mortgage holder will recover nearly all of the revenue from the sale whilst the third and fourth mortgage holders receive little. These lower priority mortgage holders may therefore sell their rights to *yakuza*.

The final way in which *yakuza* may come to occupy a property is by simply pretending to be a legitimate company or ordinary occupants.

In order for leaseholders' rights to be effective, they must have been established prior to the decision to sell the property in question. Frequently, therefore, the contract is forged to predate the announcement of auction. Forged contracts usually contain clauses empowering the occupant to sub-lease and alter the building's interior. Such forgeries are difficult to detect if the *yakuza* group is working in conspiracy with the owner or has hijacked the company.

Once occupation has been achieved, the standard practice is to advertise the fact by displaying *yakuza* affiliation from windows and on doorplates. Alternatively, an armoured public-announcement truck festooned with right-wing paraphernalia parked outside the property provides a clear signal to prospective purchasers. A name card, showing gang affiliation, may be inserted in the public notification of sale.

If these tactics prove insufficient, more direct intimidation remains an option, though this runs the risk of criminal prosecution. More sophisticated occupation specialists may prefer to entrench their position by establishing a factory on the site and claiming special rights due to the scale of capital investment. If the aim is to reduce the value of the property, this may simply be achieved by damaging it in some way or dumping industrial waste around it.

The increasing number of cases of property subject to civil execution procedure shows the potential for this type of activity. During the bubble period there were between 1,500 and 2,000 new cases each year dealt with by the Tokyo district court. By 1993, this figure had increased to about 6,000 and, in the first eight months of 1998, 5,100 (Ishibashi 1998: 119). Moreover, the low economic costs and legal risks, combined with the high potential rewards, of this business make it an attractive form of *shinogi*.

Like many other areas of *yakuza* activity, gangster occupation of buildings can be highly difficult to deal with under the law. In particular, the way in which Japanese law provides greater protection to tenants than landowners enables this type of activity to be profitable to *yakuza*. However, under the criminal law, cases of forged documents, altering official documents, and forcibly obstructing civil proceedings can be prosecuted. In addition, in recent years the courts have become prepared to interpret intimidation more flexibly. This can be seen from the 1991 Matsuyama district court ruling that the insertion of a *yakuza* name card into the binding of a report on the particulars of real estate for sale was intimidation (Konishi 1997: 110).

In most cases, however, the onus is on the civil law to deal with cases of *yakuza* occupation of property. Here, also, there is perhaps a tendency to a more robust application of the available laws by the authorities. This is suggested by the first case of forced eviction of *yakuza* from an occupied property in July 1997. The Housing Loan Administration Corporation (HLAC, *Jūsen Kinyō Saiken Kanri Kikō* or *Jūkan Kikō*)[6] successfully persuaded Kumamoto District Court that the occupation by *yakuza* members of rooms in a mansion block was tantamount to auction obstruction as the value of the property had fallen dramatically as a consequence. The following month, the HLAC won a case in Kanazawa forcing *yakuza* to vacate premises used as a gang office (Konishi 1997: 99). In addition to the more robust stance taken by the courts, credit for these successes should be attributed to the

HLAC. Under its ex-lawyer president, Nakabo Kōhei, the HLAC adopts the uncompromising stance *vis-à-vis* this problem that has been conspicuously lacking in Japanese banks.

There is also evidence that, in recent years, the police have attached greater priority to *yakuza* activity of this type. In February 1996, the NPA set up the *Kinyū Furyō Saiken Kanren Jihan Taisaku-shitsu* (Finance and Bad Debt-Related Crimes Countermeasures Room) to deal with this problem. Possibly as a consequence of this, the number of arrests made by the police for crimes of this type has risen dramatically since 1995. This is shown in Table 6.1. It is probable that this increase reflects this change in priority rather than a change in the level of actual crimes of this type. Despite the rise in arrests, it should be noted that the absolute numbers are small in proportion to the scale of the problem.

Although the legal climate in which auction obstruction occurs is slowly changing, it still remains a significant problem for the resolution of Japan's bad-debt crisis. Even if the occupation is clearly illegal, it is difficult to deal with. As will be discussed in greater depth in Chapter Seven, this is because the civil-law procedures to deal with problems of this type function so slowly and expensively, that it is frequently more cost-effective either to pay the occupants to leave or to hire another *yakuza* group to solve the problem.

Konishi likens the relationship between obstruction and its legal countermeasures to that between a virus and its vaccine: The virus quickly evolves immunity to the latest vaccine (1997: 109). As has been shown in preceding chapters, the same could be said for *yakuza* countermeasures generally.

Table 6.1 Arrests for *Yakuza* finance- and debt-reclamation-related crimes 1994–2000

	1994	1995	1996	1997	1998	1999	2000
Total	8	18	55	79	85	102	117
Debt-reclamation-related	6	13	51	77	74	—	98
Finance-related	2	5	4	2	11	—	19

Source: Keisatsu Hakusho (1999–2001).

Loss-Cutting—*Songiri*

In addition to auction obstruction, another development in *yakuza* economic activity, which can be directly attributed to the economic consequences of the bubble's bursting, is the appearance of loss-cutting specialists (*songiriya*). The way in which *songiri* operates is perhaps best illustrated by an example cited during an NHK special investigation into *yakuza* business associates. During the bubble period, financial institution 'A' lent ¥350 m to company 'B' managing a mansion block. With the collapse in the bubble economy, the company was unable to repay the loan, and the collateral became worth a fraction of the outstanding debt.

At this stage, the *songiriya* appeared. Having gained the appropriate powers of attorney from the financial institution, this individual negotiated with the debtor and persuaded it to settle the debt with a payment of ¥40 m (merely 11.4 per cent of the outstanding debt not including interest payments). The debtor paid a further ¥20 m to the *songiriya* as thanks for reducing its debt burden by so much.

This type of activity is legal. This leads to the question, why is it an activity dominated by *yakuza* and their business associates? The answer to this is that, although it is not illegal, to be effective, it relies on the implied threat of *yakuza* association. The further obvious question is why creditor and debtor do not negotiate directly. Each would have been better off by ¥10 m if they had cut out the middleman and settled the debt with a ¥50 m pay-off. It seems likely that the reason that this does not happen is the debtor has, in some way, a connection with a *yakuza*. In other negotiations, covertly filmed during the programme, this was indeed the case.

The figures given in the NHK example seem questionable. More plausible are those given by Hinago (1998: 166) in which his *songiriya* interviewee suggests a debt of ¥5 bn might be reduced to ¥3 bn for which the *songiriya* might receive 3 per cent (¥90 m). This seems in line with the 3 per cent commission that *yakuza* typically received for *jiage* services or from construction companies. Hinago's source also claims that, with the exception of Tokyo Mitsubishi Bank, all of the large banks are prepared to deal with *songiriya*.

Regardless of which of these two sources is more accurate, it is clear that this business is highly lucrative. The *songiriya* interviewed during the NHK special claimed an annual income of over ¥100 m.

It is important to note that the post-bubble developments in *yakuza* economic activity require a degree of financial expertise. Though there will always exist a niche within the organised criminal economy for those whose skills are confined to the deployment of violence, the opportunities for such individuals within this new environment are now reduced. Whilst the *yakuza* elite may be economically secure, what will the implications be for an under-employed mass of unskilled *lumpen-yakuza*? This becomes especially pertinent when we consider that the *Bōtaihō* specifically targets those activities that make use of the implicit threat of these thugs being unleashed. The unequal nature and highly divergent levels of ability within *yakuza* society is a most important consideration in our evaluation of the effects of economic and legal changes on it. This should be remembered during the following discussion on the implementation of the *Bōtaihō*.

The *Bōtaihō*

Even before the introduction of the new law, the *yakuza* were taking measures to minimise any adverse impact on their operations. Of the large syndicates, the Yamaguchi-gumi took by far the greatest steps to prepare for the new law (Mizoguchi 1992*b*: 246). Towards the close of 1990, at a monthly meeting (*teireikai*) attended by all members of the first-level group of the Yamaguchi-gumi, the executive committee (*shikkō-bu*) warned those assembled that a new law was under consideration. In order to protect the headquarters from the threat of RICO-style seizure, it was decided to purchase third-generation boss Taoka's house and register it in the names of all direct members. To this end, at the beginning of 1991, each member contributed ¥10 m ($74,000) (Yamada 1994*b*: 183–4).

At the monthly meeting on 5 March 1991 (by which time the 'basic considerations' had been published), discussion went on for longer than usual, and it was reported, had concentrated on ways in which to deal with the proposed new law. The day after the meeting, the executive committee sent fax messages to each of the sub-bosses responsible for the regional blocks, instructing them that gang signs were to be removed from the outside of all gang offices. By 10 March, roughly half of the 1,500 Yamaguchi-gumi gang offices around Japan had complied with this (Yamada 1994*b*: 183–6). This was clearly to pre-empt the provisions of what became Article 29 of the *Bōtaihō*, which made the display of gang paraphernalia susceptible to the threat of a Public Safety Commission injunction.

In addition, each regional block was instructed to set up a study group to examine the new law's provisions. This increased the importance of the regional blocks, which had hitherto largely existed for the twin purposes of ensuring good communications and fostering amicable relations between the various groups within a certain geographical area (in much the same way as the Kantō Hatsuka-kai). Just before the implementation of the *Bōtaihō*, the monthly meeting of all direct group members was also cancelled in favour of block-level meetings. The new law therefore stimulated the move to an increasing role for the regional blocks and we can therefore say that the law has caused not only operational change, but also organisational restructuring within the Yamaguchi-gumi.

Under the guidance of the criminal defence lawyer Endō Makoto, the headquarters also formed an eleven-man study group including the *wakagashira*, Takumi Masaru, and headquarters' chief, Kishimoto Saizō.

At the April 1991 general meeting, the direct members were issued with further instructions to sever all connections with the police, not to cooperate with them at all, and not to let them into gang offices without a search warrant. Although the Yamaguchi-gumi had long had a far worse relationship with the police of Osaka and Hyōgō prefecture than that enjoyed between the more politically savvy Tokyo syndicates and the MPD, a limited degree of communication and cooperation had existed. Following the April directive, all such cooperation officially ceased.

Whilst it severed its relations with the authorities, the Yamaguchi-gumi put effort into establishing better relations with the other major criminal syndicates. During May and June, senior executives played golf and had meals with their peers in the Inagawa-kai and Sumiyoshi-kai. On 27 September 1991, senior representatives of the four largest syndicates, the Yamaguchi-gumi, the Inagawa-kai, the Sumiyoshi-kai, and the Aizu-kotestu, held a '*gokudō* summit' at a restaurant in the Asakusa area of Tokyo. At this meeting it was agreed, amongst other things, not to cause annoyance to ordinary members of the public, not to invade each other's territory, and not to accept as gang members those individuals who had been expelled from other groups. It was clear that the *bōryokudan* were, above all else, attempting to minimise the risk of inter-syndicate conflict (Mizoguchi 1992*b*: 252; Yamada 1994*b*: 406; *Japan Access* 13 January 1992).

The following year, on 22 February, a larger, secret '*gokudō* summit' of about forty senior *yakuza* figures was held somewhere in the Kansai area. As well as the bosses of the four syndicates mentioned above, in attendance were the leaders of the other three syndicates ear-marked by the police for the first wave of designation under the *Bōtaihō*. These were the Kyōsei-kai, the Gōda-ikka, and the Kudōrengō Kusanō-ikka (based in Hiroshima, Yamaguchi, and Fukuoka prefectures, respectively). Together, these syndicates comprised over half of the total *yakuza* strength as identified by the police. Apart from a general agreement to refrain from intergroup conflict and upsetting the ordinary public, it is not clear what was discussed at this meeting (Yamada 1994*b*: 245–6). However, from the widely different reactions to the process of designation, it is reasonably clear that no workable agreement as to a common front in opposition to the *Bōtaihō* was achieved.

In addition to high-level diplomacy within the *yakuza* world, the Yamaguchi-gumi launched a charm-offensive aimed at affecting public opinion. As part of this strategy, the syndicate donated money, including ¥10 m from Watanabe Yoshinori, to various charities and emergency appeals (something that Taoka had done in the mid-1960s just after the launch of the first summit strategy but had not been carried out since).[7] The Yamaguchi-gumi also set up a political organisation 'The National Purification League' (*Zenkoku Kokudo Jōka Dōmei*), supposedly having the purpose of eradicating drugs. To establish this league, as well as provide a fighting fund to deal with the new law, all direct members were required to pay ¥20 m in addition to their normal *jōnōkin* (Mizoguchi 1997: 57).

In January 1992, Yamaguchi-gumi *wakagashira* Takumi Masaru sent a secret fax message to each of the 115 direct members instructing them that they were each to establish a corporate identity with the headquarters sited in the subgang's offices. The deadline for this was the end of the month. Although the message ended with instructions that it be destroyed once the contents had been confirmed, the full text was leaked to the press. As a consequence of this, sensitive messages are no longer sent by fax but are transmitted by word of mouth or telephone (Yamada 1994*b*: 240).

The urgency of this message reflects the strong sense of unease at the time that the new law would make it impossible to operate gang offices. Under Article 15, in the event of an intergang conflict, offices could be closed for 3 months. If the office in question also housed a registered business, however, forced closure of the premises might be opposed on the grounds that it infringed economic freedoms. This unease as to the security of offices was matched with widespread pessimism amongst *yakuza* that a number of their traditional income sources would be completely severed under the new law (interview criminal defence lawyer, Kōbe 1998).

By the beginning of February 1992, over half of the direct Yamaguchi-gumi groups had followed these instructions and had registered companies.[8] Most of these were ostensibly involved in finance, construction, real-estate, and bar/restaurant management (the sectors long associated with *yakuza* front companies). There were, however, a few exceptions from this pattern including companies managing old-folks' homes, ceremonial events halls, a missing-persons-retrieval agency, and aerobics classes (Yamada 1994*b*: 240–1). The organisation's headquarters had itself set up a joint-stock company in March 1991. Under the directorship of one of the syndicate's senior executives, Katsuragi Masao, the company (named 'Yamaki') was involved in leasing reception halls, managing golf practise ranges, and dealing in men's jewellery (Mizoguchi 1992*b*: 251).

Other gangs formed religious groups. An executive from the Yamaguchi-gumi first-level group Hisshin-kai, for example, made himself a missionary of the 'Watoku-kyōkai' and installed a branch at the gang office. There were also numerous articles, later confirmed by interviews with legal experts and police sources, reporting that many *yakuza* gangs were forming right-wing political organisations.

In February, the month before the law came into force, the Yamaguchi-gumi leadership produced a guide to the *Bōtaihō*, 'Concerning the New *Bōryokudan* Law' (*Bōryokudan Shinpō ni Tsuite*), which was distributed to all sub-groups. This document provided the reader with advice as to how to avoid the provisions of the law. Within the month, police in the Hyōgo area had managed to seize a copy (*Reuters News Service* 18 February 1992).

These various preparatory measures imposed a certain degree of strain on relations within the syndicate. In particular, the financial cost of setting up a company, combined with making payments for the purchase of Taoka's house, the establishment of the drug-eradication group and the *Bōtaihō* countermeasures fund, caused a certain degree of resentment amongst Yamaguchi-gumi direct members (interviewees, Osaka 1998; Tokyo 1999). Because these changes followed closely after the appointment in 1989 of Watanabe Yoshinori (second-generation boss of the Yamaken-gumi) as successor to fourth-generation boss Takenaka Masahisa, much of this resentment has been directed at the new leadership. Mizoguchi (1992*b*: 253) suggests that the reason for the leak in information concerning the Yamaguchi-gumi's preparations for the new law can be explained by this unhappiness.

The *Bōtaihō* can therefore be said to have had a significant impact on the Yamaguchi-gumi. This impact was most immediately visible in terms of changes in the syndicate's establishment of various legal fronts but extended to important changes in diplomatic relations with both other syndicates and the legitimate world. Perhaps of only marginally less importance is the psychological impact wrought by the threat of this new law; not only was the organisation put on the back foot but, within the syndicate itself, there were rumblings of discontent at the ever-increasing demands for money from the headquarters leadership.

The two big syndicates on the eastern plain, the Sumiyoshi-kai and the Inagawa-kai did not show the same degree of concern as the Yamaguchi-gumi. One Tokyo-based gang leader interviewed on television claimed that 'the new law might be a nuisance but it won't really have much effect on us *yakuza*, we'll just take new titles like president and manager' (*Reuters News Service* 2 March 1992).

This difference in attitude is perhaps due to the less confrontational, more politically sensitive, posture adopted by the Kantō syndicates. As mentioned in Chapter Five, the Inagawa-kai leadership blamed the Yamaguchi-gumi for being the cause for the introduction of the law; so it is possible that they also felt that the main brunt of the law would be borne by the Yamaguchi-gumi as well. It should, however, be noted that thorough structural reorganisation was less necessary for the Tokyo syndicates as many subgroups had operated behind business fronts for some time before 1992. Ishii Susumu, to take the most well-known example, had juggled his business affairs between numerous front companies.

Although it does not seem to have been spurred by paranoia about the new law, the Sumiyoshi-kai underwent major organisational change at this time. In 1993, following the death of president (*sōsai*) Hori Masao in 1990, the group formally dropped *rengō* from its name. At the same time, it gave up its federal structure in favour of a centralised hierarchical structure. This was sealed by the exchange of father–son sake cups between the new boss (Nishiguchi Shigeo) and the bosses and *wakagashira* of the group comprising the old federation (Shinoda 2002: 34–9). Within the *yakuza* world, federally structured organisations are extremely rare; generally they end up either splitting up or end up with one individual gaining ascendancy (*Jitsuwa Jidai* March 2002: 139).

Introduction of the *Bōtaihō*—Designation

The difference between east and west can also be seen in the attitudes taken by the big three syndicates towards designation. On 10 April 1992, public hearings were held in Tokyo and Kōbe under the provisions of the *Bōtaihō*. At the Tokyo hearings Tanaka Keizō, representing the Inagawa-kai, declared that 'we are *yakuza*, not crime organisations. Ours is a chivalrous group that dates back through history.' Nishiguchi Shigeo, head of the Sumiyoshi-kai, urged for caution in the application of the law, arguing that foreign crime syndicates might displace the *yakuza* were they to be undermined. He further asserted that 'if you disturb the balance, the drug problem will increase'. Inagawa-kai executive, Mori Izumi, took a more legalistic approach arguing that the law infringed constitutionally guaranteed human rights (Yamada 1994*b*: 247; *Reuters News Service* 10 April 1992). However, the Tokyo syndicates' more politically accommodating attitude is reflected by Tanaka's statement that 'whatever the law might be, the laws decided on by the state are humbly and solemnly accepted'. Once they had been designated as *bōryokudan*, the Tokyo syndicates accepted the fact.

In contrast, the Yamaguchi-gumi adopted a more aggressive stance. In a 30-minute presentation to the Hyōgo Prefectural Public Safety Commission, Yamaguchi-gumi *wakagashira*, Takumi Masaru, attacked the new law on three grounds. The first of these was to assert that the Yamaguchi-gumi was a chivalrous organisation (*ninkyō-dantai*) imbued with the spirit of helping the weak and crushing the strong. In support of this line, he mentioned the gang's re-assertion of public safety on the streets of Kōbe straight after the war, as well as the more recent efforts to eradicate drugs, and donations to victims of natural disasters.

The second argument adopted by Takumi was the rejection of the law's validity on the grounds that it conflicted with the constitution. These arguments have been discussed in detail in Chapter Five, but essentially concern the principles of equality before the law and freedom of association.

The third ground for the syndicate's ineligibility for designation was a more subtle organisational point. Takumi asserted that the Yamaguchi-gumi itself only consisted of the (at that time) 115 direct members, all of whom had ritually exchanged cups with the fifth-generation boss, Watanabe. The Yamaguchi-gumi had no direct control over, or responsibility for, the activities of the members of the various subgroups. Consequently, it was inappropriate to simultaneously designate the direct Yamaguchi-gumi group and its various subgroups.

Although the chivalrous group and unconstitutional defences were essentially the same as those adopted by the Inagawa-kai, the Yamaguchi-gumi differed in that they refused to accept the legal validity of designation, and launched a suit at Kōbe District Court to challenge the new law. Similarly, groups in Fukuoka, Naha, and Kyoto took legal action in an attempt to overturn the law. This is illustrative of the difference in general cultural characteristics between the *yakuza* in the west and east of Japan.

One notable exception to this pattern is the behaviour of small Osaka-based gambling organisation, the Sakaume-gumi. This group, which numerous interviewees from both sides of the law asserted had very good diplomatic relations with the authorities, adopted the same acquiescent stance exhibited by the Kantō groups. At the public hearing concerning the group's designation, the top executive representing the Sakaume-gumi stated that 'it is the duty of the people to obey the laws decided on by the state. If the Sakaume-gumi fulfils the conditions for designation, then we will have no option but to accept it' (*Shūkan Jitsuwa* 14 October 1999).

On 4 March, the NPSC confirmed that all of the big three syndicates satisfied the criteria for designation, and on 23 March their designation as *bōryokudan* was published in the Official Gazette. The following month, the Yamaguchi-gumi appealed to the NPSC to review its decision. After this appeal was rejected in October, the Yamaguchi-gumi met with its legal team and the case was submitted to Kōbe District Court on 26 November. After nine hearings, spread out over more than two years, it was finally decided, at the Yamaguchi-gumi top executives meeting in January 1995, to drop the case. Three months later, the Hyōgo Prefectural Public Safety Commission held public hearings on the re-designation of the Yamaguchi-gumi; the syndicate did not send a representative to argue its case.

Those gangs which did pursue their legal challenges of the *Bōtaihō* to a final verdict all met with no success. Whilst the plaintiffs had argued that the rights guaranteed by the constitution were absolute, the defendants argued that they were conditional. In the rulings given by all the courts concerned, the judges, whilst recognising the rights of the various plaintiffs, stressed that these rights were circumscribed by the rights of others:

It is difficult to deny that *bōryokudan* rely on violent activities and, accordingly it is clear that they exist by violating the basic human rights of individuals. To externally manifest this philosophy is unpardonable. Even though there is the basic human right of freedom of expression, which is guaranteed by the constitution, it is only proper that this be intrinsically limited to accord with other human rights. Moreover, it is understood that, for the general welfare of society, i.e. 'to preserve the safety and peace of civic life', it is permitted to have reasonable limitations on the smallest scale necessary (Fukuoka District Court 28 March 1995, in Yamaguchi 1997*a*: 70).

Because the *Bōtaihō*'s system of administrative regulation imposed only light penalties for violations, and the freedom to be member of a *bōryokudan* group itself was not denied, the restrictions were seen as limited, reasonable, and necessary. The argument that legal rights and freedoms can be reasonably limited in order 'to preserve peace and social welfare' was based on a Supreme Court ruling of 22 June 1983: 'What it is that makes this limitation accepted as necessary and reasonable, should be decided on the degree to which the limitation is necessary for the public good, the quality and contents of the restricted freedoms, the real nature of the restrictions and their comparative weights' (Yamaguchi 1997*a*).

Naha and Kyoto District Courts' rulings, of 17 May and 29 September, respectively, both concurred with the decision of Fukuoka.

The Aizu-kotetsu group in Kyoto also attempted to have its designation overturned on technical grounds. In February 1997, following

204   **The Japanese Mafia**

the retirement of Takayama Tokutarō and the succession of Zugoshi Toshitsugu, the syndicate officially changed its name from Yondaime (fourth-generation) Aizu-kotetsu to Godaime (fifth-generation) Aizu-kotestu. Because of this change in name, the group appealed to Kyoto District Court that the designation was no longer valid. This was rejected by the District Court in July and, after the syndicate had appealed, by the Kyoto High Court in September. In October, the Aizu-kotetsu abandoned its attempt to overturn its re-designation as a *bōryokudan* (*Keisatsu Hakusho* 1999: 185–6).

By March 1993, 18 groups had successfully been designated as *bōryokudan*. According to police statistics, these groups accounted for 44,340 full members (*kōsei-in*). Of this total, the big three syndicates comprised 38,500 men (87 per cent). The figures for 2000 (*Keisatu Hakusho* 2001) show that the number of designated *bōryokudan* groups currently stands at 25 comprising 39,500 *kōsei-in* (of which about 29,300 men (74 per cent) were big three syndicate members). Although this is rarely made clear in the police statistics, some groups that the police consider to be *bōryokudan* remain undesignated. In 2000, these accounted for 9 per cent of total *yakuza kōsei-in*. Although there is a dearth of information on these undesignated groups, it is likely that they are small, locally based groups. The designated *bōryokudan*, as of June 2001, are shown in the Appendix.

Effects of the *Bōtaihō*

Between January and February 1993, just eight months after the law's introduction, the NRIPS conducted interviews of 1,440 *yakuza* arrestees throughout Japan to evaluate the impact of the *Bōtaihō* (Tamura et al. 1993). Although we can expect a certain degree of bias in that these arrestees might be expected to say whatever they judged most likely to accelerate their release,[9] there are interesting differences between the various syndicates. Whilst there was a strong consensus amongst all groups that police controls and public criticism had become harsher following the law's introduction, Yamaguchi-gumi members were generally more pessimistic than those of other groups and had taken greater steps to avoid falling victim to the new law by studying its provisions, reorganising their groups, and removing nameplates from gang offices. The pessimism of the Yamaguchi-gumi interviewees was interpreted by NRIPS as being due to the fact that group's status was the main focus of the police's anti-*yakuza* efforts. This suggests that the greater sense of crisis felt by the Yamaguchi-gumi before the law's introduction was justified.

To see whether this pessimism was justified, let us look at what has happened to the *yakuza* since the NRIPS survey was conducted.

Yakuza Strength

If we look at police statistics for *yakuza* strength over a period 1989–2000 (see Table 6.2) we can see that, following 1991, there was a significant decline in numbers of *yakuza kōsei-in*.

However, this decline is partly explained by the restructuring that *yakuza* groups undertook to evade the provisions of the law. Many full members officially retired, or were 'expelled' from their gangs only to continue operations as before under the guise of a political organisation or as a 'business-brother' (*kigyō-shatei*). It is significant that over the same period the total value of *yakuza* strength, as recognised by the police (*jun-kōsei-in* and *kōsei-in*), did not decline by nearly as much. Clear evidence for this is shown by the significant *increase* in *jun-kōsei-in*, or peripheral members over the same period (25 per cent between 1991 and 1996). This increase did not reflect a jump in the number of apprentices. Rather, these 'new' *jun-kōsei-in* were full gang members seeking to evade the provisions of the new law by relinquishing formal membership.

Some interviewees, such as Yamanouchi and Mizoguchi, question the figures provided by the police as to the trends in *yakuza* numbers since the introduction in the law. The argument they present is that the real level of gang membership is lower than that suggested by the police statistics, which are massaged upwards to justify existing budgetary allocations. Mizoguchi (2000: 23) suggests that the category of *jun-kōsei-in* is inflated to imply that the overall number of *yakuza* has remained roughly constant. Given that there are no independent data to back up this theory it is difficult to know the extent to which it is

Table 6.2 *Yakuza* strength 1989–2000

	1989	1990	1991	1992	1993	1994	1995	1996	1997	1998	1999	2000
All	87,300	88,300	91,000	90,600	86,700	81,000	79,300	79,900	80,100	81,300	83,100	83,600
Full	66,700	68,800	63,800	56,600	52,900	48,000	46,600	46,000	44,700	43,500	43,900	43,400
Jun	20,600	19,400	27,200	34,000	33,800	33,000	32,700	33,900	35,400	37,800	39,200	40,200

Source: Hanzai Hakusho (1999–2001).

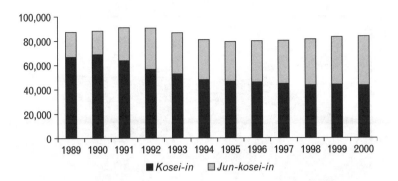

correct. Informal interviews with individuals from places as diverse as Roppongi and San'ya suggest big drops in the numbers of *yakuza* visible on the streets over the last decade. This need not necessarily mean a decline in actual numbers; it might alternatively be that *yakuza* are adopting a lower profile in a changed legal and economic environment. As will be shown later, this is undoubtedly a factor.

Disbandment

Alongside the fall in *yakuza* numbers, since 1991 there has been a rise in the number of groups disbanding. Whilst some of these cases were merely due to *Bōtaihō*-avoidance tactics as groups re-formed as political or social movements, others are genuine and directly attributable to problems in maintaining financial viability under the *Bōtaihō*. However, this need not be a socially advantageous development; if the individuals displaced do not personally mend their ways. According to police statistics, between 1991 and the end of 2000, 1,971 gangs (numbering 16,350 *kōsei-in*) disbanded. Over the same period the total decline in *yakuza* was only 7,400, so it seems likely that many of these individuals are reabsorbed by other gangs. In addition others form loose criminal associations or become lone-wolves (*ippiki-ōkami*). Consequently, the declining number of groups has not yielded a corresponding decline in the total criminal workforce.

In Figure 6.1 we see that the process of oligopolisation by the three big syndicates has been slowed, but not completely stopped, following

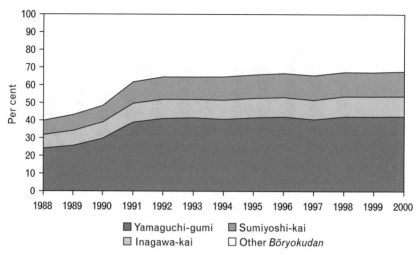

Fig. 6.1 Oligopolisation by Big Three syndicates

the introduction of the *Bōtaihō*. This contrasts with the effects of the summit strategies of the 1960s and 1970s, which, by having a disproportionately heavy effect on smaller gangs, ultimately encouraged big-syndicate expansion. Aggressive Yamaguchi-gumi expansion into such areas as north east Japan during the late 1980s was largely quelled, at least for the time being, by the introduction of the *Bōtaihō*.

Intergang Conflict

The suggestion that the *yakuza* have adopted a lower profile since the introduction of the new law has already been prompted by the pre-implementation diplomatic measures taken by the main groups to limit intergang conflict. To what extent have such conflicts actually been affected since the introduction of the *Bōtaihō*? If we look at the NPA data for intergang conflicts between 1980 and 2000 (Figures 6.2 and 6.3), we can see a clear break between the two decades; in 1991 the number of conflicts fell by over a half; the average number of conflicts per year between 1991 and 2000 was under a third of the corresponding figure for the previous decade.[10]

Although the new law did not come into effect until the following year, the fact that a new anti-*yakuza* law was being prepared was common

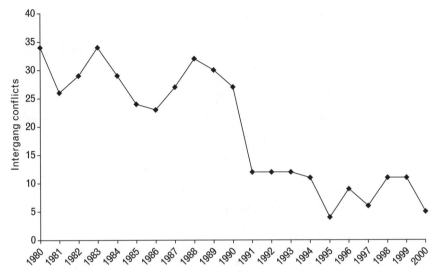

Fig. 6.2 Intergang conflicts 1980–2000

Source: *Keisatsu Hakusho* (1989–2000).

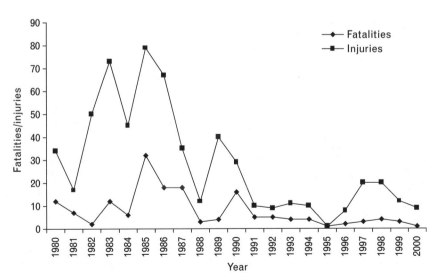

Fig. 6.3 Fatalities and injuries in intergang conflicts 1980–2000

Source: *Keisatsu Hakusho* (1989–2000).

knowledge from the beginning of 1991 when the 'basic considerations', on which the law was based, was published. As mentioned above, the various gangs were preparing for the new law before it came into effect and a pre-emptive drop in intergroup conflict is one example of this.

In addition, there is universal belief amongst interviewees and commentators, on both sides of the law, that once conflicts arise they are resolved much more quickly than before. Frequently, resolution is achieved through arbitration, and the payment of money by the party judged to be in the wrong. This assertion is also corroborated by the available police data. Of the 230 recorded conflicts between 1983 and 1990, 172 (75 per cent) were resolved within a week; 90 per cent of the 93 conflicts recorded in the following 10 years were resolved within one week (*Bōtaisaku-bu* 2002: 15–16).

Although the figures for the 1980s are erratic and distorted by the effects of the *Yama-Ichi tōsō*, the levels of violence of intergang conflict (as measured by fatalities and injuries) is also lower in the 1990s. This is of course to be expected given that the number of conflicts has decreased.

Dividing the total injuries and fatalities by the number of conflicts, as in Figure 6.4, tells us the relative bloodiness of these conflicts. Although there is considerable variance in these figures, we should note that *yakuza* conflicts generally are remarkably unbloody. Typically a conflict

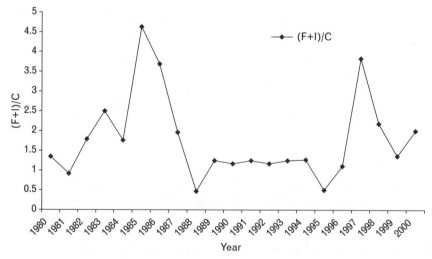

Fig. 6.4 Fatalities and injuries per conflict 1980–2000

results in the death or injury of between one and two gang members. This is despite firearms' being used in the vast majority of incidents. Rather than indicating poor weapon-handling skills, this reflects the ritual nature of much *yakuza* conflict. For the most part such warfare is limited to the symbolic firing of shots at the office exterior or gang crest, followed by a similar retaliation. Only in the minority of cases does the level of hostility increase beyond this. Even during the exceptional conflict of the Yamaguchi-gumi and Ichiwa-kai, only twenty-five fatalities and seventy injuries occurred in the course of 300 incidents, spread out over five years. By the standards of organised crime in Colombia or Russia, such stuff must seem tame indeed.

It is probable that this comparative pacificity is a product of the settled, mature state of organised crime in Japan. The period of rapid expansion of *yakuza* groups in the period up to 1963 was characterised by much greater violence between competing groups. Once groups have established their reputation for violence, it becomes paradoxically less necessary to deploy actual violence on a routine basis. At the same time the costs of all-out warfare, in the current context of more potent law enforcement and well-established rivals, means that ritual displays of non-lethal conflict allowing each side to evaluate who roars the loudest, have become the norm.

In contrast, in such countries as those of the former Soviet Union, where organised crime has mushroomed, in the fertile conditions of ineffective policing, abundant market opportunities, and a supply of under-employed males trained in the use of violence, and where a stable equilibrium has not become established, the opposite will be true.

The imperative to reduce violent conflict between the various *yakuza* syndicates, and thereby avoid police retaliation, also encouraged further diplomatic efforts following the introduction of the *Bōtaihō*. The most visible manifestation of this was the cementing of friendly relations through the creation of brotherhood bonds (through the ritual of *sakazuki* discussed in Chapter Two) between high-ranking personnel of different groups.

In June 1993, a relationship group (*shinseki-engumi*) was formed between Watanabe, Takayama Tokutarō (fouth-generation boss of the Aizu-kotetsu), and their top executives in order to stop conflict between the two groups. Despite their best efforts, however, conflict was not eradicated. In February 1996, a three-way brotherhood *sakazuki* took place between Kuwata Kenkichi, assistant Yamaguchi-gumi

wakagashira, and head of the Yamaken-gumi, Okimoto Tsutomu, leader
of the Hiroshima-based Kyōsei-kai (with which the Yamaguchi-gumi
had fought the infamous *jinginaki takakai* in the 1960s), and Zugoshi
Toshitsugu, fifth-generation boss of the Aizu-kotetsu. Officiating in the
capacity of guardian (*kōkennin*) was Watanabe Yoshinori.

In much the same way that the brotherhood relationship between
Yamaken (then Yamaguchi-gumi *wakagashira*) and Ishii Susumu in
1972 had cemented relations and prevented conflict between the
Yamaguchi-gumi and Inagawa-kai, the triple *sakazuki* of Kuwata,
Zukoshi, and Okimoto was seen as stabilising relations amongst the
western syndicates (Yamada 1998: 228).

In September 1996, a brotherhood *sakazuki* took place between the
two most high-ranking gang leaders in Japan, Watanabe Yoshinori,
and Inagawa Chihiro, third-generation boss of the Inagawa-kai.
Although in many ways this exchange was less important than the
triple *sakazuki* in that it was re-affirming a pre-existing relationship,
the fact that it was between the two most important *yakuza* in Japan
gave it greater weight. An attack by a Yamaguchi-gumi member on an
Inagawa-kai interest would become an affront to the dignity of
Watanabe, demanding recompense. This is reflected in the
Yamaguchi-gumi executive committee's directive to direct members
following the brotherhood ceremony, instructing them to respect the
Inagawa-kai's territorial integrity.

This policy of '*sakazuki* diplomacy' shows a clear contrast to the
earlier strategy of aggressive expansion adopted primarily by the
Yamaguchi-gumi (though also shown by the other two big syndicates)
up to the time of the *Bōtaihō*. The attempt by the Yamaguchi-gumi and
the other western syndicates to achieve peaceful coexistence can be
seen as the adoption of the diplomatic norms of the Kantō syndicates
exemplified by the Kantō Hatsuka-kai.[11]

However, as we shall see below, there are limits to peaceful
coexistence.

Bōtaihō Injunctions

Following the introduction of the *Bōtaihō*, the combined number of
administrative orders (*chūshi meirei* and *saihatsu bōshi meirei*) issued by

the Public Safety Commissions increased steadily. Rather than suggesting that the *yakuza* have shown an increasing propensity to flout the provisions of Article 9 of the new law, the obvious reason for this is that it has taken time for victims of so-called unfair *bōryokudan* demands to understand how the law applies to their own personal circumstances. The apparent levelling off of this increase since 1999 suggests that the process of dissemination is approaching its upper limits (given the existing level of public awareness and educational activity by the regional Centres for the Elimination of *Bōryokudan*). The annual numbers for repetition-prevention orders (*saihatsu bōshi meirei*) shows much greater variance than that of stoppage orders (*chūshi meirei*) though given that the former are roughly twenty times rarer, this is neither particularly surprising nor significant.

Under the *Bōtaihō*, an administrative order merely tells the individual infringing the provisions of the law to desist from the relevant activity. Provided that the individual then complies with the order, then no further penalties are incurred. Apart from the intangible costs to reputation, infringing the provisions of the *Bōtaihō* therefore carries no loss, and potential gains. To *yakuza*, constantly under pressure to raise money, it is likely to be a chance well worth taking.

Taken together, the various categories covered by Article 9 account for the bulk of injunctions issued under the provisions of the *Bōtaihō* (Figure 6.5). Of these, the most prominent are the demands for protection

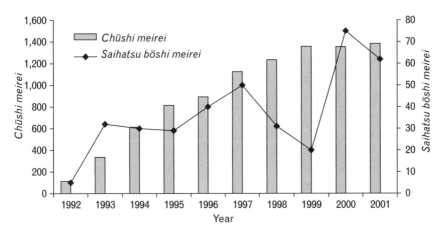

Fig. 6.5 *Bōtaihō* injunctions 1992–2000
Source: *Bōtaisaku-bu* (2002).

money/bodyguard fees, demands for gifts/donations, and demands for written waivers from existing obligations. Surprisingly, given the level of attention to auction obstruction in recent years, this type of activity has received a negligible number of injunctions. Perhaps this is because cases of auction obstruction tend to be dealt with primarily by the existing commercial and criminal codes.

The other class of *Bōtaihō* injunctions that feature heavily in the statistics is that dealing with forcible recruitment and the obstruction of gang members wishing to leave the organisation. Unfortunately, the statistics do not reveal whether recruitment or secession is the larger; it seems probable that it will be the latter. The statistics provided by the regional Centres for the Eradication of *Bōryokudan* (discussed later) show that more inquiries and discussions deal with secession obstruction than forcible recruitment. This suggests a degree of dissatisfaction amongst the *yakuza* workforce and pressure on gang leaders to maintain manning levels.

Demands by leaders that subordinates amputate fingers or have tattoos are so low as to be negligible. This seems to be indicative of the trend away from the use of *yubitsume* amongst groups, in preference for fines, as a form of punishment. It is questionable whether tattoos have ever been systematically demanded by bosses. Horishi, an Osaka-based tattoo master (and, to one who has seen his work, no other title seems appropriate), argues that many modern-minded bosses actually encourage their subordinates not to have tattoos so that their future may not be confined to traditional *yakuza* activities. Apparently, some even mention to their minions that the time may come when they wish to leave the *yakuza* and a tattoo would present a major barrier to employment in a legitimate business.[12]

However, the overwhelming majority of *yakuza* met during the course of the fieldwork were extremely proud of their tattoos and insisted on showing them off. The Yamaguchi-gumi subgroup visited in Osaka had gone to the trouble of purchasing a disposable camera precisely for this purpose. In another case, an Inagawa-kai subgroup leader even removed his shirt in a busy hostess bar near Nagoya so that I could admire the artwork. The idea that *yakuza* members are dragged kicking and screaming into the tattoo studio is not credible.

It is also noteworthy that the number of injunctions concerned with gang offices is also extremely low. This might seem to suggest that *yakuza* groups have, like the *Yamaguchi-gumi*, instructed all gang offices to remove offending paraphernalia. However not all gang offices have done so. This researcher has seen the emblems of designated *yakuza* outside at least two gang offices whilst Yamanouchi asserts that various subgroup offices similarly run the risk of injunctions (interview Osaka, July 1998). In this respect, therefore, the new law is clearly not being enforced as rigorously as it might be.

Figures for injunction by group for 2000 are given in the Appendix. When adjusted to injunctions per 1,000 members, these show that the Yamaguchi-gumi and Inagawa-kai receive above average numbers of injunctions per member and the smaller gangs (taken as a group) tend to have less.

Injunction Violations

From 1992 up to the end of 2000, a total of 13,160 injunctions (12,782 *chūshi meirei*, 378 *saihatsu bōshi meirei*) had been issued under the provisions of the *Bōtaihō*. Despite this high number, the incidence of injunctions being violated is very low; as of 2000, there had been a total of thirty-five reported injunction violations. This low number is to be expected in that, once an injunction has been issued, it should be clear to the perpetrator that the game is up and continuation of the proscribed activity is highly likely to result in a penalty.

Whilst the low number of violations suggests that injunctions, once imposed, are generally respected, recent trends suggest that this respect is declining slightly. Until 1995 there had only been one case of a *Bōtaihō* injunction's being violated. The following year this jumped to six and over the next five years averaged 6.8 violations per year.

Arrests

As was mentioned in Chapter Four, the *Bōtaihō* was significant not merely for the administrative regulations it imposed on the *yakuza* but because it had a wider symbolic importance in that, for the first time, a law explicitly identified the *yakuza* as a social evil to be eradicated.

Police White Papers since 1992 routinely identify the introduction of the law as a turning point stimulating the police to renew their *yakuza*-eradication efforts. This is apparently to be achieved through a coherent three-pillared strategy (*sanbonbashira*), making pro-active and aggressive use of the existing criminal law and the *Bōtaihō* combined with the broader social approach of the regional Centres for the Eradication of *Bōryokudan*.

This being the case we should expect to be able to see this reflected in the *yakuza* arrest statistics. These do not however seem to support this argument. If we look at the figures for full members (*kōsei-in*), we see that arrests actually decline consistently throughout the period 1988–2000. This is actually not surprising as the number of *kōsei-in* itself declined following the introduction of the *Bōtaihō*. This cannot entirely be the explanation, however; the decline in arrests precedes the new law, whilst between 1986 and 1990 the number of *kōsei-in* was increasing. Given that the ratio of *kōsei-in* to *junkōsei-in* changed over the decade, it is perhaps more useful to look at these categories collectively as in Figure 6.6.

For all *yakuza* (including *jun-kōsei-in*), arrest figures are reasonably stable over the last decade, averaging around 32,000 per year (31,054 in 2000). Although arrests rose in 1992 and again in 1993, the increases were small (5 and 3.4 per cent, respectively), so are hardly compelling evidence of a sudden switch to more aggressive use of existing police powers to combat the *yakuza*. Though perhaps, given that the *yakuza*

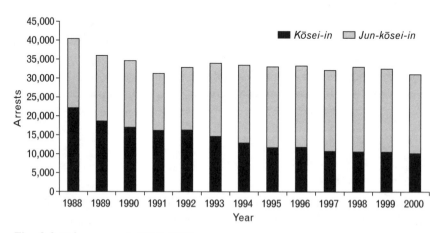

Fig. 6.6 *Yakuza* arrests 1988–2000

Source: *Keisatsu Hakusho*.

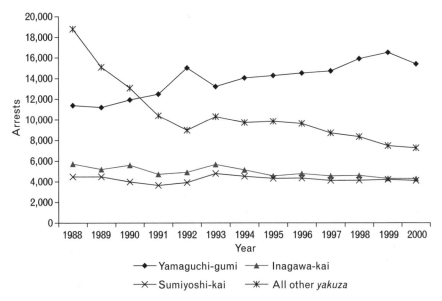

Fig. 6.7 Arrests by syndicate 1988–2000

Source: Keisatsu Hakusho.

were trying to avoid antagonising the police at the time of the new law's introduction, the fact that it rose at all, might be interpreted as significant.

What is more significant is the pronounced rise we see in the arrests for Yamaguchi-gumi members following the introduction of the *Bōtaihō*. In fact this syndicate more than accounts for all of the 1992 arrest increase; in 1992 Yamaguchi-gumi arrests rose by 20 per cent: the corresponding figure for all other *yakuza*, excluding the Yamaguchi-gumi, actually *declined* by 5 per cent (Figure 6.7).

Over the decade as a whole Yamaguchi-gumi arrests increased steadily by 29 per cent over the 1990s whilst that of the other two syndicates remained constant. Arrest figures for non-big three *yakuza* gangs dropped by 68 per cent over the same period. This is not explained by changes in the size of these two populations. If we compare arrests per member per year for 1990 and 2000 (Table 6.3), we see a big jump in the arrest probability for members of the big three syndicates. Given the static nature of the two Tokyo-based gangs' arrest figures, this increase is entirely due to increased arrests of Yamaguchi-gumi members. Over the same period, arrest probabilities for non-big-three *yakuza* fell by more than half.

Table 6.3 Arrest probabilities (arrests/member/year) 1990–2000

	1990	2000
Big three syndicates	0.50	0.79
Non-big-three gangs	0.29	0.14

It should be clear from Figure 6.7 and Table 6.3 that the collective arrest figures do not lend credence to the suggestion that the police have made more aggressive use of the existing criminal law to combat the *yakuza* collectively following the introduction of the *Bōtaihō*. However, it does seem clear that there has been far greater pressure put on the Yamaguchi-gumi over the decade. This suggests that the main focus of the *Bōtaihō* was the Yamaguchi-gumi. As if to make the point, the day the law came into effect Osaka police made a high-profile search of the gang's Kōbe headquarters.

Police antipathy towards this syndicate of course preceded this law. One Yamaguchi-gumi third-level boss interviewee did not identify the *Bōtaihō* as marking a sea-change in police attitudes towards his group, which had been 'extremely bad' for many years. In a limited sense, he said, the new law actually ameliorated operating conditions for him in that some activities that would formerly have resulted in an arrest, now merely become subject to an injunction.[13] This boss's assertion seems at odds with the supposed rationale for the *Bōtaihō's* introduction; that of dealing with *yakuza* activities that could not be dealt with by the existing body of laws. Assuming he was telling the truth here (and *Jitsuwa Jidai* May 2002: 20 notes that this view is not uncommon amongst *yakuza*), this seems supporting evidence that the police are primarily interested in regulating, rather than combating, the *yakuza*.

One thing that is striking about the level of *yakuza* arrests is how high they are. Given a total *yakuza* population of 83,600 in 2000, a gang member's probability of arrest is 37 per cent. This might lead us to expect that, within a few years, the police would manage to round up most of the country's gangsters. However, this would only work if *yakuza* arrestees were incarcerated for lengthy sentences. However, whilst the police arrested 32,511 *yakuza* members in 1999, in the same year the prosecutors processed only 8,077 *yakuza*. Of these, 6,213 were prosecuted (*Hanzai Hakusho* 2000: 523; *Keisatsu Hakusho*

2001: 131). The vast majority of these arrests therefore amount to no more than short, admittedly unpleasant, spells in police custody.

Crime Trends

As has been discussed in previous chapters, legal changes concerning *yakuza* activity tend to have been the major spur to their evolution; rather than eliminating the *yakuza* problem, these laws have pushed crime syndicates into alternative areas of criminal activity. To what extent can the same be said for the *Bōtaihō*?

First, what impact has there been on the *Bōtaihō*'s main areas of concern, the violent intervention in civil disputes, and protection-type activities? Because the *Bōtaihō* was introduced to plug the gap in pre-existing law, there are no satisfactory police statistics on the levels of *minbō*-type activities before the *Bōtaihō* came into effect. Examining the data on *Bōtaihō* injunctions does not help us greatly as we have no idea as to the level of reporting rates. The information provided by NRIPS' investigation of *yakuza* arrestees does suggest a broadly positive impact in that gang members are trying to avoid trouble with ordinary members of the public.

Assuming that purely predatory *yakuza minbō* has broadly declined as a consequence of the *Bōtaihō*, what is the situation for protection-type activities in which the *yakuza* are providing a service to a consumer?

The most obvious subcategory of this type is the traditional *yakuza shinogi* of taking protection money from Japan's enormous bar, club, and restaurant industry.[14] In an attempt to ascertain the post-*Bōtaihō* level of *yakuza* protection of this industry, the NPA commissioned the Social Safety Research Foundation (*Shakai Anzen Kenkyū Zaidan*) to conduct a study of the industry. The research project was carried out between January and February 1998 and consisted of a postal survey of 5,000 eating and drinking establishments throughout Japan.

The main findings of this survey were that 12.4 per cent of respondents claimed experience of violent demands from *yakuza* (84 per cent did not, 3.6 per cent no answer). Of these demands, 86.1 per cent included demands that various products be bought, 13.5 per cent involved demands for *shobadai* (a charge for the use of space), 3.1 per cent were demands that people be employed and 7 per cent covered miscellaneous demands.

In 37.1 per cent of cases of violent demands, the premises in question acceded to these demands. This suggests that only 4.6 per cent (12.4 × 0.371) of respondents were paying protection money and so on to *yakuza*. However, as Mugishima Fumiō, the director of this research project and formerly of NRIPS, stressed when he provided me with a copy of the report, the worth of these findings was severely undermined by the poor response rate of 17.5 per cent. Mugishima himself was inclined to believe that the true rate of protection payment in this industry was considerably higher notwithstanding the effects of the *Bōtaihō*.

Worryingly, 10.3 per cent of respondents (who might be expected to represent the more responsible part of the wider survey population) subscribed to the view that the *yakuza* are 'a necessary evil and (I) would not like them to disappear'. As one former bar owner (and later Yamaguchi-gumi third-level boss) stated in interview, were he to have telephoned the police requesting help with difficult customers, he would not have expected a positive reaction (interview, Osaka August 1998). In this situation there is a clear market opportunity for alternative sources of protection and the existence of this market has not itself been affected by the appearance of the new law.

Ujihara, a bar owner and Yamaguchi-gumi business brother from a provincial city near Nagoya, also corroborated this analysis. As a *yakuza*-associate (he described himself as 'half-*yakuza*') he had no requirement to pay protection money but, during a 1998 interview, he claimed that, of the 2,500 eating/drinking establishments in the entertainment area of his city, 30 per cent were currently paying protection money of between ¥20,000–50,000 per month to the *yakuza*. Assuming an average of ¥30,000, this yields a total annual income to the local *yakuza* of ¥270 m. Although this income had been affected by the introduction of the *Bōtaihō*, Ujihara suggested that economic factors were of greater significance. During the years of the bubble economy, there had been 4,000 hostess clubs and snack bars in this entertainment district. Revenue for Ujihara himself was down 25 per cent on the previous year.

Ujihara claimed that following the introduction of the *Bōtaihō* some clubs had attempted to sever relations with *yakuza*. In order to maintain a protective umbrella in case of trouble, these establishments had encouraged off-duty policemen to frequent their premises with the enticement of cheap drinks. Ujihara asserted that this cure was worse than the disease as, in his experience, policemen ranked alongside teachers and doctors as the worst behaved customers and the ones most likely to cause trouble with his girls.

Ujihara escorted me round various clubs, at one of which I was fortunate enough to see some trouble resolution in operation. In response to a call from the club's mama-san, Tsura, the boss from the protecting Inagawa-kai subgroup, arrived to pacify a drunken and unruly customer. Although the vigorous tongue-lashing this boss dealt out (in the plain view of the customers) was hardly the most discreet means of resolving the situation, it was not more intrusive than police intervention would have been. In terms of response time, it is highly unlikely that the police would have matched Tsura. More importantly, given that the incident itself was a relatively minor altercation, it is not clear that the police would have involved themselves anyway.

When I returned the following year (1999), Ujihara explained that the situation had changed out of all recognition. Due to a concentrated police drive on excluding *yakuza* from the prefecture's hospitality industry, many bars in the area had cut all links with their former protectors.[15] Through their exercise of the Public Morals Law (*Fūeihō*), police are able to exert considerable influence over these businesses. It seemed from Ujihara's description that this drive had had a far greater impact on the 'water trades' than the *Bōtaihō* seven years earlier. It is not clear how drinking establishments maintain their security in this new environment.

As has been described above, following the collapse of the bubble some financial institutions have made use of *yakuza* loss-cutting services whilst others have attempted to use *yakuza* to recover outstanding debts (though in the case of Sumitomo bank, with a less than satisfactory outcome). The succession of large-scale *sōkaiya* scandals that have been brought to light in recent years shows that business has found it very difficult to free itself from the protection/predation of Japanese organised crime.

Just how difficult this was, is illustrated by an incident in February 1994 in which Suzuki Juntarō, the head of Fuji Film Corporation's 'General Affairs Department', was stabbed to death. It was widely speculated at the time that the company had been attempting to cut links with *sōkaiya* extortionists and Suzuki's death had been the result.

Although the police have recently had periodic campaigns putting pressure on Japanese companies to rid themselves of *sōkaiya*, and many claim to have done so, as Nomura did in 1991, this has been easier said than done. Between 1996–1997 several high-profile incidents, involving such major firms as Ajinomoto, Nomura Securities, Takashimaya, and Mitsubishi Cars, occurred to demonstrate this. In the Takashimaya case, the large retailing company was found to have paid out ¥160 m to a group of *yakuza/sōkaiya* in order to maintain quiet shareholders' meetings between 1994 and 1995. It was further revealed that, in the seven years up to 1996, the chain had made a total of ¥700 m in illegal payments to *yakuza* (originally to quell fake social movements) and partners in a price-fixing (*dango*) ring (Iwahashi 1998: 6; *Jiji Press Newswire* 22 May 1997, 6 June 1997).

The Nomura scandal was on a far larger scale. Between 1994 and 1996, Dai-ichi Kangyō Bank (DKB) lent ¥26 bn to Koike Ryūichi, a well-known *sōkaiya* since the 1970s, with practically no collateral. With some of this money, Koike purchased 300,000 shares of Nomura Securities. From this position as a significant shareholder, Koike was able to extort ¥320 m from Nomura. As well as several arrests and indictments of senior DKB and Nomura executives, this incident resulted in the suicide of one DKB man involved in initially arranging the loan. The plot became yet thicker when Koike admitted to investigating prosecutors that three other major securities companies had also given him money (*Reuters News Service* 4–10 July 1997). Coming, as it did, on the eve of Japan's financial 'big bang', this scandal, showing persistent organised crime penetration of the mightiest financial institutions in the land, did not bode well for Japan's bid for a transparent and globally competitive financial system.

Why did DKB provide Koike with such an enormous uncovered loan? A possible explanation may be found by looking at Koike's background. Koike inherited his power from a right-wing extortionist and publisher, Kijima Rikiya, who in turn was a protégé of the infamous Kodama Yoshio. Koike's ascendancy was apparently telegraphed to the business community at the wedding of Kijima's son. At the reception, attended by a mixture of *sōkaiya*, top *yakuza* bosses, and big business executives, Koike was placed at a special table for the most important gang leaders and famous singers. Backing up Koike was a *yakuza* group, which provides him with credibility (but which also exploits him) (*Shūkan Gendai* 23 August 1997). It seems probable that it was the existence of Koike's backers that made it possible for him to 'borrow' the initial money from DKB. Koike was eventually sentenced to nine months in prison and a ¥690 m fine (*Kyōdō News Agency* 21 April 1999).

The following year Japan Airlines (JAL) was involved in a *sōkaiya*-related incident. Despite claiming to have cancelled all subscriptions to *sōkaiya* publications, they had overlooked one contract they had with a plant-leasing company. This was in fact a cover for *sōkaiya* payments mounting to ¥23 m over a three-year period (*Keisatsu Hakusho* 1999: 155). Geoffrey Tudor, a spokesman for JAL, claims that the police now are serious about *sōkaiya* and have recently put more pressure on companies to cut their links with these people (interview Tokyo, 1998).

Alongside this stern police guidance to company General Affairs Departments, the more aggressive attitude can also be seen by the heavy police presence at the company annual general meetings, which are increasingly being held on the same day. At the 1998 round of AGMs the Tokyo police deployed 5,000 officers to deal with only around 100 *sōkaiya* actively participating in the meetings (*Shūkan Jitsuwa* 2 July 1998). The overall numbers of *sōkaiya* have, according to police statistics, also fallen in recent years and by 1997 stood at 900 members and thirty groups. Only half of these identified individuals attended company AGMs in 1997 (Yokouchi 1998: 38).

In a 2000 postal survey of large businesses carried out by the National Centre for the Eradication of *Bōryokudan*, an attempt was made to evaluate the current levels of *bōryokudan/sōkaiya* activity in this area. Of the 3,000 companies surveyed, 1,977 replied (giving a surprisingly high response rate of 66 per cent). Of these respondents, 44 per cent claimed that, in the past, they had received demands for money from *bōryokudan/sōkaiya* or fake social or political movements. Of the respondents, 101 firms (5 per cent) (27.5 per cent for companies with less than 100 employees) admitted that they had paid all or part of the money demanded whilst a further 6 per cent declined to answer that question. Of the 101 companies, eighty-one were prepared to answer questions concerning the amount they paid out and in most cases the sums were less than ¥100,000. Only eleven had paid more than ¥1 m and none had given out more than ¥100 m (www1m.mesh.ne.jp/BOUTSUI/bou1/g1.htm). However, in a similar survey the previous year two companies had confessed to paying more than ¥100 m, in one case exceeding this sum by a factor of ten (*Asahi Shinbun* 19 May 1999). If we make the assumptions that non-respondents are more likely to retain links with *yakuza/sōkaiya* groups, and that some respondents may not be entirely truthful,[16] we can confidently conclude the actual level of corporate payments is higher than that suggested by this survey.

One sector of the corporate world that continues to transfer signific- ant funds to *yakuza* syndicates despite the impact of Japan's decade long recession is the construction industry. Although private-sector investment in construction has suffered massively following the collapse of the bubble, public-sector construction investment has expanded to take up much of this shortfall. Consequently, total con- struction investment held steady for the first half of the 1990s and, even though declining in nominal terms by 13.5 per cent between 1990 and 1998, at over ¥70 trillion, is hardly a negligible sum. According to Yamada Hitoshi,[17] 'probably 30–50 per cent of public-works projects in Japan now involve payoffs to gangs, and these vary from about 2 to 5 per cent of the total construction cost' (*Forbes* 3 February 1999). Assuming the lower bounds of this estimate yields a sum of ¥200 bn for 1998 ($1.5 bn).

As we have seen by now, the *yakuza* are swift to adapt to changing opportunities; so it should be no surprise to see that the elite economic-*yakuza* have also attempted to exploit the 'new-economy'. One area in which the internet can be of interest to gangsters is in the provision of pornography. Although this can be lucrative in its own right, it can be additionally so when customers' credit-card details can be obtained or they can be presented with overcharged bills. The National Consumer Affairs Centre of Japan has experienced a growing number of complaints about such bills in recent years; in an eight- month period in 2001, complaints about spurious bills for Internet sites and access numbered 12,944 (*Mainichi Shinbun* 12 February 2002). Although these firms are not typically directly run by *yakuza*, they generally enjoy a relationship with *yakuza* protectors who provide the intimidation necessary to get unhappy victims of these fake-charge scams to pay-up (Mizoguchi interview January 2003).

The frenzy surrounding hi-tech stocks of the late 1990s and early 2000s also attracted the attention of business-*yakuza*. In October 2000, with the arrest of a senior executive (and *yakuza* business brother) of one of the first companies registered on the Tokyo Stock Exchange's Mothers' market, it became apparent that *yakuza* had jumped on the dot.com bandwagon. The executive, since found guilty, had kidnapped a colleague after disputes over company strategy. According to police sources cited in the *Financial Times* (10 April 2001), both Nasdaq Japan (in Osaka) and Mothers' have had other *yakuza*-related incidents in recent years. During the dot.com bubble, the standards for listing on these markets were less stringent than for the the more established exchanges, and this made them relatively easy targets. *Yakuza* groups currently seem to be paying less attention to this market. In part this is due to the collapse of the tech-stock boom but the Osaka and Tokyo stock exchanges, in conjunction with the police, have also tightened the rules for listing on these markets.

The elite of the *yakuza* world with access to financial know-how and resources and/or an established reputation as a credible provider of protection therefore seem to have endured the lean years of the 1990s. What has happened at the other end of the *yakuza* hierarchy? It seems clear that the *Bōtaihō* has been broadly effective in raising the costs to *yakuza* of engaging in purely exploitative *minbō*-type *shinogi* targeting those engaged in legitimate activities. Of course, those operating outside of the law remain highly vulnerable to *yakuza* predation. In the light of this reduced market, how have *lumpen-yakuza* members tried to maintain their income levels?

Since the introduction of the *Bōtaihō*, two disturbing trends have appeared in the crime statistics that suggest that *yakuza* members displaced by the new law have become reliant on income generated from activities that present social problems equal to, or greater than, the ones they replace: drugs and robbery.

If we look at the police statistics for drugs offences since the beginning of the Heisei period, we see that from 1995 there has been a significant rise in the number of arrests for amphetamine-law violations. Since 1996, with the figure standing close to 20,000, the police consider that Japan is currently experiencing the third postwar period of epidemic amphetamine abuse (Higuchi 1998; *Keisatsu Hakusho* 1998: 131). Although the number of arrests in 1998 dropped below the 1996 level, the police still view the current situation as severe. From the fact that over half of the arrestees are first-time offenders, the police infer that the market is still growing (*Keisastu Hakusho* 1999: 96). The *yakuza* feature prominently amongst the figures for amphetamine-related offences; roughly 40 per cent of all such arrests are of *yakuza*, whilst this offence accounts for one quarter of all *yakuza* arrests[18] (including *jun-kōsei-in*) (*Keisatsu Hakusho* 2001: 86, 131).

The figures for amphetamine seizures do not follow such a simple pattern, reflecting the importance of serendipity in uncovering large shipments, but, if we compare the average level of seizures for 1988–1992 with that for 1993–1998, we see a clear difference. Between 1988 and 1992 an average of 174.9 kg was seized each year; the corresponding figure for the following five years was 354.0 (*Keisatsu Hakusho* 1999: 95). In both 1999 and 2000, seizures exceeded one tonne (1,976 and 1,027 kg, respectively) (*Keisatsu Hakusho* 2001: 84). As we would expect, increase in supply has been matched by a major drop in street-prices from ¥10,000 per shot in the 1980s to ¥2,000 by the end of the decade. This price-drop supports the contention that this third period of amphetamine abuse is supply-pushed rather than demand-led.

Independent estimates of current levels of consumption suggest a market of as many as 1.2 million users, and police from the NPA drugs-countermeasures section do not feel this to be an exaggeration (Ōhashi 1998: 16). There are several special characteristics of this new period but perhaps the most significant is the alarming proportion of first-time offenders, and in particular youngsters, amongst the arrestees. This is seen as being due to greater preparedness amongst dealers to sell indiscriminately to junior and high-school students (of which 60 per cent of customers are girls). The rapid increase in consumption amongst this group is illustrated by a fivefold jump in arrests of high-school students between 1994 (41) and 1996 (214).

Because of this younger, less-experienced, market, since 1998 purity levels have started to drop (interview Mizoguchi, 1999). This development of a younger clientele has also led to a move away from intravenous injection as the main form of taking the drug. Currently, amphetamines may be drunk mixed with juice, inhaled as a vapour, or ingested as a lozenge. Although the main source of supply is now China, the Golden Triangle has started producing amphetamine lozenges called '*yābā*', which may also contain heroin or LSD (Higuchi 1998).

Following rain-damage to its opium-poppy crop in 1996, North Korea has also become a major source of amphetamines with an estimated capacity of up to 15 tonnes (Perl 1998: 84–5). In January 1998, Thai officials seized 2.5 tons of ephedrine (an amphetamine-precursor chemical) destined for North Korea. Furious North Korean diplomats argued that the shipment was wanted for the legitimate purpose of making cough medicine. According to UN drugs officers, in 1998, a total of 50 tonnes of ephedrine were ordered by North Korea (*Bangkok Post* 13 May 1999; *Korean Herald* 12 May 1999; *U.S. News and World Report* 15 February 1999). The NPA estimates that 43.7 per cent of total amphetamine seizures in 1999 originated from North Korea (*Kyōdō News* 2 April 2000).

In the media and also the police literature, much is made of the importance of Iranian drug-peddling organisations in this third-epidemic period. It is these groups that are held to be responsible for the indiscriminate sale of drugs to minors. Yet, if we look at the statistics for arrests of Iranian dealers compared to *yakuza* dealers, the relative importance of the two becomes apparent.

These figures clearly show that, in terms of numbers, the Iranians account for a very small proportion of total arrests. If these Iranians occupied the apex of the distribution pyramid then indeed they might be appropriately apportioned a greater level of significance than the low numbers would otherwise warrant. However, as Ōhashi admits, they generally operate as street-level traders receiving their supplies from *yakuza* wholesalers (1998: 22). The dominant position occupied by the *yakuza* at the upper levels of the supply chain can be shown by the fact that, of the 549.0 kg of amphetamines seized by the police in 1998, 466.0 kg (85 per cent) was seized from *yakuza* (*Keisatsu Hakusho* 1999: 98).

Although the general contempt among *yakuza* for drug-dealing *yakuza* as weaklings lacking the ability and courage to earn money in more manly ways remains, the removal of alternative opportunities has meant that many *yakuza* have latched on to this business as a means of survival. Even the large syndicates, which formally prohibit their members from participation, have found themselves unable to prevent this. We can see this from the periodic directives from the Yamaguchi-gumi's executive committee instructing sub groups not to have anything to do with drugs.

During the course of one of my earliest interviews, I proposed to a career NPA officer that one side-effect of the *Bōtaihō* might have been to exacerbate the amphetamine problem. The interviewee showed a mild degree of irritation at this suggestion and advised the researcher not to spend too much time worrying about such journalistic interpretations. It is, however, hard to believe that the increase in amphetamine-dealing is not connected to the closure of other sources of revenue. The journalistic sources, so decried by the NPA interviewee, regularly make this connection.

MDMA (ecstasy), hitherto unmentioned in police white papers, has suddenly come to be a cause for police concern in 2000 with seizures totalling 77,076 tablets. However, this market seems to be primarily dominated by foreigners rather than *yakuza*; this development cannot therefore be attributed to the effects of the *Bōtaihō*.

The other conspicuous trend in the crime statistics in recent years is the increase in thefts by organised gangs. The incidence of arrests of *yakuza* members for theft jumped by almost 100 per cent, from 13,016 to 24,838, between 1991 and 1997, and this the police do accept is, at least in part, a side-effect of the *Bōtaihō* (Yasuda 1998: 27–8). In particular, the number of such cases involving ten or more individuals has shown a massive increase from below ten in the preceding years to sixty in 1997 (*Jitsuwa Jidai* December 1998).

During 1997 the NPA identified eleven theft rings composed of *yakuza* members. One arrested member admitted to the police that '*katagi* (non-*yakuza* citizens) have started issuing victims' reports so we can't make money as we used to'. This individual also claimed that, to quickly raise the money required for monthly *jōnōkin* payments in the harsh environment of the depressed economy and the *Bōtaihō*, many gang members were resorting to drug-dealing (*Yomiuri Shinbun* 20 April 1998).

Of particular concern is the increase in the sort of violent, professional robbery, which had hitherto been practically unheard of in modern Japan. In 1993, there were six robberies of armoured delivery cars compared to a total of five in the preceding three years. In 1994, there were nine, including one in Hyōgo prefecture in which two robbers made off with ¥541 m in cash (*Keisatsu Hakusho* 1995: 153). Three years later, the number of such raids had risen to twenty four. In seventeen of these cases firearms had been discharged. In 1998 the number of delivery-car robberies was eleven (in three of which guns were fired) (*Keisatsu Hakusho* 1998: 154–5, 1999: 123).

Yakuza groups are also establishing specialist groups stealing luxury cars to order and providing them with fresh key cylinders, plates, and papers before selling them on for 15–20 per cent of showroom price. One 23-man group (Yamaguchi-gumi-related) processed over eighty cars in this way before being arrested (*Jitsuwa Jidai* December 1998). In 1999, car thefts, stable in preceding years at around 35,000 per year, increased to over 43,000. In the following year, they had further increased to more than 56,000 (*Keisatsu Hakusho* 2001: 114). Stolen cars are exported not just to neighbouring countries; during an eight-month period in 2000, 865 cars stolen in Japan were located as far away as Africa, South America, and the Middle East. 672 of these vehicles were discovered in Britain which, like Japan, drives on the left (*Daily Yomiuri* 25 January 2001). Other groups specialise in diggers and trucks for the market in China and Russia, where a truck can fetch as much as ¥3 m (Iwate police 1998).

Some *yakuza* have themselves become victims of theft-gangs. One group, which operated in the Tokyo area, specialised in targeting the homes of gang bosses. It is not clear how many fell victim to this group, as to have reported to the police would have resulted in a loss of face. Eventually the group's leader, who had been expelled from a syndicate, committed suicide, and his followers gave themselves up to the police. Other such groups, composed of former *yakuza*, are still said to exist (*Jitsuwa Jidai* December 1998). One defence lawyer remarked that many of his gang-boss clients admit to now feeling unsafe on the streets (interview Osaka, June 1998). When I met some of the same individuals, they were quick to blame the increase in robbery on expelled *yakuza* but claimed that these renegades were no match for the strength of the *yakuza*.[19]

Ironically, the self-restraint on intergroup conflicts that the large *yakuza* syndicates had exercised as a response to the *Bōtaihō*, in certain respects made the streets less safe. Because firearms were no longer as essential, financially embarrassed *yakuza* members started selling their handguns to ordinary members of the public including, according to a police spokesman, professors, office-workers, and students. In one case in November 1994, a patient used such a weapon to shoot his surgeon due to dissatisfaction with a hernia operation (*Reuters News Service* 25 October 1994, 10 November 1994).

Traditionally, the *yakuza* had involved themselves in illegal activity but had a code of morality. In this code, theft was seen as something shameful, and as we saw in Chapter One there are good reasons for this. To what extent this traditional code was actually adhered to is debatable but it is a fact that in earlier times theft was not a recognised source of *yakuza* income. This development is another major step in the evolution of organised crime in Japan, of similar magnitude to the shift from traditional *yakuza shinogi* to *minbō*.

Cut-Backs

It should be clear from the above that many *yakuza* groups are currently suffering considerable financial hardship. In recognition of this fact, at the Yamaguchi-gumi direct-members' meeting (*teireikai*) on 5 April 1994, the attendees were instructed to show restraint in holding the traditional *yakuza* ceremonies, collectively known as *girikake*, at which the participants are expected to make large cash donations. The following July, the monthly *jōnōkin* dues payable by first-level group members to the organisation were dropped by ¥200,000 to ¥650,000. This cut did not apply to the top-level executives, who were still deemed to have a stable income (Yamada 1994*b*: 306). In January 1998, *jōnōkin* for directly affiliated members of the Yamaguchi-gumi was further reduced to ¥500,000, whilst that expected of executive members dropped to ¥700,000 (Herbert 2000: 155).

Yamada, broadly sympathetic to the Yamaguchi-gumi, reports that many subgroups slashed *jōnōkin* payments by as much as 50 per cent (Yamada 1994*b*: 293). News reports, however, indicate that other subgroup bosses responded to their own financial hardship by raising the *jōnōkin* burden of their subordinates (*Asia Intelligence Wire* 22 October 1999). This is putting a lot of strain on the various organisations and encouraging the sort of desperate measures outlined above.

It is also clear that the *yakuza* are trying to curb excessive expenses. Some groups have given up manning their offices round the clock under the *tōban* system. Others have started employing non-*yakuza* to man their telephones therefore freeing *kumi-in* to concentrate on finding money. In common with the rest of Japanese society, the *yakuza* have felt the need to rein in their entertainment expenses. Most severely hit are those at the bottom, over half of whom are currently dependent on the earnings of others (Yamada 1994*b*: 293).

Ujihara notes that those *yakuza* members with stable and high incomes are increasing the wealth disparity within syndicates by lending money to their less-fortunate colleagues (interview 1999). This causes problems of intra-organisational harmony, especially in cases of default. Since September 1994, the Yamaguchi-gumi executive committee has forbidden intra-syndicate money lending.

Bōryokudan Eradication Centres

As well as increasing the scope of controls on *yakuza* activity, the *Bōtaihō* also made provisions for the establishment of Centres Promoting the Eradication of *Bōryokudan* (*bōtsuisen*). The main functions of these centres are to provide the following: counselling on *yakuza*-related problems; training for company employees particularly susceptible to violent *bōryokudan* demands; literature and posters increasing public awareness of the threat of *bōryokudan* and the available countermeasures; advice and assistance for *bōryokudan* members wishing to leave their gang and return to straight society.

The first of these centres actually predates the *Bōtaihō* by several years as Hiroshima prefecture had created the *Bōryoku Tsuihō Hiroshima Kenmin Kaigi* in 1987. By the time the new law was passed, eight other prefectures had followed suit due to the favourable evaluation of Hiroshima's centre. With the implementation of the *Bōtaihō*, the remaining administrative areas quickly created their own centres with Niigata being the last to do so in July 1992 (Sumida 1997: 207).

All of these centres enjoy the legal status of foundations (*zaidan hōjin*) and receive no central government funding. Sumida (1997: 208) suggests that they are largely dependent on donations (tax-deductible) from private business. However, in the case of the two centres visited by the researcher (Kanagawa and Iwate) the vast bulk of their endowments came from local government. Half of Kanagawa's ¥500-m fund came from the prefectural government, 40 per cent from the city, town, and village assemblies, and only 10 per cent came from business. In Iwate just under a quarter of the ¥632-m fund was derived from business.

Although the researcher was not shown a breakdown for the figures in Kanagawa, in Iwate by far the biggest single private contributor was the local *pachinko* industry (nearly 5 per cent of the total fund). This seems natural in the light of the historical relationship between this business and the *yakuza*. However, it is hard to avoid the conclusion that the control that the police wield over *pachinko* through the Public Morals Law (*Fūeihō*) also encourages generosity on the part of the *pachinko* association.

The formal organisation of these centres is closely wedded to the prefectural and police hierarchies, with the posts of president and vice president being held by the governor and director general of the prefectural police, respectively. At the operational level, however, the centres are effectively police concerns being situated in the regional police headquarters and staffed by retired police officers. In this respect, it is impossible to ignore the observation made by several academic interviewees (Katō, Nishimura et al.) that one of the underlying motives behind the establishment of these centres was to provide *amakudari* (post-retirement job) positions for retired police officers.

No doubt the police can defend their close association with the regional centres in that they have the requisite experience to most effectively fulfil the duties of the *bōtsuisen*. In addition, they have the advantage of being the one organisation impervious to *yakuza* intimidation. These justifications notwithstanding, I find it hard to reject the cynical institutional empire-building interpretation.

Alongside the full-time staff (four in Kanagawa, three in Iwate), there is a team of part-time counsellors (*sōdan yakuin*) (totalling eleven in Kanagawa and nine in Iwate) composed of lawyers, probation officers, youth-guidance officers, and retired policemen. Nationally there were a total of 680 such counsellors by 1997 (Sumida 1997: 214).

In 1998, counsellors from the regional centres conducted 12,450 separate discussions with members of the public (see Appendix QP). However, two-thirds of all official *yakuza*-related discussions are actually conducted by the police. If we remove general discussions concerning the *Bōtaihō* and the work of the centres themselves, and confine ourselves to discussions concerning concrete problems, this proportion rises to over three-quarters. This might suggest that, at least in terms of counselling activity, these centres are only of marginal importance. The potential argument that some individuals may be unwilling to talk to police officers is weakened by the close police links enjoyed by the centres in terms both of facilities and personnel.

Another of the key responsibilities of the centres is to provide training in appropriate techniques for responding to *yakuza* demands. In recent years, over 50,000 individuals have received such training every year (*Keisatsu Hakusho* 1998: 188, 1999: 161; Sumida 1997: 220). Most of these trainees were employed in legitimate industries susceptible to *yakuza* victims: finance/insurance, construction, real estate, and game centres (*pachinko*). In Iwate there were also a high number of taxi drivers, parcel-delivery company employees, car salesmen, and petrol-pump attendants, trained in 1997.

Training consists of an afternoon's package of lectures introducing the trainees to the current state of the *yakuza* and the provisions of the *Bōtaihō*. This is followed by a video portraying various (quite convincing) scenarios involving *minbō*. In conclusion, there is a 45-minute lecture on mental preparation, reaction to *yakuza* demands, and the availability of the centres and police for discussion (training program Kanagawa centre). Trainees are also presented with manuals to take away for further study and phone numbers for the centre and police. The police white papers state that role-playing exercises are also part of the training but this did not appear on the Kanagawa program, and the Iwate centre claimed that this was only available for those attending the refresher course (three years after the initial one).

Although the reality of the training does not seem to quite match the expectations raised by the description of this aspect of the centres' work in the police/centre literature, police white papers routinely give examples of employees' making use of their training (e.g. Keisatsu Hakusho 1999: 161). It is, however, questionable to what extent the trainees' employers themselves were actually taking *yakuza* countermeasures seriously. In February 1993, the police surveyed 3,061 big businesses with a response rate of 77 per cent. Of the respondents, only 25 per cent claimed that they were taking steps to prevent falling victim to *yakuza* demands (Sumida 1997: 220). It is to be expected that the non-respondents were even less scrupulous.

More importantly, training company employees in how to deal with *yakuza* demands is of dubious worth if the same companies are themselves making use of these groups. As we have seen, in the past, businesses and politicians have frequently dealt with *yakuza* demands by calling on the services of other similar groups. Recent incidents suggest no great grounds for optimism that this practice is in significant decline.

Rehabilitation

The other major duty of the regional centres is to promote the secession and rehabilitation of *yakuza* members. Given the current financial hardship experienced by many *yakuza* members, this would appear to be an ideal opportunity to persuade them to leave. However, insofar as this hardship is economically determined (rather than due to the *Bōtaihō*), the centres are faced with a catch-22 problem: because of the recession, seceders have little hope of alternative employment; if the economy were booming, *shinogi* would be better and there would be little incentive to leave.

As of mid-1998, the police and centres had managed to persuade approximately 4,250 gang-members to leave their groups since the introduction of the *Bōtaihō* (*Keisatsu Hakusho* 1999: 159). The most important factor contributing to the successful rehabilitation to society of these individuals is their ability to find legitimate employment. To this end, each prefecture has a Social Rehabilitation Strategy Council (*Shakai Fukki Taisaku Kyōgikai*) composed of representatives of the centres, police, prison service, probation service, and the local employment security office.

In addition, a number of industries cooperate with these councils by offering assistance in providing employment to *bōryokudan* seceders. By 1996, an impressive total of 5,190 companies were helping in this way (Sumida 1997: 217). However, of the 4,250 gang leavers, only 540 (13 per cent) have found work through the good offices of the councils and the cooperating companies (*Keisatsu Hakusho* 1999: 159–61). These dismal figures may not reflect the entire situation. A follow-up survey conducted in 1993 showed that, of the 1,064 individuals persuaded to leave gangs by the police or centres in the first year of the *Bōtaihō*, 621 (58 per cent) had found work within three months. A further 7.5 per cent were actively looking for work, whilst the same proportion had no strong motivation to find work or were doing nothing. The fate of the remainder was unclear (Sumida 1997: 217).

Given the state of the Japanese economy at the time of writing (December 2002), it is highly unlikely that, were a similar survey to be conducted now, it would yield results as favourable to the centres. In both Iwate and Kanagawa, the researcher found rehabilitation rates even lower than those of the 1998 police white paper. At the Kanagawa centre during 1997, about 400 separate discussions were held with *yakuza* members about leaving their group. Of these, only ten members actually left.

Over the same period the Kanagawa police managed to persuade thirty-four *yakuza* members to leave. The greater effectiveness of the police is due to the fact that most of these leavers are in custody and will receive greater leniency if they agree to leave their gangs. Because of the high likelihood of deception there is a need to check up on gang leavers. Unfortunately, the Kanagawa police can only conduct surveys within their own prefecture and, consequently, it was not clear what happened to many of these individuals, though the interviewees suggested that many of them returned home or possibly joined gangs in other areas.

Since the introduction of the Bōtaihō, nine yakuza members had, by 1998, left gangs in Kanagawa and had found work. Of this total, four had quit; so only five were still known to be in gainful employment, most of them in the construction industry. In Iwate, only two former yakuza had found work through the social-rehabilitation council and one had since rejoined his gang.

Iwate also runs a more specialised scheme for former tekiya (outdoor stall-holder) yakuza. Until the end of the Shōwa period, the yakuza in Iwate had been overwhelmingly involved in tekiya activities and had been broadly tolerated by the police. In 1991, Kuwata of the Yamaken-gumi arrived in Iwate and 'invited' the most prominent gang to join his group. Once this had happened, the other yakuza groups in Iwate felt compelled to join one of the large syndicates for their own protection.

Alarmed at this development, the police started to take more aggressive measures against the yakuza. One of these steps was to prevent yakuza participation in festivals—hitherto the traditional economic bedrock of the tekiya. To help those that agreed to leave their gangs, three stall-holders' unions (essentially legitimised tekiya groups) were set up under police guidance. The impact of this change has been mixed. Under this new system, the allocation of stall sites is no longer determined by seniority within the yakuza world. Allocation by drawing lots, though fair, introduces an element of uncertainty as traders cannot gauge in advance how much stock they require. Consequently, place-allocation is now determined through negotiations with the police and festival organiser (interview Morioka, 1998).

Since non-yakuza stall-holders are now able to participate in festivals, an element of competition has been introduced, which has reduced profits. Harada, the director of one of the unions and former Sumiyoshi-kai man, claimed that his sales had dropped by 30 per cent since 1992, though he accepted that the bubble had been the largest factor behind this.

Income has also been affected by the recent trend for some festivals to restrict participation to local inhabitants in order to keep things clean. Interestingly, the fees for cleaning and electricity have also increased now that they are no longer set by the *yakuza*. Whereas they would formerly range from ¥2,000 to ¥10,000 per day, currently they may be as much as ¥30,000. On the other hand, now that he has left the Sumiyoshi-kai, Harada no longer has the financial burden of paying *jōnōkin*, taking his turn at the office-manning (*tōban*) rota and attending various yakuza ceremonies. Harada estimates that this cost him a total of ¥2 m per year.

Although the net effect of these changes means that Harada is no better off materially, he was keen to stress that the current situation was preferable and that his wife and children were much happier now he had left the Sumiyoshi-kai. He also praised the police for the help they had given him in going straight. Because the interview was conducted with two policemen sitting close by, it is not clear to what extent credence can be given for this last affirmation. It is, however, clear that this is one area in which rehabilitation is likely to be successful as there is no change in the individual's basic business.

The problem with rehabilitation of retired *yakuza* is that many of them are practically unemployable. In general, they possess low educational qualifications[20] and, according to most police interviewees, are lazy with little willpower. The additional stigma of a criminal record, tattoo, and amputated fingers, mean that the employment available to them tends to be confined to construction-type work. Given the depressed state of the construction industry this sort of employment is currently very uncertain and many former *yakuza* have ended up living rough on the streets of San'ya and Kamagasaki (interviews San'ya 1998, corroborated by observation of half-finished tattoos and truncated fingers amongst the inhabitants).

In a 1994 NRIPS investigation (Yonezato et al. 1994) into the factors promoting secession and rehabilitation, it was found that essentially those factors encouraging the former also assisted the latter. In particular, they drew attention to a negative correlation between age and successful rehabilitation; younger members are far better able to leave and adapt to legitimate employment. They are also less likely to bear tattoos and amputated fingers. The findings noted that counselling and a supportive environment were also highly important to both secession and rehabilitation; so in this respect there is clearly a role for the centres to perform.

In order to remove the stigma of tattoos and missing fingers, it is now surgically possible to remove the former and replace the latter. This is, however, highly expensive. A fake finger typically costs ¥50,000, transplanting a toe ¥100,000, and tattoo removal ¥20,000 per cm^2. Neither the police nor the centres can help *yakuza*-leavers with these expenses; the most they can do is provide living expenses for a couple of days (¥10,000–20,000) whilst the seceder finds his feet (Kanagawa centre).

Internal Conflict

The considerably reduced opportunities to make money in the current climate have also resulted in increased disputes over *shinogi* between members of the same syndicate. Although same-syndicate member-ship might be thought to prevent this, the main focus of loyalty is to one's immediate gang rather than to the wider syndicate. Syndicate membership does, however, provide a mechanism for the rapid resolution of conflicts of this type (interviews Yamaguchi-gumi sub-bosses, Osaka 1998).

When such trouble does occur, as far as the Yamaguch-gumi is con-cerned, settlement is currently determined according not to the merits of the case but to the relative strength of the disputants. In this sense, intragroup conflicts are essentially the same as intergroup ones. Within the Yamaguchi-gumi the strongest organisations are the Yamaken-gumi and, until 1997, the Nakano-kai. The ascendancy of the Yamaken-gumi, combined with the constant demands for money from the fifth-generation leadership, itself drawn from the Yamaken-gumi, has caused discontent amongst the other groups within the syndicate (interview Fujimura, Osaka 1998; interviews Mizoguchi, 1998, 1999).

Some illustration of this discontent is given in the interview of an unidentified former Yamaguchi-gumi senior executive interviewee of Mizoguchi (1997: 258):

If we talk about the Yamaguchi-gumi, Watanabe san just shows favouritism to his allies and the view has taken hold that he is trying to make the Yamaguchi-gumi into a Yamaken-gumi chain. At the moment Takumi (*wakagashira*) is around so somehow or other it keeps going without splitting up. But Takumi is sick[21] so it is a question of what happens if he dies. There is a real possibility that it will break up.

On 28 August 1997, Takumi was shot dead in the coffee shop of a Kōbe Hotel, where he had been discussing the proposed new organised-crime countermeasures law (*soshiki hanzai taisaku hō*) with headquarters chief Kishimoto Saizō (who had been unharmed in the attack). No other recent incident within the *yakuza* world more clearly illustrates the way in which political, economic, and personal rivalries within large syndicates strain the bonds holding these groups together. Given the types of people who rise within such organisations, this is perhaps inevitable within a large syndicate such as the Yamaguchi-gumi.

Suspicion for Takumi's shooting quickly fell on the Nakano-kai when the get-away car was traced to a member of one of its subgroups. The reaction of Yamaguchi-gumi leadership, however, showed confusion and indecision. After weighing up the available evidence, three days after the incident Watanabe punished Nakano Tarō, the 1,700-man-strong Nakano-kai's leader, with expulsion (*hamon*). His group was similarly treated.

The following day police from Hyōgo, Kyoto, and Osaka police forces launched coordinated searches of Yamaguchi-gumi and Nakano-kai offices. The NPA also assembled *yakuza* specialists from police forces throughout Japan for an emergency meeting in Hyōgo prefecture. Given that it was widely felt that this event could trigger off another internal war of the magnitude of the Yamaichi War of the 1980s, the police were evidently keen to prevent the conflicts from escalating.

Nakano apparently met his expulsion with equanimity and reportedly told his top executives that he would probably be reinstated within 2–3 years. At the same time, many other groups within the syndicate felt that this punishment was insufficiently severe and, on 3 September, Watanabe felt compelled to completely sever all relations (*zetsuen*) with Nakano. Even before this change, revenge attacks on Nakano-kai offices had started but, from 4 September onwards, these increased, causing the Yamaguchi-gumi headquarters to contact all block chiefs with orders to prevent such attacks. This order had little effect and the attacks continued. On 30 September, the headquarters issued a second, sterner, warning that 'if groups attack Nakano-kai-related buildings, we will deal with the leaders of superior groups'. This directive also failed to prevent retaliatory action.

In response to these attacks, the police took vigorous measures with frequent and widespread searches of both Yamaguchi-gumi and Nakano-kai offices and houses. Between Takumi's shooting and 17 October, the police made at least 910 separate searches and eighty-seven arrests directly related to the *vendetta* shootings (Yamada 1998: 453–63). An Osaka-based delivery-driver friend of mine also recalled massive police security around prime targets during this period.

It is worth noting that, despite the provisions of the *Bōtaihō* allowing for the closure of gang offices at times when they present a threat to the safety of the general public, during this period only one gang office was subject to such an order when, on 1 December, the Nakano-kai headquarters was closed. Perhaps this was due to confusion as to the status of the Nakano-kai as it was not then a designated *bōryoku-dan* in its own right (designated July 1999).

Perhaps the most significant police action of this time was the arrest of Kuwata Kenkichi, head of the powerful Yamaken-gumi, on 26 December for violation of the firearms and sword regulation law (*jōtōhō*). This was important because, at the time of arrest, Kuwata was not himself armed but subordinates travelling in a separate vehicle were. The police argued that, as their superior, Kuwata shared criminal liability. A month before, the police had tried to arrest two other top executives, Tsukasa Shinobu and Takizawa Takashi, on similar legal grounds, but they had managed to escape, though several *kumi-in* were arrested and found to be armed. Tsukasa gave himself up in June the following year but Takizawa was only arrested in July 2001 after being on the run for just under 4 years.

This more flexible interpretation by the prosecutors of conspiracy is indicative of a shift to a more generally aggressive tone of law-enforcement *vis-à-vis* these syndicates. For this change to impact significantly on the *yakuza*, the prosecutors' interpretation must be shared by the courts. The judicial reaction has however been mixed: Kuwata was found guilty by the Tokyo district court in March 2000 and sentenced to seven years; this decision was upheld by the Tokyo High Court in October 2001 (*Jitsuwa Dokyumento* December 2001: 20). Tsukasa, however, was found not guilty on the same charge, and the prosecutors appealed to the Osaka High Court. As of mid-2002, both this appeal and Takizawa's case were still in progress.

As we can see, the killing of Takumi has therefore had a profound impact on the leadership of the Yamaguchi-gumi, which the weekly press still refer to as in a 'state of paralysis'. We can see this from the chart in Appendix B, which lists the top executives of the organisation. Takumi, the man who had been responsible for the day-to-day running of the organisation, was dead. His role was temporarily filled by head-quarters chief Kishimoto Saizō. Nakano was expelled; Kuwata was imprisoned; Takizawa and Tsukasa were both fighting cases; Hanabusa, Furukawa, and Kuramoto were ill (Kuramoto died the following year on 4 December).

Kuwata had been Takumi's chosen successor as *wakagashira*, but later refused the post. At the time of writing, December 2002, this all-important post remains unfilled, with Kishimoto operating as '*waka-gashira* representative'. According to the strict hierarchy consciousness of the *yakuza* world, Kishimoto is ineligible for the role of *wakagashira* as he has a brother relationship with Watanabe whilst a prerequisite is that he should be a *kobun* (fictive son).

By the spring of 2002, it had been decided to appoint a new *waka-gashira* and top executives. This was not eventually carried out due to fallout following the fatal beating of a Kōbe University of Mercantile Marine student by Yamaguchi-gumi subgroup members after an argu-ment over their boss's car parking. After a staggeringly inept police reaction to this incident, the mayor of Kōbe publicly called on the police to toughen up their *yakuza* countermeasures, and the police chief of Kōbe equally publicly asserted that all his resources would be dedicated to this end.

In this climate, the Yamaguchi-gumi judged it best not to antagonise the police by strengthening their organisation's top management level, and the proposed promotions were postponed,[22] though, in the summer, one new *waka-gashira-hōsa* (assistant under-boss) was finally installed (*Jitsuwa Dokyumento* June 2002; Mizoguchi private correspondence).

Why did Nakano kill Takumi? The weekly press abound with theo-ries. What is clear, however, is that there was personal enmity between the two men. Nakano is a highly aggressive, argumentative man (known as '*kenka* Tarō'—literally 'quarrel Tarō') whilst Takumi was a much smarter, politically adept 'economic *yakuza*'. For some years, Nakano had been busily expanding into Kyoto in order to take advan-tage of the massive public-works projects, such as the construction of Kyoto's ¥150 bn new railway station, then under way. This had inevitably brought him into conflict with the local Aizu-kotetsu, and, in July 1996, Nakano was attacked by a squad of Aizu-kotetsu hit-men. Nakano's bodyguard shot and killed two of the assailants, successfully foiling the attack.

A peaceful reconciliation was quickly brokered between the two groups by Takumi and Zugoshi (then the *wakagashira* of the Aizu-kotetsu), with one of Zugoshi's subordinates offering an amputated finger by way of apology. Nakano, still helping the police with their enquiries, was not involved with this settlement and, once released, wanted revenge, not amicable settlements. Takumi, however, forced him to accept this situation despite the massive slight to the dignity and reputation Nakano felt this represented to both himself personally and the syndicate as a whole.

This personal animosity is not however sufficient reason for the killing. The most plausible theory, and the one widely held by informed interviewees, as to why Takumi actually was killed is that he had become too powerful within the organisation. One interviewee close to the Yamaguchi-gumi believes that Nakano operated on his own initiative but was convinced that he was doing a favour for Watanabe. This would explain both the confused reaction of the leadership and Nakano's conviction that he would shortly be readmitted to the Yamaguchi-gumi.

The circumstances surrounding the death of Takumi and its aftermath are enlightening for a number of reasons. First, the incident illustrates the tensions currently within the Yamaguchi-gumi leadership. This is an almost inevitable consequence of the size and composition of the syndicate; all of the top executives are leaders of their own power groups. In this respect, the Yamaguchi-gumi resembles a feudal monarchy with powerful barons to whom the king is in thrall. This is in marked contrast to the strong central leadership of third-generation boss Taoka, who had single-handedly created the modern Yamaguchi-gumi through military conquest.

This incident is also important because it helps explode another *yakuza* myth concerning loyalty and the sanctity of the *oyabun–kobun* relationship. Once it became clear that the Nakano-kai was not going to be re-admitted to the Yamaguchi-gumi, and with the pressure of police searches and Takumi-gumi retaliation making it practically impossible to earn money, it became clear to many in the Nakano-kai that their group had no future. By 10 October, of the sixty-four sub-groups originally comprising the Nakano-kai, only fifteen remained. These groups expressed the wish that they realign themselves with other groups within their former syndicate. When, later that month, the top executive committee lifted its ban on re-admission of Nakano-kai subgroups, many of them flocked to the Yamaken-gumi headquarters. The Nakano-kai itself has since shrunk to a tiny rump group of Nakano's closest associates and, as of June 2001, numbered only 170 men.

Although this behaviour is perfectly rational, both economically and in terms of self-preservation, in terms of traditional *yakuza* ethics of unquestioning obedience to one's boss and endurance, the Nakano-kai falls short of the ideal. During the early stages of this incident, the popular press had made much of the Nakano-kai's reputation as being a heavily armed, hard-fighting group with plenty of *teppōdama* (literally 'bullets'—members supposedly ready to risk their lives for the cause). When put to the test, however, the subgroups quickly fled to the security of the main syndicate.

Takumi's death also throws into relief the limits of control that the central executive exercises over the rank-and-file membership. Despite the repeated instructions not to commit revenge attacks on Nakano-kai facilities, they continued unabated. The fact that other executive-committee instructions have to be repeated suggests that lack of control is not confined to this particular event. If we look at the repeated demands from the top executives/executive committee not to have anything to do with drugs, not to have anything to do with *jūsen*, not to have anything to do with 'business terrorism', the picture of an organisation that is constantly struggling to keep control over its members emerges.

In Chapter One, we noted Schelling's observation that one possible advantage of organised crime over disorganised crime is that the organisation internalises the costs of increased law enforcement that would otherwise be externalities to the individual perpetrator. It is argued here that the Yamaguchi-gumi leadership is trying to square the circle in that it makes these demands on its members whilst continuing to place unrealistic financial burdens on them. In the current hostile legal and economic environment, the imperative to make money transcends all other considerations including the prohibitions of both legal and underworlds.

This problem is by no means unique to the Yamaguchi-gumi; due to the problems in making money in the comparatively harsh environment of the 1990s, *yakuza* gang members are inevitably drawn to money-making activities that incur high costs to the organisation itself. The increased reliance on drugs and theft as a source of income for lower ranking *yakuza* discussed earlier is an obvious example of this phenomenon.

The strain imposed by tougher business conditions has not just been experienced at the intra-organisational level. Prior to the introduction of the *Bōtaihō*, the large syndicates, fearing the new law's provisions, had agreed to nurture the path of peaceful coexistence. There are however clear limits to the extent to which this can be achieved. As we have seen, a significant proportion of *yakuza* business is based on providing actors, in both the under- and upperworlds, with protection from other *yakuza*.

The likelihood of intergroup conflict is increased by the comparative paucity of economic opportunities in the 1990s; if there is enough money around for everybody, then sharing is easier. Even within Tokyo, where the Kantō Hatsuka-kai has maintained a tolerably high level of intergroup harmony, there are now signs of strain. Prior to the current economic hardship of the *yakuza* world, severe penalties would be imposed on members of gangs comprising the Kantō Hatsuka-kai should they use guns against fellow members. Such actions would not infrequently result in irrevocable expulsion (*zetsuen*). More recently, these rules have apparently been interpreted more mildly and at a time when the need for them is more pressing than ever (*Jitsuwa Dokyumento* December 2001: 16–25).

In 2001, there was a rash of trouble between members of the Kantō Hatsuka-kai. Most notable of these was a highly publicised shooting of Sumiyoshi-kai bosses at a gang funeral in August 2001. One subgroup boss was killed and another injured along with another gang member. The assailants, an Inagawa-kai subgroup boss and one of his *kobun*, had attended the funeral as mourners and were apprehended by others attending the ceremony. Two days later another Sumiyoshi-kai boss was fatally shot outside his mistress's apartment in what was seen as a related attack (*Mainichi Daily News* 20 August 2001; *Agence France Press* 19 August 2001). For the two largest and most powerful groups within the Kantō Hatsuka-kai to come to blows has severe implications for the organisation; both of these big syndicates alone is considerably larger and more powerful than the other members combined and they cannot be bullied into line as would be the case for a conflict between two smaller groups.

Even when trouble does not include one of the big syndicates, it seems that the Kantō Hatsuka-kai's ability to resolve conflict has been seriously undermined. In March 2001 three senior members of a Kokusui-kai sub-group were expelled for opposing the syndicate's change from a federal to a centralised structure. The following month, exchanges of gunfire between the two factions started and went on intermittently throughout the summer and autumn. Sumiyoshi-kai-chō Fukuda Hareaki apparently attempted to mediate but both disputants refused this offer (*Asahi News Service* 7 July 2001; *Mainichi Daily News* 12 October 2001).

From the inception of the Kantō Hatsuka-kai in 1972 until the bursting of the bubble, the Tokyo *yakuza* had only experienced favourable economic conditions and, given a steadily expanding pie, the self-imposed limitations were acceptable to the association's members. In the recession of the late 1990s and early 2000s such forbearance is increasingly hard to sustain. Whilst this association is now seen as lacking its former potency, there is one good reason for its continued existence; it presents a united front in the face of the threat posed by Yamaguchi-gumi advances on the capital.

Continued Eastwards Expansion

If we look at Nakano's behaviour in moving into Kyoto, we can see that the tendency to ignore directives extends to the highest reaches of the Yamaguchi-gumi; Kuwata had become a brother of Zugoshi, and Yamaguchi-gumi members were consequently instructed to avoid causing trouble with the Aizu-kotetsu. Similarly, the brotherhood exchange between Watanabe and Inagawa carried the understanding that the Yamaguchi-gumi would keep out of Tokyo.

Though the Yamaguchi-gumi maintained this fiction by not opening gang offices, many subgroups operate in the Tokyo area through business fronts. In addition, many Yamaguchi-gumi groups have established offices in the surrounding prefectures. Tokyo police estimated in 1999 that 500 Yamaguchi-gumi men (in seventeen groups) were operating in the capital.

The syndicate has been actively trying to expand into Tokyo since the end of the 1980s but the pace of this process is said to have slowed slightly since the death of Takumi.[23] The forces causing this expansion, however, are still present. Most important of these is the fact that the Kansai area is so heavily populated with Yamaguchi-gumi men chasing limited opportunities that those not belonging to one of the stronger subgroups have little chance to progress as they are unable to deploy violence against fellow syndicate members. The other reason is that there is, *yakuza* say, five times as much money available to the *yakuza* in Tokyo as in the Osaka-Kōbe area (interview criminal defence lawyer, Osaka, August 1998).

Consequently, in recent years there have been a number of small conflicts between Yamaguchi-gumi sub-groups and Kantō gangs. In the first half of 1998, there was a running spat between the Matsuba-kai and a Yamaguchi-gumi group following the shooting of a Matsuba-kai advisor in Tsukuba city. This was followed in October of the same year by a conflict between the Sumiyoshi-kai and Yamaguchi-gumi Konishi-ikka (*Shūkan Taishū* 16 November 1998, *Shūkan Jitsuwa* 12 November 1998). In June 1999, in a two-day-long flash-fire of retaliatory attacks, the Konishi-ikka clashed with the Kokusui-kai in sixteen separate incidents in Tokyo and adjacent pre-fectures. This last conflict is of interest as it was the first time in which the police made use of provisional injunctions (*kari meirei*) prohibiting the use of five separate gang offices. The police, fearing widespread escalation of this conflict, also sent warnings to all prefectural police headquarters and mobilised 600 men to stand watch over 260 separate gang-related facilities (*Shūkan Jitsuwa* 24 June 1999).

Although these conflicts are generally resolved through the mediation of the Kantō Hatsuka-kai and the Yamaguchi-gumi representative responsible for the Kantō block (block-*sekininsha*), it is easy to understand the police reaction. The movement of Yamaguchi-gumi groups into Tokyo can only upset the balance, now increasingly precarious, maintained by the Kantō Hatsuka-kai. It is not clear what the initial causes of these var-ious conflicts were, but there have been several cases in which Kantō *yakuza* groups have occupied buildings and the owners have brought in Yamaguchi-gumi groups to remove them. More recently, an article in *Asahi Evening News* (21 August 1999) reported that the Yamaguchi-gumi's Asakawa-kai subgroup was attempting to take over the illegal porno-graphic video market in Tokyo's Kabuki-chō entertainment district.

Conclusion

Given the enormous impact of the bubble's collapse on *yakuza* finances, it is extremely difficult to quantify, with any degree of preci-sion, the impact of the *Bōtaihō* on Japan's organised-crime syndicates.

Although the bursting of the bubble economy has seriously undermined many, formerly profitable, areas of *yakuza* activity, the rapid
evolution of new types of business to take advantage of this changed
environment clearly illustrates the highly fluid nature of organised
crime. Despite the problems of disentangling the effects of these two
events, it is clear that the *Bōtaihō* has had significant effects on the
yakuza.

Perhaps most encouraging of these is that, to the extent that a
formerly grey area has become subject to controls, the *Bōtaihō* has been
effective. In cases of purely predatory *yakuza* 'violent demands' in
which no service is provided to the victim, the *Bōtaihō* now provides a
legal remedy. The increase in numbers of injunctions issued under the
provisions of the *Bōtaihō*, combined with the extremely low rate of
injunction violation, shows that, within these limited parameters, the
Bōtaihō may be positively evaluated.

However, for cases in which the victims of *yakuza* violent demands
are themselves operating outside, or at the margins of, the law,
recourse to the *Bōtaihō* is not an option. For such individuals as illegal
foreign workers and street prostitutes, *yakuza* protection, and or predation, therefore continues as before. Perhaps more significant is the
continued existence of an active demand for the *yakuza*'s protective
services from various sectors of the legitimate world (as the succession
of *yakuza*-related scandals unfolding at the time of the *Bōtaihō*'s introduction and after illustrates). Given the existence of this demand, it is
highly unlikely that *yakuza* interaction with the legitimate world will
ever entirely disappear, regardless of administrative orders or other
legal prohibitions.

In many cases the main protective function provided by these
groups is to squash other *yakuza* or right-wing groups. This immediately begs the question why the consumers of *yakuza* protection do not
instead make use of the law to resolve their initial problem. One
answer to this is that these individuals themselves are frequently
tainted by scandal, criminal involvement, or earlier *yakuza* connection,
making them reluctant to seek legal, and public, redress. As discussed
in earlier chapters, the second reason is of course that the costs of
employing such legitimate mechanisms still exceed those of informal
dispute resolution.

As we saw from the immediate reaction of the various *yakuza*
syndicates to the *Bōtaihō*, the threat of gang-office closure at times of

inter-syndicate conflict has been a broadly effective inducement for these groups to quickly resolve their differences peacefully when conflict arises. The two *yakuza* 'summits' of 1991 and the subsequent '*sakazuki* diplomacy' suggest a trend for the western syndicates to adopt the less confrontational norms of the Tokyo-based groups. This is a direct consequence of the *Bōtaihō*.

Despite the pacifying effects of the *Bōtaihō*, there are limits to which this control function can remain viable, as the reaction to Takumi's murder in 1997 shows. The apparent inability of the Yamaguchi-gumi's leadership to exercise total control over subgroups can also be seen from the strident directives repeatedly issued by the executive committee. This has become increasingly significant as subgroups, suffering from the combined effects of the *Bōtaihō* and economic recession, become more dependent on proscribed, and hitherto disparaged, sources of income such as amphetamine trading and organised theft, despite instructions to the contrary from their superiors.

This increase in drugs and theft crimes, in addition to the disorganised activities of former *yakuza* members, is a partial vindication of the thesis put forward by Ino Kenji and others that the *Bōtaihō* will exacerbate the crime situation in Japan. Given that we have seen that previous organised-crime countermeasures have pushed *yakuza* members out of certain activities into others, this is not entirely surprising. However, Ino's thesis can be no more than only partially vindicated. This is due to two separate considerations. First, we lack an acceptable calculus to determine whether the drop in one category of crime accompanied by a rise in another represents a net gain or loss to society; second, we cannot exclude the contributory role of extraneous economic factors to the recent evolution of the *yakuza*.

It is also highly likely that Yamaguchi-gumi headquarters' control will be subject to further strain in the near term, as Yamaguchi-gumi subgroups, frozen out of the crowded economic niches available in the Kansai area, turn to the capital in greater numbers in search of new sources of income. This will in all probability test the 'peaceful-coexistence' and conflict-resolution mechanisms of the modern *yakuza* close to breaking point.

7

Yakuza, Law and the State

If we look at the relationship between the *yakuza* and the police over the last five decades, a number of conclusions can be drawn. The first of these is that this relationship has been dynamic rather than static. Second, the *yakuza* is not a monolithic organisation but is a collective term for a number of different groups, and these have developed different strategies *vis-à-vis* their relationship with the upper world. Third, it is perhaps also a mistake to view the police as a monolithic organisation. There are two main dividing lines within the police organisation, one vertical, the other, horizontal. The vertical cleavage lies between the security (*kōan*) and the criminal-investigation (*keiji*) police. The horizontal line separates the elite bureaucratic 'career' police from the rank-and-file police officers responsible for carrying out the actual tasks of policing. Let us look at each of these considerations in greater detail.

The *yakuza*–police relationship prior to the first summit strategy of 1964 most closely approximates to an unambiguously symbiotic pattern suggested in much of the literature. Lest the reader form too rosy a view of this period, it should also be noted that this era was also characterised by intense intergang conflict. However, within areas of stability, gangs tended to adopt a cooperative attitude towards the police, doing such things as surrendering suspects to the police (*migawari*), exchanging information with the police and keeping non-gang trouble-makers off the street. It should be remembered that these last two 'services' were more to remove any potential rivals, show their effectiveness as suppliers of protection and keep the police from actively policing the group's territory, than a desire to be good citizens.

After the first summit strategy, the picture becomes much less clear. As a broad generalisation, since the first summit strategy the relationship between the *yakuza* and the police has gradually worsened. Not only have police countermeasures become stricter but the *yakuza* have also diversified into progressively less tolerable business activities. Following the introduction of the *Bōtaihō*, the flows of information and limited cooperation that most *yakuza* groups had extended to the police essentially dried up. Furthermore, from the empirical observation that the main factor driving the evolution and business diversification of the *yakuza* has been police action, it must be concluded that a thesis of simple *yakuza*–police symbiosis is untenable.

Within the various *yakuza* groups, there has been a wide degree of diversity in their relations with the authorities. The commonly accepted wisdom is that the groups in western Japan are more combative in their police relations than the groups in Tokyo and the rest of eastern Japan. In particular the distinction is made between the behaviour of the Yamaguchi-gumi in the Kōbe-Osaka area and that of the Tokyo syndicates. The most notable exception to this generalisation is the old, Osaka-based Sakaume-gumi, which has long been seen as having good diplomatic links with the police.[1]

This difference in behaviour is perhaps best illustrated by contrasting the aggressive military expansion of the Yamaguchi-gumi with the Tokyo gangs' creation of the conflict-minimising mechanism: the Kantō Hatsuka-kai. Whilst the Inagawa-kai and Sumiyoshi-kai have also expanded throughout Japan, the Yamaguchi-gumi has been far more active in this field. Within Iwate prefecture, many groups joined a Tokyo-based syndicate (mostly Sumiyoshi-kai) as a defence against the Yamaguchi-gumi, and it is probable that this pattern has occurred elsewhere. Apart from police intervention, the expansion of the Yamaguchi-gumi has been the most significant destabilising factor within Japanese organised crime over the last fifty years.

As might be expected, this east–west divide can also be seen in the way that the police treat *yakuza* arrestees. In the Osaka area, this has long been robustly physical, making use of *jūdō* strangulation techniques, punching, and kicking. This, apparently, has been much rarer in Tokyo (and is now also rarer in Osaka) (*Shūkan Jitsuwa* 16 April 1998; interviews Osaka, June 1998).

Just as it is not always appropriate to treat the *yakuza* as a single entity, it is important to recognise that the Japanese police force is not a monolithic organisation but composed of various constituencies. The first cleavage line we should consider is that between the security bureau (*kōan-kyoku*) and the criminal investigation bureau (*keiji-kyoku*). The security police are primarily concerned with counter-intelligence, terrorism, and political subversion whilst, as their name suggests, the *criminal investigation* bureau is concerned with more conventional policing.

These different responsibilities are reflected in the different attitudes these two bureaux have had to the *yakuza*:

The *criminal investigation* bureau of the NPA has long had the desire to destroy the *bōryokudan*. The security bureau has felt that it was more important to deal with the communists and for that reason there was the view that they should make use of the *bōryokudan* (interview Yamada, Tokyo, June 1998).

Anti-*bōryokudan* specialist lawyer Yamada Hitoshi, who first alerted me to the importance of this bifurcation, also notes that, following the end of the Cold War, the consciousness of the senior personnel at the security bureau has changed. Yamada notes, however, that the same cannot be said to apply universally to security bureau officers working at prefectural police headquarters (1998).

This mirrors the conflicting perspectives and priorities held by the elite NPA bureaucrats within the criminal investigation bureau, and by the operational prefectural police officers actually conducting the business of street-level law enforcement and crime detection. Discussions with members of Iwate prefecture's *bōryokudan*-counter-measures squad (*bōtai-shitsu*) suggested a nostalgia for the days before the *Bōtaihō*'s introduction when they would enter gang offices and sit down for a cup of coffee, a cigarette, and the chance to find out what was going on. It is easy to see how this flow of information would encourage a *quid pro quo* attitude at the grass-roots level, with officers rewarding cooperative or well-behaved groups with less rigorous law enforcement.

As has been mentioned in the theoretical chapter, this relationship need not necessarily be reinforced by bribery; it is rather a pragmatic realisation that such a relationship yields results. Whilst this pragmatism has undoubtedly declined in recent years (especially following the severance of diplomatic links with the introduction of the *Bōtaihō*), it is probably at street-level that the vestiges of *yakuza*–police accommodation are most enduring. In discussions with communist activists in the slum areas of San'ya and Kotobuki-chō, these individuals were firmly convinced that mutually beneficial police–*yakuza* links continue: 'When we are fighting the fascists (*yakuza*), the police shields are facing towards us!' (activist, interview San'ya July 1998).

In these areas, and in Osaka's Kamagasaki, policing is a highly sensitive affair and the possibility of the homeless day-labourers' rioting is ever present.[2] In such conditions, it is easy to see how the various resident *yakuza* groups may be seen as a secondary consideration, or even a useful bulwark against an unpredictable and volatile group of men with nothing left to lose. In October 1990, a riot broke out in Kamagasaki (Airin) when it was discovered that police were taking money from local gangs to provide advance warning of raids on gambling operations. The shiny marble and steel fortress that was built to replace the police station damaged during this riot, speaks volumes about the relationship between the police and inhabitants of the day-labourers' markets.

Given the number of players and the diversity of interests, attempts to model police–*yakuza* relationships in a game-theoretic way would therefore require a far more complex model than that suggested by Celantini et al. as mentioned in Chapter Two.

Whilst laws have all had non-trivial effects on the criminal activities they specifically targeted, and have had a significant effect on the overall numbers of *yakuza* over the last half century, they have not, neither individually nor collectively, dealt the *yakuza* a terminal blow. Instead, the surviving groups have developed new sources of income. Given that the consequences of these new activities have often been socially undesirable, it is by no means clear that fewer, badder, *yakuza* are to be a preferred policy outcome to more but nicer *yakuza*.

The rapid displacement of organised criminals from one set of business activities to another due to legal changes is one of the difficulties facing those framing anti-organised-crime laws raised in Chapter Five. As the commentaries provided by police officers at the time of the *Bōtaihō*'s creation, and their favourable view of America's RICO statutes, make clear, they were themselves aware of this problem. Why then did they not create a more robust, RICO-style, anti-organised-crime regime at the time they installed the *Bōtaihō*?

There are two possible answers to this question: first, the organisational preferences of the police themselves; second, impediments in the then existing legal system. Both of these considerations yield us interesting evidence as to norms and trends in Japanese law enforcement and Japan's legal culture. Let us look at them in turn.

Policing Norms and the *Bōtaihō*

As has been mentioned above, the *Bōtaihō* was drafted under the auspices of the National Police Agency rather than the Ministry of Justice. Moreover, the application of this law is effectively conducted entirely by the police up to the point that injunctions are violated whereupon criminal prosecution by the courts may be undertaken. In this way, the *Bōtaihō* provides the police with autonomous regulatory power over the *yakuza*. This administrative role is very much in the traditions of the Japanese police.

Under the Administrative Police Regulations (*gyōsei keisatsu kisoku*) of 1875 which, with minor alterations, remained in force until 1945, the police not only held power for the prevention of crime and the arrest of offenders but also held administrative jurisdiction over nearly every aspect of economic and social life. The police were responsible for the licensing of bars, restaurants, and brothels, ensuring that regulations concerning health, sanitation, religion, agriculture, construction, and forestry were adhered to, regulating trade union organisations and labour disputes and keeping the population under surveillance through a process of regular surveys. Indeed, police supervision over the lives of the citizen was 'so strict that it even dictated when and how he must clean his house' (Wildes 1954: 181). Later, due to the demands of total war on Japan's industrial base, the police also acquired responsibility for administering the allocation of economic resources and rationing food.

Although the Administrative Police Regulations formally separated the police from the judiciary, they kept the power to promulgate ordinances as well as a number of quasi-judicial powers. The 1885

Law of Summary Procedure for Police Offences (*Ikeizai Sokketsu Rei*) empowered police station chiefs to act as prosecutor and judge for minor offences carrying penalties of up to 30-days' imprisonment or a ¥20 fine (Ames 1981: 9–10; '*Nichibenren* 1995: 2–3; Aldous 1997: 22–7).

Not only did the police in Meiji Japan have the ability to operate in a semi-judicial capacity; they were also able to make law. Under Article 9 of the 1889 Meiji Constitution, the police were empowered to issue 'ordinances necessary for the carrying out of the laws, or for the maintenance of the public peace and order, and for the promotion of the welfare of the subjects' (Bayley 1976: 36). This was supposedly circumscribed by the provision that executive-derived administrative law could not contravene statute law (produced by the Diet). However, this did not in fact present an obstacle to the expansion of administrative law as statute law tended to be vaguely worded (Aldous 1997: 27).

In short, the prewar police were the powerful, centralised pillar of the Ministry of Home Affairs (*naimu-shō*), a super-ministry with a vast area of jurisdiction. The police therefore held considerable administrative powers in addition to their law-enforcement function. Even when exercising this law-enforcement role, the police showed a distinct preference for using the law in an administrative fashion. Moreover, the police held considerable powers to prosecute, and adjudicate on offenders independently of the Ministry of Justice. Under the Meiji Constitution there were no provisions for accountability, democratic or otherwise, for the police, and this was reflected in police attitudes towards the people that can best be summarised by the oft-used expression *kanson-minpi* (respect the authorities and despise the people).

Consequently, with the defeat of Japan in 1945, the police, alongside the military and the *zaibatsu* (industrial conglomerates), were seen by the SCAP (Supreme Commander of the Allied Powers) authorities as one of the main targets of reform necessary for the democratisation of Japan. There was, however, an inherent strain within the occupation authority's policies towards Japan in that SCAP administration was to be conducted indirectly, that is via the existing governmental apparatus, including the police force. This presented SCAP with a problem; 'by administering change through the prewar governmental structure, the Americans, whether they liked it or not, were legitimising that very structure' (Aldous 1997: 46). There was the additional problem of combining the demands of democratic reform with efficient administration and social stability in conditions of near total economic collapse and political dislocation.

As discussed in Chapter Two, this disruption of the police played a major part in ensuring that Japanese society in the immediate postwar era was deficient in sources of public protection. This deficiency was in turn a crucial factor encouraging the development of alternative sources of protection. It was soon recognised that attempts to decentralise the police had failed and, at the end of the 1940s, the authorities started planning a return to a national service. Police recentralisation was given greater priority in 1950 with the combination of communist victory in China followed by the outbreak of the Korean War. It was the threat of political radicalism, rather than the symbiotic relationship between criminal gangs and the police or chronic police inefficiency, that finally stimulated police reorganisation.

Re-centralisation was not, however, completed until 1954 with the new Police Law, which laid out the structure of the Japanese police today. Under the 1954 Police Law, a system of prefectural police forces was instituted. Each of these prefectural forces was to be under the supervision of a prefectural Public Safety Commission. Central coordination was to be conducted by the National Police Agency (NPA or *Keisatsu-chō*), which was itself under the supervision of the National Public Safety Commission.

Although the letter of the 1954 law suggests a reasonably high degree of decentralisation, Ames (1981: 216–7) points out that, in reality, the NPA retains control over the prefectural police; senior personnel within the regional forces are appointed, paid, and controlled by the NPA and key areas of police financing are covered by the NPA. The Security Police (*kōan keisatsu*), who are responsible for counter-intelligence, the surveillance of political extremists, the riot police (more politely known as rapid mobilisation troop or *kidōtai*), and all other matters concerning internal national security, are also controlled directly from Tokyo.

It could therefore be argued that the Japanese police reverted to their prewar centralised structure. Indeed one could say that, because they are no longer under external bureaucratic control, as a bureau of the *naimu-shō*, but an independent agency in their own right, they have acquired even greater levels of autonomy. The 1954 Police Law provides for democratic accountability for the police through the system of Public Safety Commissions. Here, however, a distinction must be made between *tatemae* (surface appearance) and *honne* (reality). Bayley (1976: 192) identifies the *tatemae*, stating that the Public Safety Commissions 'have exclusive authority over the discipline and authority and dismissal of all police officers'. Ames (1981: 218) takes a more cynical view of the commissions:

In many ways, however, the Public Safety Commission system serves to mask the total independence of the police and the almost complete lack of formal checks on the power and operation of the police establishment (the *honne*). The prefectural and national Public Safety Commissions ostensibly function as buffers between police and politicians to prevent undue bias and untoward influence, yet they do not insure public control over the police organisation.

Part of the problem for this concerns a degree of ambiguity over the wording of the 1954 Police Law. The English translation of the law states that 'the Prefectural Public Safety Commission shall supervise the Prefectural Police' (Article 38 paragraph 3). The Japanese version uses the term *kanri*, which can be translated variously as 'administration; management; control; supervision; superintendence' (Kenkyūsha's New Japanese English Dictionary). This is interpreted by both the police themselves and most academics as no more than setting broad policy:

The supervision carried out by the commission does not extend to concretely impinging on the powers of the police, but, through setting the basic policy of management, (the commission) conducts prior and post facto oversight...The direction of police officers is carried out by the chief of metropolitan or regional police (Tanoue in '*Nichibenren* 1995: 240).

However, even within the parameters of this restricted interpretation, the commissions fail to carry out their duties. Various laws (such as the traffic laws, the sword and firearms control law, and the public morals law) empower the prefectural Public Safety Commissions to issue and withdraw licences, order business closure and, in the case of the *Bōtaihō*, designate *bōryokudan*. However, the commissions have no offices or powers of investigation, and their members lack the expertise to carry out these functions. Consequently, the various duties of these commissions are delegated to the relevant police department.

The membership of the commissions has traditionally been an honorary role for pillars of the community. The '*Nichibenren*'s 1995 book on the police reveals that commission members (excluding Tokyo) are overwhelmingly recruited from the local financial and business elites

(68 per cent), the second most significant group being medical practitioners (14 per cent). Amongst the other members there were two religious figures and the head of a tea-ceremony school. Their average age is 67.7, whilst the eldest member was 85 (*Nichibenren* 1995: 243–4). Although political neutrality is supposedly maintained by ensuring that no two members of any commission belong to the same political party, in reality these individuals have tended to share a conservative world view (Ames 1981: 219). A random sample of twelve public safety commissions taken in December 2002 suggests marginal change: the mean age of the sample was 67.2; half of the total sample comprised business/financial figures, medical doctors, academics, lawyers, school-teachers, and other public worthies made up the rest; 12 per cent of commission members were women.[3]

With respect to an expanded administrative role for the police, here too we can see a trend towards a return to Meiji policing patterns. A number of laws, notably the Law on the Proprietisation and Regulation of Business Affecting Public Morals (*Fūzoku Eigyō nado no Kisei Oyobi Gyōmu Tekiseika nado ni Kan-suru Hōritsu*, more usually known as *Fūeihō* or, in English, Public Morals Law) of 1948, provide the Public Safety Commissions with authority to issue, and withdraw, licences to a number of businesses. As the commissions are effectively rubber stamps for the various prefectural police forces, this means that effectively the police have regulatory power over various areas of the social and economic fabric of Japan. For example, the *pachinko* industry, (which accounts for roughly 4 per cent of Japan's GNP) bars, restaurants, and massage parlours, come under the provisions of this law. In order to reduce congestion in the court system, the police also have administrative powers for punishing minor traffic offences.

Seen within the context of a tradition of wide-ranging administrative powers and a desire to recreate them, the rationale behind the structure of the *Bōtaihō* makes sense. Miyazawa Setsuo, author of the most penetrating study of police investigative practices, sees this expansion of administrative police powers as part of a conscious policy on the part of the NPA. The 'Japanese police have always tried to re-establish it(self) as a "*seisaku kanchō*" or a governmental agency with substantive policy mandates like the pre-war "*Naimu-shō*" or the Ministry of Interior. *Bōryokudan Taisaku Hō* can be understood as a step in its continuing effort' (private correspondence 15 November 1998).

The choice of administrative law over criminal law provides the police with total control over the exercise of the *Bōtaihō*. Although nominally operated 'at the discretion of' the prefectural Public Safety Commissions, we have seen that this effectively means that the law operates totally within the ambit of the police and independently of the judiciary. Seen in this way, it becomes immediately apparent why the prefectural Centres for the Eradication of *Bōryokudan* have ended up as organisations operating within the existing police structure. The task of designating regional centres is at the discretion of the Public Safety Commissions and, consequently, the centres have ended up as part of an expanding police empire.

As was shown in Chapter Six, there are a number of laws, which pre-date the introduction of the *Bōtaihō*, including provisions for sequestration of the proceeds from crime and the punishment of *minbō* type offences, that could be employed more proactively to mount an effective anti-*bōryokudan* campaign. The debate on OC countermeasures was also informed by other legal models, in particular the potent RICO statutes. However, these strategies were rejected. This was not because they showed less promise than administrative measures in controlling the *bōryokudan* but because the *Bōtaihō* provided for greater police autonomy and extended their sphere of administrative control.

The trend of expanding police power can also be seen in its relationship with other state agencies. 'By virtually all measures police power inside the government has been increasing greatly' (Katzenstein 1996: 62). Senior NPA bureaucrats have attained powerful positions within the Defence Agency (*Bōei-Chō*) and the Imperial Household Agency (*Kunai-Chō*), and the NPA also successfully posts junior bureaucrats to other agencies and ministries whilst remaining relatively closed to postings from outside. Within the Cabinet Secretariat (*Naikaku Kanbō*) the power of the police *vis-à-vis* other agencies has also grown. More than a quarter of the posts within the secretariat were held by NPA personnel by the early 1970s, including control over two of the most important posts. Over half of the Cabinet Information Research Office posts are held by NPA personnel. Perhaps the most striking illustration of the increasing status of the police is the ranking amongst Tokyo University graduates applying for elite bureaucratic careers. Since 1965, the NPA has risen from bottom of the list to the top alongside the Ministry of Finance and the Ministry of International Trade and Industry[4] (Katzenstein 1996: 62).

In many ways therefore we can see that the modern Japanese police shows many traits of its predecessors. This is succinctly put by Ames:

The present police establishment in Japan is an imperfectly blended amalgam of the authoritarian, powerful and highly centralised prewar police system and the 'democratic' and decentralised postwar system. The prewar system was based on a Franco-German model of a national police force on a level above the people, and the postwar system was patterned after an American or British model of small-scale police forces on the same level with the people. The former is closer to the *honne* (reality) of the police system, and the latter is ultimately a mere *tatemae* (façade) (1981: 215).

The *Bōtaihō* should be seen as part of this process towards police-reclamation of their prewar administrative role. Given that the existing system of Public Safety Commissions fails to provide adequate control and democratic accountability over the police, this trend presents cause for concern.

Another way in which police regulatory power generates uneasiness is the power this gives them over various industries. In some cases, this can make the police appear to be taking over industries formerly protected by *yakuza*. In Chapter Four, the way in which the police had used their regulatory power over the pachinko industry to set up prize-exchange and prepaid-card systems under the auspices of organisations run by retired police officers was mentioned. The private security industry, in many ways analogous to the *yakuza* business, is another field that is regulated by the police; it should be no surprise to find supra-industry organisations, staffed by retired police officers and to which all businesses in the industry must belong. The hospitality industry is also regulated by the police through their mastery of the public morals law. Whilst it might be argued that it is preferable to have these industries in the domain of the police rather than that of the *yakuza*, this does cause anxiety. It also serves to remind us that the police and the *yakuza* are ultimately rivals in the market for protection. There is, however, evidence that, despite police aspirations for an increase in their administrative role, there are countervailing trends in Japanese society which suggest that this ambition will not be met.

The first of these reasons is that the whole police system has come under increased scrutiny since the late 1990s following a succession of police scandals, botched cover-ups, and police whistleblowers revealing slush-funds and other irregularities (see e.g. Ochiai 2000; Tsuchimoto 2000; Johnson 2003). In an attempt to restore public confidence in this formerly respected institution, the Police Law was partially amended to provide for greater oversight by the public safety commissions. However, this amendment is 'largely cosmetic and unlikely to stimulate significant reform' (Johnson 2003: 32).

Another trend that is potentially antagonistic to expanded administrative police power is the increased emphasis on criminal law provisions and this will be discussed in greater depth later. Just one example of this trend can be seen in the introduction of the anti-organised crime laws in 1999.

The Three Anti-Organised Crime Laws

The second reason why the authorities did not establish a more aggressive RICO-style regime in the early 1990s, was that the Japanese police lacked many of the investigative tools necessary to build a case leading to a successful prosecution of a criminal organisation's collective membership for its various criminal activities.[5] Foremost amongst these are procedures allowing for the interception of communications. Article 21 of the Constitution guarantees that 'the secrecy of any means of communication (shall not) be violated'. However, it seems the legal status of wire-tapping is not quite so clear-cut. According to a retired elite police bureaucrat interviewee, police wiretaps can, subject to a court order, be conducted in extraordinary circumstances in which there are no other means to gain evidence. It was stressed in the course of the interview that this has only happened in drug-related cases (interview Tokyo, June 1998).[6]

In 1999, the Japanese authorities came closer to American-style organised-crime control with the passage of three laws intended to combat the *yakuza* as well as other criminal groups such as the Aum Shinrikyō doomsday cult (responsible for the 1995 subway sarin nerve gas attack). These laws, collectively known as the *soshiki hanzai taisaku sanpō* (the three organised-crime countermeasure laws or, inevitably, *sotaihō*), consisted of: *Soshiki Teki na Hanzai no Shobatsu Oyobi Hanzai Shueki no Kisei nado ni Kan-suru Hōritsu* (Law Concerning the Punishment of Organised Crimes, the Regulation of the Proceeds of Crime and other such things); *Hanzai Sōsa no tame no Tsūshin Bōjū ni Kan-suru Hōritsu (Tsūshin Bōjū-hō* or Law Concerning Intercepting

Communications in Order to Investigate Crime); *Keiji Kisō-Hō no Ichibu o Kaisei-suru Hōritsu* (Law Concerning the Partial Reform of the Code of Criminal Procedure).

Taken together, these three laws go some way to creating the aggressive organised-crime-countermeasures that hawkish 'control-lobby' critics of the *Bōtaihō*, such as Katō, called for. Owing to the controversial nature of these laws, particularly the constitutionally questionable wire-tapping law, these laws met with a certain degree of resistance at the legislative stage, were widely criticised by lawyers and academics and took considerable time to pass through the legislative process. However, by international standards, the wire-tapping measures allowed by the law are mild.

Under the provisions of the wire-tapping law, communications (including Internet and mobile-telephone traffic) may, subject to warrant, be intercepted if the police have reasonable grounds to believe that information is being exchanged in the furtherance of certain kinds of criminal activity and there is no other way in which this evidence might be acquired. The types of criminal activity are limited to: drug-law violations; trading in firearms; smuggling; and organised-crime-related homicide. Warrants can only be issued by judges of district courts and are limited to a ten-day period. Extensions may be granted but the total period of interception cannot exceed 30 days. Client–lawyer and doctor–patient conversations are specifically excluded from communications that may be tapped. To ensure that these conditions are observed, all intercepts must be carried out in the presence of a neutral observer. Two recordings are made of all intercepted communications. One of these is signed by the observer and sent to the authorising court, the other is retained by the investigating agency to build their case. Those who have been subject to a wire-tapping investigation must be informed of this fact in writing within thirty days of the end of the period of interception (Kurokawa 2000: 61–84).

The second law, which for the sake of brevity is usually called the *Soshikiteki Hanzai Shobatsu-Hō* (Organised-Crime Punishment Law), has two key components. The first of these allows for the increased severity of punishments imposed on those found guilty of committing crimes to further the interests of a criminal group. For example, the minimum penalty for murder as laid out in the criminal code is a period of three years' imprisonment,[7] under the new law, the minimum is increased to five years. Similarly, the penalties for fraud and intimidation (normally consisting of a maximum sentence of ten years) change to a minimum of one year and a maximum of life if found to be conducted to further the interests of a criminal group or organisation. Extortion increases from a minimum sentence of three to five years.

The increased penalties of this law can be seen as part of a wider trend in Japanese sentencing patterns. Although still mild by comparison with such prison-happy regimes as the United States or Britain, these have been getting harsher. One lawyer interviewee identifies this process as becoming increasingly apparent from the end of the 1980s, with a media campaign, echoing the sentiments of the police and prosecutors, that sentences were too light. In response to this, judges have delivered progressively heavier sentences. This informant illustrates this with reference to the punishments received by those found in possession of a firearm:

25 years ago, when I first became a lawyer, this would typically receive a fine of about 100,000 yen. Quite soon after that it was increased to imprisonment but this would invariably be a suspended sentence. About ten to fifteen years ago the penalty became one year imprisonment and soon after that it was increased to one and a half years. The Sword and Firearms Control Law was changed quite soon after that and the penalty for possession of one handgun became three years (five if found with ammunition). If we look at the cases of Tsukasa and Kuwata,[8] where one of Kuwata's *kobun* was found in possession, the prosecutor is recommending ten years (interview Kōbe, July 1999).

The second part of the organised-crime punishment law greatly increases the range of assets that can be seized as proceeds of crime and creates a system of supplementary charge (akin to a penalty tax) that can be imposed on those who have profited from crime but whose identifiable assets have an entirely and demonstrably legitimate provenance. The provisions of this law are restricted to the following types of criminal activity: drug-trafficking; serious crimes (such as murder and handling explosives); organised crime (prostitution, gambling, bookmaking, pornography, helping illegal foreign workers); fraud and breach of trust offences; money-laundering, corruption of civil servants, and hijacking. Pre-prosecution freezing of assets (to prevent capital flight once a suspect has been arrested) and a requirement on financial institutions to report suspicious transactions are also provided for in this law (Harada and Inohara 2000: 37–54).

The third of the new organised-crime laws, the partial revision of the code of criminal procedure law, consisted of small changes to the code to ensure that the other two laws might be effective. For example, greater protection is afforded to witnesses, translators, and others involved in criminal prosecutions; their identities, addresses, and places of work need not be made public. Minor reform of the code was also required concerning the admissibility of transcripts of intercepted communications as evidence in trial (Harada and Inohara 2000: 54–6).

Law, Legal Culture and the *Yakuza*

The two sections above suggest two different, and potentially antagonistic, trends in the Japanese criminal justice system. On one hand, we have a police force wishing to expand its traditional role of exerting autonomous regulatory control over Japanese society: on the other, we see a more recent expansion of formal legal sanctions taking Japan closer to what Japan's G8 partners see as a global standard in their shared battle against organised crime. As this suggests, this second development is in part due to foreign pressure (just as the introduction of the *Bōtaihō* had been encouraged by international considerations). As we shall see below, however, there are perceptible shifts in Japanese legal culture suggestive of more profound influences.

Both the police regulatory tradition and the more recent increase in the scope of formal law *vis-à-vis* the *yakuza* lead us to a consideration of central importance to any examination of the relationship between the *yakuza*, law, and the state in Japan. This is that Japan is typically portrayed as showing an extreme reluctance to make use of formal legal procedures, and this tendency can be seen in both criminal and civil law. Tanaka (1976: 255), for example, asserts that 'the number of civil suits per capita brought before the courts in Japan is roughly between one twentieth and one tenth of the figures for the common law countries of the United States and Great Britain'.

Although a quarter-century has elapsed since Tanaka's observation, Japanese use of law remains lower than in European countries and, *a fortiori*, the United States. For example, compared to other countries the number of legal professionals (judges, prosecutors, and lawyers) in Japan is tiny. In 1998, Japan had one legal professional for every 5,995 head of population. This compares to ratios of 1:1,641 for France; 1:724 for Germany; 1:656 for Great Britain; and 1:285 for the United States (*Yomiuri Shinbun* 3 August 1998).

The posited reasons for these can be essentially broken into three arguments: Culturalist; institutionalist the rational litigant. Noda (1976*b*: 307), a Japanese legal scholar, expresses the former view as follows:

We Japanese tend to feel uncomfortable with a black-or-white type of adjudication, if a Japanese loses in a lawsuit, being of emotional inclination, he is bound to be embittered against the winner, and even against the judge. We do not want to leave the embers of a grudge smouldering. We would rather pay a small price... and let bygones be bygones. This explains why a large majority of cases that are brought to court are settled through compromise. This is very indicative of the peculiar character of the Japanese.

Elsewhere, Noda (1976*a*: 160–74) argues that the Japanese are an emotional, intuitive, and subjective people characterised by a preference for non-rational patterns of thought. This 'Oriental spirit' is the antithesis of the dry, analytical reasoning, which Noda sees as characterising European law. Owing to this, 'even after the reception of European law, the logical conception of law did not take root easily in their mentality' (1976*a*: 165).

Rather than looking to law for the adjudication of conflicts, culturalist interpretations, see conciliation, rooted in traditional social values and customs, as being the main engine of resolving such disputes. In particular, a preference for harmony (*wa*) and a reluctance to jeopardise existing social relations, encourages a spirit of compromise in which the enforcement of one's own individual rights is seen as a selfish lack of consideration of the other disputant's position (Noda 1976*a*: 181; Tanaka 1988: 195). 'There is a strong expectation that a dispute should not and will not arise; even when one does arise, it is to be solved by mutual understanding' (Kawashima 1963: 44).

As the previous chapters have hopefully demonstrated, Japan is not a country devoid of disputes, nor has their resolution always been conducted in the most conciliatory of fashions. The 'myth of the reluctant litigant' has been attacked most famously by Haley (1978, 1991), who argued persuasively that, historically, the Japanese have not been at all reluctant to exercise their legal rights; the apparent aversion to use of law is due to institutional obstacles imposed by the authorities who saw increased litigation as endangering social stability:

The primacy of private law in nineteenth-century Western legal systems and the consequent emphasis on justiciable rights meant that intrinsic to the new (post-Meiji-restoration) Japanese legal order were a set of premises quite antithetical to fundamental precepts shared by Japan's social and political elites. As lifeless abstractions, legal rights would have perhaps caused little concern, but their exercise in court could only be perceived as a threat to Japan's social and political order (Haley 1991: 84).

Consequently, there was a gradual process of forcing the public away from litigation. This was effected by the introduction of laws forcing potential litigants to resolve conflicts by formal conciliation rather than through the courts. This process was later reinforced by the 1949 Lawyers Law (*Bengoshi Hō*), which ensured that entry into the profession (including judges and prosecutors) was restricted to those graduating from the Legal Research and Training Institute (*Shihō Kenshū Sho* or LRTI).

For most of the postwar period admissions to the LRTI have been limited to around five hundred trainees each year although many thousands apply (with a success rate of around 2 per cent) (Johnson 2002: 90). The 1949 *Bengoshi Hō* has therefore dramatically limited the supply of judges and prosecutors, the results of which can be seen in the figures given above showing the very low per capita population of judges in Japan *vis-à-vis* Europe and America.

The result of this has been to severely clog Japan's courts with a massive backlog of suits leading to a judicial system, which is both extremely slow and expensive to use. In 1990, the average civil case in a district court took 11.9 months for completion; a typical first appeal in the appellate court took a further 13.2 months. Appeals to the Supreme Court take even longer; 211 cases out of the 1,376 under consideration by the Supreme Court had been first docketed more than ten years ago. In one exceptional case, judgement was finally given 25 years after the initial docketing (Oda 1992: 79–81).

This chronic delay presents a significant deterrent to a potential litigant. Further obstacles are presented by the financial costs of bringing a case to court. Given the strictly controlled supply of lawyers, their services do not come cheap. Moreover, when awarding legal costs to the victor, judges, until recently, included only witness costs and the costs of the various legal stamps, not lawyers' fees. Since lawyers' fees usually account for 80 per cent of the total costs, even if a case is won, the burden of legal fees may offset any benefit gained (Yamaguchi and Soejima 1997: 72–3). Access to a lawyer becomes even harder in outlying rural areas because the overwhelming majority of practising lawyers are registered in Tokyo and Osaka.

The institutionalist view therefore argues that these serious obstacles prevent otherwise potentially litigious disputants from making use of the law. Most proponents of this view accept the basic premise of the traditional culturalist view that 'the law cannot be structuring the way (the Japanese) live their lives'. Some go so far as to say it is 'bankrupt' (Ramseyer and Nakazato 1989: 267–8).

In contrast, the 'rational litigant' explanation for low Japanese litigiosity asserts that, despite the disincentives to litigation, law is not irrelevant to the ways in which individuals resolve disputes. In Japan, judges strive to make decisions consistent with clear precedents and guidelines. This makes the outcome of cases highly predictable. Given that the costs of litigation are also known to both parties to a dispute, it should be straightforward for them to reach an agreement that leaves them both better off than had they gone to court. Ramseyer and Nakazato (1989) test this hypothesis by comparing out-of-court settlements and expected judicial decisions for traffic accident torts. Their findings suggest that 'neither ethical values nor high costs dull the willingness of victims to assert their legal rights' (1989: 273). Even in other types of dispute where there is less consensus as to expected judicial decisions the absence of a jury system and the considerable efforts judges make to achieve consistency, ensure that decisions are more predictable than those obtaining in Anglo-American legal systems.

Despite their apparent inconsistency, it seems that all of these views have some relevance to explaining low Japanese litigiosity. The culturalist view does indeed reflect the normative expectations that Japanese people show when pressed to explain this phenomenon; even when the existence of conflict does appear to undermine their argument, the belief that open disputes *should* be avoided remains widespread. Such a social belief ultimately becomes self-fulfilling; even those who do not share this norm will behave in accordance with it if they believe that everyone else shares it. The disincentives to litigation demonstrated by the revisionists are more tangible.

Regardless of ultimate cause, it should be apparent that aversion to the use of formal law is of considerable significance to the *yakuza*. If we see the central business of the *yakuza* to be protection then the failure of the state to afford a system by which citizens can seek to protect their interests and redress grievances provides a market niche to those who would provide such a system privately. As shown in Chapters Four and Six, in the absence of efficient public conflict resolution mechanisms, the *yakuza* have extended their business interests to areas such as bankruptcy-management, *jiage*, collection of debts, *sōkaiya* activities, and a myriad of other civil disputes. These are all areas in which the *yakuza* provide just such a system of 'dark side...private ordering' (Milhaupt and West 2000). Of course, those who find themselves on the wrong side of private ordering lack a mechanism for seeking redress for exactly the same reasons that encourages such private ordering in the first place.

One might argue that, if the culturalist argument is correct then the aversion to conflict resolution would extend to private as well as state mechanisms. However, one of the points about private protection, is that it is private in both senses of the world enabling the better-protected party to 'put a lid on that which stinks'. The appearance of harmony may be preserved. The outcome of dispute resolution in such a system is not dependent on the merits of the case (or, more cynically, on who can afford the better lawyers) but on who can afford the stronger *yakuza*. Alas, such data would not be forthcoming, but it would be fascinating to do a study, along the lines of Ramseyer and Nakazato's rational-litigant work, looking at the comparative costs and pay-offs of litigation *vis-à-vis* private, *yakuza*, resolution (though note that West (1999) has applied such rational actor analysis to the *sōkaiya* business).

Whilst both institutional and normative barriers to using litigation remain higher than in either the United States or Britain, there is a perceptible trend to their lowering. The number of those admitted each year to the LRTI has progressively increased from five hundred and in 2001 reached 1,500 (Johnson 2002: 90). At the same time, there has been a rise in the level of litigation in a number of significant areas.

In 1993 the Commercial Code was amended in ways which facilitated shareholders' lawsuits against company management for malpractice. First, it significantly reduced the level of stamp tax demanded when filing this type of suit. Second, it enabled successful litigants to claim their legal costs (Davis 1996: 142). As a consequence of this there has been a spate of shareholder-derivative actions against companies. *The Economist*'s survey of business in Japan (27 November 1999) notes that since 1993 there have been more than 1,000 such cases 'and the numbers are still rising'. Of particular relevance here are lawsuits against failed *jūsen* and companies, which have paid out money to *sōkaiya* racketeers.

This is relevant to *yakuza* interests in the *sōkaiya* business in two ways. First, it raises the potential costs to companies of paying-off

Table 7.1 Civil litigation 1975–2000

Year	Newly received civil litigation cases (thousands)
1975	164
1980	220
1985	379
1990	228
1995	421
1996	441
1997	453
1998	518
1999	519
2000	520

Source: *Tōkei Kyoku* (2000).

sōkaiya. Second, however, it provides an alternative means by which those with inside knowledge of company malfeasance may profit from that information. Such a state of affairs may, of course, still leave a niche-market for *yakuza* who would protect companies from *sōkaiya*-turned-litigant.

As Table 7.1 shows, there has been a big increase in litigation in Japan and this has not been confined to shareholder-derivative actions. This trend is likely to continue as the 'restructuring' of the Japanese economy imposes the whip hand of market forces into more and more areas of formerly cosy business practices. In the past, companies with established relationships would try and settle disputes informally, much as culturalist legal scholars argued, as they would not want to jeopardise their future relationship. Such a spirit is becoming rarer.

Increased use of law to resolve disputes and protect interests is bad news for the *yakuza*. The more disputes are resolved through the formal channel of the law, the smaller the share of the market for protection, or private ordering, enjoyed by the *yakuza*. Ultimately, such a trend could leave the *yakuza* with only illegal market transactions left to protect.

Even more significant is the way in which members of the public are now launching civil suits against the *yakuza* themselves. Although there had been incidents of such lawsuits before the introduction of the *Bōtaihō*, the new law has made such cases easier. The prefectural *bōryokudan*-eradication centres, set up under the *Bōtaihō*, can advise potential litigants, introduce them to lawyers and lend them money with which to launch a suit.

Civil suits against *yakuza* generally take two broad types: first, those demanding that a *yakuza* group vacate a building or stop using premises as a gang office; and second, those seeking compensation for an injury suffered at the hands of a *yakuza* member or group. This second category is especially potent in that it can be used to sue a gang boss for acts committed by one of his subordinates. This is made possible by Articles 715 and 719 of the civil law, which cover employer's responsibility (*shiyōsha sekinin*) and collective-illegal-acts responsibility (*kyōdo fuhō kōi sekinin*), respectively (Yamaguchi 1997b: 92).

One example of this type of suit is the case in which the parents of the high-school student killed mistakenly during the Okinawa war (mentioned in Chapter Five) sued the boss of the Okinawa Kyokuryū-kai, as well as the boss of the subgroup responsible, under Article 715 of the civil law. In October 1996, after a five-year legal battle, the parents were successful and the judge ordered that the gang bosses pay compensation of ¥58 m ($532,000) (*Keisatsu Hakusho* 1997: 197).

In a similar judgement reached in September 2002, a Yamaguchi-gumi subgroup boss and two of his subordinates were ordered to pay ¥82.5 m to the dependants of Fujitake Takeshi, a plain-clothes police officer shot in 1995 after being mistakenly identified as an Aizu-kotetsu member. The two subordinates had already been convicted of the murder. Fujitake's relatives had also sued Watanabe Yoshinori, the overall boss of the Yamaguchi-gumi, but the court had decided that he could not be held responsible as the syndicate had not been fighting the Aizu-kotetsu, only the subgroup (*Mainichi Shinbun* 11 September 2002).

In another case, in Saga, a married couple involved in the *unten daikō*[9] business, sued a *yakuza* group boss and his brother for compensation totalling ¥3,575,000 with respect to a succession of incidents, including a slashing attack on the woman's face and chest, the death of their cat, and intimidation of their drivers. The reason for these attacks had been that the couple had opposed moves by the gang to organise an association of all the local *unten daikō* businesses from which it planned to extract a managerial fee. Although they were ultimately successful, it took 10 years from the attacks to the judge's final verdict (Yamaguchi 1997b: 81–4).

The landmark *yakuza*-related civil case was the Ichiriki-ikka incident in Hamamatsu-chō. The Ichiriki-ikka was a subgroup of the Kokuryō-ya, an old gambling organisation dating back to the Edō period but which had more recently joined the Yamaguchi-gumi. In 1983, this Ichiriki-ikka set up an office in Ebizuka-chō, a residential area of Hamamatsu city in Shizuoka prefecture. This office was a black five-storey building equipped with steel plates over the windows, observation cameras, and the inevitable gang-affiliation plaque featuring the gold diamond of the Yamaguchi-gumi. This building loomed menacingly over the surrounding area and quickly became known as 'the black-building'.

From August 1985, the local residents launched a movement to drive out this office. Frequently, gang offices are rented property and it is possible to use legal measures to close them for either breach of contract or non-payment of rent. In the case of the Ichiriki-ikka, however, the office was owned by the gang boss. Owing to the lack of effective legal machinery by which they could expel this *yakuza* group, the movement staged demonstrations and sit-ins outside the gang office and ran a campaign of stickers and posters.

In November of the following year, the Ichiriki-ikka took the unusual step of initiating a suit against nine of the leaders of this movement demanding ¥10 m compensation.[10] A locally recruited team of lawyers, bolstered by help from the *Nichibenren*'s anti-*minbō* committee, decided that it would be possible to launch a counter-suit on the grounds that the existence of the gang office infringed the human rights of the local residents. In response to this counter-suit, in July 1987, the head of the local residents' legal team was seriously injured in a knife attack. Other prominent members of the movement were subject to intimidation and attacks.

The main legal arguments deployed by the gang in court were highly similar to those that were later to be used by various *yakuza* in their doomed legal fight against designation under the *Bōtaihō*. These were that the Ichiriki-ikka was not a criminal organisation but a 'chivalrous group' (*ninkyō dantai*) and that the local residents' movement was perpetrating an infringement of the gang's constitutionally guaranteed rights of freedom of association, property rights, and equality before the law. They also argued that the residents' rights were an abstract thing and not a recognisable legal right.

Despite these arguments, on 9 October 1987, the district court found for the litigants of the counter-suit and issued a provisional injunction demanding that the gang refrain from using the black building as a gang office. However, use of the office continued as before, and on

20 October, the residents' committee appealed to the court demanding ¥5 m for each day that the Ichiriki-ikka continued to use the premises as an office. The defendants argued that gang members were not assembling at the building but merely spontaneously coming and going. This being the case, the injunction did not apply.

One month later, the court provided a more precise definition of action covered by the earlier injunction, which effectively prevented continued use of the office. The defendants appealed to the Tokyo High Court and then, when this appeal was rejected, to the Supreme Court. Finally, on 19 February 1989, the Ichiriki-ikka abandoned its case, reached a peaceful settlement agreeing to all of the resident's demands and left the area.

This incident is significant for a number of reasons. First, it was the first time in which a *yakuza*-owned, rather than rented, office had been driven-out (*Nichibenren* 1998b: 53). Second, this was a citizen-initiated movement (though it later came to garner large-scale police support with several thousand police mobilised throughout Ebizuka-chō). The *Nichibenren*'s account of this incident (from which the above is largely derived) claims that the resolve of the residents was only increased by the gang's attempts to intimidate them. This public solidarity in the face of a hostile *yakuza* group shows what can be done by a motivated and united public. Raz (1996: 228–9) suggests, however, that behind this solidarity was enormous social pressure on uncommitted residents to join the movement and this pressure was backed up by the potent sanction of ostracising non-participants.

Third, it shows that, even where no criminal laws were being violated, the law extant prior to the introduction of the *Bōtaihō* could be successfully applied to restrict the use of gang offices. This should not be taken, however, as evidence that the *Bōtaihō* was merely a public-relations exercise rather than a law with a genuine role to play. It should be remembered that the new law's provisions were wider than just the imposition of limitations on the use of gang offices. Furthermore, the fact that the local residents' fight lasted three long years contrasts with the much quicker application of administrative orders to restrict usage of gang offices. It is perhaps more plausible to suggest that the eventual success of restricting usage of the Ichiriki-ikka's gang office led to the introduction of similar measures in the provisions of the *Bōtaihō*.

Fourth, due to the unusual spectacle of a _yakuza_ group launching a legal suit against a citizens' movement, this incident attracted enormous media and public interest (Raz argues that it was actually inflamed by the media (1996: 230)). This incident therefore was also influential in changing the public consciousness of _yakuza_ groups. The fact that the local residents successfully forced the Ichiriki-ikka to give in, showed the Japanese public that there was nothing inevitable about local _yakuza_ gang offices. This factor is immensely important. As has been argued in earlier chapters, _yakuza_ groups are highly reliant on their reputation. Once the Ichiriki-ikka had been driven out of Ebizuka-chō, it was seen by rivals, customers, and intended prey alike, as weak and unable to provide credible protection. Owing to this fatal loss of reputation, the Ichiriki-ikka disbanded soon after this incident (interview Hoshino, Yokohama, 1998).

It is probable that this damage to the gang's credibility was, to a certain extent, also translated to _yakuza_ at large in the public consciousness. It was observed in the Chapter Six that the general public is becoming less afraid of the _yakuza_. Whilst it is obviously a positive development, this change in consciousness may actually encourage greater levels of violence. As the threat of violence is no longer sufficient to achieve acquiescence, _yakuza_ groups may feel compelled to deploy actual violence to achieve their immediate aims as well as _pour encourager les autres_.

It should be apparent from the cases described above that proactive use of the civil law presents an extremely powerful device against the _yakuza_. For gang bosses to be held accountable for the actions of their subordinates and liable for compensation _vis-à-vis_ predatory actions, is of potentially far greater usefulness than the _Bōtaihō_. Given that the criminal law may not allow for the successful prosecution of gang superiors (though, as the cases of Tsukasa, Kuwata, and Takizawa show, even here we see greater flexibility of interpretation), the use of civil law is evaluated here as a development with grave consequences for the _yakuza_.

The increased reliance on formal legal mechanisms for dealing with problems in both the civil and criminal spheres has been matched with increased levels of crime. Japan used to be considered a criminological oddity in that it uniquely managed to combine increasing urbanisation with a declining crime rate. Figure 7.1, showing the trend in Japan's crime rate and total criminal law violations known to the police, demonstrates that this is no longer the case.[11]

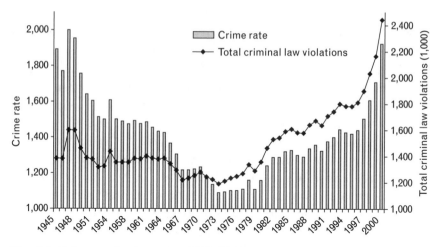

Fig. 7.1 Crimes and crime rates 1945–2000

Source: Hanzai Hakusho.

Whilst it is beyond the scope of this book to test explanatory hypotheses for this development, it is my belief that Japan's increasing criminality is due to weakening power of social control forces in Japanese society.[12] It is these forces had hitherto facilitated the resolution of conflict through informal channels. As these have become less efficacious, the demand for more formal legalistic remedies has increased.

In his study of the Japanese police, Ames suggested that in some way Japanese society 'polices itself' (1981: 228). What does this mean? In his influential book, *Crime, Shame and Integration* (1989), Braithwaite argued that Japan succeeds in controlling crime through a process of 'reintegrative shaming'. Braithwaite makes the distinction between shaming which is 'followed by efforts to reintegrate the offender back into the community of law-abiding or respectable citizens through words or gestures of forgiveness or ceremonies to decertify the offender as deviant' (reintegrative shaming) and that which 'makes no effort to reconcile the offender with the community' (stigmatisation) (Braithwaite 1989: 100–1). Braithwaite's theory would explain why the Japanese criminal justice system makes comparatively little use of the formal sanctions at its disposal. However, the rather benevolent image he holds of Japan's law-enforcement seems at odds with the more critical findings from research carried out by Miyazawa.

Miyazawa (1997) in particular has questioned the applicability of Braithwaite's theory to Japan. Whilst they agree that informal social processes, rather than formal judicial mechanisms or legal sanctions are the key to understanding low Japanese criminality, Miyazawa differs in that he proposes a much less cosy view of the way in which society treats deviants. Miyazawa argues that social control is exerted in Japan through groups such as schools and companies. He characterises these organisations by 'their extremely harsh treatment of members who defy the existing power structure and social arrangements' and asserts that 'Japanese people conform because they know that conformity will be highly rewarded while non-conformity costs enormously' (Miyazawa 1997: 7–8). Braithwaite himself admits that the prospect of reintegration is backed up by enormous informal sanctions against those who do not conform (1989: 158). Having seen, during two years working in a junior high school in Iwate prefecture, the treatment meted out to children showing such dangerous signs of deviancy as the wrong coloured shoelaces, I feel compelled to agree.

These informal controls are reinforced by peer pressure due to the fact that responsibility, and consequent sanctions, are often held at a group, rather than an individual level. This shows a clear similarity to the intra-village extra-legal controls exercised in Tokugawa Japan described by Haley (1991: 170–5).

Over recent decades a process of increased tolerance of diversity and individualism has slowly appeared in Japan. This can be seen in such phenomena as the 'new people' (*shinjinrui*), 'my home-ism' (*mai hōmu-shugi*), young drifters (*freeters*), and job-hoppers. Weakening of traditional social bonds can also be seen in the increasing rate of divorce (by a factor of 2.32 between 1970 and 1997) and the massive jump in international marriages (by a factor of 5.11) over the same period. At the same time, the declining importance of the lifetime employment system and greater opportunities for foreign travel and study have, respectively, lowered the costs of nonconformity and increased exposure to alternative lifestyles.

Whether or not this analysis adequately explains Japan's rise in criminality, it is the view put forward by the authorities themselves. Announcing yet further hikes in crime rates (not to mention declining arrest rates), the 2002 white paper on crime directly attributed the increase on the breakdown in community links.

It is tempting to see factors of informal social control as explaining not only Japan's past low criminality, but also the apparent paradox of the coexistence of low criminality with a large and conspicuous *yakuza* fraternity; those very pressures making social exclusion so expensive to the individual outcast are those that encourage such individuals to associate themselves into organised-crime groups. As these control mechanisms breakdown there are consequences for *yakuza* recruitment. The social pressure on those rebels and misfits, who would formerly have ended up in the ranks of the *yakuza* 'in order to survive in a very rigid society, has become considerably lower'. Such individuals can now 'drift around at society's margin with less problems' (Wolfgang Herbert private correspondence 8 February 2000).

An increasingly hostile relationship between the authorities and the *yakuza* obviously further reduces the attractiveness of *yakuza* membership to potential recruits. The demographic profile of the *yakuza* is an increasingly ageing one as the process of *bōryokudan banare* (movement away from the *bōryokudan*) mentioned in Chapter Two continues.

Of course, this movement away from the *yakuza* and the destabilising effects of increased law-enforcement efforts undermines any social control role the *yakuza* themselves played in Japan. If criminals stay within the membership of criminal gangs, then the gang leadership has an interest in limiting the criminal activities of both members and non-members to those that do not unnecessarily antagonise the authorities within gang-territory. By the same token, it will discourage activities which harm gang-protectees or their customers. As the number of criminals outside of *yakuza* groups increases, control becomes harder: as the prospect of police rewarding good behaviour declines, the time-horizon of gangsters declines and social control becomes less attractive than short-term revenue maximisation.

Conclusion

The *yakuza* of the twenty-first century must therefore contend with a number of different challenges. Not only do they have to face the double punch of the burst bubble and the *Bōtaihō*, they also have increased legal problems in the shape a pincer attack: from the side of criminal law the three new anti-organised crime laws and a trend to a harsher sentencing regime; from the civil law increased competition in the market for dispute resolution and, for bosses, the risk that they may have to pay damages for the misdemeanours of their minions. To add insult to injury, it seems that the police are muscling-in on *yakuza shinogi* as well.

The prospects for the *yakuza* in this harsh environment look bleak indeed. As we saw in Chapter Six, the twin effects of the burst bubble and *Bōtaihō* have been to push the *lumpen-yakuza* into hitherto disparaged activities such as theft and amphetamine dealing whilst the elite of the economic-*yakuza* and their business brothers have managed to find ways of turning Japan's depressed condition to their advantage. This, combined with the incompatible demands imposed by gang leadership for their subordinates to restrict their fund-raising activities to ones that do not unnecessarily antagonise the authorities at the same time as earning enough to pay their monthly *jōnōkin*, has resulted in serious inter and intraorganisational strain. The weakening of the Kantō Hatsuka-kai (which had formerly been credited with keeping the streets of Tokyo comparatively free of *yakuza* conflict) in recent years is one example of this.

Despite the current recession, Japan remains a very rich country. The continued existence of illegal markets where at least some of this vast wealth end up will ensure that the *yakuza* will never entirely disappear. However, a more hostile legal climate and a reduced scope for offering private fixing services in upper-world disputes, will result in the *yakuza* being less conspicuous than they were in the twentieth century. When they intervene in the upper world they will not be immediately recognisable as *yakuza*.

Japan's wealth is particularly pronounced when compared to that of its immediate neighbours. The influx of criminal groups from Russia, China, Vietnam, Taiwan, and Korea, already a process that has generated considerable media alarm in Japan will continue. Whilst, in some cases, these groups coexist with the *yakuza* in mutually beneficial trading arrangements, this is not always so. With the *yakuza* in their current predicament, control over parts of Japan's illegal markets must surely be a tempting proposition to some of these foreign groups. Whilst there are clear barriers to entry for non-indigenous criminals setting themselves up as suppliers of protection in Japan, these need not be insurmountable and, given the potential pay-offs, worth trying to overcome.

Stories surface occasionally in the weekly magazines suggesting that *yakuza* groups make use of foreign hit-men. This suggestion of a lack of suitable personnel amongst Japan's incumbent organised-crime groups implies that they are vulnerable to attack by groups composed of men reared in countries where life is harder and cheaper than it has become in Japan. Moreover, among many of Japan's neighbours there are systems of national military conscription providing a ready pool of men with a comparative advantage in the use of, and greater propensity to, violence. We can expect to see attempts ethnic succession within Japanese organised crime occuring in the early decades of the twenty-first century.

Yakuza groups will either have to coopt foreign rivals or engage in outright competition with them. Either way, these groups will encounter more aggressive countermeasures from the law-enforcement authorities. As we have seen, public toleration of organised crime is adversely affected by high-profile intergang conflicts, especially when members of the public are caught up in them. Even if the process of ethnic succession is a peaceful process of sub-contracting and recruitment, foreign criminal groups are likely to attract greater public antipathy than native ones, as we have seen from the widespread perception of early twentieth-century American organised crime as an 'alien-conspiracy'.

The destabilising of Japan's organised crime world, due to the various social, legal, and foreign factors outlined above, will undoubtedly engender more violence. Whilst this is not likely in the short term to result in the sort of mafia-on-state violence witnessed in Sicily, ultimately leading to the murders of Borsellino and Falcone, the claim that the *yakuza* are indeed the Japanese mafia becomes one justifiable not purely on the theoretical grounds of their provision of protection, but in terms of their increasingly and unambiguously sociopathic behaviour.

Appendix A—Designated *Bōryokudan* Groups

Yakuza groups (As of June 2000)	Headquarters	Leader	Geographical extent	Strength 1992	Strength 2000
Godaime Yamaguchi-gumi	Kōbe	Watanabe Yoshinori	National	23,100	17,500
Inagawa-kai	Tokyo	Inagawa Kakuji[a]	National	7,400	5,100
Sumiyoshi-kai	Tokyo	Nishiguchi Shigeo	National	8,000	6,200
Yondaime Kudorengo Kusano-ikka	Fukuoka	Nomura Satoru	3 Prefectures[b]	600	520
Sandaime Kyokuryū-kai	Okinawa	Ōnaga Yoshihiro	1 Prefecture	430	270
Okinawa Kyokuryū-kai	Okinawa	Tominaga Kiyoshi	1 Prefecture	570	370
Godaime Aizu Kotetsu	Kyoto	Zugoshi Toshitsugu	4 Prefectures	1,600	1,200
Yondaime Kyōsei-kai	Hiroshima	Okimoto Tsutomu	1 Prefecture	330	280
Rokudaime Goda-ikka	Yamaguchi	Nukui Kanji	4 Prefectures	370	190
Yondaime Kozakura-ikka	Kagoshima	Hiraoka Kiei	1 Prefecture	190	120
Sandaime Asano-gumi	Okayama	Kushida Yoshiaki	2 Prefectures	150	120
Nidaime Dōjin-kai	Fukuoka	Matsuo Seijirō	4 Prefectures	510	530
Shinwa-kai	Takamatsu	Hosoya Kunihiko	2 Prefectures	80	70
Sōai-kai	Chiba	Shin Meiu	3 Prefectures	430	460
Sandaime Yamanō-kai	Kumamoto	Ikeda Tetsuo	1 Prefecture	100	70
Sandaime Kyōdō-kai	Hiroshima	Morita Kazuo	6 Prefectures	(230)	200
Sandaime Taishū-kai	Fukuoka	Ōma Raitarō	1 Prefecture	(150)	120
Rokudaime Sakaume-gumi	Osaka	Shin Keiretsu	6 Prefectures	(450)	340
Kyokutō Sakurai Sōke Rengo-kai	Shizuoka	Serizawa Yasuyuki	7 Prefectures	(500)	370
Kyokutō-kai	Tokyo	Sō Keika	17 Prefectures	(2,300)	2,000
Azuma-gumi	Osaka	Kishida Kiyoshi	2 Prefectures	(210)	180
Matsuba-kai	Tokyo	Ri Shunsei	10 Prefectures	{1,800}	1,500
Kokusui-kai	Tokyo	Kudō Kazuyoshi	8 Prefectures	{580}	540
Nakano-kai	Osaka	Nakano Tarō	8 Prefectures	—	170
Nidaime Fukuhaku-kai	Fukuoka	Wada Makio	4 Prefectures	—	340

[a] Although the 1998 *Keisatsu Hakusho* gives Inagawa Kakuji as the leader of the Inagawa Kai, he has officially retired and his son, Chihiro, is third-generation boss of the syndicate. ( ) 1993 figures. { } 1994 figures.

[b] For simplicity prefecture here refers to all administrative areas (tō, dō, fu, ken).

Appendix B—Yamaguchi-gumi top executives post Takumi

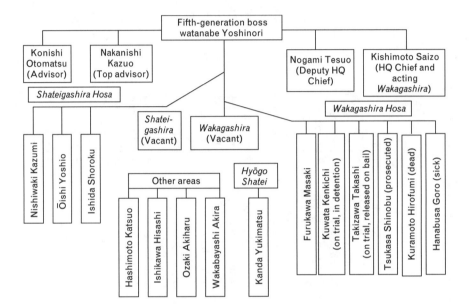

Appendix C—Main Syndicate *Sakazuki* Relations

West Japan

East Japan

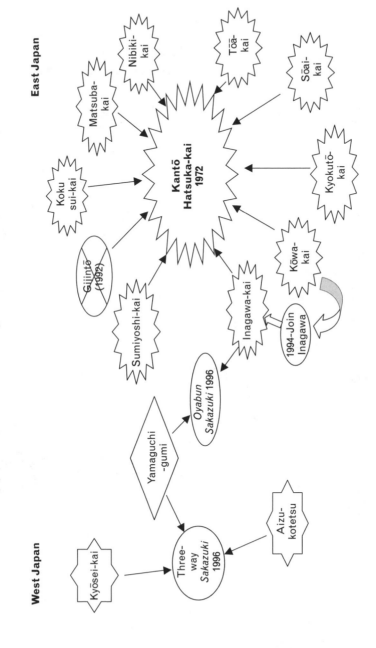

Appendix D—Chronology of significant *Yakuza* events

1960	1961	1962	1963	1964	1965	1966	1967	1968	1969
AMPŌ RIOTS			Kantō-kai set up	First summit strategy	Kantō-kai disbands				
Eisenhower visit cancelled			*Yakuza* letter to political leaders	Tokyo Olympics					

1970	1971	1972	1973	1974	1975	1976	1977	1978	1979
Second summit strategy	*Yakuza-sōkaiya* start to link-up	Ishii & Yamaken brotherhood			Third summit strategy				
		sakazuki							
Start second amphetamine epidemic		Kantō-Hatsuka-kai set up							

Appendix D (continued)

1980	1981	1982	1983	1984	1985	1986	1987	1988	1989
Taoka dies		Reform commercial code	*Sarakin* Law	Takenaka Masahisa becomes fourth-gen Yamaguchi-gumi boss	Takenaka dies	G7 summit Tokyo Co-Operation on anti-drugs measures	UN drugs conference	UN anti-drugs convention	Kaifu-US 'Global anti-drugs partnership'
		Yamaken dies			Plaza accord start of strong yen period			Recruit scandal	
				Start of Yama-ichi war	Yama-ichi war	Yama-ichi war	Yama-ichi war	Yama-ichi war	Ichiwa-kai disbands end of Yama-ichi war
				Peak of second amphetamine epidemic				Decline in amphetamine abuse	
				Ishii released from prison	Ishii sets up companies	Ishii sets up Nomura account	Kōmintō incident		Watanabe Yoshinori becomes fifth-gen Yamaguchi-gumi boss Ishii buys Tōkyō-Dentetsu
				Kodama dies	Ishii acquires Iwama country club				

1990	1991	1992	1993	1994	1995	1996	1997	1998	1999
Hachiōji War	*Bōtaihō* passed by diet in May	*Bōtaihō* comes into effect	*Bōtaihō revised*	Fuji film executive killed	Kōbe earthquake	Kuwata-Zugoshi-Okimoto Three-way *Sakazuki*	Second revision of *Bōtaihō*		Organised-crime counter measures law passed
Bubble economy bursts	Ishii dies	Sagawa Kyūbin scandal emerges	Kanemaru arrested	Sumitomo Bank Nagoya Branch manager killed	Aum-Shinri-kyō subway gas attack	*Watanabe-Inagawa Sakazuki*	Takumi killed		
Ishii enters hospital and retires			Sumitomo bank branches attacked		*Jūsen* problem hits	Start of third period of epidemic amphetamine abuse	Yamaguchi-gumi leadership paralysis begins		
Inagawa Chihirō becomes third-gen boss of Inagawa-kai			Hanwa Bank executive shot	Yamaguchi-gumi *Jōnōkin* reduced		Nakano shot	Zugoshi becomes fifth-gen boss of Aizu-kotetsu		
Okinawa War	Okinawa war (June—high school boy shot)	Okinawa War							

Appendix E—*Bōtaihō* injunctions by group 2000

Groups	Injunctions	/1,000 men
All groups	2,036	52.5
Big three	1,682	57.4
Big syndicates (>1,000 members)	1,814	53.9
All small groups (<1,000 members)	222	42.7
Godaime Yamaguchi-gumi	996 (43)	58.0
Inagawa-kai	339 (16)	69.7
Sumiyoshi-kai	272 (16)	45.7
Nidaime Kudōrengō Kusanō-ikka	14	26.4
Rokudaime Gōda-ikka	14 (3)	89.4
Godaime Aizu Kotetsu	27 (3)	27.3
Yondaime Kyōsei-kai	7	25.0
Yondaime Kozakura-ikka	8	66.7
Nidaime Dōjin-kai	39 (1)	75.5
Sandaime Kyokuryū-kai	10	37.0
Okinawa Kyokuryū-kai	14	34.1
Sandaime Asano-gumi	9	75
Shinwa-kai	1	14.3
Sōai-kai	12	26.1
Sandaime Yamanō-kai	5	71.4
Nidaime Kyōdō-kai	5 (1)	33.3
Sandaime Taishū-kai	1	7.7
Rokudaime Sakaume-gumi	9	32.1
Kyokutō Sakurai Sōke Rengō-kai	5	13.9
Kyokutō-kai	51 (2)	31.2
Azuma-gumi	15 (2)	100
Matsuba-kai	43 (6)	32.7
Kokusui-kai	39 (2)	78.8
Nakano-kai	1	5.8
Nidaime Hakufuku-kai	5	14.7

(~) refers to *saihatsu bōshi meirei*
Derived from *Keisatsu Hakusho* (2001).

Appendix F—*Bōryokudan*-related discussions (Police and Centres) 1998

	Police	Centres	Total
Discussions concerning Article 9 of the *Bōtaihō*	7,636	3,056	10,692
Demands for money taking advantage of weakness	672	218	890
Unfair demands for contributions	1,322	794	2,116
Unfair demands for subcontracting work	238	63	301
Unfair demands for protection money	493	82	575
Unfair demands for bodyguard fees	336	21	357
High interest rate debt-collection	225	183	480
Unfair debt-collection	802	346	1,148
Unfair demands for exemption of liabilities	833	279	1,112
Unfair demands for loans	162	27	189
Unfair demands for trading on credit	82	7	89
Unfair demands to purchase shares	11	1	12
Unfair land-sharking (*jiage*)	26	20	46
Auction obstruction	89	61	150
Unfair intervention on negotiations	337	215	552
Unfair demands for money on some pretext	2,008	739	2,747
Discussions concerning 'semi-violent demands'	3	—	3
Discussions concerning secession & forced-recruitment	1,269	532	1,801
Secession	856	472	1,328
Demands/enticements to join *bōryokudan*	413	60	473
Discussions concerning gang offices	901	409	1,310
Forbidden activities	25	16	41
Grievances/requests for crackdowns etc.	555	75	630
Prevent arrival/force withdrawal of gang office	102	86	188
Eviction	219	232	451
Discussions concerning other unfair *bōryokudan* acts	11,649	2,161	13,810
Acts covered by criminal law	3,691	868	4,559
Acts covered by special laws	1,435	171	1,606
Other activities	6,523	1,122	7,645
Discussions concerning the *Bōtaihō*	2,587	6,292	8,879
Concerning the *Bōryokudan* Eradication Centres	204	3,134	3,338
Other	2,383	3,158	5,541
Total	24,045	12,450	36,495

Source: *Keisatsu Hakusho* (1999).

Notes

Chapter 1

1. For a balanced and extremely well-researched discussion of the relative merits and demerits of prohibition with specific respect to illicit drugs, interested readers are directed to MacCoun and Reuter's excellent *Drug War Heresies* (2001).
2. The reason for this shift will be discussed in later chapters.
3. It should however be noted in reality the distinction can become blurred: some bouncer teams operating in Britain are obliged to pay a tax to local criminal groups for the right to conduct business; other bouncers exploit their territorial monopoly of violence to tax 'licensed' drug dealers operating in their club; this industry notoriously attracts criminal and violent elements (Morris 1998). In Japan, such men would belong to *yakuza* groups. Under the Private Security Industry Act 2001, the UK bouncer industry is now subject to closer regulation with the aim of eradication of such problems.
4. A fascinating account of the social control mechanisms deployed by the Provisional IRA to uphold their fief is provided by Hamill (2002). These groups enhance their role by actively discouraging members of their respective communities from making use of their rival supplier of protection, the state (Hamill, private correspondence).
5. Or mafia-protectee.
6. Arnold Rothstein (1882–1928), the most influential Jewish gangster of 1920s America and famously the man on whom the character Meyer Wolfsheim was based in F. Scott Fitzgerald's *The Great Gatsby* (cf. Cohen 1999).
7. It should be noted here that the hospitality afforded researchers by mafia/*yakuza* interviewees to researchers may also create obligations potentially clouding academic objectivity.
8. 'The mandatory secret ballot is a scheme to deny the voter any means of proving how he voted. Being stripped of his power to prove how he voted, he is stripped of his power to be intimidated. Powerless to prove whether or not he complied with a threat, he knows—and so do those who would threaten him—that any punishment would be unrelated to the way he actually voted' (Schelling 1980: 19).
9. Cases in which intelligence and military agencies strike collusive agreements with mafia groups in foreign countries are specifically excluded from this discussion, though examples are legion.
10. For example, the 1950 Kefauver Committee discovered that the local police were actively employed by the OC group running the gambling

wire service in Miami, to ensure that only affiliated gamblers remained in business (Reuter 1983: 124; Schelling 1984: 164–5).

Chapter 2

1. Interestingly, some *yakuza*, a social category not usually associated with progressive social causes, played an active role in some of these riots. Interviewed later, participating *yakuza* bosses from Kōbe claimed they were altruistically distributing the rice they had taken from rice merchants to local housewives and were not personally profiting from their actions (Lewis 1990: 128). Whether or not these *yakuza* were acting altruistically (and such behaviour might be seen as good advertising), it is clear that these *yakuza* bosses were not slow in taking advantage of an opportunity to engage in socially legitimised extortion.

2. The rationale for groups like the Kokuryū-kai was primarily to promote Japanese expansion in East Asia. However, the activities of many of the so-called '*tairiku-rōnin*' (continental masterless samurai), who were ostensibly forwarding this goal, were unambiguously criminal. One notable case is the Russophile, Konstantin Ivanovich Nakamura, who ran gambling, prostitution, and drug businesses with apparent immunity in Harbin. Even when he was charged with the robbery of drugged clients at his barber shop and the sexual abuse of the 13-year-old daughter of his girlfriend, the courts immediately dropped the cases due to his connections (Jennings 1996: 52).

3. It might be expected that the introduction of the Prostitution Prevention Law (*Baishun Bōshi Hō*) in 1957 benefited the *yakuza* by increasing the dependence of the sex industry on its protection. However, it should be noted that the law was sufficiently filled with loopholes for much of this business to remain within the law. Furthermore, legal or not, this type of business is particularly liable to consume protection from informal, extralegal sources.

4. These show that over the period 1965–1985, the proportion of working-age Japanese between ages 20–29 dropped from 31% to 22%, whilst that of the *yakuza* fell from one-half to a quarter. The relative changes in the proportion over forty also suggests that *yakuza*-ageing outpaces that of the general population. Between 1966 and 1985 the percentage of *yakuza* over forty rose from 14% to 37% compared to 41% to 51% for the wider working-age population (*Tōkei-kyoku* 2001: 46).

5. The career of Kodama is a case study of the interaction between the worlds of politics and *yakuza*. After an apprenticeship in various ultra-nationalist organisations interspersed with three prison terms, Kodama spent the war as an agent of the Imperial Japanese Navy charged with securing essential raw materials. To this end, he created the Kodama Kikan, which amassed enormous wealth including interests in precious metals, industrial diamonds,

fisheries, forestry, mining, and opium. So successful was the Kodama Kikan that Kodama was able to finance not only the Shanghai branch of the *Kempeitai*, but an extensive intelligence network throughout the sphere of his operations from Manchuria to Indochina (Hunziker and Kamimura 1994: 48).

At the end of the war, the Navy, keen to distance itself from the activities of the Kodama Kikan, effectively handed it over to Kodama. With this vast personal fortune he was able to set himself up as a key *kuromaku* (behind-the-scenes power-broker) linking together the extreme right-wing, organised crime, and mainstream politics. According to Kaplan and Dubro, after his release from prison, Kodama also had extensive links with American intelligence agencies (1986: 68–9). One of Kodama's first, and most significant, postwar political acts was to provide ¥160 m to finance the formation of a new political party at the request of Hatoyama Ichirō. Aided by the further financial support of Kodama, Hatoyama was later to become prime minister (1954–1956), as did another Kodama protégé, Nakasone Yasuhiro (1982–1987). The Liberal Party merged with the Democratic Party in 1955 and this conservative coalition successfully monopolised political power for the next four decades.

Alongside his political interests, Kodama set up a business, the Midori Kikan, which specialised in strike-breaking and labour intimidation. Kodama was also a central figure in the formation in 1963 of the Kantō-kai, an ill-fated federation of *yakuza* groups in the Tokyo area. Initially, this had been intended to be a pan-Japanese *yakuza* alliance with a decided political emphasis. However, the Yamaguchi-gumi refused to have anything to do with it and the organisation disbanded in 1965 due to internal dissent and the police summit strategy.

On another occasion, Kodama was instrumental in making peace between the fierce rivals, the Yamaguchi-gumi and the Inagawa-kai. Only the breaking of the Lockheed bribery scandal in 1976 displaced Kodama from his role as supreme political organised-crime fixer.

6. Ten thousand and thirty-one officers, mainly senior, had been purged from the force and many others had left; recruitment of suitable replacements was hampered because demobilised servicemen were ineligible and former police officers were not considered desirable (Wildes 1954: 184).

7. Similarly, following the investigation into the Tokyo underground sarin nerve gas attack in 1995, the police's reputation for competence has been seriously dented.

Chapter 3

1. *Kōmon* tend to have a brother relationship with the boss and, prior to the boss's inauguration, may actually have been senior to him within the organisation.

2. Strictly speaking, between 1969 and 1982, the name of this organisation was Sumiyoshi-rengō (Sumiyoshi federation), and between 1982 and 1993 Sumiyoshi-rengō-kai. Thereafter, the group formally dropped *rengō* from its name becoming the Sumiyoshi-kai (Shinoda 2002: 34–9).

3. Gang names are given in their most modern form. At the time, the Sumiyoshi-kai and the Kokusui-kai were known as the Sumiyoshi-rengō-kai and the Nippon Kokusui-kai, respectively.

4. Promotion is not, however, a purely rational, meritocratic process; former Ichiwa-kai sub-boss Fujimura asserts that the most important factor in determining promotion within *yakuza* groups is whether the boss likes you or not (interview Osaka, 1998).

5. Presumably of less significance in recent years in which the shaved head has been fashionable amongst many *yakuza*.

6. Although written in a highly polite and slightly archaic language, when compared to the sample *hamon-jō* cited by Iwai (1963: 223), it seems that in the intervening three decades the language has become less formal; classical Chinese verb endings, for example, are no longer used.

7. This term carries slightly negative associations with the medieval practice of tattooing convicted criminals. For this reason tattoo artists prefer to talk about *horimono* whilst *yakuza* themselves refer to their tattoos as *monmon* (Herbert, private correspondence).

8. Because of the organisational structure of the Yamaguchi-gumi, the head family will hold its *koto hajime* ceremony on 13 December, second-level groups will hold their own within a few days of that, and so on.

9. Though, as mentioned in the previous chapter, politician–*yakuza* links have become less noticeable in recent decades, examples of politicians attending *yakuza*-related ceremonies still occur (for example, in 2000, Prime Minister Mori was forced to admit that he had acted as match-maker to the marriage of a retired *yakuza's* son four years earlier (*The Independent* 23 June 2000).

10. Yamada also asserts that, after subtracting costs, the money is passed on to the deceased's real family.

11. The polite euphemism for *burakumin*.

12. As we might expect, however, delinquency has historically been higher amongst victims of discrimination; DeVos's work suggests rates for *burakumin* and Korean youth, respectively, at four and seven times that of the general population (DeVos 1980: 162).

13. Traditionally, the relationship between university *karate* clubs and the *yakuza* was exploitative—but in the other direction; during the 1950s and 1960s, hardcore student *karate-ka*, including the author's teacher, would pick fights with *yakuza* as a way of field-testing their technique.

14. Whilst membership also incurred costs, it also gave him a licence to engage in more lucrative illicit activities.

15. For an examination of the complex messaging implied by *yakuza* self-presentation, see Raz (1992).
16. The term '*yakuza*-style' tattoos is used here to refer to traditional, continuous body tattoos typically covering the shoulders, back, and chest. Small, discrete (though not necessarily discreet!), western-style tattoos, including western prison tattoos, have a similar signalling function, but do not send exactly the same signals.
17. In a 1993 study, *yakuza* arrestees were categorised according to whether or not they (a) had tattoos and (b) wished to leave their gang. The tattoo rates for those wishing to leave and wishing to stay were 63 per cent and 71 per cent, respectively (*Zen-bōtsusen* 1994: 33).
18. Although such detailed figures are not available for the other two large syndicates, police estimates suggest that the 2,900 executives of the Inagawa-kai paid a monthly average of ¥137,000 yielding an annual total headquarters income of ¥4.77 bn. Within the Sumiyoshi-kai 2,500 executives paid an average monthly fee of ¥52,000, which provided an annual income of ¥1.56 bn. The lower level of Sumiyoshi-kai *jōnōkin* reflects the flatter management structure of that particular syndicate.

Chapter 4

1. In discussion *yakuza* also frequently use the term '*mendō o miru*', meaning look after or look out for, when referring to this type of protection.
2. Corporate entertainment expenses alone in 1985 stood at ¥3.85 trillion ($16.1 bn).
3. These factors are even stronger in Hong Kong where an estimated 12 % of the total cost of, for example, skyscraper construction is consumed by protection and bribery payments (Booth 1999: 243).
4. Coincidentally, 3 per cent was also the sum typically paid to LDP cliques in exchange for public construction contracts (Johnson 1995: 216–7). The high costs of corruption within the Japanese construction industry, combined with the inefficiency it engenders, go some way to explaining why it costs nine times more to build a road in Japan than in the United States (McCormack 1996: 35).
5. Street stalls selling jewellery are monopolised by Israeli organisations. Stalls are usually manned by young Israelis in need of funds for their post-military-service travels. These organisations operate as territorial franchises, and traders generally purchase their supplies of jewellery from the regional boss, to whom they also pay a percentage in exchange for their spot.

6. Although the first epidemic period was over in Japan, its effects lingered elsewhere; American troops stationed in Japan became acquainted with injected amphetamine usage in Japan. Many of them brought this habit back home with them and, as college students on the G.I. Bill, used amphetamines as an aid to pre-examination cramming. This 'laid a foundation for the later patterns of (American) amphetamine abuse' (Rawlin 1968: 51–65).

7. Of the total 45,038 arrests for solvent abuse violations in 1988, 40,472 were juveniles (*Keisatsu Hakusho* 1999).

8. Within *tekiya* groups, territory is known as *'shima'* (island) rather than *nawabari*.

9. Usually known more colloquially as *ninpu* (coolies). It should be noted, however, that not all day labourers are unskilled navvies as steeple-jacks (*tobi*) and other skilled craftsmen are also employed in this way.

10. For comparison, prostitution itself is legal in Britain but soliciting, kerb-crawling, advertising, and managing brothels are all illegal. Similarly, in many European countries prostitution is legal but circumscribed with legal restrictions. The most bizarre of these is the legal requirement under Greek law that prostitutes must retire by 55 (*The Times* 28 August 1999).

11. This claim is not entirely convincing as *yakuza* seem to find the capital for investing in equally costly projects. It seems more likely that they prefer their visible capital investments to be made in areas less dependent on police toleration.

12. A charity running hostels for, and otherwise assisting, runaway prostitutes.

13. Similar phenomena exist in Italy (*disturbatori*) and South Korea (*chongheoggun*).

14. The main and oldest group, the *Buraku* Emancipation League (*Buraku Kaihō Dōmei*), is associated with the Socialist Party, whilst the Liberal Democratic Party countered this by forming the All Japan *Dōwa* Association (*Zen-Nippon Dōwa Kai*) in 1960, and in 1970 the Communist Party established the *Buraku* Emancipation League National Liaison Conference (*Buraku Kaihō Dōmei Seijōka Zenkoku Renraku Kaigi*). The All Japan *Dōwa* Association disbanded in 1986 amidst internal squabbles.

15. The Special Measures Law expired on 31 March 2002. Because of a widespread resentment felt by non-*burakumin* at the scale of resources pumped into *buraku* communities under this law (¥105 billion in fiscal 2001), *burakumin* activists felt it prudent not to press for the law's extension.

16. When he tried to have his book on the Japanese police published in Japanese, Ames was subject to considerable pressure to excise all references to *burakumin*. Only after changing publishers was he able to publish the unexpurgated version.

17. While dirty 'legitimate' companies make themselves vulnerable to *yakuza* extortion or, as in the case of Chisso, *yakuza* protection from the irate victims of pollution.

Chapter 5

1. See Chapter Seven.
2. Whilst organised crime countermeasures in these three jurisdictions consist of more than this simple device, the Japanese authorities, when considering their own legal options, considered criminalisation to be the central plank of organised crime-specific law in Europe.
3. With the passage of the Proceeds of Crime Act 2002, Britain has also dramatically increased the scope for its own ability to seize the assets of criminals. As is the case in the United States, the burden of proof in civil proceedings concerning the confiscation of assets is considerably lightened.
4. Whereby law-enforcement officers maintain tight surveillance over shipments of illegal goods rather than seizing them at the port of entry. This reveals a greater section of the distribution chain, thereby maximising potential arrests.
5. An assumption that is more reasonable for OC groups than individual, disorganised criminals as a whole.
6. *Amakudari*, literally descent from heaven, refers to the practice of retired bureaucrats securing employment in the industries they formerly regulated or in quangos set up by their respective ministries.

Chapter 6

1. As mentioned in Chapter Two, this type of business is also highly susceptible to delays and pilfering. As a consequence, Sagawa Kyūbin also paid Ishii Susumu, head of the Inagawa-kai, to protect deliveries against these eventualities.
2. This need not necessarily follow. When targeting banks with propaganda trucks, right-wing groups frequently refuse money from their first victims so as to make it easier to collect money from future victims.
3. Yamada Hitoshi, head of the Japan Bar Association's *Bōryokudan* Countermeasures Committee, suggests that the proportion of LDP parliamentarians with links to extreme right-wing groups is between 10% and 20% (interview Tokyo, 1998).
4. Japanese banks had traditionally confined themselves to a business clientele and had ignored small businesses and individual consumers.
5. Changes in accounting regulations introduced in the fiscal year 1999–2000 (requiring Japanese companies to consolidate the finances of subsidiary companies in their annual accounts) and the following financial year (in which assets must be valued at market value rather than book cost) were

expected to partially alleviate these problems (*Economist* 27 December 1999). It is not clear that this expectation has been met.

6. The quasi-governmental organisation set up in 1996 to dispose of the problem loans of the *jūsen* debacle. This later became the Resolution and Collection Corporation (RCC or *Seiri Kaishū Kikō*).

7. The Yamaguchi-gumi later achieved a notable public-relations coup following the catastrophic Hanshin earthquake of 1995. Whilst the national government was dithering as to how best to respond to this crisis, the Yamaguchi-gumi was distributing free food, disposable babies' nappies, milk, and water from outside its Kōbe headquarters (Yamada 1998: 243–308; *Reuters News Service* 22 January 1995).

8. The fact that not all direct groups had met Takumi's deadline suggests that control within the Yamaguchi-gumi is by no means absolute. Events to occur later show this even more clearly.

9. This is a problem police interviewees acknowledged elsewhere with respect to *yakuza* arrestees expressing a desire to secede from gangs.

10. 9.3 and 28.8, respectively.

11. The main intergroup relations amongst the major designated *yakuza* groups are given in the Appendix.

12. One major inconvenience to tattooed *yakuza* is that they are unable to use course bathing facilities following a round of golf (a sport highly popular amongst *yakuza*).

13. This may go some way to explaining why *kōsei-in* arrests have declined since the introduction of the *Bōtaihō* (but probably not by much given that the trend precedes 1992 by several years).

14. Despite declining by 14% from its 1992 peak, corporate entertainment expenses in Japan during 1997 totalled ¥5.3 trillion ($44 bn).

15. It is probable that this crackdown was triggered by the amendment of the Public Morals Law in 1998.

16. Senior company management may deliberately adopt a policy of ignorance by giving broad discretionary powers to its General Affairs Department and not asking too many questions.

17. Head of the Nichibenren's anti-*minbō* committee.

18. Both these ratios have been stable over the preceding decade with means of 44% and 22% and standard deviations of 1.4 and 2.1, respectively.

19. In discussions with criminal defence lawyers, it became clear that the way in which *yakuza* presented themselves to their lawyer was very different from the way in which they portrayed themselves to me. To the former they stressed that they were essentially legitimate businessmen trying to get by in a hostile environment, whilst to me there seemed greater emphasis on projecting an impressive *yakuza* image.

20. Although, amongst the younger generation of *yakuza* recruited in the bubble years, university graduates are not unheard of.

21. Diabetes and liver disease.

22. The contrast between the Yamaguchi-gumi's organisational woes and the state of the Sumiyoshi-kai is striking. Two years after its abandonment of a federal system in 1993, the group promoted a new cohort of younger executives in their late forties and early fifties. At the same time, it adopted a regional-block system similar to those of the other two big syndicates. In 1998, the group underwent an organisational 'big bang' with the replacement of Nishiguchi by the younger Fukuda Hareaki, a young executive committee, and minor change in committees. Looking at the Sumiyoshi-kai, *Jitsuwa Jidai* (March 1999: 14–15) observes that in comparison many other *yakuza* groups are redolent of the last days of the Tokugawa.

23. This is more likely to be due to the increased police pressure on the syndicate and the executive-level confusion, rather than a deliberate change of policy.

Chapter 7

1. Despite these amicable relations, this group has been in decline for several decades. Unable to compete with the vastly superior brand-recognition of the Yamaguchi-gumi, the Sakaume-gumi has failed to attract new recruits. In Autumn of 1999, the sixth-generation leader of this group disappeared with debts in excess of ¥1 bn (*Shūkan Jitsūwa* 14 October 1999).

2. Fowler (1996: 41–2) reports that over a dozen riots occurred during the 1960s in San'ya alone.

3. Compiled from the profiles of the PSC websites for Tokyo, Osaka, Kyoto, Saitama, Okinawa, Nagasaki, Hyōgo, Hiroshima, Shizuoka, Iwate, Wakayama, and Aomori. Sample size 41.

4. Now known as the Ministry of Economy Trade and Industry.

5. As mentioned in Chapter Six, the police had initially wanted RICO-style sequestration of assets when drafting the *Bōtaihō* but it had been felt that, given the lack of judicial exercise of this law, allowing for sequestration under the provisions of the *Bōtaihō* was inappropriate.

6. The police have not in the past, however, confined electronic surveillance to drugs cases. In 1986, the telephone line of the head of the international section of the Japan Communist Party was found to be tapped by a serving officer of Kanagawa prefecture's branch of the Security Police. The police, however, denied systematic participation (*Nichibenren* 1995: 203–4). Despite the clear illegality of this act, the prosecutors' office did not pursue the case following an apology from senior police officers (van Wolferen 1989: 199).

7. And can extend to life imprisonment or the death penalty.

8. Top executives of the Yamaguchi-gumi arrested in 1998 for violating the Sword and Firearms Control Law (see Chapter Five).

9. *Unten daikō* is the Japanese term for businesses providing a taxi and spare driver to take the customer and his/her car home after an evening's drinking.

10. Suggesting, perhaps, that even the *yakuza* are not immune to this increased propensity to litigation.

11. Even if this is partially explained by increased reporting rates, it supports the argument that citizens are now relying on official state sources of protection and dispute resolution rather than informal private alternatives.

12. Tanioka Ichirō (1997) has attempted to test whether control theory is applicable to Japan by adapting American tests of this theory. Whilst his results suggest that control factors are indeed significant, what we are interested in here is the decline in the power of these factors over recent decades.

Bibliography

Abadinsky, H. (1983) *The Criminal Elite* (Westport, Conn: Greenwood Press).
—— (1994) *Organised Crime* (Chicago: Nelson-Hall).
Albanese, J. (1995) *Contemporary Issues in Organized Crime* (Monsey, NY: Criminal Justice Press).
Aldous, C. (1997) *The Police in Occupation Japan: Control, Corruption and Resistance to Reform* (London: Routledge).
—— and Leishman, F. (1997) 'Policing in Post-War Japan: Reform, Reversion and Reinvention', *International Journal of the Sociology of Law*, 25.
—— —— (1999) 'Police and Community Safety in Japan: Model or Myth?', *Crime Prevention and Community Safety: An International Journal*, 1/1 (Leicester: Perpetuity Press).
Alexander, H. and Caiden, G. (1985) *The Politics and Economics of Organised Crime* (Lexington, MA: D.C. Heath).
—— (1985) 'Organised Crime and Politics', in H. Alexander and G. Caiden (eds.), *The Politics and Economics of Organised Crime* (Lexington, MA: D.C. Heath).
Alletzhauser, A. (1990) *The House of Nomura* (London: Bloomsbury).
Ames, W. (1981) *Police and Community in Japan* (Berkeley: University of California Press).
Amir, M. (1986) 'Organized Crime and Organized Criminality Among Georgian Jews in Israel', in R. Kelly (ed.), *Organized Crime: An International Perspective* (Totowa, NJ: Rowman and Littlefield).
Amnesty International (1998) *Amnesty International Report (1998): Japan*.
Anderson, A. (1995) 'Theories of the State and the Origin of Criminal Organisations', in G. Fiorentini and S. Peltzman (eds.), *The Economics of Organised Crime* (Cambridge: Cambridge University Press).
Arlacchi, P. (1983) *Mafia Business: The Mafia Ethic and the Spirit of Capitalism* (London: Verso).
Ashworth, A. (1992) *Sentencing and Criminal Justice* (London: Weidenfeld and Nicolson).
—— (1994) 'Sentencing', in M. Maguire, R. Morgan, and R. Reiner (eds.), *The Oxford Handbook of Criminology* (Oxford: Oxford University Press).
Baer, J. and Chambliss, W. (1997) 'Generating Fear: The Politics of Crime Reporting', *Crime, Law and Social Change*, 27.
Bailey, P. (1996) *Postwar Japan: 1945 to the Present* (Oxford: Blackwell).
Baum, D. (1996) *Smoke and Mirrors: The War on Drugs and the Politics of Failure* (Boston: Little, Brown and Company).
Baumol, W. (1995) 'Gangs as Primitive States (Discussion)', in G. Fiorentini and S. Peltzman (eds.), *The Economics of Organised Crime* (Cambridge: Cambridge University Press).

Bayley, D. (1976) *Forces of Order: Police Behaviour in Japan and the United States* (Berkeley, CA: University of California Press).

Beasley, W. (1990) *The Rise of Modern Japan* (London: Weidenfeld and Nicolson).

Bell, D. (1965) *The End of Ideology* (New York: Free Press).

Benedict, R. (1967 [1946]) *The Chrysanthemum and the Sword: Patterns of Japanese Culture* (London: Routledge & Kegan Paul).

Bessatsu Takarajima 56 (1986) *Yakuza to Iu Ikikata: Toshi no Soko ni Hisomu Otokotachi no Monogatari* (Tokyo: Takarajima).

Bessatsu Takarajima 157 (1992) *Yakuza to Iu Ikikata: Kore ga Shinogi Ya!* (Tokyo: Takarajima).

Bessatsu Takarajima 337 (1997) *Yakuza to Iu Ikikata: Nihon Koku-shakai* (Tokyo: Takarajima).

Bessatsu Takarajima 374 (1997) *Za Tōsan* (Tokyo: Takarajima).

Blakey, G. (1985) 'Asset Forfeiture Under the Federal Criminal Law', in H. Alexander and G. Caiden (eds.), *The Politics and Economics of Organised Crime* (Lexington, MA: D.C. Heath).

Block, A. (1986) 'A Modern Marriage of Convenience: A Collaboration Between Organised Crime and US Intelligence', in R. Kelly (ed.), *Organised Crime: An International Perspective* (Totowa, NJ: Rowman & Littlefield).

Blok, A. (1974) *The Mafia of a Sicilian Village 1860–1960: A Study of Violent Peasant Entrepreneurs* (Cambridge: Polity Press).

Boku, M. (1997) 'Bōryokudan Taisaku Hō no Igi to Kadai', in T. Fujimoto (ed.), *Bōryokudan Taisaku Hō Shikōgo Gonen no Bōryokudan Taisaku* (Tokyo: Issei Insatsu).

Booth, M. (1990) *The Triads* (London: Grafton).

—— (1999) *The Dragon Syndicates: The Global Phenomenon of the Triads* (London: Doubleday).

Bornoff, N. (1994) *Pink Samurai: An Erotic Exploration of Japanese Society* (London: Harper Collins).

Bōryokudan Taisaku Roppō (1997) See *Keisatsu-chō Keiji-kyoku Bōryokudan Taisaku-bu*.

Bōtaisaku-bu see *Keisatsu-chō Keiji-kyoku Bōryokudan Taisaku-bu*.

Braithwaite, J. (1989) *Crime, Shame and Integration* (Cambridge: Cambridge University Press).

Brill, H. and Hirose, T. (1969) 'The Rise and Fall of a Methamphetamine,' Epidemic: Japan 1945–1955', *Seminars in Psychiatry*, 1: 179–94.

Burgess, R. (1984) *In the Field: An Introduction to Field Research* (London: Routledge).

Buruma, I. (1984) *A Japanese Mirror* (London: Penguin Books).

Celantini, M., Marrelli, M., and Martina, R. (1995) 'Regulating the Organised Crime Sector', in G. Fiorentini and S. Peltzman (eds.), *The Economics of Organised Crime* (Cambridge: Cambridge University Press).

Center for Strategic and International Studies (1997) *Russian Organized Crime* (Washington, DC: Center for Strategic and International Studies).

Chambliss, W. (1992) 'Consequences of Prohibition: Crime, Corruption and International Narcotics Control', in H. Traver and M. Gaylord (eds.), *Drugs, Law and the State* (Hong Kong: Hong Kong University Press).

Chu, Y. (2000) *The Triads as Business* (London: Routledge).

Clifford, W. (1976) *Crime Control in Japan* (Lexington, MA: Lexington Books).

Cohen, R. (1999) *Tough Jews: Fathers, Sons and Gangster Dreams* (London: Vintage).

Constantine, P. (1993) *Japan's Sex Trade: A Journey Through Japan's Erotic Subcultures* (Tokyo: Yenbooks).

Cortazzi, H. (1993) *Modern Japan: A Concise Survey* (London: Macmillan).

Cressey, D. (1969) *Theft of the Nation* (New York: Harper and Row).

—— (1972) *Criminal Organisation* (New York: Heineman Educational Books).

Dalby, L. (2000) *Geisha* (London: Vintage).

Dale, P. (1986) *The Myth of Japanese Uniqueness* (London: Croom Helm).

Davis, J. (1996) *Dispute Resolution in Japan* (Den Haag, Holland: Kluwer Law International).

DeVos, G. (1973) *Socialisation for Achievement* (Berkeley, CA: University of California Press).

Doi, T. (1973) *The Anatomy of Dependence* (Tokyo: Kodansha International).

Dower, J. (2000) *Embracing Defeat: Japan in the Aftermath of World War II* (London: Penguin).

Edelhertz, H. (1987) *Major Issues in Organized Crime Control* (Washington, DC: US Department of Justice).

Endō, M. (1992) *Kaidoku: Bōryokudan Shinpō* (Tokyo: Gendai Shokan).

Fijnaut, C. (1990) 'Organised Crime: A Comparison Between the United States of America and Western Europe', *British Journal of Criminology*, 30/3.

Finch, A. (2000) 'Criminal Statistics in Japan: The White Paper on Crime, Hanzai Hakusho and Hanzai Tōkeisho', *Social Science Japan Journal*, 3/2.

Fiorentini, G. and Peltzman, S. (1995) *The Economics of Organised Crime* (Cambridge: Cambridge University Press).

Fowler, E. (1996) *San'ya Blues: Laboring Life in Contemporary Tokyo* (Ithaca and London: Cornell University Press).

Freemantle, B. (1995) *The Octopus: Europe in the Grip of Organized Crime* (London: Orion).

Friman, H. (1994) 'International Pressure and Domestic Bargains: Regulating Money Laundering in Japan', *Crime, Law and Social Change*, 21.

—— (1996) *NarcoDiplomacy: Exporting the U.S. War on Drugs* (Ithaca: Cornell University Press).

Fujimoto, T. (1997) *Bōryokudan Taisaku Hō Shikōgo Gonen no Bōryokudan Taisaku* (Tokyo: Issei Insatsu).

Fukuda, M. (1992) 'Bōryokudan Shinpō no Naiyōteki Mondai-ten', in M. Kai and K. Ōno (eds.), *Kiken na Bōryokudan Taisaku-hō* (Osaka: Bōryokudan Taisaku-hō Shinpojiumu Jikkō Iinkai).

Gambetta, D. (1993) *The Sicilian Mafia: The Business of Private Protection* (Cambridge, MA: Harvard University Press).

—— and Reuter, P. (1995) 'Conspiracy Among the Many: The Mafia in Legitimate Industries', in G. Fiorentini and S. Peltzman (eds.), *The Economics of Organised Crime* (Cambridge: Cambridge University Press).

—— (forthcoming) *Crimes and Signs: Essays on Underworld Communications* (Cambridge, Massachusetts: Harvard University Press).

Garon, S. (1997) *Moulding Japanese Minds: The State in Everyday Life* (Princeton, NJ: Princeton University Press).

Gilbert, N. (1993) *Researching Social Life* (London: Sage).

Giuliani, R. (1987) 'Legal Remedies for Attacking Organized Crime', in H. Edelhertz (ed.), *Major Issues in Organized Crime Control* (Washington, DC: US Department of Justice).

Goffman, E. (1959) *The Presentation of Self in Everyday Life* (London: Penguin Books).

Grossman, H. (1995) 'Rival Kleptocrats: The Mafia versus the State', in G. Fiorentini and S. Peltzman (eds.), *The Economics of Organised Crime* (Cambridge: Cambridge University Press).

Haley, J. (1978) 'The Myth of the Reluctant Litigant', in *Journal of Japanese Studies Vol. 4 No.1*.

—— (1991) *Authority Without Power: Law and the Japanese Paradox* (Oxford: Oxford University Press).

Hamill, H. (2002) *Hoods and Provos: Crime and Punishment in West Belfast* (Unpublished DPhil Thesis, Department of Sociology, University of Oxford).

Hanzai Hakusho—see *Hōmu-shō*.

Harada, Y. and Inohara, S. (2000) 'Soshikiteki Hanzai Shobatsu-hō Oyobi Keiji Kisō-hō no Ichibu Kaisei suru Hōritsu no Gaiyō nado ni Tsuite', in *Keisatsu-gaku Ronshū*, 53/1 (Tokyo: Tachibana Shobō).

Hartcher, P. (1998) *The Ministry: The Inside Story of Japan's Ministry of Finance* (London: Harper Collins Business).

Hasegawa, F. (1988) *Built by Japan: Competitive Strategies of the Japanese Construction Industry* (New York: Wiley-Interscience).

Hayashi, N. (2000) 'Sotai-hō Seiritsu Zakkan', in *Keisatsu-gaku Ronshū*, 53/1 (Tokyo: Tachibana Shobō).

Hellman, D. and Alper, N. (1993) *The Economics of Crime* (Needham Heights, MA: Simon & Schuster).

Herbert, W. (1990) 'One Day in the Life of a Day Labourer', *Kansai Time Out* February.

—— (1991) '*Yakuza* in the Nineties: A Tradition in Crisis', *Kansai Time Out* March.

—— (1992) 'Conjuring Up a Crime Wave: The "Rapid Growth in the Crime Rate among Foreign Migrant Workers in Japan" Critically Examined', *Japan Forum*, 4/1.

—— (1995) 'Tattooing Japanese Style', *Kansai Time Out*, May.

Herbert, W. (1996) *Foreign Workers and Law Enforcement in Japan* (London: Kegan Paul International).

—— (2000) 'The *Yakuza* and the Law', in J. Eades, T. Gill, and H. Befu (eds.), *Globalization and Social Change in Contemporary Japan* (Melbourne: Trans Pacific Press).

Herzog, P. (1993) *Japan's Pseudo-Democracy* (Sandgate: Japan Library).

Hess, H. (1998) *Mafia and Mafiosi: Origin, Power and Myth* (London: Hurst and Company).

Hicks, G. (1994) *The Comfort Women: Japan's Brutal Regime of Enforced Prostitution in the Second World War* (New York: W.W. Norton).

Higuchi, T. (1998) Paper presented to *Keisastu Seisaku Gakkai, Soshiki Hanzai Kenkyū Bukai*, Tokyo.

Hinago, A. (1992*a*) 'No to Ienai Pachinko-nin', in Bessatsu Takarajima 157, *Yakuza to Iu Ikikata: Kore ga Shinogi Ya!* (Tokyo: Takarajima).

—— (1992*b*) 'Onna-korogashi Abura Jigoku', in Bessatsu Takarajima (ed.) 157, *Yakuza to Iu Ikikata: Kore ga Shinogi Ya!* (Tokyo: Takarajima).

—— (1998) 'Songiriya, Habikoru!', in Bessatsu Takarajima (ed.) 374, *Za Tōsan* (Tokyo: Takarajima).

Hiraoka, H. (1987) 'Shakai Undō Hyōbō Goro no Torishimari', in *Keisatsu-gaku Ronshū*, 40/3 (Tokyo: Tachibana Shobō).

Hobbs, D. (1994) 'Professional and Organised Crime in Britain', in *The Oxford Handbook of Criminology* (Oxford: Oxford University Press).

—— (1995) *Bad Business: Professional Crime in Modern Britain* (Oxford: Oxford University Press).

—— Hadfield, P., Lister, S., and Winlow, S. (2002) 'Door Lore: The Art and Economics of Intimidation', *British Journal of Criminology*, 42: 352–70.

Home Office (1995–1998) *Criminal Statistics: England and Wales (1994–7)* (London: HMSO).

Hōmu-shō (1989–1999) *Hanzai Hakusho* (Tokyo: Ōkura-shō Insatsukyoku).

Hōmu-shō Keijikyoku Keijihōseika (1997) *Soshikiteki Hanzai to Keiji Hō* (Tokyo: Yūhikaku).

Hori, Y. (1983) *Sengo no Uyoku Seiryoku* (Tokyo: Keisō Shobō).

Hoshino, K. (1971) *Organized Criminal Gangs in Japan—The Subcultures of Organized Criminal Gangs* (unpublished seminar paper Northwestern University, Evanston, Illinois).

—— (1994) 'Bōryokudan Hanzai no Henka to Tenbō', in *Hanzai to Hikō*, 100: 129–48 (Tokyo).

—— Mugishima, F., and Kiyonaga, K. (1971) 'Bōryokudan ni okeru Gishiki to Shugyō', *Kagaku Keisatsu Kenkyūjo Hōkoku*, 2/2 (Dec.).

Huang, F. and Vaughn, M. (1992) 'A Descriptive Analysis of Japanese Organised Crime: The Bōryokudan from 1945 to 1988', *International Criminal Justice Review*, 2.

Human Rights Watch (2000) 'Owed Justice: Thai Women Trafficked into Debt Bondage in Japan', http://www.hrw.org/reports/2000/japan/6-sec-6–7-8.htm.

Hunziker, S. and Kamimura, I. (1994) *Tanaka Kakuei: A Political Biography of Modern Japan* (Los Gatos, CA: Daruma International Press).

Ianni, F. (1972) *A Family Business: Kinship and Social Control in Organised Crime* (New York: Russell Sage Foundation).

—— (1974) *The Black Mafia: Ethnic Succession in Organised Crime* (New York: Simon and Schuster).

Igarashi, F. (1986) 'Forced to Confess', in G. McCormack and Y. Sugimoto (eds.), *Democracy in Japan* (Armonk, New York: M. E. Sharpe).

Ino, K. (1992*a*) 'Kenryoku to Yakuza no Rekishi', in Bessatsu Takarajima (ed.) 157, *Yakuza to Iu Ikikata: Kore ga Shinogiya!* (Tokyo: Takarajima).

—— (1992*b*) 'Bōryokudan Shinpō no Mondai-ten', in M. Endō (ed.), *Kaidoku: Bōryokudan Shinpō* (Tokyo: Gendai Shokan).

—— (1993) *Yakuza to Nihonjin* (Tokyo: Gendai Shokan).

—— (1994) *Bōtaihō ka no Yakuza* (Tokyo: Gendai Shokan).

Ishibashi, S. (1998) 'Fudōsan ni Tai-suru Shikkō Bōgai no Genjō', in *Keisatsu-gaku Ronshū*, 51/12 (Tokyo: Tachibana Shobō).

Iwahashi, O. (1998) 'Bōryokudan Crimes and Countermeasures' (Paper given at Kobe Pre-congress, Twelfth International Congress on Criminology), 19–21/August.

Iwai, H. (1963) *Byōri Shūdan no Kōzō* (Tokyo: Seishin-Shobō).

—— (1974) 'Delinquent Groups and Organised Crime', in T. Lebra and W. Lebra (eds.), *Japanese Culture and Behaviour* (Honolulu: University of Hawaii Press).

—— (1986) 'Organised Crime in Japan', in R. Kelly (ed.), *Organised Crime: An International Perspective* (Totowa, NJ: Rowman and Littlefield).

Jacobs, J. (1994) *Busting the Mob: United States V. Cosa Nostra* (New York: New York University Press).

—— Friel, C., and Radick, R. (1999) *Gotham Unbound: How New York City was Liberated from the Grip of Organized Crime* (New York: New York University Press).

Jennings, J. (1997) *The Opium Empire: Japanese Imperialism and Drug Trafficking in Asia, 1895–1945* (Westport, CT: Praeger).

Johnson, C. (1972) *Conspiracy at Matsukawa* (Berkeley, CA: University of California Press).

—— (1995) *Japan: Who Governs? The Rise of the Developmental State* (New York: W.W. Norton & Company).

Johnson, D. (2002) *The Japanese Way of Justice* (Oxford: Oxford University Press).

—— (2003) 'Above the Law? Police Integrity in Japan', *Social Science Japan Journal* Vol. 6. No. 1.

Johnson, E. (1997) *Criminalization and Prisoners in Japan: Six Contrary Cohorts* (Carbondale: Southern Illinois University Press).

JUSRI (*Toshi Bōhan Kenkyū Sentā*) (1990) *Hanzai no Higaisha Hassei Jittai ni Kan-suru Chōsa Hōkokusho* 1/1.

Kai, M. and Ōno, K. (1992) *Kiken na Bōryokudan Taisaku-hō* (Osaka: Bōryokudan Taisaku-hō Shinpojiumu Jikkō Iinkai).

Kaplan, D. (1996) *Japanese Organized Crime and the Bubble Economy*, The Woodrow Wilson Center Asia Program, Occasional Paper No. 70, 13 December.

—— and Dubro, A. (1986) *Yakuza* (London: Addison-Wesley Publishing).

—— and Marshall, A. (1997) *The Cult at the End of the World: The Incredible Story of Aum* (London: Arrow Books).

Katō, H. (1991) ' "Soshiki Hanzai" ni Tai-suru Hōteki Taiō ni Tsuite', *Jurisuto*, 985.

—— (1992) *Soshiki Hanzai no Kenkyū: Mafia, Ra Koza Nosutora, Bōryokudan no Hikaku Kenkyū* (Tokyo: Seibundo).

Katzenstein, P. (1996) *Cultural Norms and National Security: Police and Military in Postwar Japan* (Ithaca: Cornell University Press).

—— and Tsujinaka, Y. (1991) *Defending the Japanese State: Structures, Norms and the Political Responses to Terrorism and Violent Social Protest in the 1970s and 1980s* (Ithaca: Cornell East Asia Series).

Kawai, N. (1999) *Japan Almanac 2000* (Tokyo: Asahi Shimbun).

Kawashima, T. (1963) 'Dispute Resolution in Contemporary Japan', in A. von Mehren (ed.), *Law in Japan: The Legal Order in a Changing Society* (Cambridge, MA: Harvard University Press).

Keisatsu-chō (1989–2001, 1991*a*) *Keisatsu Hakusho* (Tokyo: Ōkura-shō Insatsukyoku).

—— (1991*b*) *Hanzai Tōkeisho: Heisei San-nen no Hanzai* (Tokyo: Ōkura-shō Insatsukyoku).

Keisatsu-chō Keiji-kyoku Bōryokudan Taisaku-bu (1997) *Bōryokudan Taisaku Roppō* (Tokyo: Tokyo Hōrei Shuppan).

—— (2002) *Bōtaihō Shikō Jū-nen*.

Keisatsu Hakusho—see *Keisatsu-chō*.

Kelly, R. (1986) *Organised Crime: An International Perspective* (Totowa, NJ: Rowman and Littlefield).

Kersten, J. (1993) 'Street Formation, *Bosozoku*, and *Yakuza*: Subculture Formation and Societal Reactions in Japan', *Crime and Delinquency*, 39/3.

—— (1996) 'Culture, Masculinities and Violence Against Women', *British Journal of Criminology*, 36/3.

Kitaguchi, S. (1999) *An Introduction to the* Buraku *Issue: Questions and Answers*, (Richmond Surrey: Japan Library).

Kleiman, M. (1985) 'Drug Enforcement and Organised Crime', in H. Alexander and G. Caiden (eds.), *The Politics and Economics of Organised Crime* (Lexington, MA: D.C. Heath).

Komiya, N. (1999) 'A Cultural Study of the Low Crime Rate in Japan', *British Journal of Criminology*, 39/3.

Konishi, Y. (1997) 'Bōryokudan ni yoru Shikkō Bōgai', in T. Fujimoto (ed.), *Bōryokudan Taisaku Hō Shikkō-go Go-nen no Bōryokudan Taisaku* (Tokyo: Hitosei).

Kurokawa, S. (2000) 'Tsushin Bōjū-hō no Kaisetsu', *Keisatsu-gaku Ronshū*, 53/1 (Tokyo: Tachibana Shobō).

Kyōdō (Tsūshin) (1993) *Riken Yūchaku: Seizaibō—Kenryoku no Kōzu* (Tokyo: Kyōdō News Service).

Lebra, T. and Lebra, W. (1974) *Japanese Culture and Behaviour* (Honolulu: University of Hawaii Press).

Levi, M. (2002) 'The Organisation of Serious Crimes', in M. Maguire, R. Morgan, and R. Reiner (eds.), *The Oxford Handbook of Criminology*, 3rd edn. (Oxford: Oxford University Press).

—— (1998*a*) 'Perspectives on 'Organised Crime': An Introduction', *The Howard Journal*, 37/4 (Nov.).

—— (1998*b*) *Analysing 'Organised Crime' and State Responses: Some Reflections on Murky Waters*.

Levitt, S. and Venkatesh, S. (2000) 'An Economic Analysis of a Drug-Selling Gang's Finances' in *The Quarterly Journal of Economics Vol. CXV August 2000*.

Lewis, M. (1990) *Rioters and Citizens: Mass Protest in Imperial Japan* (Berkeley, CA: University of California Press).

Lupsha, P. (1986) 'Organized Crime in the United States', in R. Kelly (ed.), *Organized Crime: An International Perspective* (Totowa, NJ: Rowman and Littlefield).

Mabuchi, M. (1997) *Ōkura-shō wa Naze Oitsumerareta no ka* (Tokyo: Chūkō Shinsho).

MacCoun, R. and Reuter, P. (2001) *Drug War Heresies: Learning from Other Vices, Times, and Places* (Cambridge: Cambridge University Press).

Machiavelli, N. (1983 [1532]) *The Prince* G. Bull (trans.) (London: Penguin Books).

Maguire, K. (1993) 'Fraud, Extortion and Racketeering: The Black Economy in Northern Ireland', in *Crime, Law and Social Change*, 20.

—— (1997) *Crime, Crime Control, and the* Yakuza *in Contemporary Japan*.

Maguire, M., Morgan, R., and Reiner, R. (1994) *The Oxford Handbook of Criminology* (Oxford: Oxford University Press).

Maltz, M. (1985) 'Towards Defining Organised Crime', in H. Alexander and G. Caiden (eds.), *The Politics and Economics of Organised Crime* (Lexington, MA: Lexington Books).

—— (1990) *Measuring the Effectiveness of Organized Crime Control Measures* (Chicago: The Office of International Criminal Justice).

Mayhew, P., Elliot, D., and Dowds, L. (1988) *The 1988 British Crime Survey* (London: HMSO).

—— and White, P. (1996) *The 1996 International Crime Victimisation Survey* (London: Home Office and Research Directorate. Research Findings No. 57).

McCormack, G. (1986) 'Crime, Confession, and Control in Contemporary Japan', in G. McCormack and Y. Sugimoto (eds.), *Democracy in Contemporary Japan* (Armonk, NY: M. E. Sharpe, Inc).

—— (1996) *The Emptiness of Japanese Affluence* (Armonk, NY: M. E. Sharpe).

Merton, R. (1964) 'Anomie, Anomia and Social Interaction: Contexts of Deviant Behaviour', in M. Clinard (ed.), *Anomie and Deviant Behaviour* (New York: The Free Press).

Milhaupt, C. and West, M. (2000) 'The Dark Side of Private Ordering: An Institutional and Empirical Analysis of Organized Crime', *University of Chicago Law Review*, 67/1.

——Ramseyer, J., and Young, M. (2001) *Japanese Law in Context: Readings in Society, the Economy and Politics* (Cambridge, MA: Harvard University Press).

Ministry of Justice Web-site—http://www.moj.go.jp/ENGLISH/PPO/ ppo_01.htm.

Mitchell, R. (1976) *Thought Control in Prewar Japan* (Ithaca: Cornell University Press).

——(1996) *Political Bribery in Japan* (Honolulu: University of Hawaii Press).

Miyagi, K. (1992) 'Shinpō Seiritsu no Keika to Futai Ketsugi', in M. Endō (ed.), *Kaidoku: Bōryokudan Shinpō* (Tokyo: Gendai Shokan).

Miyazaki, K. (1994) 'Gangsters and Businessmen: The History of a Turbulent Marriage', *Tokyo Business Today*, Dec.

Miyazawa, S. (1992) *Policing in Japan: A Study on Making Crime* (Albany, NY: State University of New York Press).

——(1997) 'The Enigma of Japan as a Testing Ground for Cross-Cultural Criminological Studies, draft for version later reprinted', in D. Nelken (ed.), *Comparative Legal Cultures* (Aldershot: Dartmouth).

Mizoguchi, A. (1985a) *Yamaguchi-gumi vs. Ichiwa-kai* (Tokyo: San'ichi Shobō).

——(1985b) *Chi to Tōsō* (Tokyo: San'ichi Shobō).

——(1986) 'Urashakai no Seiji-keizaigaku', in Bessatsu Takarajima 56. (ed.), *Yakuza to Iu Ikikata* (Tokyo: Takarajima).

——(1990) *Godaime Yamaguchi-gumi* (Tokyo: San'ichi Shobō).

——(1992a) 'Yonchōen Sangyō o Mushibamu, Fuhōtōki no Amai Mitsu', in Bessatsu Takarajima 157 (ed.), *Yakuza to Iu Ikikata: Kore ga Shinogiya!* (Tokyo: Takarajima).

——(1992b) 'Yamaguchi-gumi to Bōryokudan Shinpō', in Bessatsu Takarajima 157 (ed.), *Yakuza to Iu Ikikata: Kore Ga Shinogiya!* (Tokyo: Takarajima).

——(1994) *Chaina Mafia: Bōryū no Okite* (Tokyo: Shogakkan).

——(1997) *Gendai Yakuza no Ura-chishiki* (Tokyo: Takarajima).

——(1998) 'Kigyō o Kui-tsukusu "Yami Sekai" no Jūnin-tachi', in Bessatsu Takarajima 374 (ed.), *Za Tōsan* (Tokyo: Takarajima).

——(2000) *Yakuza wa Ika ni Henbō Shita ka?*, in *Jitsuwa Jidai* September 2000.

Morgan, R. (1994) 'Imprisonment', in M. Maguire, R. Morgan, and R. Reiner (eds.), *The Oxford Handbook of Criminology* (Oxford: Oxford University Press).

Morgan, W. (1960) *Triad Societies in Hong Kong* (Hong Kong: Government Press).

Morishita, T. (1997) 'Hikakuhōteki ni Mita Soshiki Hanzai Taisaku Rippō', in *Nichibenren* (ed.), *Chūkai: Bōryokudan Taisaku Hō* (Tokyo: *Minjihō Kenkyū-kai*).

Morris, S. (1998) *Clubs, Drugs and Doormen*, Police Research Group, Crime Detection and Prevention Series Paper 86.

Morton, J. (1992) *Gangland: London's Underworld* (London: Warner).

Mugishima, F. (1998) *Inshoku-ten Eigyō ni Kan-suru Ankēto* (Tokyo: Shakai Anzen Kenkyū Zaidan).

——Hoshino, K., and Kiyonaga, K. (1971) 'Bōryokudan-in no Yubitsume to Irezumi', *Kagaku Keisatsu Kenkyū-jo Hōkoku*, 12/2 (Dec.).

Muncie, J., McLaughlin, E., and Langan, M. (1996) *Criminological Perspectives* (London: Sage).

Nakagawa, H. (1992) 'Sono Otoko wa Mihatenu Yume wo Otta', in Bessatsu Takarajima 157 (ed.), *Yakuza to Iu Ikikata: Kore ga Shinogiya!* (Tokyo: Takarajima).

Nakamura, T. (1981) *The Postwar Japanese Economy: Its Development and Structure* (Tokyo: University of Tokyo Press).

National Police Agency (1997) *Police of Japan* (Tokyo: National Police Agency).

Nelli, H. (1986) 'Overview', in R. Kelly (ed.), *Organised Crime: An International Perspective* (Totowa, NJ: Rowman and Littlefield).

Nichibenren (*Nihon Bengoshi Rengō-kai*) (1995) *Kenshō: Nihon no Keisastu* (Tokyo: Hyōronsha).

——(1997) *Chūkai: Bōryokudan Taisaku Hō* (Tokyo: Minji-hō Kenkyū-kai).

——(1998a) *Bōryokudan Hyakutō-ban* (Tokyo: Minji-hō Kenkyū-kai).

——(1998b) *Bōryokudan Jimusho Haijō no Hōri* (Tokyo: Tachibana Shobō).

Noda, Y. (1976a) *Introduction to Japanese Law* (Tokyo: University of Tokyo Press).

——(1976b) 'The Character of the Japanese People and their Conception of Law', in H. Tanaka (ed.), *The Japanese Legal System: Introductory Cases and Materials* (Tokyo: Tokyo University Press).

Ochiai, H. (2000) 'Who Polices the Police?' *Japan Quarterly*, April–June.

Oda, H. (1992) *Japanese Law* (London: Butterworths).

Ōhashi, W. (1998) 'Genka no Yakubutsu Jōsei ni okeru Tōmen no Kadai', *Keisatsu-gaku Ronshū*, 51/5 (Tokyo: Tachibana Shobō).

Okumura, H. (1997) *Sōkaiya Sukandaru* (Tokyo: Iwanami Shoten).

Onda, S. (1985) *Nihon no Dai-oyabun Jūsan-nin no Kanzen Deeta* (Tokyo: Seikai Ōraisha).

Oppler, A. (1976) *Legal Reform in Occupied Japan: A Participant Looks Back* (Princeton, NJ: Princeton University Press).

Park, W. (1997) 'Explaining Japan's Low Crime Rates: A Review of the Literature', *International Annals of Criminology*, 35 (1/2).

Parker, L. (1984) *The Japanese Police System Today: An American Perspective* (Tokyo: Kodansha).

Pearce, F. (1976) *Crimes of the Powerful: Marxism, Crime and Deviance* (London: Pluto Press).

Pearson, G. and Hobbs, D. (2001) *Middle Market Drug Distribution*, Home Office Research Study, 227.

Perl, R. (1998) 'The North Korean Drug Trade: Issues for Decision Makers', *Transnational Organized Crime*, 4/1 (London: Frank Cass).

Pinker, S. (1998) *How the Mind Works* (London: Penguin).

Pistone, J. (1997) *Donnie Brasco: My Underworld Life in the Mafia* (London: Hodder and Stoughton).

Polo, M. (1995) 'Internal Cohesion and Competition Among Criminal Organisations', in G. Fiorentini and S. Peltzman (eds.), *The Economics of Organised Crime* (Cambridge: Cambridge University Press).

President's Commission on Organized Crime (1986) *The Impact: Organized Crime Today* (Washington, DC: US Government Printing Office).

Ramseyer, J. and Nakazato, M. (1989) 'The Rational Litigant: Settlement Accounts and Verdict Rates in Japan', *Journal of Legal Studies*, 18 (Chicago, IL: University of Chicago Press).

———— (1999) *Japanese Law: An Economic Approach* (Chicago, IL: University of Chicago Press).

Randolph, J. (1995) 'RICO—The Rejection of an Economic Requirement', *The Journal of Criminal Law and Criminology*, 85/4 (Northwestern University).

Rawlin, J. (1968) 'Street Level Abuse of Amphetamines', in J. Russo (ed.), *Amphetamine Abuse* (Springfield, MA: Charles C. Thomas).

Raz, J. (1992) 'Self-presentation and Performance in the *Yakuza* Way of Life', in R. Goodman (ed.), *Ideology and Practise in Modern Japan* (London: Routledge).

—— (1996) *Yakuza no Bunka-jinrui-gaku* (Tokyo: Iwanami Shoten).

Rebovich, D. (1995) 'Use and Avoidance of RICO at the Local Level: The Implementation of Organized Crime laws', in J. Albanese (ed.), *Contemporary issues in Organised Crime* (Monsey, NY: Criminal Justice Press).

Reuter, P. (1983) *Disorganised Crime: The Economics of the Visible Hand* (Cambridge, MA: MIT Press).

—— (1985) 'Racketeers as Cartel Organisers', in H. Alexander and G. Caiden (eds.), *The Politics and Economics of Organised Crime* (Lexington, MA: D.C. Heath).

—— and Hagga, J. (1989) *The Organisation of High-Level Drug Markets: A Study of the Economics of Drug Dealing in Washington D.C.* (Santa Monica, CA: Rand).

Richardson, B. and Flanagan, S. (1984) *Politics in Japan* (Boston, MA: Little, Brown & Company).

Rosoff, S., Pontell, H., and Tillman, R. (1998) *Profit Without Honor: White Collar Crime and the Looting of America* (Upper Saddle River, NJ: Prentice Hall).

Saga, J. (1991) *Confessions of a Yakuza* (Tokyo: Kodansha International).

Saikō Saiban-sho Jimukyoku (1998) *Shihō Tōkei Nenpō 2 Keiji-hen Heisei 9-nen* (Tokyo: Hōsō-kai).

Sakurada, K. (1993) '*Yakuza* Learn New Tricks, But Companies Fail to "Just Say No" ', *Tokyo Business Today*, November.

—— (1994a) '*Yakuza* Storming the Corporate Ship', *Tokyo Business Today*, April 1994.

Sakurada, K. (1994b) 'Murder Most Foul', *Tokyo Business Today*, December.

Sālā (1996) *Sālā Q & A: Sherutā Sannen-Kan no Katsudō kara Mieta Mono*.

Sato, I. (1991) *Kamikaze Biker: Parody and Anomy in Affluent Japan* (Chicago, IL: University of Chicago Press).

Saxonhouse, G. (1979) 'Industrial Restructuring in Japan', *Journal of Japanese Studies*, 5/2.

Schelling, T. (1984) *Choice and Consequence* (Cambridge, MA: Harvard University Press).

——(1980) *The Strategy of Conflict* (Cambridge, MA: Harvard University Press).

Schilling, M. (1996) '*Yakuza* Films: Fading Celluloid Heroes', *Japan Quarterly*, 43/3.

Schlesinger, J. (1997) *Shadow Shoguns: The Rise and Fall of Japan's Postwar Political Machine* (New York: Simon and Schuster).

Seymour, C. (1996) Yakuza *Diary: Doing Time in the Japanese Underworld* (New York: Atlantic Monthly Press).

Shikita, M. and Tsuchiya, S. (1992) *Crime and Criminal Policy in Japan: Analysis and Evaluation of the Showa Period* (Germany: Springer Verlag).

Shimamura, T. (1992) Bōryokudan Shinpō ni Tai-suru Bengoshi-kai no Torikumi, in *Kiken na Bōryokudan Taisaku-hō* (Osaka: *Bōryokudan Taisaku-hō Shinpojiumu Jikkō Iinkai*).

Shinoda, K. (2001) *Yamaguchi-gumi VS Keisatsu-chō* (Tokyo: Take Shobō).

——(2002) *Nihon Yakuza Chizu* (Tokyo: Take Shobō).

Shinozaki, Y., Takebana, Y., Narita, Y., and Miyazawa, K. (1991) 'Bōryokudan Taisaku Hō o Megutte', in *Jurisuto No. 985*, 1 September (Tokyo: Yūhikaku).

Sibbitt, E. (1997) 'Regulating Gambling in the Shadow of the Law: Form and Substance in the Regulation of Japan's *Pachinko* Industry', *Harvard International Law Journal*, 38.

Skaperdas, S. and Syropoulos, C. (1995) 'Gangs as Primitive States', in G. Fiorentini and S. Peltzman (eds.), *The Economics of Organised Crime* (Cambridge: Cambridge University Press).

Stark, H. (1981) *The Yakuza: Japanese Crime Incorporated* (Ph.D. Thesis, University of Michigan).

Sterling, C. (1995) *Crime Without Frontiers: The Worldwide Expansion of Organised Crime and the Pax Mafiosa* (London: Warner Books).

Stille, A. (1996) *Excellent Cadavers: The Mafia and the Death of the First Italian Republic* (London: Vintage).

Sumida, Y. (1997) 'Bōryokudan Haijō Katsudō', in T. Fujimoto (ed.), *Bōryokudan Taisaku Hō Shikkō-go Go-nen no Bōryokudan Taisaku* (Tokyo: Hitosei).

Sutherland, E. (1937) *The Professional Thief* (Chicago, IL: University of Chicago Press).

——and Cressey, D. (1966) *Principles of Criminology* (New York: J.B. Lippincott).

Szymkowiak, K. (1994) '*Sōkaiya*, An Examination of the Social and Legal Developments of Japan's Corporate Extremists', *International Journal of the Sociology of Law*, 22.

——(1996) *Necessary Evil: Extortion, Organized Crime and Japanese Corporations* (Unpublished Ph.D. Thesis, University of Hawaii).

——(2002) Sōkaiya: *Extortion, Protection and the Japanese Corporation* (London, M. E. Sharpe).

——and Steinhoff, P. (1995) 'Wrapping Up in Something Long: Intimidation and Violence by Right-Wing Groups in Postwar Japan', *Terrorism and Political Violence*, 7.

Takagi, M. (1988) *Shin-Dōwa Mondai to Dōwa Dantai* (Tokyo: Doyō Bijutsu).

Tamura, E. (1981) *Yakuza no Seikatsu* (Tokyo: Oyamakaku Shuppan).

Tamura, M. (1988) 'Kakuseizai no Ryūtsū Kibō o Suitei-suru', *Keisatsu-gaku Ronshū*, 41/10.

——(1992) 'The *Yakuza* and Amphetamine Abuse in Japan', in H. Traver and M. Gaylord (eds.), *Drugs, Law and the State* (Hong Kong: Hong Kong University Press).

——Hoshino, K., Uchiyama, A., and Yonezato, S. (1993) 'Bōryokudan Taisakuhō no Bōryokudan ni Oyobosu Eikyō to Kumi-in no Ridatsu', in *Kagaku Keisastu Kenkyū-jo Hōkoku*, 34/2 (Dec.).

Tanaka, H. (1976) *The Japanese Legal System: Introductory Cases and Materials* (Tokyo: Tokyo University Press).

——(1988) 'The Role of Law and Lawyers in Japanese Society', in H. Tanaka (ed.), *The Japanese Legal System* (Tokyo: Tokyo University Press).

Tanioka, I. (1997) 'Social Control Theory in Japanese Society', *International Annals of Criminology*, 35—1/2.

——(1998) *Gendai Pachinko Bunkakō* (Tokyo: Chikuma Shinsho).

Tanzi, V. (1995) 'Corruption: Arm's-length Relationships and Corruption', in G. Fiorentini and S. Peltzman (eds.), *The Economics of Organised Crime* (Cambridge: Cambridge University Press).

Task Force on Organized Crime (1967) *Task Force Report: Organized Crime* (Washington, DC: US Government Printing Office).

Thompson, T. (1995) *Gangland Britain* (London: Hodder and Stoughton).

Tōkei-kyoku (Statistics Bureau) (1985–2001) *Nihon Tōkei Nenkan (Japan Statistical Yearbook)* (Tokyo: Ōkura-shō Insatsu-kyoku).

Toshi Bōhan Kenkyū Sentā (1991) *Hanzai no Higaisha Hassei Jittai ni Kan-suru Chōsa Hōkoku-sho*, 1/1, Tokyo.

Traver, H. and Gaylord, M. (1992) *Drugs, Law and the State* (Hong Kong: Hong Kong University Press).

Tsuchimoto, T. (2000) 'Light and Shadow in Japan's Police System', *Japan Quarterly*, April–June.

Uchiyama, A. (1989) 'Bōryokudan-in no Keizai Kiban ni Kan-suru Kenkyū', *Kagaku Keisastu Kenkyū-jo Hōkoku*, 30/1 (July).

Uchiyama, A. and Enomoto, Y. (1992) 'Bōryokudan Yobigun Shōnen no Bōryokudan he no Sesshoku Katei no Bunseki', in *Kagaku Keisastu Kenkyū-jo Hōkoku*, 33/1 (July).

—— and Hoshino, K. (1993) 'Bōryokudan no Bōryokudan Fukuji-bunka he no Dōchō', in *Kagaku Keisatsu Kenkyū-jo Hōkoku*, 34/2 (Dec.).

——— Tamura, M., and Yonezato, S. (1993) 'Bōryokudan Taisakuho Shikogo no Bōryokudan-in no Seikatsu Henka', in *Kagaku Keisastu Kenkyū-jo Hōkoku*, 34/2 (Dec.).

—— Okeda, S., Hoshino, K., Harada, Y., and Mugishima, F. (1992) 'Shonen ni Tai-suru Bōryokudan no Eikyō ni Kan-suru Kenkyū', in *Keisatsu Kagaku Kenkyū-jo Hōkoku*, 33/2 (Dec.).

van Wolferen, K. (1989) *The Enigma of Japanese Power* (London: Macmillan).

Varese, F. (1996) 'What is the Russian Mafia?' in *Low Intensity Conflict and Law Enforcement Vol. 5 No. 2*.

—— (2001) *The Russian Mafia: Private Protection in a New Market Economy* (Oxford: Oxford University Press).

—— (2003) 'Mafia', in I. Mclean and A. McMillan (eds.), *Concise Oxford Dictionary of Politics* (Oxford: Oxford University Press).

Vaughn, M., Huang, F., and Ramirez, C. (1995) 'Drug Abuse and Anti-drug Policy in Japan', *British Journal of Criminology*, 35/4.

Vogel, E. (1979) *Japan as Number One: Lessons for America* (Cambridge, MA: Harvard University Press).

von Mehren, A. (1963) *Law in Japan: The Legal Order in a Changing Society* (Cambridge, MA: Harvard University Press).

Watanabe, O. (1980) 'Gendai Keisatsu to Sono Ideorogii', in S. Kinbara, J. Kobayashi, and H. Takahashi (eds.), *Gendai Shihonshugi Kokka 2 Gendai Nihon no Kokka Kōzō* (Tokyo: Ōtsuki Shoten).

—— (1985) 'Gendai Nihon Keisatsu no Keisei—"Kindaika" kara "Nihonka" he', in *Shakai Kagaku Kenkyū*, 37/5 (Dec.).

West, M. (1999) 'Information, Institutions, and Extortion in Japan and the United States: Making Sense of *Sōkaiya* Racketeers', *Northwestern University Law Review*, 93/3.

Whyte, W. (1993) *Street Corner Society: The Social Structure of an Italian Slum – 4th Edition* (Chicago: University of Chicago Press).

Whiting, R. (1999) *Tokyo Underworld: The Fast Times and Hard Life of an American Gangster in Japan* (New York: Vintage).

Wildes, H. (1948) 'Underground Politics in Post-War Japan', *The American Political Science Review*, 42/6 (Dec.).

—— (1954) *Typhoon in Tokyo: The Occupation and its Aftermath* (London: George Allen & Unwin).

Winlow, S., Hobbs, D., Lister, S., and Hadfield, P. (2001) 'Get Ready to Duck: Bouncers and the Realities of Ethnographic Research on Violent Groups', *British Journal of Criminology*, 41: 536–48.

Woodall, B. (1996) *Japan Under Construction: Corruption, Politics and Public Works* (Berkeley, CA: University of California Press).

Woodiwiss, M. (1990) *Organised Crime, USA: Changing Perceptions from Prohibition to the Present Day* (Pontefract: Lofthouse Publications).

Woronoff, J. (1990) *Japan as Anything But Number One* (London: Macmillan).

Yajima, S. (1992*a*) 'Totta-mono ga Kachi Ya!', in Bessatsu Takarajima 157 (ed.), *Yakuza to Iu Ikikata: Kore ga Shinogi Ya!* (Tokyo: Takarajima).

—— (1992*b*) 'Oikondare!', in Bessatsu Takarajima 157 (ed.), *Yakuza to Iu Ikikata: Kore ga Shinogi Ya!* (Tokyo: Takarajima).

Yamada, K. (1994*a*) *Godaime Yamaguchi-gumi no Sugao* (Tokyo: Futabasha).

—— (1994*b*) *Godaime Yamaguchi-gumi ga Yuku!* (Tokyo: Futabasha).

—— (1998) *Godaime Yamaguchi-gumi no Gekiryū!* (Tokyo: Futabasha).

Yamadaira, S. (1992) *Yakuza Daijiten* (Tokyo: Futabasha).

—— (1993) *Yakuza Daijiten*, vol. 2 (Tokyo: Futabasha).

Yamaguchi, H. and Soejima, T. (1997) *Saiban no Himitsu* (Tokyo: Yōsensha).

Yamaguchi, T. (1997*a*) 'Bōryokudan Taisaku Hō ni Kan-suru Hanrei no Dōkō', in T. Fujimoto (ed.), *Bōryokudan Taisaku Hō Shikkō-go Go-nen no Bōryokudan Taisaku* (Tokyo: Hitosei).

—— (1997*b*) 'Bōryokudan-in ni Tai-suru Minji Kisō', in T. Fujimoto (ed.), *Bōryokudan Taisaku Hō Shikkō-go Go-nen no Bōryokudan Taisaku* (Tokyo: Hitosei).

Yamanouchi, Y. (1992*a*) 'Moshimoshi Akemi Desu. Aoishiro, 205-go-shitsu ni Hairimashita', in Bessatsu Takarajima 157 (ed.), *Yakuza to Iu Ikikata: Kore ga Shinogiya!* (Tokyo: Takarajima).

—— (1992*b*) 'Kagirinai SEX no Yorokobi o Motomete', in Bessatsu Takarajima 157 (ed.), *Yakuza to Iu Ikikata: Kore ga Shinogiya!* (Tokyo: Takarajima).

Yasuda, M. (1993) *Yakuza de Naze Warui* (Tokyo: Seinen Shokan).

Yasuda, T. (1998) 'Soshiki Settō no Genkyō to Kongo no Taisaku', *Keisatsu Kōron* Part 1 (April), Part 2 (June).

Yokouchi, I. (1998) 'Saikin no Kenkyo Jirei nado kara Mita Sōkaiya no Jittai', *Keisatsu-gaku Ronshū*, 51/4 (April) (Tokyo: Tachibana Shobō).

Yonezato, S., Tamura, M., Hoshino, K., Uchiyama, A., and Kurusu, H. (1994) 'Bōryokudan-in no Ridatsu oyobi Shakai Fukki o Shinsoku-suru Yōin ni Kan-suru Kenkyū', in *Keisatsu Kagaku Kenkyū-jo Hōkoku*, 35/2 (Dec.).

Young, J. (1981) 'Thinking Seriously about Crime: Some Models of Criminology', in M. Fitzgerald, G. McLennan, and J. Pawson (eds.), *Crime and Society* (London: Routledge Kegan Paul).

—— (1994) 'Incessant Chatter: Recent Paradigms in Criminology', in M. Maguire, R. Morgan, and R. Reiner (eds.), *Oxford Handbook of Criminology* (Oxford: Oxford University Press).

Zen-Bōtsusen (Zenkoku Bōryoku Tsūihō Undō Suishin Sentā) (1994) *Bōryokudan-in no Ridatsu to Shakai-fukki ni Kan suru Kenkyū.*

Index

Abadinsky, H. 20, 98, 152–3, 155
accounting regulations, changes in 291
Administrative Police Regulations (*gyōsei keisatsu kisoku*) of 1875 252
aetiology of mafias 13–16
ageing composition of *yakuza* groups 51
agricultural cooperatives (*nōkyō*) 186
Aizu-kotetsu group 197, 203, 212, 244
Ajinomoto 222
Aldous, C. 58, 253
Alletzhauser, A. 127, 135
All Japan *Dōwa* Association (*Zen-Nippon Dōwa Kai*) 290
amakudari ('descent from heaven') 64, 232, 291
America *see* United States
American Mafia 17
American-style organised-crime control 259
  see also RICO
Ames, W. 56, 61–3, 64, 80–2, 91, 253–5, 258, 272, 290
amphetamines 105, 144
  abuse 99
    first epidemic period 99
    second epidemic period 49, 99
    third epidemic period 225, 227
  -based stimulants 98
  -consuming population, usage frequency of 102
  lozenges (*yābā*) 226
  -related offences 225
  seizures, NPA estimates of total 227
  as a source of income 49
Ampō disturbances 170
Anglo-American legal system 265
aniki–shatei relationship 67
anti-*bōryokundan* campaign 257
anti control lobby 169–71
anti-money-laundering measures 145
anti-organised crime laws, three 259–62
anti-*sōkaiya* measures 126
anti-*yakuza* laws 140, 208
Araki-gumi 56, 62, 67

Arlacchi, P. 24
arrests
  drugs-related 99–100
  of early gamblers 40
  for finance and bad-debt related crimes 194
  gambling 106
  post-*Bōtaiho* 215–9
  and problem of OC countermeasures 146, 148–9
  of summit strategy 47, 90
  by syndicate 217
  for violent crimes 46
  waste disposal 134–5
  during Yama-ichi *tōsō* 50
artificial kinship relationships, system of 68
Association for the Study of Security Science 10
auction obstruction–*kyōbai bōgai* 191–4
Aum Shinrikyō doomsday cult 259
  subway sarin nerve gas attack 259
Australian Financial Review 186

bad-debt problems 27, 185–90, 194
Baer, J. 4
bakuto organisations 37, 41, 43, 70, 138
  shift into alternative economic activities 44
bankruptcy
  in Japan 123
  management 122–4, 190–1, 266
Banzuiin, C. 38
Battō-tai 55, 142
Baum, D. 154
Bayley, D. 63, 253, 255
Bell, D. 25, 80
black market 43–4
Blok, A. 24–5
Boku, M. 168
bookmaking, illegal, 107–8
Booth, M. 31, 83, 105, 289
Bornoff, N. 63
Borsellino, P. 6